Regulation through Litigation

W. Kip Viscusi
Editor

AEI-BROOKINGS JOINT CENTER
FOR REGULATORY STUDIES
Washington, D.C.

Regulation through Litigation may be ordered from:
Brookings Institution Press
1775 Massachusetts Avenue, N.W.
Washington, D.C. 20036
Tel.: 1-800-275-1447 or (202) 797-6258
Fax: (202) 797-6004
www.brookings.edu

Library of Congress Cataloging-in-Publication data

Regulation through litigation / W. Kip Viscusi, editor.
   p. cm.
Includes bibliographical references and index.
  ISBN 0-8157-0610-3 (cloth : alk. paper) —
  ISBN 0-8157-0609-X (pbk. : alk. paper)
  1. Citizen suits (Civil procedure)—United States. 2. Delegated legislation—United States. 3. Class actions (Civil procedure)—United States. 4. Public policy (Law)—United States. I. Viscusi, W. Kip.
  KF8896.5 .R44 2002
  347.73'53—dc21   2002005335

9 8 7 6 5 4 3 2 1

The paper used in this publication meets minimum requirements of the American National Standard for Information Sciences—Permanence of Paper for Printed Library Materials: ANSI Z39.48-1992.

Typeset in Adobe Garamond

Composition by Northeastern Graphic Services
Hackensack, New Jersey

Printed by R. R. Donnelley and Sons
Harrisonburg, Virginia

Foreword

This volume explores a new phenomenon that links law and regulation. It reviews a recent class of litigation involving guns, tobacco, and other products in which the stakes have become huge, running into hundreds of billions of dollars in the case of tobacco. The large scale of the litigation allowed litigants to use their financial leverage to force changes of a policy nature, including regulatory policies and excise taxes.

The emergence of the regulation through litigation phenomenon poses new sets of questions for scholars and policymakers. Under what circumstances is it appropriate to foster broad policy changes through such litigation? Should these efforts be viewed as a form of financial blackmail, or should one treat the litigation as simply a new policy tool that overcomes perceived inadequacies in the political process? Addressing such issues is important because of the unprecedented financial stakes but also because of the novel questions that such suits raise with respect to the appropriate division of labor between the courts and existing governmental institutions responsible for regulatory and tax policy.

To address these issues, the American Enterprise Institute-Brookings Institution Joint Center for Regulatory Studies convened a conference on April 26–27, 2001. The scholars who participated reflected diverse points of view. Some view the regulation through litigation phenomenon critically, while others believe that it fills glaring gaps in the existing regulatory structure. The chapters and the commentaries suggest that in many instances there is substantial disagreement, much of which may stem from the different role of litigation in different contexts. At the same time, the authors share many common concerns, such as the importance of judging policies based on norms involving a comparison of benefits and costs of different policy alternatives so as to assess whether some policies make society better off. The empirical and theoretical frameworks presented in this volume are intended to provide a foundation for assessing the regulation through litigation phenomenon.

This volume is one in a series commissioned by the AEI-Brookings Joint Center for Regulatory Studies to contribute to the continuing debate over regulatory reform. The series addresses several fundamental issues in regulation, including the design of effective reforms, the impact of proposed reforms on the public, and the political and institutional forces that affect reform. We hope that this series will help illuminate many of the complex issues involved in designing and implementing regulation and regulatory reforms at all levels of government.

The views expressed here are those of the authors and should not be attributed to the trustees, officers, or staff members of the American Enterprise Institute or the Brookings Institution. The AEI-Brookings Joint Center is supported by grants from foundations, corporations, and individuals. That information can be found at aei.brookings.org.

Shortly after the conference, one of the discussants at the conference—Professor Gary Schwartz of UCLA Law School—underwent emergency surgery and died shortly thereafter. His commentary in this volume reflects the kind of precise and inventive legal scholarship that characterized his many fundamental contributions and which set a standard of excellence for all of us working in the law and economics field.

ROBERT W. HAHN
ROBERT E. LITAN

AEI-Brookings Joint Center for Regulatory Studies

Contents

vii

Regulation through Litigation

W. KIP VISCUSI

1 | *Overview*

The recent lawsuits involving cigarettes, guns, and other products have created a new phenomenon. Such litigation results in negotiated regulatory policies to settle the suit or serves as a financial lever to promote support for governmental policies. The allocation of responsibilities for policy becomes blurred, as litigation becomes the mechanism forcing regulatory changes. The policies that result from litigation almost invariably involve less public input and accountability than government regulation.

In many policy contexts there is an interaction between regulation and litigation. Many of the economic rationales for government regulation pertain to various forms of market failure, such as inadequate consumer information or failure to account for externalities to parties outside of a market transaction. These same forms of market failure often lead to litigation as well, as injured parties seek to obtain damages for the harms that have been inflicted on them because of a lack of appropriate recognition of their economic interests by the party inflicting the harm.[1] The policy task is to coordinate the influences of these two different sets of social institutions, recognizing their different strengths and different functions. In each case, however, the ideal level of harm is not zero. A risk-free society

This research was supported in part by the Sheldon Seevak Research Fund and the Olin Center for Law, Economics and Business.
1. In some instances plaintiffs may also seek damages even if negligence is not alleged.

is neither feasible nor desirable because of the inordinate costs of eliminating risk.

The potential importance of the interaction between regulation and litigation is not a new issue. This overlap of institutional responsibilities and functions was a central theme of an American Law Institute study on tort liability published a decade ago.[2] Traditionally the focus has been on broad conceptual issues, such as the potential for institutional overlap on the creation of economic incentives. The policy concerns arising from these analyses often have focused on fairly narrow policy remedies, such as the provision of a regulatory compliance defense for firms that are in compliance with explicit government standards but are nevertheless subject to litigation.[3]

The different functioning of institutions that litigate and those that regulate is apparent from a look at their roles in promoting health and safety. Consider first the creation of economic incentives. Regulation is generally superior in addressing technical scientific issues because of the importance of expertise in analyzing these regulatory issues. Moreover, government regulation on behalf of society at large is especially appropriate when decisions about policy pertain to an entire product line rather than to purchase of a specific product by an individual. Design defects and hazard warnings, for example, should be assessed on a productwide basis. What any individual knows about the risks is not the key concern. Whether the firm provides adequate information within the market context for a representative purchaser to make a knowledgeable risk-taking decision is.

Difficulties arise when these matters are delegated to juries on a case-by-case basis. Recent literature has documented the failings of juries in thinking systematically about risk, as jurors exhibit a wide variety of systematic biases in assessing accident situations, such as hindsight bias in the evaluation of past actions involving risk. Government regulations will usually provide a more sound approach to promoting health than litigation does, which by its nature focuses on individual circumstances rather than the functioning of an entire product market. The stringency of government regulations may be excessive from a benefit-cost standpoint, owing to the restrictive nature of regulatory agencies' legislative mandates. When this occurs, regulatory standards for health and safety typically should not require any augmentation through judicial proceedings.

2. See American Law Institute (1991a, 1991b).
3. Firms could introduce evidence of regulatory compliance as evidence that they were not negligent. In extreme cases, regulatory compliance could be exculpatory.

If, however, regulations do not exist for a product, litigation can often help address gaps in the regulatory structure and stimulate regulatory activity. One of the most prominent examples is asbestos risks. Historically, asbestos risks had not been strongly regulated, but the emergence of a wave of asbestos litigation induced the Occupational Safety and Health Administration and the Environmental Protection Agency to set stringent regulation. In this instance, the combination of litigation and subsequent regulation led to inordinately large safety incentives. Litigation may complement regulation when it provides for a transfer of income to injured parties to address the damages incurred.

A general problem with distinct roles for litigation and regulation is that there is no formal or informal mechanism for coordinating the roles of these two institutions. That one institution is imposing economic penalties for a particular type of risk does not prevent the other from also imposing sanctions. The little coordination that does exist consists of the existence of regulatory compliance defenses, which typically are restricted fairly narrowly to punitive damages and are only pertinent in a few states. That there is a continuing inherent problem in coordinating the roles of regulation and litigation is well documented in the literature.

What is new is that the character of these coordination problems has changed dramatically since the mid-1990s. The advent of litigation about products such as tobacco, guns, and lead paint went well beyond the historical interactions of regulation and litigation that have been of concern in the literature. No longer was the issue one of litigation creating incentives that overlapped with those resulting from regulation. Rather, litigation was being used as the financial lever to force companies to accept negotiated regulatory policies as part of the litigation. Thus litigation led to regulation, but not regulation that went through the usual rule-making process as a result of a careful analysis by government regulatory agencies subject to their legislative mandates. Rather, the parties in the lawsuit negotiated regulatory changes as part of the package to end the litigation.

These negotiated solutions have also gone beyond simply specifying regulatory changes. In at least one instance the settlement has led to the imposition of what is effectively an excise tax on products. Rather than imposing a conventional damages award on the defendant, the tobacco settlement imposes charges on customers on a per unit basis in the future. Thus the settlement establishes a tax on the product payable to the plaintiff and paid for almost entirely by the consumer rather than a damages payment paid for by the defendant. Litigation against health maintenance organizations (HMOs) proposes a similar tax-like structure. Thus litigation has developed in a manner that not only usurps the traditional governmental authority for government regulation but also shifts the locus of establishing tax policy from the legislature to the parties in the litigation. Citizen interests are not explicitly represented, and, unlike the case of the regulatory changes, there is no mechanism to ensure that these outcomes are in society's best interests. Moreover, there is typically no procedure for even creating the appearance of the degree of legitimacy usually accorded to governmental policies.

If there is an error in these litigation settlements that impose regulatory and tax changes, the potential adverse consequences could be enormous. The stakes of the tobacco litigation exceeded more than $200 billion in expected penalties during the next twenty-five years. The regulatory changes also could have significant anticompetitive effects. Although other litigation involves stakes that are typically not as great as those in tobacco, in the effects on particular industries, the influences could be even greater.

Optimal Deterrence

The chapters in this book shed light on the likely consequences of regulation through litigation for insurance markets and society at large. The authors focus on various case studies.

In considering the merits of litigation it is useful to assess how it performs from the standpoint of efficient deterrence and efficient insurance. One of the chief functions of a liability system and government regulations is to establish optimal levels of deterrence. The case studies in this volume focus almost exclusively on health and safety risks for which the main economic issue is whether the incentives created lead to the appropriate levels of health and safety. The optimum level of risk is not zero but is rather an efficient level of risk that reflects the appropriate balancing between the benefits and costs of risk reduction.

Risk reduction measures should be undertaken only to the extent that their benefits exceed the costs. For example, adding a particular safety device to a machine is desirable only if the benefits of the safety device exceed the costs of modifying the product. Importantly, benefits are judged not only according to financial consequences but also more broadly on society's willingness to pay for the reductions in risks to health, as the appropriate benefit value recognizes the value of the risk reduction that goes beyond the financial effects. Safety is optimized when the *marginal* benefits equal *marginal* costs. Often there is a continuum of risk choices, such as the allowable level of exposure to toxic chemicals. As long as the incremental benefits of increased safety exceed the incremental costs, more tightening of the regulation or the imposition of liability on the firm is desirable. Regulation or litigation is excessively stringent, however, when firms are pushed to enact measures whose incremental costs outweigh incremental benefits.

The implications of policies for choices of the level of health and safety are rarely neutral. Ideally, litigation should also help create incentives for efficient levels of safety, but this objective may be compromised when the main focus of the litigation is to provide compensation.

The discussion by Kenneth S. Abraham in chapter 7 distinguishes two different types of litigation, each of which has different implications for economic incentives. Litigation that he calls "forward looking" focuses on setting up requirements on firm behavior or a funding mechanism that will directly influence incentives for the future. The settlement of the tobacco litigation was forward looking in that it led to regulatory changes and a damages formula that was largely tantamount to an excise tax on cigarettes. Similarly, the litigation involving guns, which is reviewed in chapter 3 by Phillip Cook and Jens Ludwig, is forward looking to the extent that it seeks to impose safety requirements on the design of handguns as well as restrictions on the distribution of handguns. Although the litigation against health maintenance organizations, discussed in chapter 6, is less well developed than that for cigarettes and guns, the overall model that is being adopted closely follows the one for tobacco and is forward looking in character.

Litigation that Abraham calls "backward looking" is more similar in character to conventional tort litigation. The lawsuits by women suffering problems they attribute to breast implants and the lead paint litigation against landlords fall into the backward-looking category. These suits seek to obtain compensation for parties that have been injured. Such compensation will establish payment structures that could potentially alter future incentives because firms will expect to be subject to similar sanctions from future litigation. However, if all such decisions have already been made or if the product is no longer sold, there will be no incentive effect unless these suits impinge on current behavior in some manner. Thus there will be no incentive effect for lead paint manufacturers because lead paint is no longer produced in the United States. However, the lead paint suits against landlords potentially could have an incentive effect to the extent that they affect building maintenance, efforts to remove lead paint, and warnings to tenants about lead paint risks. There may also be more general deterrent efforts for landlords beyond lead paint.

Optimal Insurance

A second potential function of social institutions dealing with risk is providing optimal insurance to those who have suffered injuries or illnesses. Regulatory policies by the federal government usually do not provide any insurance compensation for victims but instead are focused almost exclusively on establishing regulatory standards for health and safety. Insurance functions are typically handled through targeted government programs that focus on the disabled, the poor, or the elderly.

In contrast, litigation often has as its principal purpose an effort to transfer income to those who have suffered injuries. From the standpoint of optimal insurance this transfer should be sufficient to completely cover the economic loss when people have suffered a financial loss. The desirability of providing this insurance stems from individual risk aversion, which makes insurance of such losses desirable. When governmental entities have suffered economic losses, such as the medical costs attributable to tobacco that were incurred by the states, this type of insurance rationale would not be pertinent. Governmental entities should be risk neutral except for extremely large losses because they can spread these losses across a large citizenry base. Thus any optimal insurance rationale for transfers to the government must assume that the losses ultimately borne by individual taxpayers will be sufficiently great that risk aversion will come into play.

For individuals sustaining injuries and suffering illnesses, there will be financial losses and effects on individual health. The object of insurance for financial losses is to restore individuals to their pre-accident level of utility, but that objective is not pertinent to health effects.[4] Typically, it will not be desirable for an individual to purchase so much insurance as to be as well off as he or she would have been had the illness or injury not occurred

---

4. Optimal insurance satisfies the property that it equates the marginal utility of income when one is healthy to the marginal utility of income when one is ill.

because these events reduce people's ability to derive welfare benefits from additional funds. Even enormous transfers of money may not be adequate enough to restore the pre-accident welfare level to one who has become severely disabled. There is also the practical problem of ascertaining a person's psychic losses from such major injuries. Thus in the case of the breast implant litigation, there will be an insurance objective, but the proper role of the courts will typically fall short of restoring the plaintiff's pre-illness level of utility even when liability for the firm is established.

The Case Studies

This volume presents case studies of different types of litigation as well as broader analyses of the role of mass torts and class actions and their implications for economic performance. Table 1-1 summarizes each of these areas of litigation. In each case, there is some alleged shortcoming from the standpoint of efficient behavior on the part of the firm as well as an alleged or actual failure on the part of government agencies. The third column of table 1-1 indicates the remedy that is sought by the litigation or has resulted from the litigation. These remedies go beyond conventional damages payments and include measures of a regulatory character and financial penalties that will affect the cost of the product. A summary of the efficiency effects of the different product litigation appears in the last column of table 1-1.

Tobacco

By far the most noteworthy example of regulation through litigation is litigation against the tobacco industry. The most salient example consists of the suits by the state governments that sought to recover Medicaid expenses that they attributed to cigarettes. The prospective suit that has been filed by the federal government also has a similar character. These parallels no doubt led the federal government to initiate the suit and presumably also led the Bush administration to suggest that an out-of-court settlement should be the appropriate solution.

The alleged market failure that gave rise to these suits is that there is a medical cost externality that has not been fully addressed. Why governmental entities such as the states and the federal government failed to tax cigarettes adequately to reflect this cost of cigarettes is a major unanswered

Table 1-1. *Summary of Justifications for Litigation in Case Studies*

Product	Alleged governmental failure	Remedy	Efficiency effects
Tobacco	Medical cost externality to state Medicaid programs not addressed.	Lawsuits to transfer money to states; led to excise tax equivalent and negotiated regulatory changes; billions in plaintiff attorney fees.	Adverse effects based on assessment of the financial costs of smoking.
Guns	Governmental failure because of diffuse public benefits and strong interest group pressure.	Lawsuits by cities threatening penalties, with prospect of regulatory changes.	Prospective effects on gun distribution and safety devices, but experts disagree on desirability of all such measures.
Lead paint	Vigorous existing federal regulations, with lead paint ban since 1978; landlords subject to state and local regulations, but issues of efficacy and victim compensation.	Lawsuits against paint companies seeking payment for historical acts; lawsuits against landlords for current exposures seeking compensation.	Incentives for landlords to reduce exposures, fixed costs for producers.
Breast implants	In use before FDA medical device regulation and not regulated when authority extended; little company research, but company suppression of adverse information.	Lawsuits seeking compensation for morbidity effects and speculative ailments; led to FDA review and research, often exonerating the product.	Exit from market of breast implant producers, perhaps may stimulate more research on such medical devices.
Health maintenance organizations	Quality control problems of managed care not adequately regulated.	Litigation to force tobacco-type solution of premium taxes to pay off plaintiff attorneys.	Negative effect in discouraging purchase of coverage.

question. Critics allege that the lobbying power of the tobacco industry has hindered taxes from being set at appropriate levels. The risks of smoking have been well known for decades and, indeed, have been subject to annual reports by the Surgeon General and government-mandated warnings. Given the knowledge that cigarettes do increase health costs, what was the governmental failure that prevented legislatures from enacting taxes to cover these costs? Thus the fundamental question raised by these suits is why there was any need to resort to litigation rather than having traditional governmental processes address these costs.

My assessment of tobacco in chapter 2 makes two general points about this litigation. First, in considering economic cost externalities arising from cigarettes, there is no net cost imposed on the states or on the federal government, even if one excludes excise taxes. Proper recognition of the full health consequences of smoking indicates that smokers will live shorter lives than nonsmokers and consequently will generate fewer nursing home expenses and lower pension and Social Security costs than nonsmokers. Indeed, smokers are self-financing for every state and for the federal government, even excluding the role of excise taxes already in place. Thus there are no net economic damages to governments arising from cigarettes. The second major point I make is that there is no evident harm caused by the alleged wrongful conduct by the industry. Survey evidence indicates that smokers are aware of the risks posed by cigarettes and have an exaggerated perception of the risk. Thus, in terms of misinformed decisions, there is no evidence that alleged wrongful conduct by the cigarette industry led people to smoke cigarettes. Indeed, the risks of smoking have been well known and highly publicized for decades and are perhaps the most highly publicized risks in society.

Chapter 9 by Richard A. Epstein takes a somewhat different approach to the tobacco litigation. He does not question whether cigarettes are self-financing or whether people overestimate the risks of smoking. No suits by the states or the federal government have any justification in Epstein's view unless there would be an appropriate basis for litigation by the individuals who decided to smoke. He believes such litigation is without foundation because hazard warnings have been on cigarette packages for decades. Moreover, the warnings since 1969 include provisions that preempt litigation against the industry based on inadequate warnings.

The remedy that was sought in the case of the tobacco litigation involved the transfer of money to the states. As I indicated and as noted in the comments by John E. Calfee and Gary T. Schwartz, this monetary transfer did not take the form of a traditional damages payment but rather consisted largely of a penalty on future cigarettes that was tantamount to an excise tax. This "tax" was unusual, however, in that it was not assessed by any legislature but instead emerged through litigation and from bargains between the state attorneys general and cigarette industry executives. These parties also negotiated various regulatory changes, including restrictions on advertising that some view as having anticompetitive consequences. Notably, the cigarette litigation also generated enormous compensation for plaintiffs' attorneys that ran into the billions of dollars paid by particular states and hundreds of millions of dollars in compensation received by plaintiffs' attorneys. These attorney fee arrangements were controversial not only because of their size but also because state attorneys general negotiated these arrangements without any open bidding process or public scrutiny. In Massachusetts, the attorney general negotiated an arrangement that even the governor of the state regarded as excessive.

For the optimal deterrence and optimal insurance objectives just outlined, the cigarette litigation provided for no insurance of individual losses but only a transfer to states. Moreover, states should be regarded as risk neutral so that insurance does not really come into play. The incentives created on future cigarette sales include a tax on each pack that will discourage smoking generally. Whether doing so is desirable depends on one's assessment of the net economic consequences to society. At least as far as financial effects are concerned, the results I presented indicate that additional taxation is not warranted. Thus in cases affecting the states, there is no efficiency-based rationale for the tax. Moreover, the tax is not structured to provide meaningful incentives. A key drawback of the tax-like structure of the damages is that the level of the tax does not vary with the riskiness of the cigarette product in any way. If companies were to develop risk-free cigarettes in the future, then these products would be subject to the same tax even though they would entail no medical costs. Ideally, any tax system should provide incentives for safety innovation.

The shortcoming of the tax structure of the damages payment in tobacco can be traced to the fact that this arrangement did not emerge from a careful analysis of what the tax structure should be. Rather, it was simply a financial settlement of litigation that happened to take the form of a tax.

Guns

The high-stakes payoff of the cigarette litigation has not been lost on attorneys considering litigation in other areas. The next prominent example of the regulation through litigation phenomenon is the subject of chapter 3 by Philip J. Cook and Jens Ludwig. In the New Orleans guns suit, the plaintiffs allege that the companies neglected to provide adequate safety features for guns. The Chicago lawsuit has a different focus: a claim that firms created a public nuisance by not preventing illegal sales of firearms.

The financial resources of the gun industry are dwarfed by those of the tobacco industry. As a result, the stakes are much less significant as far as the overall effect on the economy is concerned. This difference in financial magnitude lead Cook and Ludwig to conclude that the object of the gun litigation is primarily to lead to regulatory changes rather than to provide financial compensation. However, this difference may simply reflect the more modest size of the gun industry. If it were not for the threatened financial sanctions, it is unlikely that the cities would have the leverage to force the regulatory changes that they are seeking through the litigation. Because this litigation is not as far along as the tobacco litigation, the ultimate emphasis on financial transfers as opposed to regulatory changes is not yet apparent. What the plaintiffs are seeking is a set of negotiated changes regarding gun distribution and safety mechanisms for guns. As Cook and Ludwig observe, some firms have already exited the industry, and others have changed ownership so that the financial consequences are significant for individual firms even if their aggregate impact on the overall economy is relatively small.

Cook and Ludwig assess the societal consequences of firearms by establishing a statistical relationship between the presence of guns to homicides. Their result: there is an additional death associated with the presence of an extra 15,000 guns. As Epstein comments, however, this simple analysis is controversial for various reasons, not the least of which is that it does not distinguish whether the guns were involved in the homicides. For example, people in high crime areas may choose to purchase guns for self-defense, but that does not imply that their guns led to homicides, which may have been committed with weapons other than guns. Epstein also notes that the fundamental difference between guns and other harmful products is that guns may have a legitimate use. The social objective is to prevent guns from being used unlawfully, not necessarily to prevent gun use overall. This focused objective, in Epstein's view, creates a policy problem of a more targeted nature than simply eliminating guns altogether.

Based on their assessment that guns impose net economic costs, which is shared by many other economists, Cook and Ludwig explore the various policy remedies proposed. These proposals include personalized technologies for guns as well as different safety mechanisms. Many of these options seem to offer great potential. The question then becomes, what market failure has prevented companies from introducing these products? One gun industry view is that the personalized gun technology and other such proposals are not as sound or as well developed as advocates such as Cook and Ludwig suggest.[5]

Although Cook and Ludwig do not explore the sources of market failure in detail, they do address the possible role of governmental failure to establish regulations that would have promoted such outcomes. They suggest that because of the diffuse public benefits from gun regulation, strong interest groups supporting gun use have thwarted the enactment of socially beneficial legislation. The result was a series of lawsuits by cities that did not need legislative approval but would nevertheless generate leverage to produce regulatory changes. As with the regulatory policies that emerged from the tobacco litigation, however, these regulatory proposals do not go through the detailed review and rule-making process that is the normal course for governmental regulations.

Lead Paint

Some of the lawyers who are veterans of the tobacco litigation became engaged in various lawsuits pertaining to lead paint. These lawsuits bore some similarities to the tobacco and gun litigation because they often involved government entities suing firms. However, the character of the litigation has been distinctive in other respects.

Chapter 4 by Randall Lutter and Elizabeth Mader distinguishes two kinds of lead paint lawsuits. The first type consists of suits against the lead paint manufacturers. These suits closely parallel the tobacco lawsuits. The second class consists of landlord-tenant suits. This litigation is more akin to standard personal injury litigation.

Consider first the suits against lead paint manufacturers. That these

5. See Beretta USA Corp (1999).

suits are being lodged at all is curious given that there has been a national ban on the use of lead paint enforced by the Consumer Product Safety Commission since 1978. Moreover, recently issued EPA standards for the presence of lead paint, which have been incorporated in rules promulgated by the Department of Housing and Urban Development, impose standards on lead paint exposures. There are also required housing disclosures of the presence of lead paint to buyers and renters and state and local regulations pertaining to lead levels. Lead paint production has not been active for twenty-four years, and exposures to historical applications of lead paint are now strongly regulated. The lead paint lawsuits in which the defendants are the lead-paint-producing companies consequently parallel the tobacco and gun litigation because they focus on historical behavior. Moreover, as with tobacco, there is often a latency period before the harm is done, so that the damages if paid may not always go to the individuals who suffered health losses but could go to other entities, such as local governments. Unlike the tobacco cases, however, there will be no excise tax financing mechanism that might influence future production of lead paint because this production has already ceased. Consequently, the lawsuits will have no influence on deterring manufacturers of lead paint from producing lead-based products. To the extent that this litigation creates any incentives, it will be by altering the expectations of firms making other products by showing them that the legal system might eventually impose costs on them long after they have ceased producing or selling certain items.

The historical claims against lead paint manufacturers have also created difficulties in assigning liability. Most likely, for example, there have been several applications of paint to a wall over time, and it is often impossible to ascertain the date of the paint application or the manufacturer of the lead paint. Some lawsuits have sought unsuccessfully to apply market share liability rules to assign responsibility for the historical applications of lead paint. These efforts have not been successful, in part because of inherent uncertainties about when the lead paint was applied and the respective market shares of different companies at different points in time. Efforts to apply similar concepts of market share liability to guns have also not been successful.

The second set of lead paint lawsuits involving landlords and tenants could potentially function quite differently as far as achieving optimal deterrence and efficient insurance. Landlords continue to make decisions about building maintenance, which in turn affects exposure to lead.

Moreover, to the extent that these lawsuits lead to compensation of people actually exposed to lead, there is potentially some insurance rationale for the litigation. As Lutter and Mader indicate, however, strong government regulations that address many of these exposure issues are already in place, thus reducing the deterrence rationale.

The pattern of lead paint litigation also yields some surprising results. Increasingly, these lawsuits lead to out-of-court settlements, but Lutter and Mader observe that despite the decline of lead levels in contaminated housing, the number of lawsuits has not diminished. Their statistical analysis suggests that higher blood lead levels do not increase the probability that a plaintiff will win the case though it does increase the magnitude of the award. Lutter and Mader, as well as the commentary in this volume by Thomas J. Kniesner, conclude that litigation is a very poor mechanism for promoting control of lead and promoting individual health, which they believe can be done more effectively through better regulatory controls on lead-based paint hazards.

Breast Implants

The role of government regulations also figures prominently in Joni Hersch's analysis of breast implants. The conventional view in the literature, which is shared by the commentary in this volume by Peter Schuck, is that the breast implant litigation epitomizes the extent to which class action litigation has led to undesirable social outcomes. According to this view, companies were punished and in one case driven into bankruptcy (Dow Corning) by claims of illnesses that were not supported by the scientific evidence. The chapter by Hersch challenges this conventional assessment by tracking the state of information at different points in time and the link of this information to litigation.

Many observers suggest that the breast implant litigation should be a nonissue for the courts because of regulation by the Food and Drug Administration (FDA). The commentary in the chapter by Epstein, for example, proposes that there should be an exemption for all products regulated by the FDA because this regulation already establishes appropriate tests of product safety. Although that point of view is certainly pertinent to prescription drugs and many medical devices, Hersch shows that breast implants were in use before there was regulation of medical devices by the

FDA. Once the authority of the agency was extended to include medical devices, the FDA never explicitly reviewed breast implants and evaluated their properties for safety and efficacy. Thus, unlike more recently regulated products, the fact that breast implants ultimately fell under the jurisdiction of the FDA in no way ensures that the FDA made the judgment that the product met adequate safety standards.

The litigation that resulted began with lawsuits involving adverse health consequences of breast implants other than life-threatening ailments. This litigation was based on well-established medical consequences of breast implants such as capsular contracture around the implants and led companies to provide hazard warnings to alert potential users of breast implants to these consequences. A more controversial and more recent line of litigation on breast implants has involved individual suits and class actions on highly speculative ailments, such as connective tissue disease, and autoimmune diseases, such as lupus and scleroderma. Plaintiffs often waged successful legal battles based on the fact that they suffered identifiable ailments and that case reports often linked the presence of breast implants to such ailments. What was missing, however, were detailed epidemiological studies demonstrating that breast implants increased the risk of severe adverse effects and made it more probable than not that breast implants were the cause of the ailments. Many critics of the breast implant litigation consequently claimed that these cases had no merit because the risks had not been documented based on large-scale epidemiological studies performed for this product.

Hersch challenges this view based on the nature of the information flows. Because government regulators never required companies to undertake this research and companies never did so on their own, she views it as inappropriate to fault the litigation based on informational shortcomings. The availability of epidemiological data is controlled by the companies. Moreover, when the first such studies did emerge, the samples were sufficiently small that one could still not rule out with any reasonable confidence the hypothesis that the use of breast implants made it more probable than not that the patient's ailments were attributable to this product. It was only after substantial additional research that the courts have now concluded that there is no legitimate scientific basis for the claims for ailments such as connective tissue disorders.

The breast implant litigation was very much in the spirit of traditional personal injury litigation in that the beneficiaries of the damage awards consisted of injured individuals. However, because of the class action character of much of the litigation, the scale of it resembled that of the suits by governmental entities against tobacco, guns, and lead paint.

Although the breast implant litigation itself did not lead to negotiated settlements that imposed regulation, it did stimulate regulatory action by the FDA. The litigation led to the production of company documents that alerted the FDA to problems with the product, including leakage of the silicone gel from the implants and concealment of these problems by the company. Moreover, it may not be entirely coincidental that FDA Commissioner David Kessler suspended the use of breast implants shortly after a major court award in a breast implant case. Kessler's decision is widely viewed as an overreaction to the scientific evidence and public pressures.

In the end the scientific consensus is that the breast implants do not pose long-term risks, and Hersch documents that breast implants remain a popular form of cosmetic surgery. However, the financial cost to the firms that produced the implants cannot be reversed. Moreover, the bottom line for efficiency is that, at least in retrospect, society is not better off. The current state of information indicates that breast implants were not seriously unsafe devices.

Health Maintenance Organizations

The same kinds of lawsuits that have been lodged against products such as tobacco and lead paint have also focused on HMOs. This development may seem curious from the perspective of evaluating risk. Tobacco is certainly a risky product. Guns are often risky, especially if they are misused. Similarly, lead paint and breast implants pose hazards. However, one would have expected that the main effect of HMOs would be to enhance health rather than to increase risk.

The focus of the most recent litigation is on the quality control problems of managed care facilities. The plaintiff group is known as the REPAIR team, which is an organization headed by a former prominent tobacco attorney, Richard "Dickie" Scruggs. What Scruggs and his colleagues are attempting to do is to impose a settlement patterned after that in tobacco. Perhaps in an effort to force a settlement, they claim their HMO litigation will threaten the entire HMO industry with bankruptcy. Thus, as in the case of many of the other litigation case studies in this volume, serious financial pressures are being brought to bear in the hopes of generating some kind of settlement: principally a tax on premiums paid by individuals purchasing managed care insurance. For tobacco, one could easily argue that the excise tax discourages consumption of a risky product. However, for HMOs the effect of any kind of premium tax will be to discourage utilization of health care, which is presumably harmful to individual health rather than beneficial. Thus extensions of the tobacco model seem especially inappropriate.

Chapter 6 by Daniel P. Kessler and Mark B. McClellan uses survey data pertaining to physician practices to explore some of the presumed analytical linkages underlying the use of litigation with respect to HMOs. Their empirical analysis suggests that there seem to be few demonstrable benefits of litigation. In fact, increased medical malpractice claims lead to defensive medicine and the use of low-benefit treatments designed to decrease the risk of litigation rather than to foster patient health. In contrast, the increased role of managed care has led to more efficient health care utilization outcomes. Moreover, as noted, the character of the financial incentives created in at least one line of litigation is not structured to promote better quality care in any sense but will simply reduce the quantity of medical care received by raising premiums.

The concept of treating HMOs as a dangerous product that should be discouraged in much the same way as society discourages the use of tobacco and handguns appears to be without any sound foundation and driven solely by the desire of attorneys to extend the concept of regulation through litigation to promote their own personal gain. As yet, there has been no settlement of this litigation, and there is no indication that it will lead to any broadly based regulatory changes other than the proposed tax on insurance premiums.

Insurance Market Ramifications

Large-scale lawsuits requiring damages payments in the billions of dollars have profound ramifications for the defendant companies, but they also have influences that extend to insurers. In some, but not all, instances, firms have purchased insurance to cover at least a portion of their losses. As Kenneth S. Abraham and the commentary on his chapter by J. David Cummins indicate, assigning responsibility for bearing the financial costs is often a highly complex matter. Many of the risk exposures that have been subject to litigation are subject to long latency periods. Although asbestos risks are perhaps the most noteworthy case, tobacco, breast implants, and lead paint also have effects that are not immediate. The levels and timing of the risk exposure from such cases create serious problems for insurance. Assigning responsibility for any given ailment is difficult, particularly when there are multiple potential causes. The role of time is important too. Did the disease result from a risk exposure that took place during the time the insurance company was writing coverage for such losses, or was it some other period? In many instances, the character of the risks was not known when insurance companies wrote the policies. As a result, the insurance premiums charged were inadequate to cover the losses that eventually emerged once new diseases were identified or new lines of litigation developed. Now that insurance companies are aware of such unanticipated costs, Abraham notes that they are beginning to raise premiums to cover such contingencies, thus boosting the cost of insurance to potential purchasers.

The character of the insurance policies that the companies are willing to write has also changed. Abraham explores the evolution of insurance contracts in the case of pollution coverage and, more generally, coverage for toxic torts. For example, did the damage done by breast implants occur "during the policy period" because that was when the patient received the breast implants? Or did the harm occur at some later date? Such latent injuries often trigger great debate as to whether the injury occurred during this policy period and what the character of exposure should be to trigger coverage. As a result of this kind of litigation, insurance contracts now typically are written to provide "claims made" coverage for a particular policy period, thus reducing the uncertainties faced by insurance companies. However, even with a narrowing of the coverage of insurance contracts that are being written, Abraham concludes that firms are charging an uncertainty tax on premiums because of the difficulty in pricing risks that have a potentially long tail.

Class Actions and Mass Torts

Although many of the studies identify problems that have arisen with respect to the large-scale litigation case studies that were analyzed, chapter 8 by David Rosenberg suggests that this litigation in some instances can be constructive. He claims that mass torts are far superior to a rash of individual cases in addressing cases that involve common questions of law, common questions of fact, common legal facts, and potential economies of scale.

Such litigation would avoid the duplication of individual lawsuits. Rosenberg also makes the novel observation that the launching of mass tort suits leads to optimal investment in the litigation by plaintiffs because it avoids the collective action problems that would otherwise be present.

In many respects the Rosenberg model is one in which the judicial system in effect is the counterpart to regulatory agencies. In much the same way as government regulators find it efficient to focus on establishing broadly based regulatory standards for certain products, it is also more efficient in Rosenberg's view to have the legal system address all such product-related concerns in a single suit rather than in a series of individual cases, thus enabling the courts to take more of a market-based perspective. Rosenberg focuses, however, on the superiority of mass torts to individual suits, rather than on the superiority of mass torts to government regulation.

One noteworthy aspect of mass torts is the all or nothing character of the potential payoffs. If firms are risk neutral, then they will be indifferent to facing a series of individual lawsuits or one large-scale lawsuit. However, this conclusion assumes away the potential for learning and changing one's litigation strategy in a series of cases. Moreover, once the stakes are in the billions, risk aversion of shareholders enters as a factor. By raising the stakes of litigation in a manner that threatens firms with bankruptcy should they lose, class actions increase firms' willingness to settle rather than put the viability of the firm at risk, especially when there is a fear of punitive damages. Thus the merits of class action may vary greatly in different situations depending on whether we relate more closely to Rosenberg's constructive world of ideal class action assumptions or to the world of Judge Richard Posner, who views these lawsuits as no more than single-class blackmail.

The analytical desirability of the Rosenberg class action model also hinges critically on his assumptions about the character of the class action. As he emphasizes, homogeneity of the cases is important. One can view his criteria for the constructive role of mass torts as a useful checklist for what conditions must be satisfied for these lawsuits to be superior to individual litigation.

Policy Prognosis

Although several contributors to this volume cite constructive roles for class actions and the phenomenon of regulation through litigation, many have identified potential problems as well. Moreover, many of these chapters have identified criteria for judging which forms of litigation are constructive and which are not. Ideally, one would like to discourage litigation that has undesirable consequences, such as usurping the traditional authority of government regulation agencies and the control of taxation by the legislature.

How constructive changes could be accomplished is more problematic. The difficulty is not one of faulty government policy. The usual calls for government reform will not be effective. However, the more that can be done to promote effective regulatory oversight of potentially risky products such as breast implants and the greater the ability of government entities to ensure appropriate quality for products such as the health care provided by HMOs, the less chance there will be of successful litigation to address these concerns. In many instances, the litigation stems from a real or perceived failure by regulators to address potential harms to society.

Directly discouraging litigation is a more difficult matter. The attorneys bringing these suits have no reason to discipline themselves and restrain from launching lawsuits that are in their financial interest but perhaps not society's. The stakes involve payoffs to them in the billions of dollars, which constitutes a considerable lure for even the most self-restrained. Changing the character of the reimbursement of attorneys to avoid the windfall gains that resulted in the tobacco litigation and are being sought in the lead paint and HMO litigation could do much to deter such lawsuits in the future. At the minimum, there should be increased public scrutiny of such fee arrangements and a competitive open bidding process for all such deals involving government entities as the plaintiffs to discourage sweetheart deals with attorneys and litigation that is driven by the prospect of windfall private gains resulting from the threat of catastrophic losses by governmental lawsuits.

Whether the phenomenon of regulation through litigation proves to be a temporary or permanent way to address risk issues will depend greatly on the extent to which the concept can be applied to other products. Alcoholic beverages, fast food, automobiles, sport utility vehicles, and other products that create risks to consumers and external risks to others are among the potential targets of litigation. Whether such litigation will ever materialize hinges largely on how the courts address such suits. Unfortunately, because the tobacco litigation was settled, we lost an opportunity for the courts to establish definitive legal guidelines for such litigation. Only time will tell whether society will continue to regulate through the courts or through more conventional processes.

References

American Law Institute. 1991a. *Enterprise Responsibility for Personal Injury—Reporters' Study, Vol. 1: The Institutional Framework.* Philadelphia: American Law Institute.
———. 1991b. *Enterprise Responsibility for Personal Injury—Reporters' Study, Vol. 2: Approaches to Legal and Institutional Change.* American Law Institute.
Beretta USA Corp. 1999. "Beretta Announces Position concerning 'Smart Gun' Technology." Corporate Press Release (January).

W. KIP VISCUSI

2 | *Tobacco: Regulation and Taxation through Litigation*

Cigarettes are subject to considerable government regulation, taxation, and litigation. The social institutions of the regulatory agencies, the legislature, and the courts exert substantial control over the marketing of cigarettes and the economic incentives facing the cigarette industry. The involvement of multiple institutions is not necessarily undesirable. Different social institutions have different strengths and potentially can target different aspects of the performance of the cigarette industry. Moreover, cigarettes remain by far the most hazardous consumer product in terms of the total mortality associated with consumption of the product. However, existence of even substantial risks does not necessarily imply that all forms of intervention are necessarily desirable. This chapter explores the different aspects of societal intervention, the incentives they create, and the degree to which there is an appropriate division of labor among these different social institutions.

Although cigarettes have long been the target of substantial regulation by the federal government and legislative restrictions imposed by Congress, it has been the litigation against the cigarette industry that has catapulted tobacco into its current prominence in the risk policy area. As a

The author acknowledges support from the Sheldon Seevak Research Fund and the John M. Olin Center for Law, Economics, and Business. Although the author has served as an expert witness on behalf of the cigarette industry, the industry did not provide any financial support for this paper.

result of the lawsuits by states against the industry, there was a settlement of $206 billion with forty-six state attorneys general. This amount was in addition to the separate settlements with four individual states for a total $37 billion. Even these record-breaking penalties have not ended the sanctions imposed by litigation, as the Florida class action against the industry led to a punitive damages award in excess of $145 billion, and individual lawsuits against the industry have now begun to succeed in some instances, whereas formerly the industry had an unblemished record of long-term success.[1]

This transformation in the liability landscape has had profound implications not only for the financial well-being of the cigarette industry and the price of cigarettes but also on the overall character of how regulations are being imposed on the industry. As part of the settlement of the litigation launched by the states, the cigarette industry agreed to a variety of regulatory restrictions as well as a settlement formula that was tantamount to an excise tax. Thus the locus of control for important aspects of cigarette policy has shifted to the judicial arena, rather than being the province of the government entities that have traditionally had responsibility for such matters.

The principal implication of this assessment is not that cigarette regulation is too lenient or too stringent. The nature of the departure from optimal policies varies considerably with the context. For example, there is no clear-cut rationale for raising cigarette taxes based on the social externalities associated with smoking. However, there is a legitimate role for additional regulation of cigarette safety by the Food and Drug Administration provided that this regulation serves a more constructive function than many past government interventions have had.[2] The most fundamental shortcoming of this set of government interventions is not in the policy realm. Rather, it is the encroachment on the legitimate functions of the legislature and regulatory agencies that has occurred because of the national settlement of the cigarette litigation on behalf of the state attorneys general. Unfortunately, this phenomenon is not unique, as the tobacco model is now being emulated in other litigation contexts.

---

1. See Marc Kaufman, "Tobacco Suit Award: $145 Billion; FLA Jury Hands Industry Major Setback," *Washington Post*, July 15, 2000, p. A1.

2. This proposal is for an extension of FDA authority rather than reliance on its current legal authority, the extent of which is a matter of some debate. See Sunstein (1998) and Merrill (1998) for alternative points of view.

The Social Costs of Smoking

The standard textbook rationale for intervening to regulate a product is that it causes harm through the externalities that it generates. If smokers are making rational choices about their own well-being, then the only externalities to be considered are those imposed on society at large, not the externalities to smokers' future selves. The degree to which smokers are making an informed choice is explored in the following pages. However, for the purposes of assessing the social costs of smoking, I follow the standard approach in the literature.[3] This focus on the social externalities not including the effects on the smoker was also that taken in the lawsuits filed against the cigarette industry by the state attorneys general and in the federal government's suit.

From an economic standpoint, calculating the social costs of cigarettes is a fairly straightforward accounting exercise. The focus is on the financial externalities associated with cigarettes, and these are readily estimable. Excluded from this calculation are the health effects on smokers because these are private costs that are fully internalized if people are making informed decisions. These health effects on smokers themselves have not been part of any of the lawsuits filed by governmental entities against the industry but rather, more appropriately, remain the province of individual lawsuits claiming that consumers of the product have been harmed by the alleged wrongful conduct of the industry. Similarly, the calculations do not include costs associated with low birth weight babies.[4]

While proper economic accounting for the costs of cigarettes follows generally accepted standard methodologies, there are some fundamental economic principles governing the calculation that often are not observed in many of the cost estimates that have been publicized. Two key principles are that costs should be net costs over the lifetime, and these costs should be discounted back to the present.

The first key aspect of the calculations pertains to how costs are tallied within any particular time period. What is pertinent to the social cost calculations is the net costs specifically attributable to cigarettes and, in the case of litigation, the costs attributable to the wrongful conduct of the

---

3. See analyses such as those in Shoven, Sundberg, and Bunker (1989); Manning and others (1989, 1991); Gravelle and Zimmerman (1994); and Viscusi (1995, 1999).

4. Evans, Ringel, and Stech (1999) provide estimates of these costs.

cigarette industry. Thus what is needed is an analysis of the trajectory of medical costs and other cost impositions of an individual with the demographic profile of a smoker and to compare this stream of costs with that of a person who smokes but is otherwise similarly situated. It is the net difference in these costs that is the cigarette-related cost, not the gross medical costs incurred by smokers. This distinction is important because smokers are risk takers in a variety of dimensions. Smokers are more willing to work on hazardous jobs, more prone to accidents, and less likely to undertake self-protective behaviors such as checking their blood pressure or flossing their teeth.[5]

It is essential to note the different length of the time frame in which costs are incurred. Because smokers die sooner than do nonsmokers, their cost trajectory is shortened. In contrast, nonsmokers will continue to incur medical costs for a period after smokers have died. Recognizing this difference in the cost trajectory is not a "death credit" as it has been labeled by some attorneys in the state cigarette litigation. Rather, it is simply a recognition of what costs are actually incurred. Somewhat surprisingly, the dominant approach taken in the state cigarette litigation against the industry was to ignore the different lifetimes and only assess the relative costs during periods in which both smokers and nonsmokers were alive. That approach will overstate the actual cost generated by cigarette smokers. Recognizing the earlier death of smokers does not imply that this premature mortality is in any way socially desirable. Rather, it is simply a recognition that if one is to undertake a calculation based on the adverse health consequences of cigarettes, then one should recognize the full effects of these consequences and not simply those aspects of these health effects that impose costs on society.

The efforts by the state governments to calculate the costs of cigarettes never addressed the substance of the lifetime cost argument but rather attempted to demonize it. With respect to my analysis, which was not prepared in connection with any litigation, the state of Mississippi offered the following critique:

> The contention of entitlement to an "early death" credit is, on its face, void as against public policy. That policy and basic human decency preclude the defendants from putting forth the perverse and depraved argument that by killing Mississippians prematurely, they provide an economic benefit to the State. No court of equity should

5. See Hersch and Viscusi (1998); Viscusi and Hersch (2001).

countenance, condone, or sanction such base, evil, and corrupt arguments. . . . The defendants' argument is indeed ghoulish. They are merchants of death. Seeking a credit for a purported economic benefit for early death is akin to robbing the graves of the Mississippi smokers who died from tobacco-related illnesses. No court of law or equity should entertain such a defense or counterclaim. It is offensive to human decency, an affront to justice, uncharacteristic of civilized society, and unquestionably contrary to public policy.[6]

What the state of Mississippi and other states ignored was that the procedure I adopted simply focuses on the medical costs and other costs of cigarettes that actually occurred. This principle is common to all calculation of damages for wrongful conduct, whether it be a cigarette case or some other kind of action. By assuming that smokers continue to have higher medical costs than nonsmokers throughout a normal life expectancy, ignoring the fact that smokers are already dead, the calculation in effect will make smokers die twice because medical costs are highly concentrated in the last years of life.

Closely related to this principle of looking at the net difference in costs between smokers and nonsmokers is that if the litigation is seeking damages for the harms resulting from alleged wrongful conduct of the industry, the appropriate concept is to focus only on the portion of the cost attributable to the wrongful conduct. This principle is not unique to cigarette litigation but is a fundamental principle of economic damages calculations more generally. In the following analysis I do not attempt to distinguish the portion of costs attributable to wrongful conduct but instead focus only on the overall financial costs associated with smoking. Within the context of any particular litigation, one would then want to examine the amount of smoking during the period under consideration and the extent to which cigarette smoking was influenced by the wrongful conduct during that period.

The second consideration is that the value of these net lifetime costs must be discounted back to present value terms. In effect, what is of concern is the present value of the stream of costs recognizing that deferred cost impacts should receive less weight on a discounted basis than more immediate impacts. Many of the most publicized cost estimates do not

6. See my analysis, Viscusi (1995); and see pp. 21 and 23 of the Memorandum Supp. State's Mot. Ruling In Limine, or Alternatively, Partial Summary Judgment, In Moore, Attorney General Ex Rel., Miss. Tobacco Litigation (24-1429), August 11, 1995.

include any discounting, leading to an overstatement of the present value of medical costs. For purposes of my calculations, I use a real rate of return of 3 percent to discount the cost effects.

Discounting has effects that involve competing influences. Focusing strictly on the medical costs associated with smoking, using a lower rate of discount, or not discounting at all will increase the present value of these medical costs, making smoking look less attractive from a societal standpoint. Plaintiffs in cigarette litigation focusing only on these medical costs consequently have an incentive to use a low discount rate in calculating these costs. Similarly, estimates by public health groups focusing on medical costs often focus on the undiscounted values.

However, using a very low rate of discount affects other cost implications of cigarette smoking as well. One of the consequences of cigarette smoking is that smokers die sooner, reducing the pension and retirement benefits that smokers will receive. This component appears as a cost reduction in the cost calculations. The chief entity affected by this premature mortality is the Social Security retirement system. A higher rate of discount places a lower weight on these reduced pension and retirement cost reductions attributable to smoking. The net consequence of these discounting influences is that higher rates of discount make cigarette smoking less attractive from a net economic standpoint, whereas lower rates of discount make cigarettes look more attractive financially. Thus, while lower rates of discount boost the cost levels if one is only concerned with medical costs, with a more comprehensive cost focus lower rates of discount have the opposite effect.

Table 2-1 summarizes the cost implications of cigarettes for different components. These costs include those borne by the federal government, state governments, and private insurers. Two sets of estimates appear. Those in the first column do not include any tar adjustment for the riskiness of cigarettes. The second column adjusts the estimates proportionally for cigarette tar levels. The extent of the link between tar and the riskiness of cigarettes remains a matter of debate. Moreover, even if one accepts a linkage of smoking risks to tar levels, whether the adjustment should be proportional or less than proportional is not clear. As a result, the estimates assuming proportionality and the estimates assuming no risk-related properties of tar can be viewed as bracketing the likely social costs of cigarettes. Those wishing to undertake their own weighting can consequently use a weighted average of these cost estimates depending on the extent of the tar adjustment one would like to make. Because the estimates are in terms of costs

Table 2-1. *Social Costs of Smoking*
Dollar costs per pack of cigarettes

Cost category	Costs with no tar adjustment for cigarette risks	Tar-adjusted estimates of cigarette costs
Total medical care	0.580	0.481
Sick leave	0.013	0.012
Group life insurance	0.144	0.121
Nursing home care	−0.239	−0.207
Retirement and pension	−1.259	−1.055
Fires	0.017	0.017
Taxes on earnings	0.425	0.344
Total net costs	−0.319	−0.289

All estimates update the 1993 cost estimates in Viscusi (1995) to 1995 data whenever possible. All estimates involve discounting using a 3 percent real rate of return. These estimates are based on Viscusi (1999).

per pack of cigarettes, they do account for the number of cigarettes smoked but not for how low-tar cigarettes are smoked.

For the sake of concreteness, let us focus on the tar-adjusted estimates of the costs of cigarettes. As it turns out, adjusting for tar levels decreases the net social attractiveness of cigarettes from a financial standpoint. The total medical care costs of smoking are forty-eight cents per pack. There is also an additional life insurance cost of twelve cents per pack. Because smokers have earlier mortality, they do not contribute payroll taxes for Social Security and Medicare after their death. This loss is thirty-four cents per pack. My calculations do not include foregone federal income tax payments because smokers are not alive to reap the benefits of these programs. The reason for including the payroll tax values is that the payroll tax component is needed in order to have balanced accounting with respect to the inclusion of the Social Security and pension component.

By far the greatest cost reduction is with respect to retirement and pension costs, which are $1.06 per pack less because of the risks associated with smoking. Because of smokers' shorter lifetimes, they also spend much less time in nursing homes, leading to an additional cost savings of twenty-one cents per pack. Overall, there is a net cost savings to society of twenty-nine cents per pack using the tar-adjusted estimates. Based on the cost estimates without a tar adjustment, the cost savings is thirty-two cents per pack. Thus the tar adjustment raises the net costs of cigarettes to society or, put somewhat differently, reduces the net cost savings.

When assessing the overall net financial externalities, the conclusion is that cigarettes are not a burden on society but in fact lead to a net cost savings. Thus, if there is going to be a rationale for cigarette taxes or other penalties, then presumably it is not because cigarettes impose a net financial burden overall.[7]

Although these calculations address the costs generated by the smokers' medical expenditures, perhaps environmental tobacco smoke externalities also generate medical costs. In my analysis I used estimates by the Environmental Protection Agency and the Occupational Safety and Health Administration of the risks associated with environmental tobacco smoke.[8] The financial costs linked to environmental tobacco smoke, even using these conservative estimates that are likely to overstate the environmental tobacco smoke risks, were negligible. These results are consistent with the direct estimates by Michael J. Moore and Carolyn W. Zhu, who also found that there is no apparent effect on the health costs for those exposed to environmental tobacco smoke.[9]

A higher cigarette cost scenario would also include people's willingness to pay to avoid the health losses associated with exposure to environmental tobacco smoke rather than simply the medical costs. Using the conservative government estimates of the health risks of passive smoking, which are likely to overstate the health risks, I found that cigarettes do not impose a net cost on society from a financial standpoint.[10] Moreover, these estimates are exclusive of the role of excise taxes imposed on cigarettes, which represent an additional financial contribution from this product.

Taxing Cigarettes

Cigarettes are one of the most heavily taxed consumer commodities. In 1998, for example, cigarette taxes were twenty-four cents per pack at

7. Estimates by Cutler and others (2000) prepared as part of the state attorney general lawsuit in Massachusetts were to the best of my knowledge unique among all of the state estimates in that they used a sound methodology to calculate lifetime costs. These estimates focused, however, only on the costs associated with Medicaid spending, which they found to be about $318 million annually. Unfortunately, they did not report a cost per pack of cigarettes.

8. Viscusi (1995).

9. Moore and Zhu (2000).

10. Viscusi (1995).

the federal level and averaged thirty-five cents per pack at the state level, for a total tax per pack of fifty-nine cents.[11] Congress revisits the federal tax issue frequently but until recently had not raised cigarette taxes since 1993. In the mid-1990s there were proposals to tax cigarettes at ninety-nine cents per pack at the federal level to fund the Clinton health care plan, with one draft health care bill proposing a tax of two dollars per pack. States have also considered increases in the cigarette tax, and several states have continued to raise the cigarette excise tax level.

Excise taxes can serve various purposes from an economic standpoint. If the product imposes a net economic externality on society, taxes can be used to align the economics incentives of the product purchaser with those that would prevail if the full social costs of the product were borne by the consumer. The taxes on cigarettes and alcohol, which are often referred to as "sin taxes," at least implicitly involve some belief that the taxes are linked to the health consequences of smoking.

Another rationale for raising taxes on cigarettes or any other product is simply to raise money. In seeking to raise funds through taxation cigarettes may be an increasingly attractive target. Smokers tend to be blue-collar workers, who vote with lower frequency than nonsmokers and consequently may have less political influence. Smokers are also an increasingly small minority of the population and a vulnerable minority given the increased social unacceptability of smoking.

Even before the recent flurry of antismoking efforts, cigarettes ranked as the most heavily taxed major category of consumer purchases.[12] The tax rate on cigarettes exceeds that on alcohol, is triple the tax rate on gasoline, and more than an order of magnitude greater than the tax rate on automobiles and utilities.

Although there have been repeated proposals to increase cigarette taxes substantially, legislators have often hesitated to impose stark increases in this tax. Two reasons contribute to this hesitancy. First, the cigarette tax is extremely regressive.[13] It is much more likely that the janitors in the Capitol will bear more of the tax than will the legislators voting for it. The usual definition of regressivity is that the poor pay a higher proportion of their income toward such a tax. For cigarettes, the situation is much worse. The poor certainly pay a higher proportion of their income, as those with

---

11. See Tobacco Institute (1998).
12. See Fullerton and Rodgers (1993, p. 74) for documentation.
13. Estimates of regressivity discussed below are based on Viscusi (1995).

incomes below $10,000 pay 1.62 percent of their income in cigarette taxes, compared with 0.08 percent of the income of people making $50,000 or more. More tellingly, the poor pay a greater absolute amount of cigarette taxes than do the wealthy because of their higher smoking rates. Thus the cigarette excise tax is regressive in proportional as well as absolute terms.

A second reason for hesitating to impose a higher tax is that increased taxes will reduce cigarette demand. Most estimates of the elasticity of demand for cigarettes are in the vicinity of -0.4 to -0.7.[14] Similar estimates of the cigarette demand elasticities for women appear in Joni Hersch and for youths in Jeffrey Wasserman and others, while estimates for the cigarette demand elasticities of minorities are reported by Philip DeCicca, Donald Kenkel, and Alan Mathios.[15] Because of this negative demand elasticity, the total amount of cigarettes purchased will diminish as the tax increases, thus decreasing the number of packs of cigarettes for which these cigarette tax revenues will be paid. Taxes that are sufficiently great to eliminate cigarette smoking or regulations that prohibit smoking altogether would lead to a loss in revenues of $5.5 billion in 1998, and even greater amounts now given the structure of the tobacco settlement and subsequent tax increases.[16]

Do the excise taxes levied by the legislators reflect the cost implications of cigarettes? Given the widespread publicity for the reports by the Surgeon General for more than three decades, it is difficult to make the case that the government entities were ignorant of the linkage between smoking and health. Moreover, there have been published economic assessments of the health costs associated with smoking for more than a decade. These studies are in the public domain. Should the state legislators or Congress choose to raise excise taxes in view of these costs, then that is certainly within their province. On a prospective basis, there is little question that the appropriate taxation of cigarettes is a legislative issue, not a judicial issue.

Table 2-2 summarizes the costs of the federal government and the state government, when these estimates focus on financial effects excluding excise taxes. The federal excise tax rate of 24.0 cents per pack is almost identical to the total medical costs associated with cigarettes of 23.6 cents per pack. Thus, even if we focus solely on the medical cost component of cigarettes alone, the excise taxes cover this cost.

14. For a survey of these studies, see Viscusi (1992).
15. Hersch (2000); Wasserman and others (1991); DeCicca, Kenkel, and Mathios (2000).
16. See Tobacco Institute (1998); Viscusi (2002).

Table 2-2. *State and Federal Governmental Burden
of Insurance Externalities*
Dollar costs per pack of cigarettes

Cost category	Federal cost estimate	State cost estimate
Total medical care	0.236	0.033
Sick leave	0.001	0.001
Group life insurance	0.004	0.005
Nursing home care	−0.145	−0.078
Retirement pension	−0.847	−0.078
Fires	0.000	0.000
Taxes on earnings	0.221	0.027
Total net costs	−0.529	−0.090

Estimates are in 1995 dollars using a 3 percent real rate of interest. See Viscusi (1999) for discussion of the methodology underlying these estimates.

There are many major components of cost reductions that the federal government reaps because of the premature mortality of cigarette smokers. The chief components are the eighty-five-cent-per-pack savings in retirement pension costs and the fourteen-cent-per-pack savings in nursing home costs. The other cost increase components include the twenty-two-cent-per-pack tax on earnings that is lost because smokers die sooner and under a penny per pack in sick leave and group life insurance costs. Overall, from the standpoint of the federal government cigarettes generate fifty-three cents per pack in cost reductions. That amount is in addition to the excise tax cigarettes smokers pay for their product.

Estimates for the average state also appear in table 2-2. As can be seen, the scale of the effects on the states is much smaller. On average, the states incur total medical costs associated with smoking of only three cents per pack. This amount is roughly an order of magnitude smaller than the level of state excise taxes on cigarettes.

As with the federal government, states also are affected by the cost reduction components. In this instance, the nursing home care costs and retirement pension cost savings are almost identical, as they are each eight cents per pack. The overall average effect on states is nine cents per pack.

Table 2-3 summarizes the cost per state and the pertinent excise tax rate for each state. In every instance, the state does not incur overall positive external costs because of smoking. Rather, there is a net cost savings. This amount is in addition to the substantial excise taxes, such as those in the

Table 2-3. *State Cigarette Smoking Externalities*
Dollar costs per pack of cigarettes

State	State excise tax rate per pack	External costs per pack
Alabama	0.165	−0.069
Alaska	0.290	−0.111
Arizona	0.580	−0.107
Arkansas	0.315	−0.075
California	0.370	−0.183
Colorado	0.200	−0.147
Connecticut	0.500	−0.147
Delaware	0.240	−0.078
Florida	0.339	−0.091
Georgia	0.120	−0.081
Hawaii	0.600	−0.091
Illinois	0.440	−0.122
Indiana	0.155	−0.084
Iowa	0.360	−0.142
Kansas	0.240	−0.127
Kentucky	0.030	−0.066
Louisiana	0.200	−0.093
Maine	0.370	−0.070
Maryland	0.360	−0.090
Massachusetts	0.510	−0.128
Michigan	0.750	−0.073
Minnesota	0.480	−0.098
Mississippi	0.180	−0.036
Missouri	0.170	−0.156
Montana	0.180	−0.064
Nebraska	0.340	−0.096
Nevada	0.350	−0.085
New Hampshire	0.250	−0.112
New Jersey	0.400	−0.088
New Mexico	0.210	−0.066
New York	0.560	−0.036
North Carolina	0.050	−0.065
North Dakota	0.440	−0.050
Ohio	0.240	−0.104
Oklahoma	0.230	−0.160
Oregon	0.380	−0.079
Pennsylvania	0.310	−0.108

Table 2-3. *(continued)*

State	State excise tax rate per pack	External costs per pack
Rhode Island	0.610	−0.123
South Carolina	0.070	−0.061
South Dakota	0.330	−0.077
Tennessee	0.130	−0.047
Texas	0.410	−0.063
Utah	0.265	−0.061
Vermont	0.440	−0.069
Virginia	0.025	−0.089
Washington	0.815	−0.076
West Virginia	0.170	−0.042
Wisconsin	0.440	−0.135
Wyoming	0.120	−0.070
Averages	0.320	−0.096

Note: All figures assume a 3 percent discount rate. These average statistics are weighted by the packs of cigarettes sold per state rather than a simple average, which is the approach used for the averages in table 2-2. All estimates are for the costs invariant to the tar level case. See Viscusi (1999) for discussion of the methodology underlying these estimates.

state of Washington, where the tax is 81.5 cents per pack. The magnitude of the cost savings varies as well from low values such as 3.6 cents per pack for Mississippi and New York to 15.6 cents per pack in Missouri and 16.0 cents per pack in Oklahoma. The extent of the cost savings varies across these states because of the different composition of the population as well as differences in state pension and medical programs.

The empirical results, including the influence of excise taxes, are even stronger.[17] If excise taxes would have been recognized in the litigation as providing an offset to the increased medical costs of smoking, then cigarettes would be self-financing. Similarly, nursing home cost savings owing to smokers' premature mortality also exceed the increased medical costs owing to smoking for almost every state. The addition of pension costs savings would ensure a complete offset. How these various factors would have been tallied or should be tallied in future cases involving other products was never resolved because the cases were settled out of court. A social loss arising from the settlement was consequently the failure to establish legal precedents that would guide future litigation against hazardous products.

17. This discussion is based on Viscusi (1999).

Irrespective of the particular state, cigarettes do not impose a net negative financial externality. Moreover, the state excise taxes provide substantial positive revenues. These results do not necessarily imply that the states did not have a valid claim in the litigation against the cigarette industry. Whether there were in fact damages depends in large part on which component costs are calculated. However, from the standpoint of fiscal policy and the desire to find the optimal Pigovian tax to levy because of cigarette externalities, there is no apparent basis for doing so because of the financial externalities generated by smoking. States and the federal government can, however, choose to impose cigarette taxes for other legitimate reasons.

Hazard Warnings

The typical division of responsibility for hazard warnings can rest with one of three different social institutions. The firm within a market context may provide hazard warnings on its own. The government may establish guidelines for hazard warnings or specify the warning language through legislative action or through the efforts of regulatory agencies acting under enabling legislation pertaining to risk information. Finally, warnings are an ongoing concern in litigation. For roughly the past forty years, tort litigation has devoted increasing attention to concerns about hazard warnings.

The rationale for hazard warnings is that they potentially can provide information to consumers to enable them to make sounder decisions about taking risks.[18] This information can be one of two forms. First, the warnings could provide information to consumers with respect to the discrete choice of whether to purchase a product or engage in a risky activity. A second type of warning provides information that is of assistance in enabling people to take precautions within a particular risky activity. Cigarette warnings have generally been of the first type in that they have attempted to alert people to the hazards of smoking rather than indicating how they should smoke. Warning information pertaining to the relative riskiness of cigarettes, such as information about tar and nicotine content, would be closer to being a warning of the second type in that it indicates how people can reduce the risk given that they will be engaging in smoking.

The fundamental principle that should guide the provision of hazard

18. For reviews of the principles for hazard warnings see Viscusi and Magat (1987); Magat and Viscusi (1992); Viscusi (1991b).

warning information is that such warnings will only be effective to the extent that they provide new information in a convincing manner. If people already know the basic message being conveyed by the warning, then the warning will not be effective. Thus warnings that serve simply as reminder warnings will not alter behavior.[19] Similarly, warnings that are not credible because they are not truthful about the risks or do not seek to provide risk information but rather simply discourage consumption will not be effective forms of risk information.

In legislation passed in 1965, Congress required that beginning in 1966 cigarette packages bear the following warning: "Caution: Cigarette Smoking May Be Hazardous to Your Health." Congress not only specified the wording of the warning but also the size of the warning lettering and its placement on cigarette packs. This warning followed closely after the release of the landmark 1964 report linking cigarette smoking to lung cancer.[20]

Although warnings are now commonplace, the idea of stamping a product hazardous was relatively novel for the 1960s. Until that time, Congress had passed very few pieces of legislation directed at warning requirements. The 1927 Federal Caustic Poison Act was the first piece of legislation to require labeling of dangerous chemicals, such as sulphuric acid, which had to bear the warning "Poison." Beginning in 1938, the Federal Food, Drug, and Cosmetic Act began warnings for food and drugs. However, much of this warning effort was directed at mislabeling of products. In some cases dangerous chemicals were being marked as having health-enhancing properties. Moreover, the focus was exclusively on imminent hazards rather than the more deferred risks associated with cigarettes. In 1947 the Federal Insecticide, Fungicide, and Rodenticide Act initiated labeling of insecticides and herbicides. In 1960 Congress extended warning authority to include over-the-counter drugs and, for the first time, passed legislation (the Federal Hazardous Substance Labeling Act) that specified warnings for flammability and radioactivity. Thus, in terms of the overall warning environment, cigarettes were being put into the same kind of category as very dangerous chemicals and other products that posed immediate risks of death or serious injury. Indeed, it was not until 1983, or almost two decades later, that the Occupational Health and Safety Administration enacted warning regulation to require the labeling of dangerous chemicals in the workplace. By almost any measure, cigarettes were at the forefront of the warning effort.

19. See, for example, Adler and Pittle (1984) for a critique of reminder warnings such as those for seatbelts.

20. See the U.S. Department of Health, Education, and Welfare (1964).

The practical consequence of this primacy is that cigarettes were being singled out as the most dangerous widely used consumer product. Moreover, the warnings indicated the product was dangerous even if used correctly as the manufacturer intended. In contrast, the danger with insecticides and pesticides, for example, only arose from product misuse.

In 1969 Congress amended the warning language to the following: "Warning: The Surgeon General Has Determined That Cigarette Smoking Is Dangerous to Your Health." This change in warning language was noteworthy in that it was accompanied by legislative language that preempted lawsuits against the industry based on claims that the warnings were inadequate. In 1984 Congress expanded the warnings to include a series of four rotating warnings that are now on cigarette packs as well as in cigarette advertising.

These warning policies have also been accompanied by advertising restrictions. Print advertising for cigarettes must include the hazard warning label. Congress has also prohibited the cigarette industry from television and radio advertisements for the product.

Advertising may have had an influence on health risk beliefs in an unexpected manner. Because of the long-standing awareness that cigarettes have adverse health consequences, cigarette advertising has long attempted to suggest that this product does not pose greater health risks than other products. These health risk mentions are substantial and date back to the 1920s and perhaps earlier.[21] Even in the 1926–29 period, cigarette advertising was making claims with respect to harm to the throat, coughs, and health more generally.[22]

Whether additional warnings are needed about the risks of smoking depends on whether people's risk beliefs are already sufficiently high given the level of risks posed. The survey evidence available suggests that not only is there risk awareness, but that people greatly overestimate the risks.[23] Consider the following results.[24] Estimates based on studies reported by the Surgeon General suggest that the risk of lung cancer owing

21. For a review of this evidence, see Ringold and Calfee (1989), Calfee (1985, 1986), and Viscusi (1992), which discuss their research and other evidence in the literature.

22. See Ringold and Calfee (1989).

23. Similar results to those reported below for the United States also hold true for Spain. Compare, for example, the results for the United States in Viscusi (1990, 1991a, 1998a, 1998b, 1998c) with those for Spain in Antoñanzas and others (2000); Rovira and others (2000); and Viscusi and others (2000).

24. The 1985, 1997, and 1998 surveys discussed below were administered by nationally recognized survey research firms, where these surveys were funded by law firms representing the cigarette industry. The 1991 survey was supported by my research funds at Duke University.

to smoking ranges from 0.06 to 0.13 over the smoker's lifetime. The assessed probability of lung cancer based on my analysis of responses to questions about the risk of smoking was 0.43 in a national survey in 1985, 0.38 in a North Carolina survey in 1991, 0.47 in a national survey in 1997, and 0.48 in a large-scale survey of Massachusetts in 1998. The general form of the lung cancer question was in terms of the risk to a group of 100 smokers. For example, in 1985 it was the following: "Among 100 smokers, how many of them do you think will get lung cancer because they smoke?"

The mortality risks associated with smoking are also seriously overestimated. Estimates based on findings by the Surgeon General suggest a total mortality risk to the smoker ranging from 0.18 to 0.36, based on an analysis that takes these health risk estimates at face value. In contrast, public perceptions of the total mortality risks of smoking were 0.54 in North Carolina in 1991, 0.50 in the 1997 national survey, and 0.54 in the Massachusetts 1998 survey. The wording of the total mortality risk question was similar to that for lung cancer. For example, the wording in the 1997 survey was as follows: "Among 100 smokers, how many of them do you think will die from lung cancer, heart disease, throat cancer, or any illness because they smoke?"

Estimates of the life expectancy loss associated with smoking are similar and also indicate overestimation of the risk but not to the same extent as for lung cancer. For example, the 1997 national survey indicated an assessed life expectancy loss of 10.1 for males and 14.8 for females. An example of the life expectancy question used to generate these estimates was the following wording in the 1997 survey: "As you may know, an average 21-year old male (female) would be expected to live to the age of 73 (80). What do you think the life expectancy is for the average male (female) smoker?"

A distinctive feature of these questions is that they elicit risk beliefs with respect to a meaningful quantitative metric. Thus in every instance there is a well-defined reference point for assessing whether risk perceptions are too high, too low, or accurate, given the current state of knowledge about the risks of smoking. In contrast, qualitative risk questions that ask consumers whether smoking, for example, is very dangerous, somewhat dangerous, or not at all dangerous, do not permit comparison with a scientific reference point to assess whether beliefs are sufficiently great, given the risks associated with smoking. These difficulties with qualitative questions are particularly great when different respondents interpret these qualitative characteristics of risk differently, as is often the case when deal-ing with risk perceptions across different educational groups and different segments of the population exposed to varying levels of hazards in the con-text of their work.[25]

The overwhelming evidence is that based on surveys using mean-ingful quantitative metrics people either have accurate perceptions of the risk of smoking or overestimate these risks. Thus in terms of creating general awareness about the risk of smoking, there is no need for addi-tional information on risk. A conclusion along these lines is not new but dates back to claims made long ago by the head of the federal agency responsible for disseminating smoking information. Daniel Horn, M.D., a leading smoking lung cancer risk researcher and the director of the National Clearinghouse for Smoking and Health, observed in 1968, "You could stand on the rooftop and shout 'smoking is dangerous' at the top of your lungs and you would not be telling anyone anything they did not already know."[26]

That it is difficult to quit smoking is also well known.[27] Would it, for example, be worthwhile to alert consumers that smoking is now labeled an addiction by the Surgeon General? Overall, 13 percent of smokers, fifteen to twenty years old, believe that smoking is addictive, 26 percent believe that it is a habit, 57 percent believe that it is both a habit and an addic-tion, and only 4 percent believe that it is neither.[28]

The government already has substantial mechanisms for providing hazard warning information, including not only product warnings for cigarettes but also regular media coverage of the annual reports by the Surgeon General and general statements by public health officials. Indeed, as the quantitative measures of risk perception indicate, the extent of these efforts has been so great that there seem to be no evi-dent informational gaps. Rather, there is evidence of great overestima-tion of the risks of smoking. Should there be any perceived need for more warnings in the future, they can presumably be addressed through legislative actions given the fact that currently the on-product warnings for cigarettes and cigarette advertising are dictated by existing laws passed by Congress.

25. See Gaba and Viscusi (1998) for empirical documentation.

26. See Nancy Sharp, "Is An End Near for Smoking?" *Syracuse Herald-American*, November 3, 1968, p. 20.

27. For an economic analysis of cigarette addiction, see Becker and Murphy (1988); Becker, Gross-man, and Murphy (1996).

28. See Hersch (1998).

Cigarette Riskiness

Although hazard warnings are designed to alert consumers to the over-all riskiness of cigarettes, tar and nicotine ratings have a narrower focus in that they address the specific risk attributes of different brands of ciga-rettes. These tar and nicotine ratings have been the major publicized mea-sure of cigarette hazards and have been associated with the most dramatic changes in smoking behavior. Whereas tar levels per cigarette were 46.1 mg in 1944, these levels dropped to 12 mg of tar by 1994.

In the 1950s companies engaged in a vigorous effort to promote cig-arettes based on their comparative riskiness. In the 1957–60 period known as "The Great Tar Derby," market competition led to substantial advertis-ing of low-tar brands as well as substantial switching of consumers to such low-tar cigarettes.[29] To make sound risk-taking decisions, one would want consumers to be informed about the relative riskiness of cigarettes so that they could better match the risk levels of the particular brand to their own risk-taking preferences and willingness to trade off risk against other ciga-rette attributes, such as taste. Unfortunately, rather than encouraging this market competition on the safety dimension, the government has long dis-couraged it. In 1960 the Federal Trade Commission brokered an agree-ment with the industry to eliminate tar and cigarette advertising. The ill-conceived character of this policy was recognized by the American Can-cer Society, which ultimately was successful in reversing the FTC position in the late 1960s. The FTC published tar and nicotine levels for cigarettes in 1967, and shortly thereafter disclosure of tar and nicotine levels became a required component of all cigarette advertising. Testing of cigarettes for their tar and nicotine levels and rating of cigarettes along this dimension remains the responsibility of the FTC, which also disseminates tar and nicotine ratings.[30]

The government has continued to have a lack of enthusiasm toward providing information to enable people to choose cigarettes based on their relative riskiness. Rather, the government emphasizes the risk-free charac-teristics of not smoking at all. Unfortunately, if people are going to choose to smoke, the government does not provide them with the kind of infor-mation that might be useful in making such decisions. Indeed, the 1989 Surgeon General's report summarized the official misgivings with respect to

29. Calfee (1985) provides an extensive discussion of this period. Also see Viscusi (1992).
30. The procedure that continues to be used is the Cambridge testing method, which was approved by the FTC in 1966. The FTC updated this testing approach in 1980.

the Premier cigarette—a cigarette product that eliminated the carcinogenic risk associated with smoking without any increase in other risk components. By any reckoning, it was clearly a lower-risk product. Nevertheless, the Surgeon General warned:

> The marketing of a variety of alternative nicotine delivery systems has heightened concern within the public health community about the future of nicotine addiction. The most prominent development in this regard was the 1988 test marketing by a major cigarette producer of a nicotine delivery device having the external appearance of a cigarette and being promoted as "the cleaner smoke."[31]

In almost every other area of cigarette policy the government has embraced technological advances that reduce risks. Somewhat surprisingly, the government has long been in a position of discouraging such innovations, as well as hindering information about relative product safety.

One noteworthy new policy on relative cigarette riskiness was the Massachusetts Tobacco Disclosure Law, known as Chapter 234 of the Acts of 1996. The provisions of this law would require the cigarette industry to disclose the toxic ingredients in cigarettes. Although this law was successfully challenged in court by the tobacco industry, the provisions of the law exemplify the kind of risk communication that is not likely to be helpful to consumers. Simply listing cigarette ingredients will not aid consumer understanding, as consumers do not know the quantity of these chemicals and do not have the expertise to map the presence of such chemicals into assessed risk levels. What is consequential is the overall riskiness of cigarettes, not a list of their components.

Perhaps inspired in part by the Massachusetts disclosure law, R. J. Reynolds began to advertise its Winston cigarette brand noting that it contains no additives. Presumably, if additives are a sufficiently great public concern to warrant the Massachusetts legislation, companies should indicate the absence of additives to aid consumers in making their brand choice. Somewhat surprisingly, the FTC filed a complaint against R. J. Reynolds for the no additives claim, indicating that it might mislead consumers into thinking the product was safer. As a result, the additive-free Winstons now include the following statement in all advertisements: "No additives in our tobacco does NOT mean a safer cigarette."[32]

31. See U.S. Department of Human Services (1989).
32. FTC file 9923025, March 3, 1999, p. 1.

On additives and on tar levels, the industry is often subject to conflicting government policies that often seem to lose sight of what should be the nation's principal policy objective, which is the promotion of consumer welfare based on informed decisions about possible risks.

The Proposed Federal Settlement

Although cigarette policy has traditionally been the focus of the legislature and regulatory agencies, in 1997 there was a landmark change in the role of the judiciary.[33] The legitimate role of the courts has been and will continue to be to provide a venue for individual smokers who claim they were wrongfully injured by cigarettes. However, a different set of cases emerged in the mid-1990s as the states filed a series of lawsuits seeking to recoup Medicaid expenses linked to cigarettes. By 1997 more than forty states had filed lawsuits against the industry, and the industry sought to consolidate these lawsuits through an out-of-court settlement. However, the proposed out-of-court settlement was not a settlement in any conventional sense. Rather, it was a proposal to impose a cigarette tax and additional regulatory restrictions on the industry.

On June 20, 1997, the cigarette industry departed from its past practice of successfully defending itself against lawsuits by offering a $368.5 billion settlement amount over a twenty-five-year period to settle these lawsuits and obtain additional protections.[34] Although this proposed resolution was never adopted by Congress, it nevertheless was instructive in that it provided the model for the final settlement that was reached and marked the beginning of this kind of negotiated settlement of other kinds of litigation.

The terms of the settlement were complex and extended far beyond the $368.5 billion price tag that was widely publicized. The industry would be paying $10 billion up front and then making annual payments rising from $8.5 billion a year initially to $15 billion after five years. Although the publicity about the proposed settlement focused on the first twenty-five years of payments, the agreement would continue in perpetuity. The most distinctive component of the settlement is that it did not

33. See Viscusi (1998a, 1998b) for earlier discussions of these proposed and final cigarette settlements as well as Schwartz (1999, 2000) for a different perspective.

34. The "Proposed Resolution" was released "for settlement discussion purposes only, June 20, 1997, 3:00 p.m." and can be accessed at www. Stic.neu.edu [August 1, 2002].

involve a lump sum payment by the cigarette industry. Rather, it involved payments that varied proportionally with the unit sales volume of tobacco products. In effect, the settlement was a negotiated tobacco tax that was equivalent to sixty-two cents per pack on cigarettes. Given the nature of tax shifting, the brunt of the tax would be borne by smokers rather than by the cigarette industry. To the extent that one was to impose a tax that would discourage smoking, these incentive effects are desirable. Some anti-smoking advocates expressed regret that it would be smokers rather than the industry itself bearing the tax. However, if the penalty had been a lump sum imposition of some form, then that would sacrifice the incentive effects that the antismoking groups also wished to preserve.

Characterizing the imposition of a new cigarette tax as a settlement amount has obvious benefits for marketing the agreement. Because conventional settlements are actually paid for by the defendants themselves, this settlement would have the appearance of imposing a cost solely on the tobacco industry. Attorneys general could sell this settlement to their constituents as a windfall for the state that would be paid for by the industry, whereas in fact it would be paid for in large part by the smokers within their state.

The approach of settling litigation through the imposition of a tax rather than a conventional damages payment bypasses the usual legislative processes for setting taxes. At that time state and federal cigarette taxes were only fifty-six cents per pack so that the tax amount that would be levied through the out-of-court settlement would exceed the total state and federal excise taxes already in place and approved by legislators. The issue that was never addressed as part of the settlement is why there was some kind of governmental failure on the part of the legislature to levy the appropriate tax. In the absence of such a failure, there is no rationale for transferring this responsibility to this group of negotiators including representatives of the tobacco industry and a group of representatives of the states' interests, including Mississippi Attorney General Mike Moore, Republican Senate Majority Leader Trent Lott's brother-in-law, and the increasingly newsworthy brother of Hillary Rodham Clinton, Hugh Rodham.

The proposed settlement also was not a settlement in any conventional sense in terms of its other provisions. Rather than Congress extending the regulatory authority of the Food and Drug Administration, this settlement would have given the FDA broad authority to regulate cigarettes as a drug. A preferable outcome would be to have Congress itself focus on broadening the FDA authority if it believes such authority should be expanded.

The Proposed Resolution would have replaced the existing set of warnings with a series of nine rotating warnings, which would have been the following:

WARNING: Cigarettes are addictive
WARNING: Tobacco smoke can harm your children
WARNING: Cigarettes cause fatal lung disease
WARNING: Cigarettes cause cancer
WARNING: Cigarettes cause strokes and heart disease
WARNING: Smoking during pregnancy can harm your baby
WARNING: Smoking can kill you
WARNING: Tobacco smoke causes fatal lung disease in non-smokers
WARNING: Quitting now greatly reduces serious risks to your health

Although warnings such as these may seem innocuous, the drafting of hazard warnings should not be a haphazard exercise. The designers should not clutter the warning space with information that is already well known. Before embarking on a warning program such as this, it is essential to ascertain what information gaps need to be filled and whether these warnings will be successful in addressing them. In the past, Congress has held hearings on tobacco risk information and has also benefited from studies undertaken by federal regulatory agencies in support of such legislation. Moreover, there is an opportunity for open debate and presentation of diverse points of view on the appropriate form that warnings should take. In contrast, the secretive deals such as those embodied in the Proposed Resolution seek to supplant the current warning policy with a negotiated set of new warnings without any evidence whatsoever on the likely effects on consumer choice.

The Proposed Resolution also included numerous other regulatory components. It would have banned outdoor advertising of cigarettes and formally retired cartoon characters such as Joe Camel and human figures such as the Marlboro Man. There also would be a $500 million annual antismoking advertising campaign launched by the federal government as well as bans of cigarette sales through vending machines and all self-service tobacco displays except in adults only facilities.

The agreement would have discouraged unregulated claims about the riskiness of various brands of cigarettes, such as "low tar" and "light" unless the company could prove that such cigarettes would "significantly reduce the risk to health." Companies were to prove that their products were safer. The proposal permitted the FDA to allow "scientifically-based specific health claims" and even would have given the FDA authority to mandate the introduction of "less hazardous tobacco products" that are technologically feasible. Whether the FDA would have encouraged the promotion and marketing of safer cigarettes under this proposal or have continued to oppose those products as nicotine delivery devices is not clear.

The bill also would have had extensive provisions directed at youth smoking, including increased penalties for violations and decreased payments to states that did not meet performance targets for the sale of cigarettes to minors. There would also be "look-back" provisions that would impose additional penalties of up to $2 billion per year if targets for underage use of cigarette products were not met. These targets were often ambitious, such as a 60 percent decline in youth smoking within ten years. The practical difficulties of such provisions arise because the cigarette industry may not have effective policy levers to reduce youth smoking, particularly if, for example, youths obtain cigarettes from their friends or from adults.

In return for these concessions, the cigarette industry not only would obtain settlement of the state tobacco suits but also would have obtained additional legal protections. The settlement would have precluded all future claims for punitive damages, all class actions, and all future claims based on addiction or cigarette dependence. Although the industry could still be sued for past conduct, suits about future conduct would be precluded.

The Proposed Resolution was never adopted by Congress. President Bill Clinton never gave the Proposed Resolution substantial support. Moreover, former public health officials such as David Kessler, former commissioner of the Food and Drug Administration, believed that if the industry could afford an additional tax of sixty-two cents per pack, then it could incur a much greater cost. Public health advocates proposed a $1.50 increase in the tax imposed on each pack of cigarettes. A bill raising federal excise taxes on each pack to $1.50 was introduced in November 1997 by Senator Ted Kennedy, leading to an estimated cost to the industry of more than $600 billion.[35] This proposal was never adopted.

35. See Barry Meier, "Tobacco Bill Being Offered by Kennedy," *New York Times*, November 10, 1997, p. A22.

Although no version of the Proposed Resolution was ever adopted by Congress, this proposal remains a watershed event in the history of tobacco litigation. For the first time, the industry volunteered to settle pending litigation, and it did so with a proposed settlement that was at a record-breaking level. However, the settlement proposal was not so much a settlement but rather a combination of an excise tax coupled with extensive regulatory provisions. Functions that had usually been addressed through legislation and regulatory policy had now become the province of the legal bargaining process.

The Settlement of the State Lawsuits

After the prospects for adoption of the Proposed Resolution began to fade, the cigarette industry began to negotiate settlements with the individual states. It reached a settlement with the state of Mississippi for $3.5 billion, Florida for $11.3 billion, Texas for $15.3 billion, and Minnesota for $6.6 billion.[36] After these initial settlements and after the prospects for congressional passage of the Proposed Resolution were eliminated, there was a settlement of the state attorneys general suits for $206 billion shortly after the November 1998 elections. This settlement was similar in many respects to the character of the Proposed Resolution except that the stakes were somewhat less, as were the legal protections given to the cigarette industry. However, the key features, which are the functioning of the settlement as an excise tax and the inclusion of some regulatory provisions, were retained.

As with the Proposed Resolution, the settlement did not take the form of a damages payment but rather was a tax linked to the total number of packs of cigarettes sold. For example, the tax level set by the settlement would be $8 billion annually from 2004 to 2007, which is tantamount to a thirty-three-cent-per-pack tax equivalent charge.[37] The tax equivalent value in other years is comparable, though the amounts differ depending on the penalty level specified in each year by the agreement. Thus the first distinctive aspect of the state settlement is that it led to the imposition of an additional per pack tax on cigarettes.

36. All settlement information for the master settlement agreement can be found at www.stic.neu.edu.

37. Recognition of costs of the four separate state settlements would increase these cost-per-pack values further. See Viscusi (1998d).

Imposing a tax on current cigarette producers would, of course, create the potential for new lower-cost entrants. Existing companies would be disadvantaged, and the states would reap fewer penalty dollars than they had expected. To prevent such losses, the master settlement agreement required that new entrants also contribute to a prospective damages fund. Since the settlement was an excise tax on future cigarette sales rather than a lump sum payment for past harms, this aspect of the settlement logic is seemingly consistent. The justification for any such payment derived from the cigarette litigation must, however, be linked to companies' wrongful conduct. New entrants presumably have not yet engaged in such wrongful conduct. The logic of the litigation consequently was abandoned by simply making the settlement a vehicle for an excise tax. Moreover, if the settlement is simply tantamount to an excise tax, why is not such a financial imposition the legitimate province of the state legislatures? Disguising the tax as a damages payment did offer the benefit of being able to sell the agreement to the public more easily than would have been the case had its true structure been better known.

There are additional serious concerns raised about prospective market competition. If new entrants develop safer cigarettes, these new products will be penalized unduly by the settlement formula. If future cigarettes were, for example, risk free, presumably there should be no tax penalty.

The master state settlement also included a wide range of regulatory reforms. Because the state settlement was not an act that would be approved by Congress, it did not include provisions such as a new set of hazard warnings for cigarettes or increased regulatory authority for the FDA. However, it did include many other regulatory actions. These included provisions that prevented the targeting of youths by cigarette marketing, bans on the use of cartoon characters such as Joe Camel in cigarette advertising, no payments by the cigarette industry for product placements in movies, bans on tobacco brand merchandise, and limitation on corporate sponsorship of events. The desirability of such efforts is not at all obvious given the competing policy objectives at stake. Limitations on cigarette advertising in effect lock in the market shares of existing companies. Besides these anticompetitive effects, limitations on cigarette advertising reduce the opportunities firms have to market to consumers cigarettes of different riskiness, thus enabling consumers to make an appropriate choice of the risk level of cigarette that they wish to consume. To the extent that cigarette advertising largely affects brand choice rather than the decision to smoke, these provisions will be an economic benefit to the existing firms in the industry but will decrease the information available to consumers that might have enabled them to make a better choice among cigarette brands.

The settlement also included funding for antismoking efforts. The cigarette industry was required to fund a foundation to reduce youth smoking, with payments totaling $250 million over ten years. The industry would also contribute funds to a national publication education fund, where the magnitude of such payments was even greater. The industry contribution would begin at $250 million in 1999 and $300 million annually beginning in the year 2000 through the year 2003 for a total of $1.45 billion.

The settlement agreement itself was a political document driven by the relative political strength of the different attorneys general bargaining on behalf of their states. Although the shares of the settlement received by each state were correlated with the medical costs incurred by the state, these costs were not the driving force behind the division of the settlement amount.

Table 2-4 provides a summary for each state of the percentage share of the medical costs related to smoking incurred in each state. The second column of table 2-4 indicates each state's share of the settlement amount specified in the settlement agreement. If states were paid directly in proportion to their medical costs, the medical cost share in the first column of table 2-4 should be identical to the settlement share in the second column. The final column of table 2-4 gives the ratio of the settlement share to the medical cost share. States with a ratio greater than 1.0 reaped a disproportionate share of the settlement relative to their share of medical costs. States with a ratio below 1.0 were not adequately compensated from a proportional standpoint. All states were overcompensated in absolute terms. Clearly there was not a proportional distribution of the settlement amount.

Of particular interest are three states that received very low levels of compensation relative to their medical costs. These include the state of Kentucky, which had a settlement payment share per percentage point of dollar loss of 0.64; North Carolina with a payment relative to medical cost loss of 0.68; and Virginia, which had a payment relative to medical cost loss of 0.75. These are the three leading tobacco-producing states in the country, and each of them received a less than proportional share of the settlement given the level of their medical costs.

In contrast, consider the state of Washington. That state received 1.4 percent of the settlement for each percentage point of medical cost loss. This disproportionate benefit amount to the state of Washington is not

Table 2-4 *Relationship between Settlement Payments and Medical Care Externalities*

State	Medical cost share	Share of settlement	Settlement share divided by medical cost share
Alabama	0.015	0.016	1.08
Alaska	0.003	0.003	1.26
Arizona	0.005	0.015	2.85
Arkansas	0.010	0.008	0.83
California	0.086	0.130	1.52
Colorado	0.012	0.014	1.14
Connecticut	0.019	0.019	0.97
Delaware	0.005	0.004	0.78
Georgia	0.032	0.025	0.79
Hawaii	0.002	0.006	2.89
Idaho	0.002	0.004	1.62
Illinois	0.056	0.047	0.84
Indiana	0.036	0.021	0.58
Iowa	0.010	0.009	0.90
Kansas	0.008	0.008	1.02
Kentucky	0.028	0.018	0.64
Louisiana	0.024	0.023	0.95
Maine	0.007	0.008	1.08
Maryland	0.020	0.023	1.12
Massachusetts	0.032	0.041	1.30
Michigan	0.033	0.044	1.33
Missouri	0.027	0.023	0.85
Montana	0.002	0.004	1.77
Nebraska	0.006	0.006	1.07
Nevada	0.005	0.006	1.19
New Hampshire	0.009	0.007	0.76
New Jersey	0.043	0.039	0.92
New Mexico	0.004	0.006	1.73
New York	0.152	0.130	0.86
North Carolina	0.035	0.024	0.68
North Dakota	0.002	0.004	1.76
Ohio	0.061	0.051	0.83
Oklahoma	0.012	0.011	0.88
Oregon	0.010	0.012	1.16
Pennsylvania	0.053	0.059	1.10
Rhode Island	0.007	0.007	0.99

Table 2-4 *(continued)*

State	Medical cost share	Share of settlement	Settlement share divided by medical cost share
South Carolina	0.014	0.012	0.84
South Dakota	0.003	0.004	1.39
Tennessee	0.029	0.025	0.86
Utah	0.002	0.005	2.06
Vermont	0.003	0.004	1.31
Virginia	0.028	0.021	0.75
Washington	0.015	0.021	1.40
West Virginia	0.010	0.009	0.92
Wisconsin	0.020	0.021	1.06
Wyoming	0.002	0.003	1.42

Florida, Minnesota, Mississippi, and Texas did not participate in the settlement, therefore report-ing zero percentage. Medical cost externality figures assume a 3 percent discount rate. See Viscusi (1999) for discussion of the methodology underlying these estimates.

unexpected since the lead individual responsible for structuring the set-tlement was Washington attorney general Christine Gregoire. Besides putting together a consensus agreement among the forty-six attorneys gen-eral, she also succeeded in bringing home more than a fair share of the set-tlement amount to her state.

What this table demonstrates is that the settlement of the litigation was very much a political settlement. It was not driven strictly by medical costs but also by the relative political power of the various participants. The other provisions of the agreement, including those pertaining to excise taxes and regulations, were also political in character.

Conclusion

The tobacco settlement led to a record-breaking damages award that functioned as a cigarette excise tax and to extensive regulation of cigarettes from a product safety and marketing standpoint. That such an outcome resulted from a process that was in many respects political in character is not in itself disturbing. Legislation enacted by Congress is also political in character. However, what distinguished the out-of-court settlement of the tobacco litigation was that these tax and regulatory policies were enacted without the usual input that accompanies the development of policies of this type.

Consider, for example, the procedures that are in place for the promulgation of federal regulations. Agencies considering a proposed rule must prepare a regulatory impact analysis of the rule and submit it to the Office of Management and Budget sixty days before posting a notice of proposed rulemaking in the Federal Register. If the regulation is consistent with the priorities of the administration and is published in the Federal Register, the public has thirty to ninety days to be made aware of the regulation and provide comments. Thus there is a formal mechanism at the very early stages of the regulatory process to engage the public in providing information pertaining to the merits of the regulatory proposal. The agency then prepares the final rule and regulatory impact analysis and must send it to the Office of Management and Budget thirty days before publishing it in the Federal Register. If the regulation is approved by the Office of Management and Budget, which is guided by an executive order that establishes well-defined principles for assessing costs and benefits of regulation, then the agency will be permitted to publish the final rule in the Federal Register. At that point, Congress has an opportunity to review the regulatory proposal should it wish to do so, where the rule would go into effect thirty days after being published in the Federal Register.

Even listing these various stages of study and review does not do justice to the scrutiny that regulatory policies receive. The regulatory impact analysis process itself often involves a detailed discussion of the benefits and costs of the regulation. These assessments are often the subject of bitter battles between the Office of Management and Budget and the regulatory agency. Moreover, there are often public hearings associated with regulatory proposals to obtain detailed information and public input on these efforts. Although all regulatory proposals that emerge from this process are not always ideal, there is a much greater opportunity for informational input and for diverse points of view to be expressed than is the case with secret deals negotiated by participants in a litigation process, such as that for the tobacco settlement. Moreover, even within the overall context of this regulatory effort, there are legislative guidelines that provide additional structure to what regulatory agencies can and cannot do, when these guidelines are the results of laws enacted by Congress.

In the case of regulation or taxes that emerged through negotiated settlements to litigation, there is no substantial public input of this type. Nor is there any guarantee that the public interest will be well represented. Consider, for example, an industry faced with the prospect of a substantial damages payment that will emerge from court cases. Other things being equal, it would be attractive to the industry to have a larger portion of that payment shared by consumers. Similarly, because the current resources of tobacco companies are more limited, it might be in the interests of the states to also prefer a tax-like structure over a longer period because they will be able to reap a greater amount of funds from the settlement than they otherwise would. Consumers, especially cigarette smokers, in all likelihood might have different preferences regarding what they view as the optimal structure of such an arrangement. However, they are not represented in this process except to the extent that cigarette companies would like to sell the product to them, and the states typically would like to discourage them from buying the product.

Unfortunately, even though the tobacco settlement was a bad model, it has spurred additional efforts of the same type. One prominent veteran of the tobacco litigation initiated a series of lawsuits against HMOs that he indicated were patterned after the Proposed Resolution. Moreover, the billions of dollars in attorneys' fees reaped by the lawyers engaged in the tobacco litigation have fueled additional litigation efforts of this type. The harm caused by this settlement consequently extends well beyond the cigarette industry itself.

COMMENT BY
John E. Calfee

Viscusi has provided a compelling argument that the most important tobacco litigation to date, brought mainly by state attorneys and involving the payment of hundreds of billions of dollars to state governments and others over many years, cannot be justified on its own grounds of recoupment of health care costs imposed by smoking. That this litigation and similar suits brought by other organizations have proceeded despite his argument (which was well known before the litigation began), and have done so with substantial political and judicial support, requires explanation and comment. The explanation lies partly in the fact that public health agencies and organizations believe that tobacco litigation is useful if not essential. My comments argue that even by the standards of the public health community, tobacco litigation appears to be unjustified.

The Public Health Community and Tobacco Litigation

Support for tobacco litigation had emerged in the public health literature by the 1980s. Not until the mid-1990s, however, did litigation become a prominent part of the public health community's battle against smoking.[38] A prominent figure in the tobacco litigation community notes that the Food and Drug Administration (FDA) played a decisive role: "The third, and current, wave of tobacco litigation began in the spring of 1994. It was initiated by the February 1994 announcement by Dr. David Kessler that the Food and Drug Administration was considering classifying nicotine and cigarettes as drugs."[39] Much of the public health community has since adopted the view that tobacco litigation is an essential part of the anti-smoking movement. A prominent 1995 editorial in the *Journal of the American Medical Association*, for example, concluded its list of the leading items in the American Medical Association's strategy against tobacco by stating, "All avenues of individual and collective redress should be pursued through the judicial system."[40] Official AMA statements have reinforced this position, and the AMA played a leading role in the assessment of the 1997 and 1998 global settlements.[41] The *Journal of the American Medical Association* has published a series of articles taking a favorable view of litigation, as have other American Medical Association journals.[42] Other public health groups have taken similar positions, including the American Heart Association, the American Public Health Association, and nonprofit health insurance entities such as Blue Shield-Blue Cross organizations.

The World Health Organization, which has worked actively with plaintiff counsel in the Minnesota litigation, seeks to make tobacco litigation part of its worldwide strategy on smoking and health, a goal that

38. This is not to say that litigation is invariably given a major role in proposed policies toward tobacco. For example, DeJong (1997), representing the Harvard Center for Cancer Prevention in the Harvard School of Public Health, barely mentions litigation as a separate element.

39. Daynard (1997).

40. Todd and others (1995).

41. American Medical Association (1997, 1998).

42. For example, see Glantz, Fox, and Lightwood (1997).

is reflected in the WHO's Framework Treaty Convention on Tobacco Control.[43]

There are reasons to think this has been of considerable practical importance. The public health community has provided prestigious expert witnesses in the state of Minnesota and Washington cases and other lawsuits. The Minnesota Blue Cross-Blue Shield and other Blue Cross-Blue Shield organizations joined the state attorneys general as plaintiffs in health care cost recovery suits. Public statements and journal articles from the AMA and other prestigious groups advocating litigation have undoubtedly inspired much of the news media's pervasive editorializing and news accounts favorable to litigation. All this may have influenced judges and jurors to adopt attitudes more favorable toward plaintiffs' cases. An indication of this influence is that state litigation, and the 1997 and 1998 settlements, seems to have generated little popular or political resistance even though consumer surveys consistently find that most people disagree with the conceptual foundations of this litigation, and attempts to implement similar measures (such as tax increases) through legislation have usually failed.[44]

Public Health Goals for Tobacco Litigation

Why has the public health community so enthusiastically supported tobacco litigation? One reason is simply to advance the main goal of the state government litigation itself, which is compensation for health care costs caused by smoking (ignoring Viscusi's assessment of the appropriateness of that objective). The most important public health goals for tobacco litigation, however, pertain to smoking itself. One goal is to increase cigarette prices in order to reduce consumption, especially by youth. The 1998 Master Settlement Agreement (MSA) was designed to raise prices in two ways, by requiring large payments (mainly to state governments) and by impeding competition. The latter is achieved by restricting advertising and promotion and by discouraging or penalizing market entry by nonsignatory firms.[45] The multitude of lawsuits still under way or yet to come, which typically seek very large damages payments, would also tend to raise prices.

43. Brundtland (2000); World Health Organization (1998).
44. Blendon and Young (1998); Joan Biskupic, "Jurors Vent Outrage at Industry," *Washington Post*, August 30, 1999, p.A1; Gallup Organization, "Tobacco and Smoking," October 9, 2001.
45. See, for example, Ayres (1998); for an updated treatment see O'Brien (2000).

A second public health goal has been to lay the basis for FDA regulation of tobacco products. An earlier global settlement, which was reached
in June 1997 but failed for lack of required congressional action, included
support for legislation to give the FDA regulatory power over cigarettes.[46]
Although litigation probably cannot provide a direct route toward FDA
regulation, it can still be a decisive influence. Negotiations over legislation
creating FDA oversight in the tobacco market could involve trade-offs
yielding stronger regulation in return for partial relief against future litigation (as was planned in the 1997 global settlement).

A third public health goal is much broader: to alter the information
environment surrounding smoking. One way to do this is through restrictions on advertising and promotion as a remedy in lawsuits. The view that
advertising restrictions will reduce smoking is widely accepted in the public health community.[47] Another tool for altering the information environment is the funding of antismoking campaigns. The MSA provides
unprecedented sums for antismoking activities by the American Legacy
Foundation, an independent industry-funded organization dedicated to
antismoking campaigns. The MSA also anticipated that state governments
would use damages payments to fund their own antismoking campaigns,
including intensive school-based campaigns. The Centers for Disease
Control has issued guidelines on this topic, but very few states have come
close to following those guidelines.[48]

Finally, the public health community sees litigation as a way to implement its view that if the public knew what the cigarette industry knew
about smoking and health, knew what the industry was up to in marketing and the design of cigarettes, and learned about the undisclosed ingredients of cigarettes, then many smokers would quit and nonsmokers
would not start. In other words, smoking can to a substantial degree be
prevented and reduced simply by letting smokers and young people know
more about the internal workings of the cigarette industry. This point was
emphasized in a 1997 *Journal of the American Medical Association* editorial by two Harvard Medical School faculty members:

> Although it is impossible to put a dollar value on this anti-tobacco publicity, history
> has shown that such revelations have had an important impact on public attitudes and

46. Redhead (1997).
47. Kessler and Myers (2001).
48. Kessler and Myers (2001).

practices regarding cigarette smoking. And time has shown that the media attention generated by high-profile trials also provides the public with an education about the hazards of tobacco and industry's duplicity. Public outrage at the greed and deception of the industry provides a powerful incentive for smokers to quit.[49]

Supporters of the Minnesota litigation argued along the same lines.

Thus the litigation process itself, and the release of millions of industry documents as a result of litigation, was expected to have a strong and independent effect on smokers' behavior, a point emphasized by the *Journal of the American Medical Association*, which has published a series of articles taking a favorable view of litigation, with the focus mainly on the industry documents.[50] The World Health Organization has taken a similar view.[51] Based on the premise that the industry is the proximate cause of smoking, the essential argument is that litigation will reveal the true magnitude of the harms from smoking, the actual dangers of nicotine addiction, and the previously unknown susceptibility of smokers to hidden marketing techniques including the details of cigarette design.

All this reflects the central tenet of the antismoking movement since the early 1980s, which is that the main causes of smoking are not social forces but cigarette marketing and how cigarettes are designed to induce and maintain nicotine addiction.

The Public Health Effects of Tobacco Litigation

Has tobacco litigation advanced public health goals? There is no reason to assume that it has, inasmuch as the litigation process is bound to involve primarily the interests of the contesting parties, which so far have usually been state governments seeking large sums and defendants seeking to minimize the net present value of those sums.

PRICES AND SMOKING.   The main market effect of tobacco litigation so far has been to raise cigarette prices, partly by requiring the payment of several billion dollars annually to state governments, and partly by reducing competition and penalizing entry. The effects of reduced competition are evident in that industry profits and stock prices have increased greatly since the MSA went into effect. Average retail prices increased by $0.96

49. Brandt and Richmond (1997).
50. See Glantz and others (1995); and other articles in the same special edition of the *Journal of the American Medical Association* on tobacco documents.
51. Brundtland (2000).

per pack, or about 44 percent between November 1998 and November 2000, while the CPI increased by only 6 percent.[52]

The long-run effects of higher prices on smoking behavior are surprisingly uncertain, however. Econometric research consistently finds price elasticities on the order of 0.3 to 0.5, but there are reasons to doubt the long-term validity of these estimates for the 15 to 25 percent of populations in advanced nations who persist in smoking.[53] Experience in nations with much higher prices or much lower disposable incomes suggests that many smokers will persist in their habit in the face of prices (relative to income) that are far higher than anything previously seen in the United States. International data collected by the World Health Organization in 1995 reveal only a very loose relationship between prices and youth smoking rates even though prices varied several-fold.[54] Smoking rates in the UK, for example, are not greatly different from those in the United States even though UK prices have long been far higher than they are in the United States even today. Smokers in very poor nations such as India and China often pay substantial portions of their disposable income for tobacco (25 percent for Chinese men, in one report).[55]

Econometric analysis of youth smoking in the United States yields mixed results. The common finding of higher smoking rates in states with lower taxes does not account for social factors that might determine smoking attitudes and tax rates. This leaves open the possibility that taxes and prices may be only weak determinants of youth smoking rates. For alcohol, research has found that the relationship between tax rates and drinking failed to hold up in longitudinal analysis, which found very small effects from changes in tax rates. One careful new study of youth smoking takes a similar approach and finds no significant effect from tax increases on youth smoking rates.[56] Another recent study, applying different data but the same idea, does find a significant effect.[57] Their results yielded, however, a price elasticity for smoking initiation of approximately 1.0, so that a 10 percent price increase would be predicted to decrease new

52. Cathleen Egan, "Tales of the Tape: Big Tobacco More Sought Than Feared," *Wall Street Journal*, September 27, 2001 [Dow Jones Newswires]; *Tax Burden on Tobacco* (2001); OECD (2001).

53. Tauras and others (2001). On the persistence of 15 to 25 percent, see Shiffman, Mason, and Henningfield (1998).

54. World Health Organization (1996).

55. See Yang and others (1999) on China; and World Bank (1999) showing that the poor in India smoke more than the relatively wealthy.

56. Tauras and others (2001); Dee (1999); DeCicca, Kenkel, and Mathios (1999).

57. Tauras and others (2001).

youth smoking by 10 percent. This result greatly overpredicts the declines in youth smoking that have occurred in the wake of an approximately 40 percent price increase. This is notable because the other components of antismoking activities generated by litigation—antismoking campaigns and a drastically altered information environment—were unmeasured in this study. That should have caused recent large price increases to generate smoking reductions that were greater, rather than smaller, than predicted.

INFORMATIONAL EFFECTS FROM LITIGATION. There are reasons to doubt that litigation has strongly affected the information environment of smoking. The limited restrictions on advertising and promotion induced by litigation are unlikely to have substantial effects. Econometric research has consistently found that large fluctuations in cigarette advertising, including the 1970 ban on broadcast advertising, have had no detectable effect on cigarette sales.[58] Even before the MSA went into effect, mass media advertising had declined to less than $700 million in 1998, leaving relatively little advertising power to be tamed.[59] Whether antismoking campaigns funded by the MSA will have strong effects on youth smoking (the primary target) remains to be seen. Earlier mass media antismoking programs have yielded mixed results, seldom with significant lasting effects.[60] Some MSA-funded campaigns have been linked to reductions in smoking by certain populations (eighth graders, for example), but so far there is little reason to expect these effects to persist.

Finally, there is the question of whether the information unleashed by litigation has altered overall attitudes and behavior regarding smoking. Surveys show little change since 1997. The Gallup surveys, for example, have asked very similar questions for many years. The percentage saying they smoked in the previous week in the 1997, 1999, 2000, and 2001 surveys were, respectively, 26 percent, 23 percent, 25 percent, and most recently, 28 percent. Even on whether manufacturers should be held liable for the harms from smoking, the proportion saying tobacco companies are mostly or completely to blame was 25 percent in May 1997 and 25 percent in July 2001, although it dropped to 20 percent in September 1999. The proportion saying smokers are mostly or completely to blame barely declined, from 64 percent in May 1997 to 61 percent in July 2001.

58. A recent review of the literature is in Calfee (2000).
59. Data from the Federal Trade Commission (annual reports).
60. Pechmann and Thomas (2000).

Youth smoking has decreased slightly in recent years after increasing through most of 1990s, but as noted, the decrease has been far less than predicted from price increases. If litigation had mobilized antismoking sentiment, youth smoking should have declined by more than predicted by demand models incorporating price changes. Even in Minnesota, where litigation was exceptionally prominent and attracted much publicity about what industry documents, youth smoking failed to decline from rates far higher than they were at the start of the 1990s and has not declined relative to smoking in other states.[61]

Per capita smoking has declined in the face of price increases but, again, not as much as one would expect from a 40 percent increase in real prices. And, again, declines should have been more than predicted from price changes, not less, if information changes were an independent force. In fact, smoking patterns in the United States have been similar to those in Canada, where antismoking activists have sought to initiate large-scale litigation with little success (so far), and in the UK, where tobacco litigation remains in its infancy.

The Emerging Costs of Tobacco Litigation

Set against the doubtful public health benefits of tobacco litigation are its emerging costs. The funding of litigation in other areas, with the litigation often using similar methods as described elsewhere in this volume, is certainly important. Whether the consequent expansion of litigation constitutes a net social cost cannot be settled here, but I note that much of the litigation launched with tobacco proceeds is explicitly couched as attempts to use litigation in place of regulation or legislation.

Tobacco litigation, of course, already comprised arguably the largest example of regulation through litigation, simply by imposing very large taxes without legislation. Others have described in detail the ways in which the MSA was structured to mimic a tax rather than damages payments. Thus payments are generated by future sales rather than past sales and would be required by firms that were not part of the settlement and had not been sued for past behavior. This was done after repeated failures to enact comparable tax increases in Congress and many state legislatures (although some states have succeeded, including California and Massachusetts). The

61. "Target Market /Good First Results against Tobacco," editorial, *Minneapolis-St. Paul Star Tribune*, September 3, 2001, p. 12A.

fact that this litigation was engineered by government agencies in states
that had refused to raise tobacco taxes strongly suggests that this by-passing
of constitutional methods must be accounted a significant cost of tobacco
litigation.

Public health uses of tobacco litigation have also introduced or magnified distortions in the intellectual environment. Public health groups,
politicians, and journals, confronted by the arguments posed by Viscusi
and other economists on health care costs from smoking, have often
greeted those arguments with scorn rather than serious analysis. This
response prevails even though some of the research supporting Viscusi's
argument has come from prestigious medical journals and the federal government.[62] State and federal health agencies, including HHS (source of the
Surgeon General's reports on smoking and health) have argued in court
that because they relied on industry marketing and public relations, they
had been deceived into lacking a reasonable appreciation of the health
harms of smoking until the 1990s. This has introduced an unnecessary element of hypocrisy in public discussions. The same is true of the popular
move among state legislatures, with active support from the Clinton
administration, to allocate substantial tobacco litigation payments to
tobacco farmers as compensation for their loss of business as tobacco sales
decline.[63] This has been done despite the fact that tobacco farmers, even
more so than the general public, have long been aware that the crops they
sold to tobacco wholesalers were used to manufacture cigarettes with all
their health risks.

Another, quite different cost of tobacco litigation has been to increase
government's stake in smoking itself. It has long been clear to antismoking activists and others that nations in which tobacco was controlled by
state monopolies have been especially reluctant to endorse or embark upon
antismoking campaigns or publicize the dangers of smoking.[64] That the
billions of dollars flowing to the states under the MSA work like a sales tax
on cigarettes means that state governments have a large stake in the con-
tinuation of smoking and the solvency of the industry. Because many
states have allocated future revenues for numerous purposes unrelated to
smoking, the nexus between MSA payments and government welfare has

62. Barendregt, Bonneux, and van der Maas (1997); Gravelle (1997).
63. Clinton (1999); David Rice, "Price of Change," *Winston-Salem Journal*, January 17, 1999, p. 1.
64. See Mackay (1997). On the important case of China, see Glenn Frankel and Steven Mufson,
"Big Tobacco's Global Reach: Vast China Market Key to Smoking Disputes," *Washington Post*, November 20, 1996, p. A1.

been strengthened. This has been noted by parties otherwise sympathetic to the antismoking movement. A striking example of this influence occurred in Florida, where the legislature passed a law to permit the industry to avoid bankruptcy after an adverse liability verdict, in order to preserve the flow of MSA payments.[65] Another cost is the distortion of the legal process. State attorney general suits put state judges, appointed by the very governments serving as plaintiffs, in a position to make rulings that, by undermining industry defenses, left the defendants with no choice but to agree to transfer immense sums to those states or risk immediate bankruptcy (because appeals would require posting of a bond equal to the entire verdict plus expected interest during the appeals process). Some states passed laws designed to facilitate tobacco liability suits. In Florida, the governor explained that he ordered state officials not to sue anyone other than tobacco firms, although the statute was written more broadly in order to deflect constitutional challenges.[66]

A very different problem is the undermining of individual responsibility on the part of smokers. Tobacco liability litigation before 1994 had always failed because juries were never persuaded that smokers should not be held responsible for their decisions to smoke. Recent tobacco litigation, including that leading to the MSA, was explicitly designed to avoid this issue.[67] That attempt was successful, as legislation and court rulings made smokers' awareness of health risks irrelevant. Other suits argue that marketing and cigarette design eliminate any role for smokers' responsibility, an argument that few juries have accepted so far. These developments tend to undermine the long-term trend toward cessation and less smoking. The argument that smokers are the victim of an addiction foisted on them weakens the primary force in reduced smoking, which is smokers' own determination to quit (there are more ex-smokers than smokers in the United States). In addition, the prospect of receiving damages payments for smoking tends to undermine incentives to avoid or quit smoking.

Another cost, difficult to assess but very important, pertains to speech and its effects. Little-noticed provisions of the MSA and a parallel agreement with U.S. Tobacco (the leading manufacturer of smokeless

65. Gordon Fairclough, "Three Tobacco Firms Agree to Post $2 Billion Bond in Tobacco Lawsuit," *Wall Street Journal*, May 7, 2001; "Who's Addicted?" editorial, *Washington Post*, March 26, 2000, p. B6.

66. Gibeaut cited in Little (2001, note 20). The Florida statute is the Medicaid Third-Party Liability Act, Fla. stat., sec. 409.910.

67. Daynard (1997).

tobacco such as snuff and chewing tobacco) severely limit manufacturers'
ability to lobby, discuss, or advertise about smoking and health. For example, the chief executive officer of U.S. Tobacco noted in an interview that,
as part of a settlement, his firm had agreed not to "debate" the health consequences of smokeless tobacco versus smoking in the "media."[68] These
measures were presumably taken in the belief that competitive speech from
tobacco manufacturers could not possibly favor public health.

The restrictions on speech, combined with the MSA's severe penalties
on the growth of nonsignatory firms and restrictions on advertising and
marketing as a result of this and other litigation, has tended to impede discussion of safer tobacco use, including the use of cigarettes employing radical technologies such as smokeless processing of tobacco, safer tobacco
variants, and tobacco alternatives such as snuff, cigars, and chewing
tobacco.[69] This perspective reflects the dominant view since 1980 in the
antismoking movement that public policy should focus exclusively on the
cessation of smoking and that marketing of safer cigarettes would be a dis-
traction if not an outright barrier to cessation. Even the minority who see
a useful role for safer cigarettes are hostile to the idea of permitting manufacturers to help market or design cigarettes. History shows, however,
that competitive marketing increases the salience of the health effects of
smoking and accelerates the development of new technologies.[70] Tobacco
litigation has essentially implemented the antismoking community's gam-
ble on cessation to the exclusion of harm reduction.

References

Adler, R., and D. Pittle. 1984. "Cajolery or Command: Are Education Campaigns an Ade-
quate Substitute for Regulation?" *Yale Journal on Regulation* 1 (2): 159–94.
American Medical Association. 1997. "Analysis, Report, and Recommendations of the
American Medical Association: Task Force on the Proposed Tobacco Settlement Agree-
ment." Chicago (July).
———. Advocacy and Communications. 1998. "Briefing Assessment of the Multi-State
Tobacco Settlement Proposal" (November).

68. Interview with Vincent Grier, Jr., chairman of the board and chief executive officer of UST, Inc.,
August 29, 2001.
69. See Shiffman, Mason, and Henningfield (1998) on potential cigarette technologies.
70. Calfee (1985); 1994 Surgeon General's report, U.S. Department of Health and Human Services
(1994).

Antoñanzas, Fernando, W. Kip Viscusi, Joan Rovira, Francisco J. Braña, Fabiola Portillo, and Irineu Carvalho. 2000. "Smoking Risks in Spain: Part I – Perception of Risks to the Smoker." *Journal of Risk and Uncertainty* 21 (2/3): 161–86.

Ayres, Ian. 1998. "Comment on Bulow and Klemperer, 'The Tobacco Deal.'" *Brookings Papers on Economic Activity.* [Comment printed separately after publication of the volume.]

Barendregt, Jan J., Luc Bonneux, and Paul J. van der Maas. 1997. "The Health Care Costs of Smoking." *New England Journal of Medicine* 337 (15): 1052–57.

Becker, G. S., and K. M. Murphy. 1988. "A Theory of Rational Addiction." *Journal of Political Economy* 96: 675–700.

Becker, G. S., M. Grossman, and K. M. Murphy. 1996. "An Empirical Analysis of Cigarette Addiction." *American Economic Review* 84 (3): 396–418.

Blendon, Robert J., and John T. Young. 1998. "The Public and the Comprehensive Tobacco Bill," *Journal of the American Medical Association* 280 (14): 1279–84.

Brandt, Allan M., and Julius B. Richmond, 1997. "Settling Short on Tobacco: Let the Trials Begin." *Journal of the American Medical Association* 278 (12): 1028.

Brundtland, Gro Harlem. 2000. "Achieving Worldwide Tobacco Control." *Journal of the American Medical Association* 284 (6): 750–51.

Calfee, J. E. 1985. "Cigarette Advertising, Health Information and Regulation before 1970." Federal Trade Commission Working Paper 134. Washington (December).

———.1986. "The Ghost of Cigarette Advertising Past." *Regulation* 10 (6): 35–45.

———. 2000. "The Historical Significance of 'Joe Camel.'" *Journal of Public Policy and Marketing* 19: 168–82.

Clinton, William J. 1999. "President's State of the Union Address, January 20, 1999." Government Printing Office.

Cutler, David M., Arnold M. Epstein, Richard G. Frank, Raymond Hartman, Charles King III, Joseph P. Newhouse, Meredith B. Rosenthal, and Elizabeth Richardson Vigdor. 2000. "How Good a Deal Was the Tobacco Settlement? Assessing Payments to Massachusetts." *Journal of Risk and Uncertainty* 21 (2/3): 235–61.

Daynard, Richard. 1997. "Litigation by States against the Tobacco Industry." Presented at the 10th World Conference on Tobacco or Health. Beijing (August).

DeCicca, Philip, Donald Kenkel, and Alan Mathios. 1999. "Putting Out the Fires: Will Higher Taxes Reduce Youth Smoking?" Department of Policy Analysis and Management, Cornell University, 14853 (June).

———. 2000. "Racial Differences in the Determinants of Smoking Onset." *Journal of Risk and Uncertainty* 21 (2/3): 311–40.

Dee, Thomas S. 1999. "The Complementarity of Teen Smoking and Drinking." *Journal of Health Economics* 18 (6): 769–93.

DeJong, William. 1997. "Prevention of Tobacco Use." *Cancer Causes and Control* 8 (supp. 1): S5–S8.

Evans, William, Jeanne Ringel, and Diana Stech. 1999. "Tobacco Taxes and Public Policy to Discourage Smoking." In *Tax Policy and the Economy* 13, edited by James M. Poterba, 1–55. MIT Press.

Federal Trade Commission (FTC). Annual. *Report to Congress Pursuant to the Federal Cigarette Labeling and Advertising Act* (www.ftc.gov.).

Fullerton, Don, and D. L. Rodgers. 1993. *Who Bears the Lifetime Tax Burden?* Brookings.

Gaba, Anil, and W. Kip Viscusi. 1998. "Differences in Subjective Risk Thresholds: Worker Groups as an Example." *Management Science* 44 (6): 801–11.

Glantz, Stanton A., Deborah E. Barnes, Lisa Bero, Peter Hanauer, John Slade. 1995. "Looking Through a Keyhole at the Tobacco Industry." *Journal of the American Medical Association* 274 (3): 219–24.

Glantz, Stanton A., Brion J. Fox, and James M. Lightwood. 1997. "Tobacco Litigation: Issues for Public Health and Public Policy." *Journal of the American Medical Association* 227 (9): 751–53.

Gravelle, Jane G. 1997. "The Proposed Tobacco Settlement: Who Pays for the Health Care Costs of Smoking?" updated April 30, 1998. Report 97-1053. Congressional Research Service.

Gravelle, Jane, and D. Zimmerman. 1994. *Cigarette Taxes to Fund Healthcare Reform: An Economic Analysis.* Report 94-214. Congressional Research Service.

Hersch, Joni. 1998. "Teen Smoking Behavior and the Regulatory Environment." *Duke Law Journal* 47 (6): 1143–70.

———. 2000. "Gender, Income Levels, and the Demand for Cigarettes." *Journal of Risk and Uncertainty* 21 (2/3): 263–82.

Hersch, Joni, and W. Kip Viscusi. 1998. "Smoking and Other Risky Behaviors." *Journal of Drug Issues* 28 (3): 645–61.

Kessler, David, and Matthew Myers. 2001. "Beyond the Tobacco Settlement." *New England Journal of Medicine* 345 (7): 535–37.

Little, Margaret A. 2001. "A Most Dangerous Indiscretion: The Legal, Economic, and Political Legacy of the Governments' Tobacco Litigation." *Connecticut Law Review* 33: 1143.

Mackay, Judith. 1997. "Battling Upstream against the Tobacco Epidemic in China." *Tobacco Control* 6 (1): 9–10.

Magat, Wesley A., and W. Kip Viscusi. 1992. *Informational Approaches to Regulation.* MIT Press.

Manning, Willard G., Emmett B. Keeler, Joseph P. Newhouse, Elizabeth M. Sloss, and Jeffrey Wasserman. 1989. "The Taxes of Sin: Do Smokers and Drinkers Pay Their Way?" *Journal of the American Medical Association* 261 (11): 1604–09.

———. 1991. The Costs of Poor Health Habits. Harvard University Press.

Merrill, Richard A. 1998. "The FDA May Not Regulate Tobacco Products as 'Drugs' Or As 'Medical Devices.'" *Duke Law Journal* 47 (April): 1071–94.

Moore, Michael J. and Carolyn W. Zhu. 2000. "Passive Smoking and Health Care: Health Perceptions Myth vs. Health Care Reality." *Journal of Risk and Uncertainty* 21 (2/3): 283–310.

O'Brien, Thomas C. 2000. Constitutional and Antitrust Violations of the Multistate Tobacco Settlement." *Policy Analysis* 371. Washington: Cato Institute (May).

Organization for Economic Cooperation and Development (OECD). 2001. "Main Economic Indicators."

Pechmann, Cornelia, and Ellen Thomas. 2000. "Anti-Smoking Advertising Campaigns Targeting Youth: Case Studies from USA and Canada." *Tobacco Control* 9 (Suppl. 2): ii18–ii31.

Redhead, C. Stephen. 1997. "The Tobacco Settlement: An Overview." Congressional Research Service (July).

Ringold, D. J., and J. E. Calfee. 1989. "The Informational Content of Cigarette Advertising: 1926-1986." *Journal of Public Policy and Management* 8: 1–23.

Rovira, Joan, W. Kip Viscusi, Fernando Antoñanzas, Joan Costa, Warren Hart, and Irineu Carvalho. 2000. "Smoking Risks in Spain: Part II – Perceptions of Environmental Tobacco Smoke Externalities." *Journal of Risk and Uncertainty* 21 (2/3): 187–212.

Schwartz, Gary. 1999. "Tobacco, Liability, and Viscusi." *Cumberland Law Review* 29 (3): 555–68.

————. 2000. "Cigarette Litigation's Offspring: Assessing Tort Issues Related to Guns, Alcohol, and Other Controversial Products in Light of the Tobacco Wars." *Pepperdine Law Review* 27 (4): 751–57.

Shiffman, S., K. M. Mason, and J. E. Henningfield. 1998. "Tobacco Dependence Treatments: Review and Prospectus." *Annual Review of Public Health* 19 (2) 335–58.

Shoven, J. B., J. O. Sundberg, and J. P. Bunker. 1989. "The Social Security Cost of Smoking." In *The Economics of Aging*, edited by D. A. Wise, 231–51. University of Chicago Press.

Sunstein, Cass R. 1998. "Is Tobacco a Drug? Administrative Agencies as Common Law Courts." *Duke Law Journal* 47 (April): 1013–69.

Tauras, John A., Patrick M. O'Malley, and Lloyd D. Johnston. 2001. "Effects of Price and Access Laws on Teenage Smoking Initiation: A National Longitudinal Analysis." Working Paper. ImapacTeen. University of Illinois at Chicago (April).

Tax Burden on Tobacco. 2001. Available from Arlington, Va.: Orzechowski and Walker.

Tobacco Institute. 1998. *The Tax Burden on Tobacco: Historical Compilation 1998.* Vol. 33. Washington.

Todd, James, D. Rennie, and others. 1995. "The Brown and Williamson Documents: Where Do We Go from Here? *Journal of the Medical Association* 274 (3): 256–59.

U.S. Department of Health, Education and Welfare. 1964. *Smoking and Health: Report of the Advisory Committee to the Surgeon General of the Public Health Service.* Public Health Service Publication 1103.

U.S. Department of Health and Human Services. 1989. *Reducing the Health Consequences of Smoking: 25 Years of Progress, A Report of the Surgeon General.*

————. 1994. *Preventing Tobacco Use among Young People: A Report of the Surgeon General.*

Viscusi, W. Kip. 1990. "Do Smokers Underestimate Risks?" *Journal of Political Economy* 98 (6): 1253—69.

————. 1991a. "Age Variations in Risk Perceptions and Smoking Decisions." *Review of Economics and Statistics* 73 (4): 577–88.

————. 1991b. *Reforming Products Liability.* Harvard University Press.

————. 1992. *Smoking: Making the Risky Decision.* Oxford University Press.

————. 1995. "Cigarette Taxation and the Social Consequences of Smoking." In *Tax Policy and the Economy*, vol. 9, edited by James M. Poterba, 51–101. MIT Press.

————. 1998a. "A Postmortem on the Cigarette Settlement." Rushton Distinguished Lecture. *Cumberland Law Review* 29 (3): 523–53.

————. 1998b. "Constructive Cigarette Regulation." *Duke Law Journal* 47 (6): 1095–1131.

————. 1998c. *Rational Risk Policy.* Oxford University Press.

————. 1998d. "Smoke and Mirrors: Understanding the New Scheme for Cigarette Regulation." *Brookings Review* 16 (1): 14–19.

————. 1999. "The Governmental Composition of the Insurance Costs of Smoking." *Journal of Law and Economics* 42 (2): 575–609.

————. 2002. *Smoke-Filled Rooms: A Postmortem on the Tobacco Deal.* University of Chicago Press.

Viscusi, W. Kip and Joni Hersch. 2001. "Cigarette Smokers as Job Risk Takers." *Review of Economics and Statistics* 83 (2): 269–80.

Viscusi, W. Kip and Wesley A. Magat. 1987. *Learning about Risk: Consumer and Worker Responses to Hazard Information.* Harvard University Press.

Viscusi, W. Kip, Irineu Carvalho, Fernando Antoñanzas, Joan Rovira, Francisco J. Braña and Fabiola Portillo. 2000. "Smoking Risks in Spain: Part III – Determinants of Smoking Behavior." *Journal of Risk and Uncertainty* 21(2/3): 213–34.

Wasserman, J., W. G. Manning, J. P. Newhouse, and J. D. Winkler. 1991. "The Effects of Excise Taxes and Regulations on Cigarette Smoking." *Journal of Health Economics* 10 (1): 43–64.

World Bank. 1999. *Curbing the Epidemic: Governments and the Economics of Tobacco Control.* Washington.

World Health Organization. 1996. *Tobacco Alert,* special issue. Geneva (April).

————. 1998. "Remarks by Director-General Gro Harlem Brundtland at the Seminar on Tobacco Industry Disclosures: Implications for Public Policy." Geneva (October).

Yang, Gonghuan, Lixin Fan, Jian Tan, Guoming Qi, Yifang Zhang, Jonathan M. Samet, Carl E. Taylor, Karen Becker, and Jing Xu. 1999. "Smoking in China: Findings of the 1996 National Prevalence Survey." *Journal of the American Medical Association* 283 (13): 1247–53.

PHILIP J. COOK
JENS LUDWIG

3 | *Litigation as Regulation: Firearms*

The recent law suits brought by local governments against the gun industry have offered several legal theories for why the industry should be held accountable for the costs of gun violence and compelled to change its practices. The first of these suits, filed by the city of New Orleans on October 30, 1998, asserts among other things that the manufacturers have neglected their duty to incorporate available safety features into the design of their products. The second, filed by Chicago, focused on marketing practices, asserting that the industry had created a "public nuisance" by neglecting to take feasible measures that would help prevent the illegal sale of its products to Chicago residents or to traffickers who supply residents.[1] Following these actions by New Orleans and Chicago, thirty other cities and counties have filed against the gun industry, claiming negligence in its marketing practices, the design of its products, or both.

The public suits against the gun industry were inspired by the success of the states' litigation against the tobacco industry in the 1990s.[2] The cigarette manufacturers ultimately settled those suits with the attorneys general,

The authors thank George Christie, Ted Gayer, Jay Hamilton, Julie Samia Mair, Jonathan Mathieu, Hank Ruth, Steve Teret, Jon Vernick, Garen Wintemute and the participants in the Brookings-AEI Joint Center for Regulatory Studies Conference "Litigation as Regulation" for helpful comments.
1. Siebel (1999, pp. 248–49); Vernick and Teret (1999, pp. 1747–49).
2. Kairys (1998, pp. 12–13); Bogus (2000, pp. 1361–72).

agreeing to some restrictions on their marketing practices and to pay the states more than $240 billion in damages over twenty-five years. The firearms industry is much smaller and more diffuse than the tobacco industry, so the financial settlement possible in these cases is more limited;[3] the primary motivation for the plaintiffs is forcing the industry to take greater responsibility for reducing the amount of damage done by its products.

If successful, this litigation could force a number of changes, including the following:

—Manufacturers would be required to modify the design of their guns to make them safer;

—Manufacturers and distributors would be required to exercise oversight of retailers, ensuring that they screen buyers carefully, keep their records in order, cooperate with authorities, exercise care against theft, and comply with the laws governing retail gun sales;

—Prices of new guns would increase because of elimination of models that do not meet minimum safety standards, additional safety features on higher-quality models, and expanded liability for manufacturers, importers, and distributors.

Of course, these same outcomes could in principle be accomplished through government regulation. Indeed, a frequently voiced objection to these suits is that the plaintiffs are seeking to circumvent the democratic process—to impose regulation without legislation. To be specific, the cities, which lack the power to regulate the industry but suffer the greatest share of the burden of gun violence, are turning to the courts to seek what Congress and most state legislatures have been unwilling to legislate.

It is not our purpose here to judge whether it is proper for local jurisdictions to seek a court-ordered remedy when the state and federal legislative process has, in the view of local officials, failed them. Nor are we going to comment on the legal merits of the plaintiffs' cases. Rather, we focus on the broader question of whether the available remedies in these cases would further the public interest. Our analysis suggests that remedies of the sort listed above are likely to have greater benefits than costs. But there are arguably worthwhile reforms that are beyond the reach of the courts and this litigation, including registering firearms and outlawing informal transac-

---

3. Total product shipments by small arms manufacturers were only $1.2 billion in 1997, with small arms ammunition shipments accounting for another $859 million. U.S. Department of the Treasury, Bureau of Alcohol, Tobacco, and Firearms (2000a). Tobacco manufacturers, however, had product shipments valued at $38.7 billion during the same year. U.S. Bureau of the Census (1999, p. 752).

tions. The litigation may prove a catalyst for legislative action in these areas; that is, litigation may influence the legislative process but will not replace it.

Filling the Gaps in Government Regulation

The plaintiffs assert that the current state and federal regulations on the firearms industry do not go far enough and in any event have not been adequately enforced. Judging such claims requires some understanding of the regulations that are currently in place.

The primary objective of federal law in regulating guns is to insulate the states from one another, so that the stringent regulations on firearms commerce adopted in some states are not undercut by the relatively lax regulation in other states.[4] The citizens of rural Montana understandably favor a more permissive system than those living in Chicago, and both can be accommodated if transfers between them are effectively limited. The Gun Control Act of 1968 established the framework for the current system of controls on gun transfers. All shipments of firearms (including mail-order sales) are limited to federally licensed dealers who are required to obey applicable state and local ordinances and to observe certain restrictions on sales of guns to out-of-state residents.[5]

Federal law also seeks to establish a minimum set of restrictions on acquisition and possession of guns. The Gun Control Act specifies several categories of people who are denied the right to receive or possess a gun, including illegal aliens, convicted felons, those under indictment, people ever convicted of an act of domestic violence, users of illicit drugs, and those who have at some time been involuntarily committed to a mental institution. Federally licensed dealers may not sell handguns to people younger than twenty-one or long guns to those younger than eighteen. And dealers are required to ask for identification from all would-be buyers, have them sign a form indicating that they do not have any of the characteristics (such as a felony conviction) that would place them in the "proscribed" category, and initiate a criminal history check. Finally, dealers are required to keep a record of each completed sale and cooperate with authorities when they need to gain access to those records for gun-tracing purposes.[6]

4. Zimring (1975).

5. The McClure-Volkmer Amendment of 1986 eased the restriction on out-of-state purchases of rifles and shotguns. Such purchases are now legal as long as they comply with the regulations of both the buyer's state of residence and the state in which the sale occurs.

6. Vernick and Teret (2000).

Besides these federal requirements, states have adopted significant restrictions on commerce, possession, and use of firearms. Twelve states require that handgun buyers obtain a permit or license before taking possession of a handgun, a process that typically entails payment of a fee and some waiting period.[7] All but a few such transfer-control systems are "permissive," in the sense that most people are legally entitled to obtain a gun. In those few jurisdictions, including Massachusetts and New York City, it is very difficult to obtain a handgun legally, while Chicago and Washington, D.C., prohibit handgun ownership. Various more modest restrictions on commerce have been enacted as well: for example, Virginia, Maryland, and several other states have limited dealers to selling no more than one handgun a month to any one buyer.

As noted, the plaintiffs seek changes in the design and marketing of firearms. The status quo in these two areas can be summarized as follows:

Design

Certain types of firearms are effectively prohibited by federal law. The National Firearms Act of 1934 (NFA) was intended to eliminate gangster-era firearms, including sawed-off shotguns, hand grenades, and automatic weapons capable of continuous rapid fire with a single pull of the trigger. The legal device for accomplishing that purpose was a requirement that all such weapons be registered with the federal government and that transfers be subject to a tax of $200, which at the time of enactment was confiscatory. Although some of these weapons have remained in legal circulation, the NFA (now amended to ban the introduction of new weapons of this sort into circulation) appears to have been effective at reducing the use of automatic weapons in crime.[8]

The Gun Control Act of 1968 included a ban on the import of small, cheap handguns,[9] sometimes known as "Saturday Night Specials." This ban was made operational through the development of the factoring criteria that assigned points to a gun model depending on its size and other qualities.[10] Handguns that fail to achieve a minimum score on the factor-

7. Peters (2000); U.S. Department of Justice (2001, p. 77).
8. Kleck (1991).
9. An important loophole allowed the import of parts of handguns that could not meet the "sporting purposes" test of the Gun Control Act. This loophole was closed by the McClure-Volkmer Amendment of 1986.
10. Zimring (1975); Karlson and Hargarten (1997).

ing criteria, or do not meet size and safety criteria, cannot be imported. However, it is legal for domestic manufacturers to assemble guns, often from imported parts, that fail the factoring criteria, and that market "niche" has been well supplied. A recent study found that one-third of new domestically manufactured handgun models did not meet the size or quality requirements that are applied to imports through the factoring criteria.[11]

In 1994 Congress banned the importation and manufacture of certain "assault" weapons, which is to say military-style semiautomatic firearms. The Crime Control Act banned nineteen such weapons by name, and others were outlawed if they possess some combination of design features such as a detachable magazine, barrel shroud, or bayonet mount.[12] The act also banned the manufacture and import of magazines that hold more than ten rounds. Existing assault weapons and large-capacity magazines are "grandfathered" and remain in legal circulation.[13]

Federal law leaves unregulated those types of firearms that are not specifically banned. Firearms and ammunition are excluded from the purview of the Consumer Product Safety Commission.[14] This exclusion is the basis for the claim that toy guns are more closely regulated than real ones. In any event, there is no federal agency that has responsibility for reviewing the design of firearms and no mechanism in place for identifying unsafe models that could lead to a recall and correction.[15] "Regulate firearms as consumer products" has become a rallying cry for gun control advocates, but Congress has taken no action on this matter to date.[16] However, there has been action at the state level: in April 2000 the attorney general of Massachusetts announced that firearms would henceforth be regulated by the same authority available to his department for other consumer products and those deemed unacceptable would be taken off the market.[17]

Massachusetts is unique in asserting broad state authority to regulate gun design and gun safety. There are a handful of states in which the legislatures have acted to restrict the permissible design of new guns

11. Hargarten and others (2001); see also Wintemute (1994).
12. Vernick and Teret (2000, p. 1197).
13. Roth and Koper (1999).
14. Vernick and Teret (2000, p. 1196).
15. Bonnie, Fulco, and Liverman (1999).
16. Firearms Safety and Consumer Protection Act of 1999 (S. 534 and H.R. 920).
17. The new rules effectively ban "Saturday Night Specials" and require that handguns sold in Massachusetts include childproof locks, tamper-proof serial numbers, and safety warnings. The new gun safety regulations affect manufacturers as well as retailers.

in a more limited way. The first important instance of this sort occurred in Maryland, with its ban on Saturday Night Specials. The Maryland legislature acted in response to a successful law suit against a manufacturer. In exchange for relieving manufacturers of small, cheap handguns from liability, the legislature created a process for reviewing handgun designs and specifying which models would be ruled out owing to concerns about size and safety. As of 2000 seven states have some version of a Saturday Night Special ban in place.[18] The Maryland legislature recently adopted another pioneering requirement, namely, that by 2003 all guns sold in that state be "personalized" in the sense of having a built-in locking device that requires a key or combination to release. California has also been active in recent years, instituting among other measures its own ban on assault weapons.

A settlement between the plaintiffs and the industry could include any number of specific safety requirements for new guns. The following are among the requirements that have been suggested:[19]

—Modify triggers so that they are "child proof"—too stiff for a six-year-old to pull;

—Incorporate a device that indicates whether there is a round in the firing chamber;

—For guns that have detachable magazines, incorporate a safety mechanism that locks the trigger unless the magazine is in place; and

—Build in a "personalization" device as standard equipment in all handguns to prevent firing by someone who is not authorized by the owner.

A more open-ended regulatory regime could also be put in place, whereby an industry-sponsored agency was created to review new models and monitor those in circulation for safety defects.

Marketing

As explained above, the distribution of firearms is regulated by the federal government under the Gun Control Act. The agency responsible for implementing these regulations is the Bureau of Alcohol, Tobacco and Firearms (ATF) in the Department of the Treasury. The ATF is charged

18. Vernick and Teret (2000, p. 1206).
19. Vernick and Teret (1999).

with licensing manufacturers, importers, distributors, and retail dealers in firearms. Federal firearms licensees (FFLs) are required to follow federal and state requirements governing all transactions and to cooperate with authorities in investigations. The ATF exercises its authority over dealers through inspections and enforcement actions. As a practical matter there are so many retail licensees—currently about 80,000—that ATF can only inspect a few percent of them in any one year.[20] Even when ATF investigators determine that a dealer is in serious violation of the law, it can be very difficult to take effective action, thanks to federal legislation (the McClure-Volkmer Act, or Firearm Owners Protection Act of 1986), which limits regulatory actions and establishes a near-impossible evidentiary requirement for successful prosecution. A vivid case in point is ATF's ten-year effort to shut down the Baltimore Gunsmith, a dealer selling 20 percent of the guns used in crime in that city.[21]

In principle, ATF's compliance efforts could be supplemented by firearms manufacturers. In fact, however, there is currently no upstream accountability in the firearms industry and hence no incentive for manufacturers to exercise oversight of the retailers who are selling their products. Manufacturers and importers do business with dealers (usually through sporting goods distributors) at arms length, without taking responsibility for determining whether these dealers are careful about complying with legal requirements governing sales.[22] By contrast, manufacturers in some other industries that sell dangerous consumer products exercise close oversight over retailers. Examples include manufacturers of spray paint, motor vehicles, explosives, and scuba equipment.

Various remedies have been suggested, including a system of industry oversight operating under court order, whereby manufacturers would require that dealers exercise due care in screening customers. This private supplement to ATF enforcement capacity would among other things provide a way around legal restrictions on regulatory actions. For example, the Firearm Owners Protection Act of 1986 limits ATF to just one unannounced inspection per FFL a year, whereas distributors could inspect dealers' books as often as deemed necessary. Manufacturers could also compel dealers to follow procedures that are currently not legally required in most states, such as a requirement that dealers protect their inventory from theft and give special training to their clerks. Manufacturers are in a

20. U.S. Department of the Treasury, Bureau of Alcohol, Tobacco, and Firearms (2000a).
21. Butterfield (2001).
22. Stewart (1999).

position to sanction wayward dealers by cutting off their supply of new firearms, based on whatever standard of proof the industry deems reasonable.[23]

Price

Since 1918 the federal government has collected an excise tax on firearms amounting to 10 percent of the manufacturer's price for handguns and 11 percent for long guns. This tax is no doubt passed along to consumers. The federal ban on the import of handguns that do not meet minimum standards of size and safety may also affect prices of the least expensive new guns, although domestic manufacturers have filled that niche.[24] In states that require a permit to purchase a gun, the price of the permit adds to the transaction cost. Design and permitting requirements may become still more important influences on gun availability in the future. Maryland's requirement that new handguns be equipped with internal locking devices by 2003 could add substantially to the cost and hence price of a new handgun.

The effect of taxes and regulations on the price of guns is not just an incidental detail but rather may have an important effect on gun sales, use, and misuse. It seems apparent (at least to economists) that the most important health-relevant outcome of the tobacco litigation has been the large increase in the price of cigarettes resulting from the financial settlement with the states. The litigation against the firearms industry may result in increased prices for several reasons. Some manufacturers may go bankrupt or choose to exit the personal firearms business, as has already occurred in the cases of several of the Ring of Fire manufacturers in southern California, as well as more reputable firms including SIG Arms and Colt.[25] Design changes and more careful marketing practices will be costly, and those costs, with the costs of litigation and expanded liability, would be

23. Another aspect of marketing that has been addressed in both the public filings and several private suits is advertising. In some cases advertising campaigns have been designed to persuade people that a gun would provide them and their families with protection from harm, a problematic claim given the evidence that households with guns are at greater risk of injury than those that are gun free. Other gun models have been advertised as well suited for those who want to use their guns against other people and get away with it.

24. Wintemute (1994).

25. The Ring of Fire manufacturers (Wintemute 1994) have supplied most of the cheap handguns in circulation in recent years. Davis Engineering and Sundance Industries have both exited from the industry.

passed on to the consumer. Higher prices would be welcome to those who believe that cheap guns are part of the problem in youth violence.[26]

Negative Externalities from the Sale of Handguns

Given that one consequence of successful litigation against the firearms industry would likely be to increase prices, this assessment begins with a brief review of the evidence on whether prices are currently too low, in the sense of understating the marginal social cost of owning or possessing a gun. If so, then there exists an inadequate incentive to economize on gun possession and use.

To illustrate, suppose the federal government increased the excise tax on handguns. The retail prices of new handguns would shift upward, and that price increase would lead to an increase in the prices of used handguns, given that they are close substitutes for new ones and in limited supply.[27] A variety of behavioral consequences would ensue, including a reduction in sales of new guns, a decision on the part of some existing owners to sell their guns, and a general increase in the level of care in protecting guns from breakage, theft, or confiscation by police. The household and individual prevalence of handgun ownership would decline. But what would be the effect on the externalities associated with gun ownership? The net externality associated with gun acquisition and possession depends on the relative importance of at least three key mechanisms: substitution, propensity to violence, and deterrence and self-defense.

Substitution

While about two-thirds of all homicides are currently committed with a gun, and 80 percent of those with handguns, if handguns became scarcer, some assailants would substitute other weapons. The evidence suggests that substitution of knives for guns in serious assaults would reduce the fatality rate substantially;[28] substitution of shotguns for handguns, however, may increase the fatality rate, although that sort of substitution may be rare in practice.[29]

26. Cook (1981).
27. Cook and Leitzel (1996).
28. Cook (1991); Zimring (1968).
29. Kleck (1984); Cook (1991).

Propensity to Violence

The probability that a gun will be used in crime differs widely depending on who is in possession. If guns become scarcer, that would affect not only the prevalence of guns but also their distribution. It is possible that violence-prone people who possess a gun under the current regime have a lower elasticity of demand than those current gun owners who are less violence prone. In that case, a tax increase on handguns would cause a larger reduction in handgun possession than in handgun violence.

Deterrence and Self-Defense

Although guns are used to inflict damage on others, they also are used in self-defense against crime. Further, the possibility that potential victims may be armed could well have a general deterrent effect on criminals. In the latter case, gun ownership may have a positive externality (in the sense that an increase in the prevalence of gun ownership in a community will reduce burglary and assault rates). The benefits of handguns will depend on whether they are more effective than alternative means of crime avoidance such as burglar alarms, dogs, pepper spray, or even long guns, about which relatively little is currently known.[30]

Thus determining the magnitude and even the sign of this externality is an empirical matter. But while there have been several empirical investigations, there is no consensus among economists. John Lott's best-selling book on the subject is *More Guns, Less Crime*, while Mark Duggan titles an article in the *Journal of Political Economy* "More Guns, More Crime." Lott's work focuses on the effects of state laws that have made it easier for individuals to obtain the permit required to carry a concealed gun legally. He offers various estimates for the effect on crimes other than homicide but in every case finds that these laws reduce the homicide rate. That reduction, he asserts, is the result of the deterrent effect; would-be assailants are deterred by the perception of a higher probability that would-be victims are armed.[31]

More directly relevant to our externality question is Lott's finding that a state's rate of gun ownership (as measured by voter exit polls) is negatively related to rates of both violent and property crimes after controlling for a list of other factors.[32] In contrast, Duggan finds that his own proxy for the

30. Cook (1991); Ludwig (2000).
31. Duggan (2001); Lott (2000); Cook, Moore, and Braga (2002).
32. Lott (2000, pp. 113–14).

prevalence of handgun ownership—subscription rates to gun magazines—has a *positive* effect on homicide rates, and no effect on other types of crime. He also offers evidence that contradicts Lott's conclusion that relaxing the rules on concealed carrying saves lives.

This is not the place to attempt a resolution of these dueling estimates.[33] However, we do offer some rough-and-ready estimates of our own for the sake of illustrating the computation of the net externality to gun ownership. Table 3-1 gives ordinary-least-squares regression results for a cross-section analysis of homicide rates in the one hundred largest counties. Since there are no county-level estimates of gun prevalence available, we use a well-validated proxy, namely, the percentage of adult (age twenty-five and over) suicides committed with a gun.[34] To control for all other influences on the homicide rate, including socioeconomic characteristics of the population and the effectiveness of local law enforcement, we include as covariates the rates of robbery and aggravated assault. (Definitions and descriptive statistics for all variables are given in appendix table 3A-1, p. 93.) The result, regardless of specification, is that gun prevalence is significantly positively associated with the homicide rate. The best "fit" is with the robbery rate as the sole covariate.

The coefficient estimate on the proxy for handgun prevalence is .65. Since all variables are in log form, that can be interpreted as the elasticity of homicide with respect to this proxy. Based on the estimated relationship between the proxy and the ownership prevalence we end up with the following result, computed at the mean values for the relevant variables: every additional 15,000 handguns in an urban county will result in an additional homicide. (This result is net of any deterrent effect.) If we focus only on homicides and conservatively value a statistical life at $1 million, then the additional social cost per handgun is $65 a year.[35]

Needless to say, there are several qualifications required. First, the regression is limited to urban counties, where rates of violence tend to be

33. See Black and Nagin (1998); Ludwig (1998, 2000); Donohue and Ayres (1999); Cook, Moore and Braga (2002).

34. This proxy was validated by correlating it with survey results for the fifty states and by other such comparisons. See Azrael, Cook, and Miller (2001). On that basis we can say that this proxy "outperforms" the others that are commonly used. Note that the proxy is not the suicide rate or the firearms suicide rate, but rather the *percentage of suicides* committed with a gun.

35. In Cook and Ludwig (2000, pp. 9–10) we argue that the costs of gun violence are not closely linked to the loss of life, since that perspective omits the value of the prevention, avoidance, and melioration efforts of public and private actors. We estimate that a 30 percent reduction in gun injuries resulting from assault would be worth $24 billion to the American public, which, it turns out, is about $1 million per injury.

Table 3-1. *Effect of Gun Prevalence on the Homicide Rate per 100,000*

Item	Regression 1	Regression 2	Regression 3
Estimated coefficients and standard errors[a]			
Intercept	−5.863	−5.835	−4.673
	(0.456)	(0.438)	(0.789)
Gun–ownership			
prevalence (percent)	0.653	0.665	0.439
	(0.105)	(0.101)	(0.188)
Robbery rate			
per 100,000	0.941	0.960	
	(0.064)	(0.042)	
Aggravated assault			
rate per 100,000	0.030		0.841
	(0.074)		(0.088)
R squared	.86	.86	.54

a. Ordinary least square regression results for the one hundred largest counties. All variables in natural log form, computed from data for 1993–96 combined.

highest. The net effect on homicide of additional guns in rural counties may well be smaller. Second, our calculations take no account of the possible effect of gun prevalence on other types of crime, including assault and burglary. (Duggan's results suggest that the narrow focus on homicide is warranted, since he finds no evidence that other crime rates are affected by changes in gun prevalence.) Third, the regression analysis may be misspecified. For example, it is possible that the cross-section structures of both homicide and gun prevalence reflect the influence of some third variable that is not well accounted for by including the robbery rate as a covariate.[36]

If the calculations presented in our (and Duggan's) paper are even roughly correct, then the implication is that gun ownership has a substantial negative externality associated with it. Households are making decisions about whether to obtain and keep a handgun based on prices that are far

36. One important candidate for such a "third variable" is the stringency of state gun control measures. The Open Society Institute recently published an index of state laws based on thirty criteria. Peters (2000). The index, which has a maximum of 100 points, ranges from 76 at the high end (Massachusetts) to −10 for Maine. A negative value indicates that the state's laws actually have the effect of undermining the minimum standards created by the federal law. The index is negatively correlated with the prevalence of gun ownership, and it is plausible that the omission of indicators of legal stringency bias the coefficient estimate on gun prevalence. For that reason we experimented with including the index as a covariate in the linear (unlogged) versions of the specifications reported in table 3-1. In each case the coefficient estimate on the index was a fraction of its estimated standard error, with little change in the other coefficient estimates. We note that the index has not been validated, and that in any event it is defined for the laws in place as of 2000 rather than in the mid-1990s.

lower than the marginal social cost. Hence there is a case for further intervention in the gun markets, either to reduce the externalities associated with
gun ownership or to increase the price and reduce the prevalence of ownership.

The Prospects for Effective Discrimination

One approach to reducing the negative externality generated by widespread gun ownership is to limit possession to those who can be trusted to
use guns safely and legally. The case for higher prices and across-the-board
restrictions on gun availability is obviated to the extent that those who are
at risk for misuse can be reliably identified and prevented from obtaining
one. The regression results reported above suggest that the current restrictions on transfer and possession, as specified in the Gun Control Act and
state laws, are inadequate, but perhaps with greater effort it would be possible to better enforce the line between "entitled" and "proscribed."

Federal policy (and the policy in most states) toward personal
firearms can be characterized as an effort to balance the interest in reducing the harms resulting from criminal and other misuses against the interest in preserving traditional sporting and household-protection uses. That
balance has been sought through regulations that prohibit possession of
firearms by people who are too young or who have a serious criminal
record, while leaving untouched almost everyone else's access to guns.
The FFLs are important in implementing this discrimination policy. It
is up to them to identify which buyers are "entitled" and which are "proscribed" and to refuse to sell to members of the latter group. One purpose of the lawsuits brought by city and county governments is to make
manufacturers take responsibility for policing dealers who sell their products.[37]

But is this remedy going to achieve a significant reduction in gun violence? Skeptics doubt that it will, either because they deny the underlying
premise of the discrimination strategy (namely, that most people can be
trusted with a gun), or because they doubt that effective discrimination
can be preserved in the face of profitable arbitrage possibilities in the secondary market.

Four positions, A, B, C, and D, as noted in table 3-2, summarize the
controversy. The strongest case for American-style gun control is position
A, which asserts that most people can be trusted with a gun and that it is

37. Vernick and Teret (1999, pp. 1748–49).

Table 3-2. *Alternative Viewpoints on a "Discrimination" Approach to Gun Regulation*

		Adequate?**	
		Yes	No
Feasible?*	Yes	A	B
	No	C	D

*Is it feasible to keep guns from legally proscribed individuals?
**Is a discrimination strategy adequate in that most people can be trusted with a gun?

feasible to deprive those who cannot be trusted without reducing general availability. Position B may be associated with the view that current gun control can have a beneficial effect but does not go far enough, while viewpoints C and D engender doubt about the efficacy of gun control. At the risk of oversimplification, we link the positions of advocacy organizations to these viewpoints as follows:

A. Brady Campaign to Prevent Gun Violence (formerly Handgun Control Inc.) and other advocates for enforcing existing regulations on gun commerce;

C. The National Rifle Association and many of the commentators who argue against gun control;[38] and

D. The Violence Policy Center, the *Washington Post* editorial board, and other advocates for handgun bans[39]

Viewpoint B is rarely espoused, although it may be the underlying view of groups that favor expanding the list of those proscribed from gun possession.

The two underlying dimensions of the viewpoints are important.

—First, who should be entrusted with firearms? Federal law denies

38. See, for example, Kates and Polsby (2000); Wright (1995); Daniel D. Polsby, "The False Promise of Gun Control," *Atlantic Monthly*, March 1994, pp. 57–60; and James Q. Wilson, "Just Take Away Their Guns," *New York Times Magazine*, March 20, 1994, p. 47.

39. See, for example, Violence Policy Center (2000); Sugarmann (2001); Bogus (2000). The *Washington Post* editorial page has argued that "legal guns are no less deadly than illegal ones. A society that tolerates the easy collection of large stashes of powerful weapons also makes an implicit decision to tolerate large body counts as some number of gun owners let the tensions of their lives overtake their self restraint. . . . Generally speaking, the sale, manufacture and possession of handguns ought to be banned." *Washington Post*, "Editorial: Legal Guns Kill, Too," November 5, 1999, p. A32.

guns to certain groups. In practice, the most important of the characteristics that define these proscribed groups are those who can be identified through administrative records in the public domain—records on felony convictions and age in particular. The law also proscribes possession by members of groups defined along other dimensions in the list—illegal aliens, users of illicit drugs, those involuntarily committed to a mental institution—but the records accessed in a standard background check are generally not useful for detecting those characteristics.

This approach, which could be called "permissive screening," would be most promising if the population divided neatly into two groups, as in the old movie Westerns: the "White Hats" (most of the adult population) and the "Black Hats" (the small minority who cause most of the trouble).[40] This view is widely asserted but has been challenged by gun control advocates.[41] For example, Carl Bogus argues that "many previously law-abiding citizens lose control in lover's quarrels, alcohol-soaked arguments, bursts of road rage, and other moments of passion, fury, or despair," so that widespread ownership of guns is inevitably dangerous.[42] Although that view is plausible, it does not comport well with available research, which suggests that the vast majority of adult killers are not "law abiding" but rather have a history of criminal behavior.[43]

The problem remains, however, that the "Black Hats" cannot always be identified in criminal history records. Several studies have demonstrated that only a minority of killers have a felony conviction on their record.[44] (Some have a documented history of violence but are not officially designated "felons," since their prior misdeeds were dealt with in the juvenile court or resulted in nothing more than a misdemeanor conviction.) As a result, it has been argued that the list of proscribed people be expanded to include, say, those with any misdemeanor conviction for violence.[45] But wherever the line is drawn, it will fail to identify some dangerous people who have avoided acquiring a criminal conviction record. So preserving a large legal sphere for gun ownership and use means tolerating a certain level of gun violence, even if the line between entitled and proscribed is defended effectively.

40. Spitzer (1998).
41. Wright (1995).
42. Bogus (2000, p. 1355). See also Zimring and Hawkins (1997).
43. Elliott (1998); Kates and Polsby (2000).
44. Sherman (2001, pp. 69–96).
45. Wintemute and others (2001).

In practice the line is located differently for different types of weapons, and for different uses. Federal law bars FFLs from selling handguns to those under twenty-one, but the age limit for rifles and shotguns is just eighteen. In every state but one (Vermont), carrying a gun concealed requires a special permit or is banned outright, whereas keeping a gun at home is more lightly regulated. As discussed above there are categories of guns that are simply prohibited—the discriminatory approach is not deemed appropriate for machine guns or dynamite or nuclear devices.

Even if the group that is entitled to own guns under a permissive system includes some dangerous people, it seems clear that a more effective defense of the line between entitled and proscribed would reduce the negative externalities associated with widespread gun ownership.[46]

—Second, is effective discrimination possible? Economic forces work to undercut the effect of any screening system. Although teenagers and felons may find it somewhat difficult or chancy to purchase a gun directly from a licensed dealer, the secondary market provides access to firearms without the necessity of undergoing a background check.[47] Primary market regulations can influence the terms on which guns are available on the secondary market; for example, anything that increases the price of a new gun in the primary market is likely to have a positive effect on prices in the used market, including the secondary market.[48] Advocates for more effective regulation of the primary market also argue that FFLs play a direct role in supplying criminals with guns. Yet the relative importance of intentional dealer misbehavior for the flow of guns into the secondary market remains unclear.

Some observers have argued that "manufacturers could identify irresponsible dealers using readily available information,"[49] since ATF trace data show that a large share of crime guns originate from a relatively small share of FFLs. And in fact criminal investigations occasionally identify dealers who have knowingly sold thousands of guns to criminals over the course of several years.[50] A recent "focused inspection initiative" undertaken by ATF selected 1,012 dealers (1.2 percent of the total) for comprehensive

46. As a logical matter, that would be true even if everyone were equally likely to misuse a gun. If 10 percent of the population were effectively proscribed, then the gun violence rate would be reduced by at least 10 percent.

47. Cook, Molliconi, and Cole (1995); Cook and Ludwig (2000).

48. Cook and Leitzel (1996).

49. Lytton, (2000, p. 1255).

50. Wachtel (1998); U.S. Department of the Treasury, Bureau of Alcohol, Tobacco, and Firearms (2000b).

compliance inspections because they had been the source of ten or more crime guns submitted for tracing in 1999 or had been uncooperative with trace requests.[51] These dealers accounted for 20 percent of all guns sold by dealers in 1999, but more than 50 percent of the successful crime gun traces were traced to them. The inspections uncovered violations in 75 percent of cases, usually involving incomplete or faulty record keeping and failure to comply with the requirement that multiple sales be reported to ATF. More important, perhaps, inspections identified sales to more than 400 potential firearms traffickers and nearly 300 prohibited persons.[52] Only 20 (2 percent) of the FFLs were recommended for license revocation, but 29 percent of those inspected were warned. Importantly, the resources devoted to this effort were far higher than usual, and the initiative is unlikely to be repeated, at least in the next few years. The industry, however, could make such a focused inspection program routine.

If successful steps were taken to close down "dirty dealers" and convince the others to exercise greater care, would gun availability to criminals be reduced? Although it does seem possible to cut back on dealers as "point sources" of guns moving directly to criminals, even under the best of circumstances dealers would not be eliminated as a source of crime guns. Even conscientious dealers cannot necessarily detect straw purchasers (those with clean records who are buying guns on behalf of proscribed people) or proscribed purchasers using false identification. And no state expects dealers to refuse sale to someone who meets the minimum conditions for legal purchase. One dealer complained that government officials "want gypsy crystal-ball tellers at the counter," but in fact the government cannot ask for much more than careful screening based on available records.[53]

More important, a crackdown on dealer misbehavior would leave open other potential sources, and those could provide a ready substitute. The 200 million guns already in private hands represent a large inventory potentially available to proscribed people in the unregulated secondary market.

Some evidence on this matter comes from a case study of Chicago following the Brady Act.[54] The Brady Handgun Violence Prevention Act, implemented in 1994, required all dealers to institute background checks of

51. U.S. Department of the Treasury, Bureau of Alcohol, Tobacco, and Firearms (2000c)

52. U.S. Department of the Treasury, Bureau of Alcohol, Tobacco, and Firearms (2000c, p. ii).

53. Devnon Spurgeon and Paul M. Barrett, "Chicago's Shots in 'Operation Gunsmoke' Marked by Misfires," *Wall Street Journal*, May 13, 2000, p. ZS-3.

54. Cook and Braga (2001).

those seeking to buy handguns from FFLs. An analysis of guns confiscated during the period 1996–99 by the police in Chicago (which prohibits handgun sales and acquisition) found that 46 percent of those manufactured before 1994 were first sold at retail out of state, especially in Mississippi and its neighboring states of the deep South. Yet few of the confiscated guns that were first sold in 1994 or later originated in the deep South—that channel was replaced by in-state Illinois sources. What changed is that the dealers operating in states that had the requirement for background checks as a matter of state law were not affected by the Brady Act, but those in Mississippi and environs had to change their practice. The new background check and waiting period made Mississippi a more costly source of handguns to traffickers, and those channels were apparently no longer profitable.

Unfortunately, this abrupt change in trafficking patterns seems to have had little effect on homicides in Chicago—the percentage of homicides involving guns did not fall after 1993.[55] Although a more refined analysis may demonstrate that there was some effect on criminal use, the evidence suggests that in this instance there were close substitutes for the pre-Brady trafficking channels.

An alternative strategy is to target the illicit middlemen who seem to be essential players in distributing guns within underground markets. Surveys of incarcerated criminals suggest that only about one-quarter of adults and 7 percent of teens obtained their most recent gun directly from an FFL.[56] The ATF trace data demonstrate that a disproportionate share of crime guns are new (more than a quarter are less than three years old), yet for the most part purchased by someone other than the criminal.[57] Moreover for tight-control jurisdictions such as New York, Washington, D.C., and Boston, the great majority of the crime guns are imported from other states, indicating that middlemen are vital to trafficking guns across state lines.[58]

Interventions aimed at the bottom of the crime-gun distribution chain might help reduce gun ownership rates among juveniles and criminals. In the past there has been little legal threat to individuals who supply guns to youths and criminals, and so making a "connection" has not been difficult. Increasingly, however, law enforcement agencies have attempted to develop intelligence on sources of guns on the street and arrest the suppliers. This

55. Cook and Braga (2001).
56. Wright and Rossi (1994); Sheley and Wright (1993); Beck and others (1993).
57. Cook and Braga (2001).
58. Cook and Braga (2001).

strategy has not been adequately evaluated but has some promise.[59] Regardless of the potential efficacy of interventions aimed at street-level underground dealers, this type of activity will (appropriately) remain the purview of ATF and local law enforcement rather than the gun industry no matter what the outcome of the city lawsuits.[60]

Is a "technological fix" possible? Analyses of firearms-trace data and interview data indicate that only a small minority of guns used by criminals were purchased new from a licensed dealer. Rather, most crime guns have changed hands one or more times following the original purchase. More than 500,000 used guns are stolen each year, and far more than that are transferred in other ways by gift, loan, or sale.[61] This vast resale market inevitably undercuts the crime prevention effect of the FFLs' screening of customers. One approach to meeting this challenge is through technology. If guns could only be fired by the original purchaser, or by someone who is authorized by that purchaser (and the relevant authorities), then the resale market would no longer be a source of guns to individuals proscribed from possessing one.[62] Engineering a practical "smart" or "personalized" gun was a priority for the Clinton administration, with millions of dollars given to different research laboratories and gun manufacturers, and some versions have begun to appear on the market.

Among the personalized designs that have been tested are the following:

—A built-in combination lock;

—A built-in locking mechanism that would only be released if the would-be shooter were wearing a special ring or bracelet and that would relock automatically otherwise; and

---

59. Koper and Reuter (1996) analyze this approach by analogy to interdiction efforts directed at illicit-drug markets and are skeptical of its potential effectiveness. Mark Moore, however, argues that the one factor of production in the market for illegal drugs that is in long-run short supply is "the process of reliably executing large financial transactions in a crooked world with no police or courts to enforce the contracts." Street-level interventions may increase the difficulty with which middlemen and end-users make "connections" in underground gun markets. The difficulty and risks of making these underground retail connections could in principle be inferred from data on the price mark-up associated with this distribution activity. See Moore (1990).

60. Evidence on the Brady Act's effects on gun crimes in Chicago tells us little about the effects of interventions aimed at street-level retailers. In principle Brady may have shifted the mix of "wholesalers" who supply guns to underground retailers, while leaving the street-level retail market unaffected.

61. Cook and Ludwig (1996).

62. Robinson and others (1998); Teret and others (1998b); Cook and Leitzel (2002).

—A built-in lock that would only be released if an embedded microchip "recognized" the shooter's thumb print.

In the first two cases someone who took the gun without the cooperation of the original owner would find it useless, assuming that no inexpensive method is available to override the lock; the owner would have to pass the combination or the ring along with the gun. Designs of the third kind would require something more than the cooperation of the original owner; the microchip would have to be reprogrammed, which would presumably require specialized equipment if it were possible at all.

Any of these designs would protect people who need to carry a loaded gun in public, including law enforcement and private security personnel, from the possibility of having someone grab their gun and shoot them with it. More interestingly, any of these designs would ensure that unauthorized transfers would be of little value to the taker; if such guns were stolen or borrowed by, say, an adolescent member of the family, they would pose little threat to the public. The designs differ with respect to the possibility of an informal, voluntary transfer: presumably the combination lock or ring could be transferred as part of a sale at a gun show or elsewhere, but the microchip would pose a larger problem.

As shown in the two-by-two matrix in table 3-2, the personalized gun offers a technological fix for keeping guns away from proscribed people and hence if it were widely adopted, it would give greater credence to positions A or B rather than C or D. Some advocates of the "diffuse risk" position have opposed the introduction of personalized technology, however, on the grounds that it would encourage some people to acquire a gun who otherwise would go unarmed for fear that some unauthorized person (a member of the family or a visitor) might find it and misuse it.[63] These advocates believe that a personalized gun might be misused by the original buyer— even if the buyer is legally authorized, he like everyone else is liable to misuse the gun. But for those who believe that the risk of misuse is concentrated among legally proscribed individuals, that possibility is not of much concern. In any event, at least so far there seems to be little market for personalized guns, perhaps in part because of the substantial additional cost.

A settlement agreement could include a stipulation that the manufacturers would invest in developing personalized-gun technology and eventually offer such models for sale.[64] A more effective stipulation would be

63. Violence Policy Center (1998).

64. The settlement ending Boston's lawsuit against Smith and Wesson included that provision (99-2590, Superior Court Dept., Suffolk County, Mass.).

that any manufacturer who offered a gun for sale after a specified date that lacked such a locking device would be liable for subsequent misuse made possible by unauthorized transfer. In neither case would the design change be a panacea, since there would remain in circulation the approximately 70 million handguns that lack this technology. But the new designs would be of some use in reducing injuries from the beginning.

Suppose there were an ideal personalization technology whereby each gun is "assigned" to the original purchaser by the dealer and cannot be transferred, except perhaps through special equipment that was limited to FFLs. The immediate result would be to eliminate straw purchases and theft of new guns. Assuming that the FFLs screened buyers effectively, the secondary market for used guns would become the only source for anyone who was legally barred from the primary market or who did not want a record kept of the purchase. That fact, together with the increase in price of new guns resulting from the personalization design, would increase the price of guns in the secondary market. Workable used guns would become increasingly scarce as the stock deteriorated and was drained by police confiscations.

The bottom line is that there is great promise for personalization technology as a means for reducing gun availability to proscribed people, especially if guns were designed so that they could not be transferred once "assigned" except through a process that could be subjected to official scrutiny.

The Limits of Litigation

A comprehensive effort to reduce gun violence in America would focus on gun design and distribution, as well as interventions to reduce gun misuse among owners. Despite the practical difficulty of strengthening existing firearms regulations in the current political environment, in principle almost any aspect of gun commerce and use is subject to legislative intervention. In contrast, the scope of what litigation might accomplish—even under the plaintiffs' most optimistic scenarios—is more limited.

The lawsuits may have their greatest impact on gun design, partly because the design of firearms is under the immediate control of the manufacturers and importers who are the defendants in these cases. As table 3-3 shows, potential design changes include increases in the minimum weight or length of handguns (designed to make guns more difficult to

Table 3-3. *Potential Direct Outcomes of Litigation against Gun Industry*

Item	Possible	Unlikely
Gun design	Changes in minimum size, weight of handguns Addition of safety features (such as "childproof" firing devices) Personalized gun technology	
Distribution/ access	Changes in effective price of guns Enhanced oversight of licensed gun dealers Limits on gun sales of one per person per month	Restrictions on gun sales to those with "risky" (but not disqualifying) background characteristics Regulation of secondary gun market transfers (for example, through licensing and registration)
Carrying/use		Changes in gun storage Changes in prevalence of gun carrying in public Gun misuse

carry concealed), safety measures such as firing devices that cannot be operated by young children, or personalization technologies.

The restrictions applying to gun sales in the primary market are implemented by retail dealers and may be indirectly influenced by manufacturers. For example, manufacturers could insist that retailers limit gun sales to one per transaction even in states that do not have such a limit mandated by law. But we are dubious that a reliable licensing system could be organized and maintained by the gun industry—that would seem to require new legislation and government participation.

Even less amenable to court-ordered change are those aspects of gun commerce and use that are entirely beyond the control of manufacturers or retailers. Since the influence of the gun industry largely ends at the gun dealer's door (except indirectly, through design), neither manufacturers nor retailers can do much to affect the flow or use of guns once they leave the primary market. The gun industry cannot on its own implement a firearms registration system to help regulate secondary market sales. Although the gun industry can require that all handgun purchasers also buy some form of locking device, it cannot require owners to lock their guns up at home. Nor can the gun industry act directly to reduce illegal carrying, which some observers argue is the most promising strategy for reducing gun crime, or enhance the probability or severity of punishment for those who misuse guns.[65]

In short, many of the changes in gun commerce and use that may be worthwhile in reducing the problem of gun violence in America will require legislation. Although litigation cannot affect these changes directly, the city lawsuits may alter the political environment in which the relevant legislative debates occur.

The Political Consequences of Litigation

Many observers have criticized the city lawsuits against the gun industry for shifting authority away from the legislative process and toward the courts, thus achieving an "undemocratic" end. For example, H. Sterling Burnett of the National Center for Policy Analysis argues, "The lawsuits threaten democracy because they would replace the will of the majority as expressed through the legislature with the determinations of an unelected judiciary."[66]

By design the American system of democracy includes institutional features to protect minority and regional interests. For example, the apportionment of the U.S. Senate ensures that voters in the mountain states are disproportionately influential in the national legislative process. Since these less populated rural states are also characterized by relatively high rates of gun ownership, the national legislative system has in some sense a built-in "pro-gun" tilt.[67]

Another institutional feature of our political system that may help protect minority interests is the lobbying process and the purchase of

65. Wilson, "Just Take Away Their Guns"; Sherman (2001).

66. Sterling H. Burnett, "Gun Lawsuits Hurt Us All," *Houston Chronicle*, editorial, December 12, 1999. In February 2001 Florida's Third District Court of Appeal denied a request to overturn a trial court ruling in favor of gun manufacturers with the assertion that the lawsuit was a clear attempt "to regulate firearms and ammunition through the medium of the judiciary." A somewhat different perspective is offered in "When Lawsuits Make Policy," *Economist*, November 21, 1998, p. 17. The editors suggest, "If gun-control advocates achieve their goals by legal threats, rather than through properly enacted legislation, it will be a Pyrrhic victory. With good reason, gun-owners will never accept their defeat as legitimate. The subject of guns will become as bitterly polarised as abortion, and just as incapable of resolution through debate or compromise."

67. Cook and Ludwig (1996); Glaeser and Glendon (1998).

access to policymakers, which enables voters to express the intensity of
their preferences. Regulation of media violence and environmental pollution produces diffuse benefits and concentrated costs, and the same may
be true for regulations to reduce gun violence.[68] Because the gains to most
people from regulations that achieve a lower risk of injury are modest, it
has not been easy to translate majority support into effective political
action.[69] The opposition to any new firearm regulations comes in part
from the gun industry, which has a large stake in resisting measures that
reduce gun sales or increase the costs of conducting business. Even minor
regulatory changes are vigorously opposed by gun rights ideologues.[70]
Regardless of whether one views lobbying activity as a desirable or undesirable feature of the U.S. political system, the end result is a legislative
outcome that often departs from "majority rules." In contrast Timothy D.
Lytton argues that "in the tort system, parties, despite differences in the
amount of resources that they can invest in litigation, are granted equal
access to decision makers."[71]

Lawsuits might also address what some might view as "undemocratic"
(and inefficient) outcomes that result from our system of assigning states
an important role in determining gun policy. Gun misuse is a regional or
national problem. Because the system put in place by the 1968 Gun Control Act fails to fully insulate states from one another, state-level decisions
to implement lax regulations on gun sales impose negative externalities on
more restrictive states because of gun trafficking. Congress may be unwilling to address these externalities given the disproportionate political influence of states with lax firearms rules, although in principle restrictive states
could bargain with or at least sue lax states to induce them to internalize
these external costs.[72] An alternative mechanism for addressing the problem is for restrictive states to litigate against the gun industry directly to
induce changes in operating practices in states with permissive gun laws.

But debates about the appropriate division of responsibility among
branches of government, and the extent to which the courts or the legis-

68. Hamilton (1998).
69. In Ludwig and Cook (2001), we estimate that two-thirds of households are willing to pay $200
or more for a 30 percent reduction in the threat of criminal gun violence.
70. Spitzer (1998).
71. Lytton (2000, pp. 1251–52).
72. This situation is analogous to the problem associated with stationary sources of air pollution
that were already in operation in 1970 (and thus are regulated by state authorities under the Clean Air
Act). Several states have filed lawsuits against one another in an attempt to reduce the external costs
associated with air-born pollutants, although a system for facilitating across-state payments is also
being considered. Portney (2000).

latures serve the public interest, however defined, may be somewhat beside the point in the current circumstances.[73] The city lawsuits are likely to influence rather than replace the legislative process in this arena.

The public lawsuits are a great threat to the financial viability of this small industry. One possible outcome, as we have discussed, is a settlement, although the industry may find that unsatisfactory; as in the case of the tobacco settlement with the states, a settlement with the public plaintiffs would not forestall private lawsuits, which may ultimately be sufficient to bankrupt the industry. Given the threat of widespread bankruptcy and withdrawal by manufacturers, Congress or the state legislatures could respond by granting the industry some sort of immunity from civil liability, much as did the Maryland legislature following the judgment against some manufacturers of Saturday Night Specials in 1985. But as in that case, the necessity of defending the industry would place gun control opponents in a position where they might have to bargain with gun control supporters. The status quo, always the easiest position to defend in the legislative process, would be shifted.

The lawsuits could thus reframe the set of realistic policy choices that are under consideration.[74] That has *not* been the case in Georgia, Arkansas, Montana, Arizona, Tennessee, Nevada, Maine, Louisiana, Texas, and several other states, in which the legislatures have barred local governments from suing the industry, or Alaska and South Dakota, which have gone still further in immunizing the industry against all sorts of civil liability. But more liberal states are not going to take this step unless gun control advocates are satisfied.

A legislative compromise prompted by the city lawsuits is not undemocratic—rather, this outcome would be the result of a democratic process in which the starting point is a foreseeably bankrupt industry rather than the current status quo (a financially viable and largely unregulated industry). Because large majorities of the American public favor stronger regulations over gun design and distribution, it would even seem that the result may be closer to what could be considered the "will of the people."[75]

73. For one effort to grapple with these issues, see Eskridge (1988). He reviews the public choice critique of legislative behavior and suggests that an activist court may help redress some legislative failings.

74. McCubbins, Noll, and Weingast (1989) discuss a related matter, namely, the influence of the position adopted by a regulatory agency which is subject to modification by the legislature. They point out that the agency establishes the status quo, and that in a legislature whose factions are defined along two dimensions that status quo position may influence the domain of legislated change that would receive majority support in the legislature.

75. Teret and others (1998a).

Conclusions

In this chapter we have avoided discussing the merit of the legal arguments that underlie the gun lawsuits, not because this is an unimportant issue but rather because we are unqualified to remark on it. Nor have we attempted to predict how the lawsuits will fare in the courts. Furthermore, we have offered only a cursory discussion of the larger philosophical issues about the appropriate division of responsibility between courts and legislatures within democratic societies. Rather, our focus has been on considering just what the lawsuits might accomplish if they were to be successful.

We have argued that firearm regulations currently in place are probably inadequate, in the sense that the current regime is characterized by large negative externalities associated with gun ownership. Of course this conclusion is contested, but we believe that most available evidence (including the new evidence we offer) supports it. That conclusion invites a discussion of just what additional regulations might be worthwhile. Clearly the evidence of market failure is not by itself sufficient to demonstrate that just any new restriction on the market is worthwhile. Ideally each possibility would be subjected to careful evaluation of its costs and benefits, acknowledging that a bad regulation could make an unfortunate situation worse.

The lawsuits are most promising in their ability to force modifications in gun design. The easiest design changes for the industry to implement—such as childproof firing mechanisms—are likely to help reduce unintentional firearm injuries. In principle the lawsuits could also compel the industry to adopt personalized gun technologies that might help address the larger problem of adolescent gun suicide and gun crime.

Changes in gun design, or even the costs associated with litigation or the threat of litigation, may result in some increase in the price of guns. If the prevalence of private gun ownership contributes to a net increase in lethal violence, higher gun prices may lead to a socially desirable reduction in gun sales and the prevalence of gun ownership.

Many of the lawsuits seek to change the distribution practices of the gun industry in an attempt to reduce the flow of guns into the secondary gun market. Industry-imposed limits on handgun sales of one per person per month might help, since the result would be to effect a marginal increase in the costs of gun trafficking with no effect on the ability of other people to keep guns for self-defense. The impetus to impose greater discipline on FFLs is based on strong evidence that some dealers are important

Table 3A-1. *Descriptive Statistics*

Variable[a]	N	Mean	Standard deviation	Minimum	Maximum
Homicide rate per 100,000	100	11.52	11.82	1.38	78.17
Robbery rate per 100,000	100	349.0	278.5	41.3	1,569.7
Assault rate per 100,000	100	511.0	308.4	44.1	1,370.1
Gun suicides[b]	99	50.1	13.4	18.1	76.4

Source: Data are from an unpublished source from the FBI's *Uniform Crime Report* (Washington).

a. Variables used in the regression analysis; one hundred largest counties, 1993–96.

b. Percent of suicides committed with firearms, for victims twenty-five years old and over during 1987–96. One county lacks sufficient observations to be included in this study.

sources of supply to traffickers and criminals. Even if these "point sources" can be closed down, our analysis of Chicago's experience following implementation of the federal Brady Act raises some doubt about the effect on gun availability and crime.

Finally, both sides of the gun issue agree that the behavior of gun owners seriously affects the overall volume of crime and gun violence, even if there is disagreement about the magnitudes (or even the signs) of the underlying relationships. Although the gun lawsuits are unlikely to have any near-term effect on storage, carrying, or gun misuse, litigation may have some indirect effect in each of these areas by strengthening the hand of gun control advocates in the legislative process.

COMMENT BY

Jim Leitzel

In the past few years, more than thirty lawsuits have been brought by local governments against firearm manufacturers, distributors, trade associations, and retailers, in addition to numerous suits by individuals. Phil Cook and Jens Ludwig grant summary judgment to the government plaintiffs in these suits and then examine potential remedies. Cook and Ludwig ask if the changes in firearm design and marketing that could result from such lawsuits will serve the public interest. The potential remedies include mandates to develop safer guns and increased oversight of retailers by manufacturers, as well as a concomitant price increase for guns. Cook and Ludwig conclude that, by and large, such measures would be desirable. Nevertheless, they continue, there are other regulatory changes to the firearms market that would also be sensible, including gun registration and incorporation of the secondary market into the regulatory regime that governs the primary market, though these changes are not as susceptible to being brought about by litigation.

The Cook and Ludwig analysis comes at a time of very good news concerning U.S. firearm violence, at least compared with most of the past thirty-five years. According to a recent Centers for Disease Control report, the firearm homicide rate fell 42 percent between 1993 and 1998.[76] Fatal firearm accidents, which have been declining for half a century, fell even more sharply than gun homicides, while the gun suicide rate also fell, by 15 percent. Despite the trends downward, approximately 31,000 gun deaths took place in the United States in 1998, with an additional 64,000 nonfatal gun injury cases treated at hospital emergency rooms. So firearm morbidity and mortality remain major problems. Indeed, we have become rather inured to what, in the recent past, would have been shocking news. Not long ago (April 14, 2001), in Elgin, Illinois, a suburb of Chicago, a lone gunman walked into a bar and shot eighteen people. My informal poll suggests that most people, even those who follow the news rather closely, know little or nothing of this tragedy. In the summer of 2000, in the park near where I live in South Chicago (Jackson Park), nine people were shot in a single incident—but none of the victims died, and even most Chicagoans, it seems, have no knowledge of this event. (The most widely known Chicago-area gun incident, the St. Valentine's Day massacre of 1929, claimed seven victims, though all seven were fatalities.) All told, the costs of gun violence in the United States, according to a reliable source, amount to some $100 billion annually.[77]

And most of these costs are not borne by the gun consumer. Cook and Ludwig take pains to argue for and document the negative externality associated with guns—their simple regression brings an interesting new datum into the analysis. Although these calculations are inherently uncertain (and Cook and Ludwig are careful to point out complicating factors), it looks as if a Pigovian excise tax on the average urban handgun would be close to

76. Gotsch and others (2001).
77. Cook and Ludwig (2000).

prohibitive, that is, it could be approximated decently by a ban on the sale of handguns. (Their conservative figure of an average of $65 per urban handgun per year, if imposed in present-value terms as a single lump-sum tax at the time of purchase of a gun expected to last for twenty years, would come to about $850, with an annual discount rate of 5 percent.) The higher prices associated with safer guns or better-supervised behavior by retailers are almost certainly a step in the right direction.

Of course, not all guns present the same danger—rather, the gun itself as well as the owner (and his or her training and environment) determine the "expected" negative externality arising from gun ownership. We subsidize the gun possession of law enforcers, and in current American circumstances, rightly so. Guns that seem to offer higher social costs relative to their social benefits (cheap handguns, extremely powerful or automatic weapons) face stricter controls.

What about the city lawsuits against the gun industry? Cook and Ludwig's table 3-3 nicely encapsulates the potential impacts these suits might have on the firearm regulatory system. I would add two observations. Perhaps the first two elements in the "Unlikely" column, restricting sales to risky but not prohibited purchasers, and regulation of secondary market transfers, are not that unlikely. Many of the city suits name gun distributors and retail sellers, as well as manufacturers, as defendants. Distributors and retailers might respond not just to pressure from their suppliers but also to the direct threat of suits. As significant levels of straw purchases might make a distributor susceptible to public nuisance suits, some retailers and distributors might come to favor regulation of secondary market trades, for instance. A second point is that there is some hope of developing a technological fix, perhaps spurred on by the lawsuits. Cook and Ludwig mention one promising remedy, the personalized gun, but perhaps the preferred technological development would be a nonlethal firearm substitute: the "phaser on stun" solution.[78]

A certain thread runs through the Cook and Ludwig analysis, though it is not stated explicitly. It is a cause for optimism, so let me give voice to it. There are many complementarities among gun regulations. The marginal value of an improvement in one control tends to increase as another control is made marginally more effective. For instance, incremental improvements in policing the secondary market make marginal improvements in oversight over scofflaw primary market dealers more valuable. If it

---

78. Hemenway and Weil (1990).

is easy for bad guys to get guns on the secondary market, then primary market controls do have a hint of futility or worse—"if guns are outlawed, only outlaws . . . " (Phil Cook and I have argued elsewhere it needn't be much more than a "hint" of futility.)[79] But if meaningful penalties on straw purchasers develop, for instance, then increased scrutiny of dealers, or one gun-per-month rules, suddenly become more valuable. (The significant laxity of oversight over dealers that has been the norm until recently might be sensible in a world of nearly unregulated secondary markets.) So the lawsuits, which might lead to the sorts of changes listed in table 3-3, will have the indirect effect of improving the operation of other, existing controls.

As an aside on the issue of scrutiny over licensed dealers, more effective oversight can now be applied simply as an artifact of the substantial decline during the past decade in the number of dealers. In 1993 there were approximately 261,000 licensed dealers, as opposed to some 80,000 in 2001. The drop in gun homicide during this same period suggests a potential connection. Much of the decline in the number of dealers is attributable to an increase in license fees, introduced as part of the Brady Act. Ludwig and Cook have previously shown that the waiting periods and background checks of the Brady Act did not significantly reduce firearm homicide.[80] Did the Brady Act nevertheless lead to a reduction in firearm homicide through its impact on the number of licensed dealers?

Another potentially relevant change in recent decades concerns the ex post punishments applied to those who misuse guns. Convictions and jail terms for gun misusers are a partial substitute for most ex ante gun regulations. (Only a partial substitute because even if such punishments were universal and costless to impose, the existence of nondeterrable or judgment-proof individuals might still provide a case for ex ante controls, as might gun accidents and suicides.) The relatively low clearance rates that currently exist for murder tend to present a stronger case for ex ante controls than existed in the 1960s when the clearance rates were much higher, even though the homicide rates are nearly the same.[81] In other words, the marginal value of ex ante controls is higher when one partial substitute, ex post punishment for offenders, is functioning less

---

79. Cook and Leitzel (1996).

80. Ludwig and Cook (2000).

81. The national clearance rate for murder was 69 percent in 1999, as opposed to 91 percent in 1965 (US Department of Justice [2000] and Regini [1997]). In Chicago, the homicide clearance rate is currently less than 50 percent, versus 62 percent in 1995. See Frank Main, "New Detective Chief Named," *Chicago Sun-Times*, April 13, 2001, p. 24.

well. But while ex post punishments tend to be substitutes for ex ante controls, the relationship is not reciprocal: not all ex ante measures are substitutes for ex post punishments. Firearm registration, gun "finger-printing" through bullet casing markings, gun personalization, and the application of primary market controls to the legal secondary market are ex ante controls that can help to increase conviction rates for those who commit violent crimes with guns.[82] So these preventive measures (to invoke the terminology of John Stuart Mill), some of which could be promoted through the city lawsuits, will also aid in the administration of punitive controls.[83]

While we are using the language of complementarities, let me address another issue. Is litigation a substitute or a complement for legislation? The typical response, I believe, is that in regulating markets, litigation is increasingly substituting for legislation. Cook and Ludwig, however, argue the case for complementarity between the lawsuits and legislation in the case of guns. They foresee a legislative compromise (between gun control proponents and the firearms industry) prompted by the lawsuits, which will take place under the threat of bankruptcy for the industry. The lawsuits can shift the status quo, Cook and Ludwig contend, to the point at which the firearms industry essentially is "endowed" with the state of bankruptcy but can purchase solvency by agreeing to some regulations. (Whether this shift in the status quo is legitimate, or is more like the shift that occurs when a robber offers you the opportunity to purchase back your life, is not addressed in the Cook and Ludwig chapter, although it might be of prime concern for many of the interested parties.)[84] So Cook and Ludwig offer what for me was a somewhat unexpected perspective. The standard Coasian-style view depicts the law as defining the system of property rights, and then bargaining takes place in reference to (or under the shadow of) the law. For Cook and Ludwig, litigation defines the property rights, and the law is the outcome of the bargain. Their approach is perhaps not that

82. Cook and Leitzel (2002) note that personalization is complementary with other ex ante controls and after-the-fact punishments.

83. Incidentally, it can be inferred from *On Liberty* that Mill, who would support the legalization of narcotics, would not view such ex ante measures as gun registration to be unallowable infringements upon personal liberty; see Mill's discussion of regulating poisons in Ryan (1997, p. 117).

84. The legitimacy of the tobacco and firearm lawsuits to achieve regulatory ends is strongly contested, of course. Wagner (1999), for instance, finds "rough justice" in the tobacco suit and settlement. Morgan (1999, p. 549) suggests that the litigation is illegitimate: "Changes in the gun industry should take place on the floors of the legislatures, not in the halls of justice, lest tort law become a vehicle for not only stomping out cigarettes and melting down guns, but also for tearing down walls of other entire industries."

unique; it has the flavor of a public-choice-style argument, employing law-suits, not lobbying, as the means by which interest groups apply pressure. Indeed, from this perspective, lawsuits are lobbying by other means.[85]

As already noted, Cook and Ludwig do not discuss the legal merits of the gun lawsuits but focus instead on the social value of the potential reme-dies. I will not discuss the legal merits, either, though I raise one point. The shifting status quo argument of the Cook and Ludwig chapter sug-gests that the regulatory changes will result not so much from plaintiffs winning the lawsuits but simply from a sufficient number of them being filed. The shift of the status quo to bankruptcy for the industry comes from having to contest lawsuits, not from paying damages. (Indeed, the lawsuits have not fared that well in court so far, and many have been pre-empted by state legislatures.) Using litigation for regulatory purposes brings up issues of just how many bites at the regulatory apple proponents of regulation are allowed. In the case of firearms, however, the pro-regulatory side can "win," it seems, without ever succeeding in managing to bite the apple, by forcing the industry to expend resources to fend off the nibbles.[86] Precedents for altered behavior by defendants brought about through lawsuits that are not won by plaintiffs already exist in the gun industry. Despite not losing any lawsuits, Colt has elected to discontinue the manufacture of small, cheap handguns, and Smith and Wesson agreed in a settlement with many cities and the Department of Housing and Urban Development to implement a code of conduct for its gun dealers and to move toward smart, personalized guns.[87] The avoidance of inter-state gun commerce rules and record-keeping requirements by firms that provided firearm "kits" was brought to an end by an unsuccessful lawsuit against one of the firms by drive-by shooting victims.[88]

One effect of the filing of the lawsuits is to create some uncertainty over what standard of care the defendants must meet to avoid being held liable for negligence.[89] An advantage of legislative standards of care is that

85. Lytton (2000) offers a sophisticated analysis of the firearms lawsuits that views them as one part of a comprehensive system of public policy formation.

86. There are claims that for many years the tobacco industry employed a strategy of raising plain-tiffs' legal costs to prevail in lawsuits filed by individual smokers. See Rabin (1993, p. 113).

87. Bogus (2000, p. 1357).

88. The case was *Halberstam* v. *Daniel* No. 95 Civ. 3323 (E.D.N.Y. 1998); see the discussion in Lytton (2000, pp. 1271-72).

89. Bogus (2000) argues for a strict liability standard ("generic liability") that would require hand-gun manufacturers to pay for the external costs that arise from the misuse of their "unreasonably dan-gerous" products, even in the absence of negligence on the part of the manufacturers.

such uncertainty is reduced. In fact, a manufacturer (even if risk neutral) facing an uncertain negligence standard will tend to undertake a socially excessive amount of care (at the margin expenditures on care will exceed their social benefits). The increase of uncertainty, then, might be another channel through which the behavior of gun manufacturers, distributors, and retailers is altered independently of the outcome of the cases. And as Cook and Ludwig indicate, one manifestation of this changed behavior might be a willingness by defendants to embrace some legislative regulatory controls that clarify the requisite standards of care.

Finally, as Cook and Ludwig note, the gun litigation appears to have been prompted by the tobacco litigation involving state attorneys general. Let me offer, in table 3-4, an impressionistic comparison of the government lawsuits between these two industries. The table is not meant to be comprehensive, and many of the entries are controversial; the purpose of the table, however, is simply to highlight some of the dimensions along which these two series of lawsuits can be contrasted and to stimulate discussion. There are similarities among the lawsuits, as well as differences. Three aspects of the suits seem most notable: the extent to which costs of product consumption are externalized, the potential profit incentive to sell to legally proscribed purchasers, and the resources available to the defendants.

Most of the costs of gun misuse are external, that is, they are not borne by the gun purchaser, while most of the costs of cigarette smoking are internal.[90] The difference in the distribution of costs suggests that the case for taxation and other controls is much stronger for firearms than for cigarettes.

Both lawsuits have as major goals the introduction of marketing changes that attempt to restrict the profit motive that could drive attempted sales to high-risk or proscribed users. Federal law requires states to prohibit tobacco sales to individuals under the age of eighteen, though many states had their own minimum age laws before the mid-1990s initiation of the federally mandated standard.[91] Cigarette manufacturers seem to have a strong incentive, in the absence of regulation, to sell to those who are under age, for a variety of reasons. First, any increase in sales is presumably

90. The claim that the bulk of the costs of smoking are internal to the smoker is itself not uncontroversial; nor, therefore, is the claim that existing cigarette excise taxes exceed the Pigovian level. See Viscusi (1998–1999), and Gruber (2001).

91. Some of the shortcomings in enforcing the ban and reporting violation data are documented in U.S. General Accounting Office (2001). The median reported state violation rate on under-age sales by cigarette retailers was 24.2 percent in 1999, a significant decline in the median violation rate from 1997, when it was 40 percent.

Table 3-4. *Comparing the Government Lawsuits against the Tobacco and Firearms Industries*

Issue	Tobacco	Guns
Costs incident to consumption	Overwhelmingly internal	Significant external costs
Influence of consumer "care" during use on harms	Rather small	Very substantial
Is consumption rational? Feedback effects?	Cigarettes are addictive; peer-group social dynamics; many repeat purchases	Arms race dynamics; addiction to lethality?; guns are durable goods
Existing excise taxes	Meet or exceed Pigovian level	Much below Pigovian level
Barriers to legislative or standard regulatory action	Exempt from Food and Drug Administration and Consumer Product Safety Commission oversight	Exempt from CPSC oversight; McClure-Volkmer limits on oversight of dealers; Second Amendment
Industry structure	Oligopoly: four dominant firms	Handful of major producers; dozens of fringe competitors
Aims of litigation	Monetary damages; marketing changes	Design, marketing damages
Plaintiff claims	Deception concerning risks of consumption; targeting children in advertising	Negligence in design, willful blind eye by manufacturers to marketing; deceptive or negligent advertising; creation of a public nuisance
Defendant strategies	"Assumption of risk" raised against individual lawsuits; raising legal costs of plaintiffs; settlement with attorneys general	Legislative overrides of litigation; settlement on design, marketing conditions; exit from personal handguns market
Defendant resources	Very substantial	Directly, rather limited; through allied groups, substantial

beneficial to the sellers, as it would be for any industry. Second, youth smoking is susceptible to cascade throughout the youth population, so one new youth smoker could bring in many new customers. Third, and most important, because of the habit-forming properties of cigarettes, the future prosperity of the tobacco industry significantly depends on current sales to young, though not necessarily under-age consumers.

Gun manufacturers and dealers also would seem to reap a financial gain by selling to proscribed users, such as children or felons, if they could do so with little risk. Much of this financial gain will still be available if the guns reach proscribed users not through the primary market but through informal secondary market exchanges, even thefts—a point that applies to cigarette acquisition by under-age youth as well. That is, the industry tends to benefit from high demand for its products, whatever the precise channel by which that demand is met. Sales that are channeled to proscribed users might even be more beneficial for the industry than sales to legitimate gun purchasers, as an increase in possession of guns by high-risk individuals would seem to spur more gun demand from both low-risk users and other high-risk users. There are even claims that guns are addictive at the individual level: "Lethality in guns is like nicotine in cigarettes—an addictive hook set deep into the irrational side of [gun industry] customers."[92]

Revenues of the tobacco industry are about $45 billion annually, whereas gun sales total about $1.4 billion a year.[93] The tobacco industry had much more at stake in its litigation than does the relatively small firearms industry. The firearms industry, however, has other "resources" available with which to counter the suits—namely, the National Rifle Association and other groups that frequently oppose gun control legislation. These groups, as much as the defendants, may have been instrumental in the state overrides of city litigation, for instance.

Resources are valuable not just for contesting lawsuits but also for investigating and elucidating desirable directions of regulatory change. (Unlike lawsuits, such paths to better policies, in a changing world, of necessity remain unsettled.) The Cook and Ludwig contribution provides an important resource for indicating preferred routes for current U.S. firearm regulation—routes that could be traveled even without city lawsuits against gun manufacturers.

92. Diaz (1999, p. 120).

93. Lytton (2000, n. 81), citing Paul M. Barrett, "As Lawsuits Loom, Gun Industry Presents a Fragmented Front," *Wall Street Journal*, December 9, 1998, p. A1.

References

Azrael, Deborah, Philip J. Cook, and Matthew Miller. 2001. "State and Local Prevalence of Firearms Ownership: Measurement, Structure, and Trends." Working Paper. Cambridge, Mass.: National Bureau of Economic Research. October.

Beck, Allen, Darrell K. Gilliard, Lawrence Greenfeld, Caroline Harlow, Thomas Hester, Louis Jankowski, Tracy Snell, James Stephan, and Danielle Morton. 1993. *Survey of State Prison Inmates 1991*. NCJ-136949. Washington: U.S. Bureau of Justice Statistics.

Black, Dan, and Daniel Nagin.1998. "Do 'Right to Carry' Laws Deter Violent Crimes?" *Journal of Legal Studies* 27: 209–19.

Bogus, Carl T. 2000. "Gun Litigation and Societal Values." *Connecticut Law Review* 32 (4): 1353–78.

Bonnie, Richard J., Carolyn E. Fulco, and Catharyn T. Liverman, eds. 1999. *Reducing the Burden of Injury: Advancing Prevention and Treatment*. National Academy Press.

Butterfield, Fox. 2001. "The Federal Gun Laws: The First Obstacle to Enforcement." Paper presented at the University of Arizona Rogers College of Law Conference on Guns, Crime and Punishment in America.

Cook, Philip J. 1981. "The 'Saturday Night Special': An Assessment of Alternative Definitions from a Policy Perspective." *Journal of Criminal Law and Criminology* 72 (4): 1735–45.

———. 1991. "The Technology of Personal Violence." In *Crime and Justice: An Annual Review of Research*, vol. 14, edited by Michael Tonry, 1–71. University of Chicago Press.

Cook, Philip J., and Anthony Braga. 2001. "Comprehensive Firearms Tracing: Strategic and Investigative Uses of New Data on Firearms Markets." *Arizona Law Review* 43 (2):1–33.

Cook, Philip J., and James A. Leitzel. 1996. " 'Perversity, Futility, Jeopardy': An Economic Analysis of the Attack on Gun Control." *Law and Contemporary Problems* 59 (Winter): 91–118.

———. 2002. "'Smart Guns': A Technological Fix for Regulating the Secondary Market." *Contemporary Economic Problems* 20 (January): 38–49.

Cook, Philip J., and Jens Ludwig. 1996. *Guns in America: Results of a Comprehensive National Survey on Firearms Ownership and Use*. Washington: Police Foundation.

———. 2000. *Gun Violence: The Real Costs*. Oxford University Press.

Cook, Philip J., Stephanie Molliconi, and Thomas B. Cole. 1995. "Regulating Gun Markets." *Journal of Criminal Law & Criminology* 86 (Fall): 59–92.

Cook, Philip J., Mark H. Moore, and Anthony Braga. 2002. "Gun Control." In *Crime: Public Policies for Crime Control*, edited by James Q. Wilson and Joan Petersilia, 291–329. ICS Press.

Diaz, Tom. 1999. *Making a Killing. The Business of Guns in America*. New Press.

Donohue, John J., and Ian Ayres. 1999. "Nondiscretionary Concealed Weapons Law: A Case Study of Statistics, Standards of Proof, and Public Policy." *American Law and Economics Review* 1 (1): 436–70.

Duggan, Mark. 2001. "More Guns, More Crime." *Journal of Political Economy* 109 (5): 1086–1114.

Elliott, Delbert S. 1998. "Life Threatening Violence Is Primarily a Crime Problem: A Focus on Prevention." *Colorado Law Review* 69 (4): 1081–98.

Eskridge, William N. Jr. 1988. "Politics without Romance: Implications of Public Choice Theory for Statutory Interpretation." *Virginia Law Review* 74 (March): 275–38.

Glaeser, Edward L., and Spencer Glendon.1998. "Who Owns Guns? Criminals, Victims, and the Culture of Violence." *American Economic Review* 88 (May): 458–62.

Gotsch, Karen E., Joseph L. Annest, James A. Mercy, and George W. Ryan. 2001. "Surveillance for Fatal and Nonfatal Firearm-Related Injuries–United States, 1993–1998." Centers for Disease Control, *Morbidity and Mortality Weekly Report*, Surveillance Summaries 50 (SS02):1–32.

Gruber, Jonathan. 2001. "Tobacco at the Crossroads: The Past and Future of Smoking Regulation in the United States." *Journal of Economic Perspectives* 15 (2): 193–212.

Hamilton, James T. 1998. *Channeling Violence: The Economic Market for Violent Television Programming*. Princeton University Press.

Hargarten, Stephen W., John S. Milne, Arthur L. Kellermann, and Garen J. Wintemute. 2001. "Impact of Current Federal Regulations On Handgun Safety Features." Firearm Injury Center, Medical College of Wisconsin (under review).

Hemenway, David, and Douglas Weil. 1990. "Phasers on Stun: The Case for Less Lethal Weapons." *Journal of Policy Analysis and Management* 9 (1): 94–98.

Kairys, David. 1998. "Legal Claims of Cities against the Manufacturers of Handguns." *Temple Law Review* 71 (1): 1–21.

Karlson, Trudy A., and Stephen W. Hargarten. 1997. *Reducing Firearms Injury and Death: A Public Health Sourcebook on Guns*. Rutgers University Press.

Kates, Don B., and Daniel D. Polsby. 2000. "The Myth of the 'Virgin Killer': Law-Abiding Persons Who Kill in a Fit of Rage." Paper delivered at the American Society of Criminology annual meeting. San Francisco.

Kleck, Gary. 1984. "Handgun-Only Control: A Policy Disaster in the Making." In *Firearms and Violence: Issues of Public Policy,* edited by D. B. Kates Jr., 167–99. Ballinger.

———. 1991. *Point Blank: Guns and Violence in America*. Aldine DeGruyter.

Koper, Christopher S., and Peter Reuter. 1996. "Suppressing Illegal Gun Markets: Lessons from Drug Enforcement." *Law and Contemporary Problems* 59 (1): 119–46.

Lott, John R. 2000. *More Guns, Less Crime: Understanding Crime and Gun-Control Laws*. 2d ed. University of Chicago Press.

Ludwig, Jens. 1998. "Concealed-Gun-Carrying Laws and Violent Crime: Evidence from State Panel Data." *International Review of Law and Economics* 18 (September): 239–54.

———. 2000. "Gun Self-Defense and Deterrence." In *Crime and Justice: A Review of Research*, vol. 27, edited by Michael Tonry, 363–417. University of Chicago Press.

Ludwig, Jens, and Philip J. Cook. 2000. "Homicide and Suicide Rates Associated with Implementation of the Brady Handgun Violence Prevention Act." *Journal of the American Medical Association* 284(5): 585–91.

———. 2001. "The Benefits of Reducing Gun Violence: Evidence from Contingent-Valuation Survey Data." *Journal of Risk and Uncertainty* 22 (3): 207–26.

Lytton, Timothy D. 2000. "Lawsuits against the Gun Industry: A Comparative Institutional Analysis." *Connecticut Law Review* 32 (4): 1247–75.

McCubbins, Matthew D., Roger G. Noll, and Barry R. Weingast. 1989. "Structure and Process, Politics and Policy: Administrative Arrangements and the Political Control of Agencies." *Virginia Law Review* 75 (March): 431–82.

Moore, Mark H. 1990. "Supply Reduction and Drug Law Enforcement." In *Crime and Justice: An Annual Review of Research,* vol.13, edited by James Q. Wilson and Michael Tonry, 109–58. University of Chicago Press.

Morgan, Doug. 1999. "What in the Wide, Wide World of Torts is Going On? First Tobacco, Now Guns: An Examination of Hamilton v. Accu-Tek and the Cities' Lawsuits against the Gun Industry." *Mississippi Law Journal* 69 (Fall): 521–59.

Peters, Rebecca. 2000. *Gun Control in the United States: A Comparative Survey of State Gun Laws.* New York: Open Society Institute.

Portney, Paul R. 2000. "Air Pollution Policy." In *Public Policies for Environmental Protection,* 2d ed., edited by Paul R. Portney and Robert N. Stavins, 77–124. Washington: Resources for the Future.

Rabin, Robert L. 1993. "Institutional and Historical Perspectives on Tobacco Tort Liability." In *Smoking Policy: Law, Politics, and Culture,* edited by Robert L. Rabin and Stephen D. Sugarman, 110–30. Oxford University Press.

Regini, Charles L. 1997. "The Cold Case Concept." *Law Enforcement Bulletin.* Federal Bureau of Investigation (August).

Robinson, Krista D., Stephen P. Teret, Jon S. Vernick, and Daniel W. Webster. 1998. *Personalized Guns: Reducing Gun Deaths through Design Changes,* 2d ed. Baltimore: Johns Hopkins Center for Gun Policy Research.

Roth, Jeffrey A., and Christopher S. Koper. 1999. *Impacts of the 1994 Assault Weapons Ban: 1994-96.* Washington: National Institute of Justice Research in Brief (NCJ 173405).

Ryan, Alan. 1997. *Mill.* W.W. Norton and Company.

Sheley, Joseph F., and James D. Wright. 1993. *Gun Acquisition and Possession in Selected Juvenile Samples.* Washington: National Institute of Justice Research in Brief (NCJ 145326).

Sherman, Lawrence W. 2001. "Reducing Gun Violence: What Works, What Doesn't, What's Promising." *Perspectives on Crime and Justice: 2000-2001 Lecture Series.* Washington: National Institute of Justice.

Siebel, Brian J. 1999. "City Lawsuits Against the Gun Industry: A Roadmap for Reforming Gun Industry Misconduct." *St. Louis University Public Law Review* 18 (1): 247–90.

Spitzer, Robert.1998. *The Politics of Gun Control.* 2d ed. Chatham House.

Stewart, David. 1999. Testimony on January 15 in *Hamilton* v. *Accu-Tek* (935 F. Supp. 1307, 1330 E.D.N.Y.).

Sugarmann, Josh. 2001. *Every Handgun Is Aimed at You: The Case for Banning Handguns.* New Press.

Teret, Stephen P., Daniel Webster, Jon Vernick, and others. 1998a. "Support for New Policies to Regulate Firearms: Results of Two National Surveys." *New England Journal of Medicine* 339 (12): 813–18.

Teret, Stephen P., Susan DeFrancesco, Stephen W. Hogarten, and Krista D. Robinson. 1998b. "Making Guns Safer." *Issues in Science and Technology* (Summer): 37–40.

U.S. Bureau of the Census. 1999. *Statistical Abstract of the United States.* Washington.

U.S. Department of Justice, Bureau of Justice Statistics. 2001. *Survey of State Procedures Related to Firearm Sales, Midyear 2000.* NCJ 186766.

U.S. Department of Justice, Federal Bureau of Investigation. 2000. "Crime in the United States, 1999." Press Release (October).

U.S. Department of the Treasury, Bureau of Alcohol, Tobacco and Firearms. 2000a. *Commerce in Firearms in the United States.*

————. 2000b. *Following the Gun: Enforcing Federal Laws Against Firearms.*

————. 2000c. *ATF Regulatory Actions: Report to the Secretary on Firearms Initiatives.*

U.S. General Accounting Office. 2001. "Synar Amendment Implementation: Quality of State Data on Reducing Youth Access to Tobacco Could Be Improved. GAO-02-74 (November).

Vernick, Jon S., and Stephen P. Teret. 1999. "New Courtroom Strategies Regarding Firearms: Tort Litigation against Firearm Manufacturers and Constitutional Challenges to Gun Laws." *Houston Law Review* 36 (5): 1713–54.

————. 2000. "A Public Health Approach to Regulating Firearms as Consumer Products." *University of Pennsylvania Law Review* 148 (April): 1193–1211.

Violence Policy Center. 1998. *The False Hope of the "Smart" Gun.* Washington.

————. 2000. *Unsafe in Any Hands: Why America Needs to Ban Handguns.* Washington.

Viscusi, W. Kip. 1998–99. "A Postmortem on the Cigarette Settlement." *Cumberland Law Review* 29: 523–53.

Wachtel, Julius.1998. "Sources of Crime Guns in Los Angeles, California." *Policing: An International Journal of Police Strategies and Management* 21 (2): 220–39.

Wagner, Wendy E. 1999. "Rough Justice and the Attorney General Litigation." *Georgia Law Review* 33 (Spring): 935–76.

Wintemute, Garen J. 1994. *Ring of Fire: The Handgun Makers of Southern California.* Sacramento: Violence Prevention Research Program, University of California, Davis.

Wintemute, Garen J., Mona A. Wright, C. M. Drake, and J. J. Beaumont. 2001. "Subsequent Criminal Activity among Violent Misdemeanants Who Seek to Purchase Handguns, Risk Factors and Effectiveness of Denying Handgun Purchase." *Journal of the American Medical Association* 85 (8):1019–26.

Wright, James D. 1995. "Ten Essential Observations on Guns in America." *Society*, March/April, 63–68.

Wright, James D., and Peter H. Rossi.1994. *Armed and Considered Dangerous: A Survey of Felons and Their Firearms (Expanded Edition).* Aldine de Gruyter.

Zimring, Franklin E. 1968. "Is Gun Control Likely to Reduce Violent Killings?" *University of Chicago Law Review* 35 (Summer): 721–37.

————. 1975. "Firearms and Federal Law: The Gun Control Act of 1968." *Journal of Legal Studies* 4 (1): 133–98.

Zimring, Franklin E., and Gordon Hawkins.1997. *Crime Is Not the Problem: Lethal Violence in America.* Oxford University Press.

RANDALL LUTTER
ELIZABETH MADER

4 | *Litigating Lead-Based Paint Hazards*

Despite dramatic declines in American children's blood lead levels and in the numbers of homes with lead-based paint, courts are busy with costly and lengthy litigation over lead-based paint hazards. Most litigation takes the form of suits by tenants against landlords, but state and local authorities have filed an unusual set of suits against paint manufacturers. These authorities are seeking to recover expenses they believe they have incurred as a result of high lead levels among local residents. Even the federal government may get involved. Hearings of the Senate Committee for Banking, Housing, and Urban Affairs in December 2001 demonstrated that Washington policymakers are becoming interested in the lead-based paint problem. Two northeastern senators are planning to reintroduce a 1999 bill that would authorize the federal government to sue manufacturers of lead or lead compounds for lead-related housing, education, and medical costs.[1]

Lawsuits against the paint manufacturers might seem an unlikely policy development because the federal Consumer Product Safety Commission

The authors thank Tim Hardy, Diane Jacob, Dennis Kim, Eileen Lee, Mark Moore, Eileen Quinn, Wes Stewart, and conference participants for helpful discussions.

1. *Lead Poisoning Expense Recovery Act of 1999*, S. 1821. Sponsor Jack Reed's office indicates that this bill may be reintroduced.

banned the sale of lead-based paint nationally in 1978, and some localities imposed similar bans much earlier. But lead, which as a metal does biodegrade, can still pose hazards in older homes where it is present. In addition, large corporations with deep pockets, including BP Amoco, have acquired some of the companies that used to sell lead-based paint. These acquisitions provide large revenue opportunities to municipalities like Philadelphia, which has recently created a new affirmative litigation unit "to seize the potential revenue benefit that could be gained by the City of Philadelphia acting as plaintiff."[2]

Should more government agencies join the lawsuits against former lead-based paint manufacturers? Is such litigation likely to solve problems associated with lead-based paint? Although we cannot offer a definitive assessment because these suits are new and ongoing, we analyze the social problems related to lead-based paint hazards and consider whether government-sponsored civil litigation is likely to solve them. We also review lawsuits against landlords and analyze the incentives such rulings give landlords to control lead-based paint hazards.[3]

We show that lawsuits against paint companies are a poor solution to social problems related to lead-based paint. They may provide increased funding, but only part of any winnings would go to children who have been harmed or to control lead-based paint hazards in residences. Lawsuits are unlikely to result in fair compensation because, if successful, they cause parties only indirectly responsible for the harm to make payments to other parties who have been only indirectly harmed. These suits provide no useful deterrent value; indeed, the only possible deterrent effect is to reduce incentives to make products that in the future might be shown to have adverse health effects. Such suits appear not to promote accountability among potential wrongdoers because they hold people accountable for past actions on the basis of new and improved scientific understanding. We also show that suits against landlords yield awards that are not very sensitive to the level of damages and payments to plaintiffs that are very large relative to the Environmental Protection Agency's (EPA) estimates of damages. Finally, we assess landlords' incentives to control lead-based paint hazards in light of current regulations and recent court cases.

2. See City of Philadelphia (2001).
3. Other chapters in this book also deal with litigation and risk to health. For further insight into product liability and public health issues, see Buzby, Frenzen, and Rasco (2001).

Overview of Hazards

Lead-related litigation occurs despite government regulation of lead-based paint hazards because of the risks such hazards pose to young children. The public health implications of lead, the existing regulations, and the economic incentives that landlords currently face to remedy these hazards are important to a discussion of lead-related litigation.

Effects on Public Health

In young children—the most vulnerable population—lead has been linked to impairment of intelligence, small-muscle control, hearing, and emotional development even at low levels where obvious symptoms are not present. At higher levels of contamination now rare among U.S. children, lead causes increasingly severe health effects including death. Table 4-1 presents a list of the health effects and the medical recommendations associated with different levels of lead contamination.[4] At low levels children's blood lead levels correlate with their IQ scores. In general, an increase in children's blood lead levels of 1 microgram per deciliter (µg/dl) is associated with a decline of about 0.26 IQ points.[5] The IQ deficit in the vast majority of children exposed to lead hazards is fewer than 2 IQ points.[6]

Blood lead levels in children have fallen dramatically in the past twenty years because of federal bans on lead in gasoline and paint and controls on lead in drinking water and consumer products (figures 4-1 and 4-2).[7] Between 1991 and 1994, fewer than 5 percent of young children between ages 1 to 5 years (about 930,000 children) had blood lead levels greater than or equal to 10 µg/dl, a level of concern established by the Centers for Disease Control and Prevention. About 0.4 percent of children between ages 1 and 5 years (some 85,000 children) had blood lead levels at or above 20 µg/dl.[8] The reductions from earlier levels reflect a remarkable public health success story.

More recent but less representative data from nineteen states' surveillance programs confirm this trend.[9] From 1994 to 1999, the geometric mean blood lead level in children 1 to 5 years old in these states decreased

---

4. See "Lead Poisoning" in *Encyclopedia Britannica* at www.Britannica.com for more information.
5. Schwartz (1994).
6. Battelle (1998).
7. U.S. Environmental Protection Agency (2001).
8. U.S. Centers for Disease Control and Prevention (1997).
9. U.S. Centers for Disease Control and Prevention (2000).

Table 4-1. *Effects of Lead on Health of Children and Medical Recommendations by Blood Lead Level*

Class	Blood lead level (μg/dl)	Health effects	Medical recommendation
I	< 10	IQ, hearing	Not considered lead poisoned.
IIA	10–14		Many children (or a large proportion of children) with blood lead levels in this range should trigger community-wide childhood lead poisoning prevention activities. Children in this range may need to be screened more frequently.
IIB	15–19	Metabolism, developmental toxicity	A child in Class IIB should receive nutritional and educational interventions and more frequent screening. If the blood lead levels persist in this range, environmental investigation and intervention should be done.
III	20–44	Decreased vitamin D metabolism, decreased hemoglobin synthesis	A child in Class III should receive environmental evaluation and remediation and a medical evaluation. Such a child may need pharmacologic treatment of lead poisoning.
IV	45–69	Colic	A child in Class IV will need both medical and environmental interventions, including chelation therapy.
V	70 or above	Anemia, nephropathy, encephalopathy, death at around 130 μg/dl	A child in Class V lead poisoning is a medical emergency. Medical and environmental management must begin immediately.

Source: U.S. Agency for Toxic Substances and Disease Registry (1992).

Figure 4-1. *Percent of Children 1–5 Years Old with Blood Lead Levels of at least 10 µg/dl*

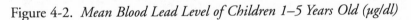

Source: Pirckle and others (1994); U.S. Centers for Disease Control and Prevention (1997, 2000).
Note: New data from nineteen unrepresentative states show that the proportion of children tested with BLLs <10 µg/dl decreased from 10.5 percent in 1996 to 7.6 percent in 1998.

Figure 4-2. *Mean Blood Lead Level of Children 1–5 Years Old (µg/dl)*

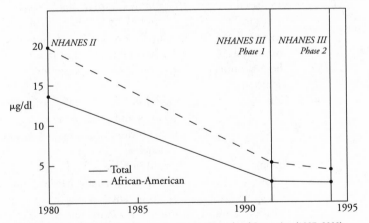

Source: Pirckle and others (1994); U.S. Centers for Disease Control and Prevention (1997, 2000).
Note: In nineteen unrepresentative states, the geometric mean blood lead level in children 1 to 5 years old decreased from 2.7 to 2.0 µg/dl between 1991–94 and 1999. Survey dates reflect the year surveys were completed.

from 2.7 µg/dl to 2.0 µg/dl, and the fiftieth percentile decreased from 2.6 µg/dl to 1.9 µg/dl. In the nineteen states providing data, the proportion of children tested with blood lead levels at or above 10 µg/dl decreased from 10.5 percent in 1996 to 7.6 percent in 1998. The proportions of children with blood lead levels above 15 µg/dl and above 20 µg/dl also decreased. These continued reductions underscore the success of more recent efforts to reduce children's lead levels.

One rarely appreciated reason for these sharp reductions in blood lead levels is the rapid drop in the number of lead-contaminated homes. Ten years ago, approximately 64 million housing units had lead-based paint. The Department of Housing and Urban Development (HUD) recently reported that an estimated 38 million homes in the United States have lead-based paint somewhere in the building.[10] Thus, during the past ten years there has been a dramatic reduction in the scope of the problem.

Despite those improvements, African American children between 1 and 5 years of age and children of low-income, urban families are still at greater than average risk. For non-Hispanic black children 1 to 5 years of age, the mean blood lead level in 1994 was 4.3 µg/dl, significantly above the mean value of 2.3 µg/dl for non-Hispanic white children.[11] The likelihood that any child between 1 and 5 years of age has blood lead levels in excess of 10 µg/dl is four times greater if the child is from a low-income, rather than a middle-income, family.[12] The most recent data also show that the problem remains concentrated on a local level. Older and poorer communities are most affected.

Existing Regulations

Concern for children with high blood lead levels has already resulted in significant federal regulation of lead hazards in housing. Owners are required to disclose any information about the presence of lead-based paint or lead hazards to prospective buyers or renters.[13] Professional lead contractors must also keep records of any work and provide copies to owners.[14] Only government-certified workers may inspect homes and abate

10. U.S. Department of Housing and Urban Development (2001).
11. U.S. Centers for Disease Control and Prevention (1997, table 2).
12. U.S. Centers for Disease Control and Prevention (1997, table 2).
13. *Code of Federal Regulation* 40, sec. 745.107.
14. *CFR* 40, sec. 745.227.

residential lead hazards.[15] Finally, owners of homes built before 1978 must provide a federally approved lead-hazard information pamphlet to prospective buyers or renters.[16]

Motivated by continuing concern for children's health, the Environmental Protection Agency in January 2001 issued uniform, numerical hazard standards for lead-based paint, dust-lead, and lead in soil.[17] The standards—which are significantly more stringent than both pre-existing guidelines and EPA's 1997 proposal—would apply to most pre-1978 housing, as well as to other facilities occupied by children.[18] They define a lead-based paint hazard to include "*Any* other deteriorated lead-based paint in any residential building or child-occupied facility or on the exterior of any residential building or child-occupied facility."[19] As a result, EPA acknowledges that "almost all" older homes where lead-based paint is present are out of compliance.[20] The agency set such a stringent standard "to alert the public to the fact that all deteriorated lead-based paint should be addressed—through use of paint stabilization or interim controls."[21] The rule also designates hazardous levels of lead in dust and soil and specified clearance levels that correspond to these hazard standards; cleanup is incomplete if these levels are not met.[22]

This rule is unusual in that EPA expects it to be enforced by third parties, including litigants and the courts. The authorizing statute makes no provision for EPA to take enforcement action, and EPA states that the rule does not, by itself, mandate any particular action.[23] The agency believes "it is likely that an indirect legal enforcement mechanism will develop through the threat of tort law liability suits."[24] EPA adds that "these standards will become part of Federal mortgage programs administered by the U.S. Department of Housing and Urban Development. . . . Furthermore,

15. *CFR* 40, sec. 745.220.
16. *CFR* 40, sec. 745.107.
17. For a critical view of this approach, see Lutter (2001).
18. U.S. Environmental Protection Agency (2001).
19. *CFR* 40, sec. 745.65(a)(4). Emphasis added. Paint is deteriorated if it is "peeling, chipping, chalking or cracking" or "otherwise damaged or separated from the substrate." See *CFR* 40, sec. 745.63.
20. U.S. Environmental Protection Agency (2001, pp. 1210, 1229).
21. U.S. Environmental Protection Agency (2001, p.1210). The agency adds that "something less than abatement and certified personnel, however, would be needed to undertake interim controls or to abate lower levels of deterioration."
22. *CFR* 40, sec. 745.65(c) and 745.227.
23. U.S. Environmental Protection Agency (2001, p. 1236).
24. U.S. Environmental Protection Agency (1998a, sec. 8.1.2).

mortgage lenders are likely to be more hesitant to fund property acquisitions if those properties exceed the standards."[25] Elsewhere EPA "expects that public and private institutions may incorporate the standards into State and local laws, housing codes, and lending and insurance underwriting standards."[26] If EPA's expectations are realized, rental housing may be in substantial compliance with the rule within a few years.

Economic analysis clearly helped in the development of EPA's rule. The agency used benefit-cost analysis to identify a range of standards from which to choose final standards. It selected its final standards "based on consideration of relevant factors, including the assumptions and tools underlying EPA's analysis, health protectiveness, cost and the effect on the overall lead risk reduction program."[27]

The agency's rulemaking nevertheless suffers from serious flaws related to its economic analysis. First, the analysis considers standards that do not correspond with the standards that EPA adopted in its final rule. The agency's analysis assumes that deteriorated lead-based paint of less than two square feet per room is not a hazard, while the rule defines as a hazard "any" deteriorated lead-based paint. Thus the rule covers many homes with lower risk than those included in EPA's economic analysis, and as a result the net benefits are likely to be much less than it estimated. Second, it does not refer to a recent housing survey from the Department of Housing and Urban Development that indicates very large reductions in the number of lead-contaminated homes in the interval 1990 to 1998–99.[28]

The EPA's estimates of the net benefits of complying with its standards (between negative $20 billion and positive $54 billion) are likely to be too high because EPA assumes that the birth of a child is the event that triggers intervention activities. The standards themselves, however, apply to all housing that may be occupied by young children.[29] For its proposed rule, EPA estimated that net benefits assuming that real estate transactions rather than births triggered abatement activity. In this case its estimates of the net benefits of the proposed rule, which is less stringent than the final rule, were negative $55 billion using one risk assessment model and negative $6.3 billion using another.

25. U.S. Environmental Protection Agency (1998a, sec. 8.1.2).

26. U.S. Environmental Protection Agency (1998b, p. 30304).

27. U.S. Environmental Protection Agency (2001, pp. 1275–76).

28. U.S. Environmental Protection Agency (2000) does not cite U.S. Department of Housing and Urban Development (2001).

29. CFR 40, sec. 745.65.

The agency's lead hazard standards are incorporated in a HUD rule that housing receiving federal assistance and federally owned housing that is to be sold may not pose lead-based paint hazards to young children.[30] The rule sets requirements for remediation based on the amount of federal funding received by property owners. The most stringent level of protection required (full abatement of lead-based paint) applies to public housing and multi-family mortgage insurance for conversions and major rehabilitations. In contrast, HUD-owned single-family properties and multifamily properties receiving rental assistance require only paint stabilization.[31] The rule also directs HUD to inspect and provide rehabilitation assistance based on the amount of federal support received by the property owner.[32]

Besides these federal regulations, various local and state laws and regulations also address residential lead hazards, but we provide only a brief summary because these provisions vary so much across jurisdictions and over time. The National Conference of State Legislatures lists thirty-eight states, all of which have paint, dust and soil standards that differ from EPA's.[33]

The structure of states' programs varies widely. New York's state law focuses on screening and notification. Massachusetts requires the owner of a residence to remove or cover lead-based materials so as to make them inaccessible to children and has a policy of strict liability that may hold property owners accountable for damages to children who are poisoned in their rental properties.[34] Rhode Island law has no such requirement or similar liability policy; instead, it makes "lead free" or "lead safe" certification a condition to licensing facilities such as schools and nurseries and requires tenant notification of lead hazards.[35] Last year Virginia enacted a law providing some immunity to landlords and owners, provided that they notify tenants or purchasers of lead hazards and comply with Virginia's lead-paint laws, the Uniform Statewide Building Code, "and applicable federal laws and regulations."[36]

Maryland has a unique lead control program. The state Lead Paint Poisoning Act, enacted in 1994, is designed to bypass the tort liability system

30. U.S. Department of Housing and Urban Development (1999, p. 50148).

31. U.S. Department of Housing and Urban Development (1999, p. 50152).

32. U.S. Department of Housing and Urban Development (1999, pp. 50203–231).

33. National Conference of State Legislatures, "Actionable Lead Levels in Paint, Dust, Soil, and Water" (www.ncsl.org/programs/ESNR/pbaction.htm [March 2002]).

34. Sargent and others (1999). For further information on state laws, see Farquhar and others (2001).

35. Sargent and others (1999); Farquhar and others (2001).

36. Code of Virginia 8.01-226.7(B) and (C).

and provide a remedial assistance program to lessen children's lead exposure while also giving limited liability to owners who comply with certain risk-reduction standards.[37] Property owners pay a nominal annual registration fee and get an inspection certificate if they perform a "risk reduction" consisting of basic maintenance procedures at turnover. If a child at the property is later found to have an elevated blood lead level, the property owner can make a "qualified offer" which, if accepted, provides up to $9,500 in relocation benefits until the child is 6 and if not covered by insurance, the property owner can also provide up to $7,500 in medical benefits until the child reaches the age of 18. By accepting a qualified offer, a child waives the right to sue. Maryland law also ensures that property owners can be insured for the amount of the qualified offer if they participate in this plan—a notable benefit, because insurance coverage for lead hazards can be uncertain. The Coalition to End Childhood Lead Poisoning, which manages this program for Maryland, reports that sixty-three offers have been made since 1996. Of these, forty-four offers have been accepted. This apparently low rate of participation may partly be explained by the fact that, of children with blood lead levels above the minimum level of 20 µg/dl necessary for eligibility, only about 15 percent live in eligible housing. Few landlords are participating in the program, despite its advantages.[38]

Local laws change over time. New York City's Local Law 38, signed into law in July 1999, replaced Local Law 1, which had been in force since 1982 and had required removal of lead paint from children's dwellings. On October 11, 2000, a state court judge struck down Local Law 38, making Local Law 1 again the applicable law.[39] Changes in the interpretation of local laws by the courts make it even more difficult to generalize about the nature of local regulation of residential lead hazards.[40]

Finally, enforcement (or the lack thereof) may result in great differences in the effective stringency of laws and regulations. In fact, questions of enforcement drove the enactment of New York's Local Law 38 in 1999.[41] In 1985 a group of petitioners brought an action to compel the

37. Maryland Reduction of Lead Risk in Housing Program, Maryland Code: Environment, sec. 6-801-6-852; article 48A, sec. 734–737; Real Property, sec. 8-208.2.
38. Wes Stewart of the Coalition to End Childhood Lead Poisoning kindly helped explain the Maryland Qualified Offer program.
39. York (2000).
40. See Kaminsky (1998, part 3) for a state-by-state review of recent decisions in lead poisoning cases.
41. Alan C. Eagle and Charlotte Biblow, "New York City's New Lead-based Paint Law May Make It More Difficult to Successfully Sue Landlords," *Mealey's Litigation Report: Lead*, November 12, 1999, pp. 16–21.

city to enforce Local Law 1.[42] During the fifteen years before the repeal of Local Law 1, the city was held in contempt of court multiple times for not promulgating regulations required by the law.[43]

These different state policies may affect blood lead levels. In a comparison of children's lead poisoning in Providence, Rhode Island, and Worcester, Massachusetts, Sargent and colleagues suggest that active enforcement of Massachusetts's more stringent policies has lowered the prevalence of high blood lead levels more than in neighboring Providence. The percentage of children with blood lead levels above 10 µg/dl was twice as high in Providence as in Worcester. The percentage of children with blood lead levels above 20 µg/dl was three and a half times higher in Providence than in Worcester. Although both states have laws mandating universal annual lead screening of children aged 6 to 60 months, lead hazard management and landlord liability vary greatly, and Massachusetts requires abatement of any lead hazard in homes built before 1978 in which children younger than 6 years live.[44]

Regulatory authorities have chosen to emphasize the preemptive avoidance of exposures that could raise children's blood lead. Although that approach has the clear benefit of prevention, it requires control of hazards in large numbers of homes. If abatement is to reduce risks of elevated blood lead *before* it occurs, hazards must be controlled at homes in which children do not have elevated blood lead levels. Indeed, attainment of EPA's stringent paint standard would require abatement of "almost all" homes built before 1978. Of course regulators' preference for primary prevention is at odds with their reluctance to embark on enforcement of mandatory standards in the millions of homes with lead-based paint. New York City relaxed its mandatory controls because it found them too stringent.

Despite the general emphasis on primary prevention of lead poisoning, it is worth mentioning the failure of existing efforts to identify and treat children with high levels of lead in their blood. The federal Health Care Financing Administration requires that all Medicaid-eligible children 1 through 5 years old be tested. Enforcement of this screening requirement has historically been very inadequate according to the congressional

42. *New York City Coalition to End Lead Poisoning* v. *Giuliani*, 42780/85 (Sup. Ct. N.Y. Co.).
43. York (2000).
44. Sargent and others (1999).

General Accounting Office, and lawsuits have been brought in Idaho and Ohio.[45]

The Economics of Controlling Lead

The economics of controlling lead-based paint hazards are different from those of other environmental risks because the primary problem occurs within a home. Almost all lead-related health hazards involve a landlord and a tenant or a homeowner's own family. Thus, safety from lead-based paint threats is not a public good, nor does it involve a classic externality like air or water pollution. Of course a complicating factor is that assessment of lead-based paint hazards is costly and health effects in most affected children are asymptomatic, so that property owners and residents may be making decisions under substantial uncertainty. Despite these complications, Coasian solutions seem applicable provided that property rights are well defined.

A primary issue is the incentives that property owners and landlords have to control lead-based paint hazards, because the available controls are at their discretion. These controls include wet-mopping, use of special vacuum cleaners, encapsulating contaminated walls or parts of doors or windows, and replacing or covering contaminated soil. Stripping or removing surfaces where lead-based paint is accessible or subject to friction is especially helpful. Of course, parents also have a role, but educational efforts aimed at parents are not very effective.[46]

Here we focus on landlords, because owner-occupied housing—with costs and benefits of controls internal to each family—seems a poor target for regulatory efforts. Moreover, recent federal disclosure regulations already address potential problems of asymmetric information about lead hazards in owner-occupied housing markets.

A self-interested landlord would generally control lead-paint hazards to the point at which the incremental costs of further controls equal the incremental benefits. The incremental costs include the costs of the contractors who inspect for lead hazards and control them. The incremental benefits involve potential increases in rent, resale value, and in the reduced risk of

45. U.S. General Accounting Office (1998); "Parents Allege Idaho Failed to Screen Children for Lead as Required by Medicaid," *Mealey's Litigation Report: Lead*, October 18, 2000, p.6; "Ohio Woman Says Managed Care Provider Failed to Test for Lead, Seeks Class Status, *Mealey's Litigation Report: Lead*, August 16, 2000, p. 6.

46. University of Rochester (1995); Battelle (1998).

uninsured litigation costs and any reductions in insurance premiums.[47] Therefore, from the landlord's perspective, efficient resource allocation dictates that the marginal increase in rent plus the additional appreciation in the value of the property, and any savings in insurance premiums, less the reduction in expected uninsured payments to plaintiffs equals the marginal cost of controlling lead hazards.

The Environmental Protection Agency has presented reasonably complete data on the marginal cost of controlling residential lead hazards, so the incremental benefits to landlords may be the key to a full understanding of the incentives to control lead-based paint hazards.[48] The effect of lead hazards on the price of renting or buying real estate is a crucial determinant of likely clean-up levels, but these effects seem small at best. We have not found a single study indicating that the presence of lead-based paint or lead-based paint hazards affects housing prices. Indeed anecdotal evidence suggests that lead hazards may affect housing prices hardly at all.[49]

Real estate appraisers take into account suspected lead hazards in only a limited way. Guidelines by the Federal Housing Authority and the Department of Housing and Urban Development state that "if the property was built before 1978, and there is evidence of cracking, chipping, peeling or loose paint, [the appraiser must] make this statement on lead-based paint: 'Property built before 1978, lead-based paint corrective measures are required.'"[50] For condominium units built before 1978 that show signs of "excessive deferred maintenance of defective paint" appraisers should prepare estimates assuming that satisfactory repairs are completed. Thus the guidelines to date do not require an assessment of the scope of the problem. For example, they do not require an assessment of lead in dust, although such lead-contaminated dust may be present if there is deteriorated lead-based paint. In general they assume that lead hazards can be controlled through conventional repairs rather than special measures.

Although insurers may adjust premiums for general commercial liability insurance according to whether buildings are known to be lead safe, it is

---

47. Kenneth S. Abraham has a further discussion of the insurance effects of regulation by litigation in chapter 7 in this volume.

48. U.S. Environmental Protection Agency (2000). Survey evidence of the market price of services to control lead hazards in specific properties does not, to our knowledge, exist.

49. We have discussed this issue with various knowledgeable professionals who all subscribe to the view that such effects have not been estimated but are in any event likely to be small.

50. Federal Housing Authority Guidelines for Appraisers, section 5.

unclear whether these adjustments are significant.[51] In addition, reductions in expected uninsured litigation costs are also likely to be of limited value, because the risk of incurring such costs seems small. Less than a hundred awards to lead-poisoned children are reported each year, although tens of thousands of children have blood lead levels above 20 µg/dl. Insurance may cover many landlords' liability, although many liability policies exclude pollution-related claims from covered claims, and insurers have gone to court to avoid having to pay damages to tenants. Currently there is substantial legal uncertainty about whether lead-based paint hazards are covered by policies that have conventional pollutant exclusion clauses. The issue is still being debated: Mealey's reports that a recent Pennsylvania decision found lead paint to be a pollutant, overturning a 1998 decision in which the pollution exemption clause was found inapplicable to lead.[52]

Thus one reason that success stories about controlling lead hazards involve only hundreds or thousands of residences, while many millions have lead-based paint hazards, is that there are weak incentives for landlords to pay for such controls.[53]

Lead Litigation

Various lawsuits concerning lead-based paint hazards have been filed in recent years. The most common lawsuit involves a child with high blood lead who sues his or her landlord. (We develop a quantitative analysis of the outcomes of such suits later in this chapter.) Other recent suits involve the alleged poisoning of a babysitter's children because of renovation to her employer's home, a child who ate a lead-based sealer used by a utility company's employee, and a product liability lawsuit for a heat gun used in renovation. In regard to government policy, however, the most interesting filings involve suits by government bodies against companies that sold lead-based paint. Although these suits are growing in number, not one has won money for the plaintiffs.

51. For an example of the information provided to insurers in this situation, see the application form of McGowan & Company, Inc. at their website, which requests information on swimming pools, boat slips, parking lots, sprinklers, and smoke detectors, as well as lead-safe certification and past damages. For a discussion of insurance coverage of lead-paint hazard reduction, see Anderson and Lewis (1997).

52. "Absolute Pollution Clause Applies to Lead-Based Paint," *Mealey's Litigation Report: Lead*, January 6, 2000, p. 6. See also Kenneth S. Abraham, chapter 7, in this volume.

53. See the U.S. Department of Housing and Urban Development Lead Office success stories (www.hud.gov/lea/successstories.html [January 2002]).

Table 4-2 summarizes ongoing lawsuits by various state and local government authorities against former lead-based paint companies. Plaintiffs include the Rhode Island Attorney General, a group of California counties in the San Francisco Bay area, two Houston school districts, counties in Texas and Mississippi, and the cities of New York, Saint Louis, and Milwaukee; Chicago is expected to file a suit soon. Peter Angelos, a prominent attorney in the tobacco litigation, is bringing one suit on behalf of Maryland homeowners and one on behalf of five lead-poisoned children. Suits have been brought in Newark, New Jersey, seventeen other New Jersey municipalities, and West Orange township. Besides these ongoing suits, approximately forty cases against various representatives of the lead paint industry have been dismissed in the past.[54]

The suits involving government plaintiffs raise new questions about the proper exercise of government authority, as other authors have noted.[55] These lawsuits can transfer substantial sums from industry to governments and may in that sense rival traditional government authorities to tax or regulate the private sector. They sidestep established constitutional processes for elected representatives to determine policy. Finally, it is unclear that the lawsuits are efficient as a compensatory mechanism because large sums go to lawyers.

In discussing these lead-related suits, we start with three accepted purposes of civil litigation: compensation, deterrence, and accountability.[56] Compensation can include reimbursement of expenses, such as those for medical treatment, as well as payments to cover pain and suffering. Compensation is accepted as a purpose of civil litigation because of a broadly held belief that it is fair that parties who wrongly harm others offer compensation for that harm. Deterrence is an important goal to the extent that certain hazards are ongoing and put people at continued risk. Civil suits can deter paint companies or landlords from future wrongdoing. Finally, by establishing rules to assess liability, the tort system provides a mechanism for society to hold wrongdoers accountable for their actions. For example, civil suits may lead to the assessment of punitive damages for egregious behavior if the jury finds the defender liable.[57]

The social problems associated with lead-based paint seem poorly suited for court-ordered remedies according to these three purposes of litigation. For mandatory compensation to be fair, a party directly responsible

54. Oral communication from Tim Hardy.
55. See, for example, Schonbrun (1997).
56. Jacobson and Warner (1999) discuss these purposes in the context of tobacco litigation.
57. See Kaminsky and others (1998) and Konigsberg (1996) for further discussion.

for harm must pay someone who suffered the harm. Yet the lawsuits in question involve parties only indirectly associated with the threats to health posed by lead-based paint. Shareholders in modern corporations have no responsibility for the historical decisions to make and sell lead-based paint a half-century ago, although the suits put them at risk of having to pay compensation. Moreover, the companies are often sued under a theory that their liability can be determined on the basis of national or regional market share over a period of decades, rather than on the basis of any physical evidence linking lead-based paint hazards to a certain brand of paint that they sold. Finally, the quality of home maintenance is crucial in determining the extent of lead-based paint hazard. Well-to-do neighborhoods generally have fewer lead-based paint hazards because superior maintenance has resulted in less deterioration of the existing lead-based paint and thus lower lead levels.

The government entities engaging in the suits also are not the parties directly harmed by lead-based paint. Lead hurts the children who ingest it and the families of those children. It only indirectly affects the school districts that serve the children and the medical institutions that may treat them. These suits thus break new ground in seeking compensation for parties harmed only indirectly. Moreover, they often seek money to abate lead hazard problems in existing housing rather than to compensate people who may have had high blood lead as a result of the lead hazards.[58] Although this approach protects young children born in the future, it offers no compensation for people unlucky enough to be born in, say, the 1990s instead of a decade later. In a sense, such a suit would benefit landlords more than children.

Federal lawsuits against former lead-based paint manufacturers could generate revenues that would not necessarily go to the people who were harmed as children or even to reduce childhood lead poisoning. The Senate bill that may be reintroduced would make the use of funds subject to requirements of the appropriations process. Thus winnings from federal suits against companies could go to fund pork barrel projects.

Local governments that are filing the suits have always had opportunities to protect themselves from these indirect costs of lead poisoning without contracting with trial lawyers. Some local governments have adopted legislation or regulations long ago, such as New York City's 1960 ban on lead-based paint for residential uses.[59] They can also impose taxes or fees such as California's tax on gasoline and paint companies. This tax

58. See table 4-2 for more information about compensation sought in various suits.
59. New York Independent Budget Office (1999).

Table 4-2. *Recent Litigation against Former Lead-based Paint Manufacturers*

Date filed	Plaintiff	Compensation sought	Contingency financing?
1989	City of New York	Compensation for housing authority, abatement at two projects.	In-house
1999	Five lead-poisoned children	Damages	Yes, with Peter Angelos's firm.
1999	Rhode Island Attorney General	Abatement and public health costs	16.33%
2000 (original Santa Clara filing)	Santa Clara County and other communities in the San Francisco Bay Area	Abatement, educational, and public health costs, punitive damages sought in all cases.	17%
2000	City of St. Louis	Damages for treating lead-poisoned children and abating hazards in public housing	Yes
2000	Two Houston area school districts	Costs of testing and remediation in public buildings	25%
2001	Milwaukee	Abatement of lead-based paint in Milwaukee homes	Reimbursement for costs, 20% of gross fund for first $20 million recovered and 15% of additional

2001	Harris County, Texas	Costs of testing and remediation in public buildings	25%
2001	Jefferson County, Mississippi	Costs of testing and remediation in public buildings	Not available
2001	City of Newark, New Jersey	Abatement of lead-based paint in Newark homes, testing and medical monitoring for all city children	Not available
2001	17 New Jersey municipalities	Indemnity for abatement carried out by municipalities	Not available
2001	West Orange township, New Jersey	Punitive and compensatory damages with interest as well as provision of funds for lead-poisoning detection and lead detection and abatement in public buildings	Not available

Note: Chicago may be planning to file a suit for damages including future remediation costs and past and future costs borne by the city health department. Financing for such a Chicago suit would probably occur in-house. A class action suit filed by eight Maryland homeowners was dismissed in the Circuit Court for Baltimore City on December 7, 2001. Source: Oral communications with lawyers and public relations personnel for the plaintiffs, *Mealey's Litigation Report: Lead*, January 9, 2002.

generates about $12 million dollars each year for risk communication, screening, and treatment.[60] Thus local governments' lawsuits are imperfect substitutes for preventive action they might have taken earlier.

Contingency fees that municipalities and other local government bodies have accepted ensure that local governments have a financial incentive to prefer litigation to other programs. These fees are significant. As shown in table 4-2, the first suits have been rapidly copied in other jurisdictions because they pose little financial risks to the local governments while offering a promise of big winnings.[61]

Contingency financing raises an interesting policy question. If states or localities have "nothing to lose," why not sue? The lawyers handling the Houston cases used this convincing argument as their first point in a letter addressed to the Region 11 Education Center, describing the opportunity to sue as "*A win-win situation*. The district has nothing to lose in adopting the proposed resolution to file suit. If we recover nothing for a district, the district will owe no attorney fees *or costs*."[62]

Broadly speaking, the primary rationale for government agencies to sue companies associated with lead-based paint appears reminiscent of Willie Horton's famous rejoinder about why he robbed banks: that's where the money is.

The second key purpose of civil litigation is deterrence, but the suits against former lead paint companies have no beneficial deterrent value whatsoever. Federal regulations have prohibited paint companies from selling lead-based paint for twenty-three years; in some localities restrictions have been in place much longer. The lead lawsuits provide no deterrent value because paint companies are not now engaged in any lead-related behavior that is potentially harmful to public health.

Yet the lead lawsuits may have much broader unintended effects on firms that produce and market goods. Holding firms liable for past actions on the basis of new scientific information may provide sweeping incentives to alter product design, production levels, or marketing practices. Any product may in the future be found less safe than current information indicates. Thus all manufacturing firms may interpret suits against former lead-based paint manufacturers as implying that they face unknown future liabilities associated with any new evidence of health risks attributable to

---

60. Steve Lawrence, "Ballot Measure Targets Product-Related Fees," October 24, 2000, *Associated Press*, Sacramento.

61. See Schonbrun (1997) for a discussion of the effect of contingency fees on class action suits.

62. See Hunt (2000). Emphasis in the original.

the current product line. In this sense these class action suits only serve to deter innovation.

There is surely new information about the risks to health posed by exposure to lead. New scientific investigations have dramatically changed the definition of how much childhood exposure to lead is considered safe. In 1970 the Surgeon General defined "undue exposure" to lead as greater than 40 μg/dl, although this level was considered asymptomatic at the time and was intended to give an adequate margin of safety to remove the affected child from the source of exposure.[63] The federal Centers for Disease Control (CDC) set a level of concern at 30 μg/dl in 1980 and then five years later lowered its level to 25 μg/dl.[64] In 1991 the CDC again lowered its level of concern to 10 μg/dl.[65] Thus there has been a fourfold decline in levels of children's blood lead that the scientific community and public health authorities perceived safe. If lead-based paint contributes to elevated blood lead levels in a systematic way, as is implicit in the risk assessment models that EPA uses for its regulatory decisions, then reductions in the levels of lead in blood that are considered safe imply reductions in safe levels of lead in paint. Thus finding that lead-based paint firms are liable amounts to holding them responsible for past actions on the basis of current information. The most plausible incentive effects of such a policy would be to deter generally the sale of products and the acquisition of plant and equipment.

A third purpose of civil litigation is to ensure that people are held accountable for their negligent misdeeds. Yet for several reasons, litigation against lead-based paint companies does not promote accountability. First, they are being sued for production and marketing decisions that they made with the approval of regulators forty to eighty years ago. Regulatory authorities whose official function was to promote public health and to protect public safety had some responsibility during their time in office. If they failed to use that responsibility, does it all then shift to the lead-based paint companies? The defense of compliance with existing regulations should carry some weight. Lawsuits by municipalities that failed to use their authority to regulate lead-based paint earlier than the federal government seem particularly opportunistic.

Second, the suits promote a Kafkaesque accountability to the extent that lead companies are being held liable for risks uncovered by scientific investigations completed after lead-based paint was sold. Irrespective of what lead-based paint manufacturers once knew, it is indisputable that

63. Berney (1993, p. 14).
64. Berney (1993, p. 28).
65. Campbell and others (1996).

scientific understanding about the risks of exposure to lead has greatly improved since 1970. In the face of such improved understanding, the accountability that the lawsuits appear to promote is akin to changing the rules of the game after the kickoff.

Finally, these lawsuits represent an abrupt departure from the cooperative approach to environmental problem solving used in the regulatory negotiations of the early 1990s.[66] The Environmental Protection Agency organized such negotiations for important rule makings to address problems like combined sewer overflows and disinfection by-products in drinking water.[67] For these rule makings the agency invited "stakeholders" to a series of public meetings to seek consensus on a specific regulatory option that EPA could then use as the basis for a regulation. Such regulatory negotiations and the difficulty of achieving consensus often delayed the promulgation of a final rule. Yet many observers believed that this process was an improvement over the conventional one because it could reduce the delays, costs, and uncertainty associated with legal challenges to final rules. In addition, regardless of the difficulties of implementing regulatory negotiations, sponsors of such negotiations and the participants themselves shared a belief that a voluntary consensus seemed intrinsically valuable. They preferred a negotiated consensus to the adversarial litigation that dogged so many environmental regulations.

Suits against former lead-based paint manufacturers, by private or government plaintiffs, fail to meet the conventional purposes of civil litigation. They also mark a sharp departure from the consensual policy development processes popular in the 1990s.

Tenant-Landlord Suits

It is useful to compare lawsuits against landlords with lawsuits against former lead-based paint manufacturers. Landlords and their insurance companies have paid awards in the millions of dollars to hundreds of children suffering from high blood lead levels. These payments, unlike those that might result from suits against former paint companies, are from the party responsible for the harm to the party that suffered the harm. The risk of losing such cases provides an incentive to landlords to control lead-based paint hazards on their properties. And such suits hold landlords accountable for hazardous conditions on their premises. Here we look more closely at lawsuits against landlords to assess the deterrent effects of such suits.

---

66. *Negotiated Rulemaking Act of 1990*, U.S. Code Title 5, chapter 5, subchapter 3.
67. See, for example, U.S. Environmental Protection Agency (1998c).

We collected data on outcomes of lawsuits against landlords from the legal professional press. Most of the cases were reported in the *Verdict & Settlement Report, Exclusive Edition* of *Mealey's Litigation Report: Lead*. This volume covers verdicts from September 1990 to September 1999 and settlements from January 1998 to September 1999. We also collected more recent data from weekly publications of *Mealey's Litigation Report: Lead* through March 7, 2001.

Mealey's summarizes litigation results reported by attorneys or in court filings. The reports typically mention the amount of any award, blood lead levels, whether the award was a settlement or court ordered. They often mention whether juries decided the awards. Juries determined about 40 percent of the cases, while another 40 percent reflected settlements.

These data suggest growth and decline in the number of children on whose behalf suits were pursued to conclusion in the nineteen nineties.[68] In the first three full years for which *Mealey's* reported lawsuits (1992–94), it reported twenty-nine cases. For the period 1995 to 1997, it reported seventy-four cases, and for the years 1998 to 2000, it reported only fifty-one cases. *Mealey's* also reported settlements systematically for the most recent years and these added substantially to the total number of cases. *Mealey's* reported ninety-two settlements for the three years 1998 to 2000. It is intriguing that lawsuits have not fallen with declines in blood lead levels and in contaminated housing, but changes in the annual number of reported cases may occur in part because of changes in *Mealey's* data collection methods.

Using these data we explore questions relating to the amount of an award given that one exists and to the probability of any award going to the plaintiff. We consider whether the awards are commensurate with the damage estimates implied by EPA and HUD models. Blood lead levels are generally a very good measure of damages, insofar as epidemiological evidence links blood lead levels in children to measures of neurological performance, such as IQ, and to other health effects. As shown in table 4-1, the Agency for Toxic Substances and Disease Registry categorizes the severity of lead-related health effects according to the blood lead levels of children. The Environmental Protection Agency and HUD use blood lead levels as the measure of exposure to lead and hence lead-related health effects in their assessments of the benefits of controlling environmental lead.

The data suggest that the awards are generous relative to the value that

---

68. We concentrate on the number of children, rather than the number of cases, because in some instances where one case covered more than one child, only one child received compensation.

federal agencies put on reducing blood lead levels. The Environmental Protection Agency has estimated that an increase in blood lead levels of 10 µg/dl lowers IQ by about 2.6 points and that each IQ point lost lowers the present value of discounted life-time earnings by about $9,500.[69] Thus, at least for changes in low levels of blood lead below 20 or 25 µg/dl, an increase in blood lead of 10 µg/dl would be associated with reductions in the present value of lifetime earnings of about $25,000. By contrast, the average award paid to children with blood lead levels of more than 10 µg/dl and less than or equal to 20 µg/dl was $524,000 in 2000 dollars, and the median award to children with this level of lead in their blood was $81,000. Awards to children with blood lead levels greater than 20 µg/dl but less than or equal to 30 µg/dl averaged $929,000; the median award to such children was about $187,000. Both the mean and median values are much larger than estimates implied by the economic models used by HUD and EPA.

Of course such large awards might make sense if they were partly punitive. In instances in which negligence is hard to detect and proof of causality is rare, significant punitive awards may make economic sense.[70] Unfortunately, we do not know what part of the awards was punitive because *Mealey's* provides virtually no information about punitive damages.

We begin our regressions with a Box-Cox procedure to choose an appropriate functional form.[71] (See table 4-3 for a description of the data used in the regressions.) We regress the award on blood lead levels, five dummy variables for the five states with the most cases, and a trend variable. For the award, the data do not reject the hypothesis of a logarithmic transformation, for which the true transformation parameter λ would be 0 (estimated $\lambda = 0.0170$, standard error $= .0281$). For the blood lead level the data do not reject an inverse transformation, for which the true transformation parameter λ would be -1 (estimated $\lambda = -1.39$, standard error $= .605$). We use this Box-Cox regression, which has dummy variables for Massachusetts, Maryland, New York, and Pennsylvania and a trend variable, to calculate the predicted award for different levels of lead in the blood of a hypothetical child.[72] As shown in figure 4-3 the Box-Cox

69. U.S. Environmental Protection Agency (2000). These values have been converted to 2000 dollars.

70. Sunstein, Kahneman, and Schkade (1998).

71. The procedure transforms a variable x according to $(x^\lambda - 1)/\lambda$. See Box and Cox (1964).

72. We assume that the child would live in New York, the state with the most lawsuits filed in 1997, which was the average year in our sample.

Table 4-3. *Description of Data Used in Regressions*

Variables	Complete sample	Sample with awards
Number of children	246	210
Mean of awards in 2001 dollars	$760,471	$891,000
(standard deviation)	($3,455,000)	($3,725,000)
Mean of average blood lead level	42.2	41.6
of child (standard deviation)	(23.0)	(19.4)
Number of entries by selected state		
Illinois	11	11
Maryland	27	21
Massachusetts	42	34
New York	127	115
Pennsylvania	16	13
Number of children with		
a poisoned sibling reported	81	71

Note: We treat siblings poisoned together as individual cases even if such children are part of a single lawsuit.

Figure 4-3. *Predicted Award by Child's Blood Lead Level*

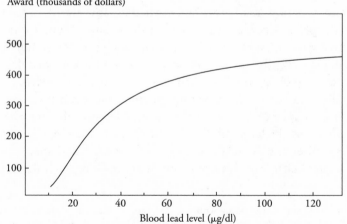

Award (thousands of dollars)

Blood lead level (μg/dl)

Note: The predicted awards are from New York in 1998 based on the Box-Cox model described in the text.

model implies that children with relatively moderate levels of lead in their blood are compensated by the judicial system more than suggested by EPA's model of damages. In addition, although the medical severity of higher blood lead levels increases—an increase of 20 μg/dl from a baseline of 40 μg/dl is worse than from a baseline of 5 μg/dl, because 25 μg/dl has essentially asymptomatic effects—the incremental compensation for higher blood lead levels falls sharply. Indeed the awards paid to children with blood lead levels of 50 μg/dl are within 20 percent of the awards paid to children with blood lead levels of 100 μg/dl. These results change little when we drop influential observations.

We present in the first column of table 4-4 an ordinary least squares regression based on the Box-Cox model but with transformations of these two variables modified so that the estimated coefficient is (-1 times) the elasticity.[73] This regression also includes dummy variables for the five states with the most lawsuits (Illinois, Maryland, Massachusetts, New York, and Pennsylvania) and an index for time. It has an R^2 equal to 0.123. We find that the elasticity of the award with respect to the blood lead level is 0.82 evaluated at the sample mean and that it is statistically different from zero but not from unity. We also find that the awards exhibit an upward trend of about 9 percent per year.

James Heckman and others have shown that such ordinary least squares estimates are biased if the error term correlates with the errors in a separate equation that determines whether any award is paid.[74] To address this selectivity bias, we present in the second column of table 4-4 our estimates based on Heckman's method, which involves simultaneously estimating the awards equation (with the transformations just described) and a probit model predicting whether any award was observed.

Ideally, the equation estimating whether the plaintiffs receive any award should include as independent variables information about the likely liability of the landlord. Was he informed of the presence of a child on the premises and about the presence of specific lead-based paint hazards? Did he fail to take timely action after receiving such information?

---

73. Before running these regressions, we divide the awards by the mean of the positive awards in the sample, and we divide the blood lead levels by the mean blood lead level of the full sample. Given these steps, it follows that the elasticity of the award with respect to the blood lead level is −b, where b is the estimated coefficient, because the blood lead level (BLL) is unity at the sample mean. Note also that d award/dBLL = −b award/$(BLL)^2$ = −b, because the award and BLL are unity at the sample mean.

74. Heckman (1976).

Table 4-4. *Regression Results, Coefficients, and Standard Errors*

Variables	Ordinary least squares	Heckman estimator
Inverse of blood lead levels	−.815*	−.807*
	(.171)	(.171)
Illinois	.197	.152
	(.571)	(.590)
Maryland	.217	.212
	(.495)	(.486)
Massachusetts	−.295	−.309
	(.438)	(.433)
New York	.157	.130
	(.395)	(.402)
Pennsylvania	−.762	−.773
	(.539)	(.531)
Date	.0924**	.0900**
	(.0521)	(.0520)
Intercept	−3.65**	−3.52**
	(1.99)	(2.02)
R squared	.123	Not applicable
Constraints on sample	Only awards > 0	None
Number of observations	210	246
		Probit regression
Medical significance BLL>15 μg/dl	. . .	1.15**
		(.462)
Sibling with high BLL	. . .	.336
		(.245)
Illinois	. . .	6.73*
		(88102)
Maryland	. . .	.0621
		(.424)
Massachusetts	. . .	.249
		(.391)
New York	. . .	.632
		(.354)
Pennsylvania	. . .	.0766
		(.493)
Year dummies ?	. . .	Yes
Rho	. . .	−.0743
		(.302)

Table 4-4. *(continued)*

Variables	Ordinary least squares	Heckman estimator
Sigma	. . .	1.42
		(.0698)
Lambda	. . .	−.105
		(.428)
Chi squared value for test of independent equations	. . .	0.06

Note: Rho is the correlation between the errors of the two equations, sigma is the standard error of the residual in the award equation here and lambda is the product of rho and sigma.

*Coefficients statistically significant at a 99 percent confidence level.

**Coefficients significant at a 90 percent level.

Were the hazards in question of a nature likely to have caused the observed blood lead levels? We lack such data.[75] Instead, we introduce into the probit equation a variable for the medical significance of the blood lead level, which we take to be levels greater than 15 µg/dl. We believe that only the medical significance of blood lead, and not levels of blood lead generally, should predict whether a child receives an award. We use 15 µg/dl because other measures of medical significance have less predictive value. We also introduce a dummy variable indicating whether any siblings were reported to have high blood lead levels, because we believe that the presence of siblings with high blood lead suggests a genuine residential hazard exists and so is likely to affect the probability of an award. Finally, because we do not anticipate any trend in the likelihood of an award over time, we introduce a set of dummy variables to model the different years in the sample.

We find that these variables generally perform as expected except that the sibling effect is not statistically significant and that many of the year effects are also not statistically significant. The elasticity of awards with respect to blood lead levels is little changed. Moreover, the estimated correlation between the error terms in the two regressions, ρ, is not statistically different from zero. Thus the selection bias appears small, and we may as well consider the ordinary least squares regression.

These data show that the courts award lead-poisoned children far more than EPA's models of damages imply, at least for moderate levels of

75. Without such data we do not think that an analysis of the likelihood of jury awards versus judgments versus settlements is worthwhile.

lead (20 µg/dl). They also show rapidly diminishing incremental damages at higher blood lead levels, a finding that seems at odds with the ladder of health effects summarized in table 4-1. A final implication is that the awards are fairly hard to predict. More than 85 percent of the variation in the (log of) awards is unexplained by the data, although blood lead levels are probably the single best measure of exposure and hence harm.

Although such litigation clearly provides incentives for landlords to control lead hazards, estimating the magnitude of such incentives is difficult. We have little information about the likelihood of the landlord making an uninsured payment to a child harmed by a lead-based paint hazard, given that such a hazard exists. This likelihood may be small, however, because some 85,000 young children have blood lead levels greater than 20 µg/dl and many hundreds of thousands of young children have blood lead levels higher than 10 µg/dl. Yet each year not even a hundred lawsuits against landlords result in awards. Moreover, only a fraction of children with high blood lead may be tenants. Thus the risk to landlords of having to make payments is clearly small, on the order of one in a thousand or less. Even if all awards were uninsured, the expected cost to the landlord of losing a lawsuit brought by a lead-poisoned child, given a child with elevated blood lead in residence, might conservatively be on the order of $500.[76] Less conservative assumptions or liability insurance that covers lead-related claims would seriously lower this estimate.

Discussion and Conclusions

Federal regulations may indirectly contribute to increased litigation. The Environmental Protection Agency expects courts, lenders, insurance companies, and localities to adopt and enforce its new standards. Indeed, we believe that key features of the EPA standards were chosen in part to facilitate other institutions' efforts to mandate them. For example, EPA adopted a bright line approach, rather than acknowledging that the appropriate level of hazard depends in part on a variety of factors such as the number and age of children and the costs of remediation, which will vary from one residence to another. These bright line standards may affect additional litigation if lawyers and courts are willing to interpret violations of

76. This illustrative calculation assumes average awards of $500,000, one hundred lawsuits concluded per year, and 100,000 children who have medically significant blood lead levels and reside in rental units.

these standards as evidence of negligence. But practical difficulties suggest limits to these effects. The standard prohibiting "any" deteriorated lead-based paint is too stringent to be met. In addition, information about lead dust levels will be irrelevant in court if not collected around the time that a child was identified as having high blood lead levels. Thus any increases in litigation may be small.

In the litigious world of environmental policy it is not surprising that EPA's standards are themselves in doubt because of a recently announced court challenge. The National Multi Housing Council and two other property-owner associations recently petitioned the U.S. District Court of Appeals for the D.C. Circuit to review EPA's lead hazard standards. The petition asks the court to review whether the Residential Lead-based Paint Hazard Reduction Act of 1992 authorized EPA to regulate all lead "regardless of the source." In essence, apartment owners object to being made responsible for cleaning up lead that is in the soil or in wind-blown dust as a result of historical use of leaded gasoline and does not result from leaded paint.[77]

The lawsuits mounted by local government agencies against lead paint companies fail to satisfy the accepted purposes of civil litigation. They would require parties only distantly responsible to pay compensation to parties who did not directly suffer harm. They would provide absolutely no meaningful deterrent value, while instead providing disincentives for manufacturing firms generally. By seeking to hold paint companies liable for historical actions in light of today's scientific understanding, they promote a distorted notion of accountability.

These lawsuits are a poor way to solve the problems associated with lead-based paint hazards. These suits have arisen in part because poorer, older communities where lead hazards are concentrated are frustrated at having insufficient resources to address lead hazards. Towns like Milwaukee and St. Louis may face huge financial burdens trying to comply with the new stringent hazard standards. And in areas with low real estate values, lead control costs may be a significant percentage of housing values, so that strict enforcement of stringent new lead standards could lead to premature abandonment of housing.[78] But lawsuits against paint manufacturers amount to a tax on deep pockets whose owners have only an

77. *National Multihousing Council and others* v. *Environmental Protection Agency*, Petition for Review by the U. S. Court of Appeals for the District of Columbia Circuit.
78. Fraas and Lutter (1996).

indirect responsibility for ills associated with lead-based paint. Even if successful, they will tend to create government programs that will work only to the extent that children with high blood lead or homes with genuine lead hazards can be readily identified. Such identification is costly, as illustrated by the difficulties with the Medicaid-sponsored tests of children's blood lead. Moreover, concerns over legal liability may provide landlords with incentives not to test for lead-based paint hazards.

More sensible controls on lead-based paint will require better incentives for landlords to control hazards. There is currently no evidence that controlling lead-based paint hazards increases the rents landlords can earn from rental property or the resale value of that property. Thus the key reason for self-interested landlords to comply with EPA's recent hazard standards may be a reduction in the risk of being sued by a tenant whose child has high blood lead levels. But these risks are too low or too likely to be insured to provide an adequate incentive.

There have been proposals to provide additional funding to remediate lead-based paint problems. A 1993 bill would have set up a federal trust fund for that purpose, but it did not make it out of committee.[79] The funds would have come from a forty-five-cent-per-pound tax on lead from U.S. smelters and lead in certain products entering the United States.[80]

One alternative approach to improving incentives would be to support lead-based paint controls with tax incentives. For example, the federal government could provide a modest tax credit for the replacement of any window frame that a certified lead inspector reports is lead contaminated. This approach would not entail large administration costs, and it would promote energy conservation while reducing lead hazards. Most important, it would address the apparent lack of incentives for landlords to control lead hazards.

Incentive-based proposals offer a few key advantages over the increasingly popular lawsuits against former lead-based paint manufacturers. They would avoid burdening today's shareholders with costs resulting from management decisions made decades ago. They would avoid adverse deterrent effects on manufacturing activity. Most important, they could provide incentives for landlords to take reasonable steps to remediate the hazards that they control.

---

79. Bill Summary and Status for 103 Cong. 1 sess., H.R. 2479, *Lead-Based Paint Hazard Abatement Trust Fund Act of 1993.*
80. 103 Cong. 1 sess., H.R. 2479.

Appendix

As noted earlier we collected data on outcomes of lawsuits against landlords from the legal professional press. Most of our cases were reported in the *Verdict & Settlement Report, Exclusive Edition* of *Mealey's Litigation Report*. This volume covers verdicts from September 1990 to September 1999 and settlements from January 1998 to September 1999. We also collected data from bi-weekly publications of *Mealey's Litigation Report: Lead* from October 29, 1999, until March 7, 2001.

The data in *Mealey's Litigation Report: Lead* required editing to be suitable for quantitative analysis. We excluded cases because of incomplete or inconsistent data. We included cases when both an award (or dismissal) and blood lead levels were given. For some children, *Mealey's* provided information on the child's gender, age, IQ, hospitalization history, the presence of lead-poisoned siblings, and residence time in the location with the alleged hazard. These data were generally reported for only a few children, however. For almost all children, *Mealey's* reported whether the award was a settlement and, if it was a court-ordered award, whether it was handed down by a judge or jury. We deleted from any analysis involving the amount of the award those cases in which *Mealey's* stated that an award amount was the simple sum of future payments rather than the cash value of future payments.

Mealey's reported only the total award for some cases involving more than one child. In such instances we divided the award equally among the children although the child with the higher blood lead levels may have received more of the award.

James Cordray, the editor of *Mealey's Litigation Report: Lead,* helpfully explained that *Mealey's* obtains litigation results from attorneys, court filings, and other news sources. Although he was unable to estimate the percentage of existing cases reported in *Mealey's*, he believes that *Mealey's* covers most of them.

COMMENT BY

Thomas J. Kniesner

Many years ago when sex was dirty and the environment was clean, I was a member of the Reagan administration's lead hazards policy working group. The consensus was that exposure to lead fit a basic justification for government regulatory intervention: a health detriment to children living near sources of lead. The issue was easy back then—to determine the most important lead sources, which would indicate the place to start reducing lead in the environment. Leaded gasoline turned out to be the main culprit because exhaust fumes contaminated the air and ground of persons living near highly trafficked roads. Lead is now gone from our gasoline and with it the largest single source of lead contaminating the environment. Today Randall Lutter and Elizabeth Mader examine how the public policy issues connected with lead hazards and children have now changed from regulation to litigation about lead paint in so-called chewable areas of rental housing. I recommend that the authors place the current lead-paint-related health problems in a context with other health problems, provide more interpretable likelihood of settlement results by presenting adjusted-odds ratios and expand their scope to include examination of the determinants of the decision mechanism (settlement, jury, or judge) and why awards are so high in relation to apparent economic damages.

Context

Many years ago policymakers and economists largely rejected tort suits as a way of allocating the costs of work-related injuries. Instead safety regulation and no-fault insurance became the way to help pay rehabilitation expenses and replace lost earnings. The same logic would seem to apply to improving public policy on health problems related to lead-based paint. Relatively well-informed adults in the workplace are nonetheless covered by the Occupational Safety and Health Administration and workers' compensation insurance programs. Because children are at risk, lead poisoning has clearer justification for regulation or no-fault insurance.

Altering the course of public policy related to health is costly, emotionally and economically, so it is important to know whether the problems caused by lead paint are serious enough to warrant re-orienting policy. Clearly the removal of leaded gas from the ecosystem has resulted in far fewer health problems related to lead. It seems crucial that Lutter and Mader not leave the reader lacking in knowledge of the extent of health and economic consequences caused by lead paint. How extensively are children affected? A severity-weighted count of children affected could be compared with a similar statistic for other health problems such as lead or arsenic in the drinking water or second-hand smoke.

Likelihood of Award

The probit coefficients in table 4-4 yield a sense of what matters sta-tistically but not economically. We care more about whether the impacts of the independent variables are large or small. Economists generally like to discuss elasticities, which are most useful when influences and outcomes are continuous. That is not the case here. When the variables we seek to connect are in the context of a probit or a logit regression, then it is becom-ing customary to express the effect of each independent variable in terms of its adjusted-odds ratio or its marginal effect. To be concrete, it is not particularly obvious what a probit coefficient of 0.632 means for New York in table 4-4. What we really want to know is how much more likely an award is in New York than in the comparison states.

Award Size

A perhaps more informative way to start would be first to estimate a censored regression model such as a Tobit or CLAD (censored least absolute deviations), which avoids pitfalls associated with incorrect empir-ical assumptions for the stochastic part of the model.[81] The Tobit or CLAD results would yield estimated average effects of the independent variables, including the case in which the plaintiffs get nothing.

Fancier yet would be a two-step semiparametric Heckit model. The procedure involves a first-stage ordinary-least-squares regression of the probability of a settlement. The researcher then uses the first-step results to produce predicted probabilities of any settlements that then appear as regressors (including their squares and cubes) that purify the second-step generalized-least-squares regression describing the level of awards won.[82] The advantage of the semiparametric Heckit procedure is that it allows separate and loosely connected models for award incidence versus award level that do not depend on any (possibly wrong) statistical distribution for unmeasured influences.

Lutter and Mader could also take fuller advantage of an opportunity to add to the empirical literature on the law and economics of liability. I would find the outcome of how the decision was reached interesting and important. The authors could offer additional valuable information by estimating a multiple logit regression that seeks to locate the relative importance of measurable factors that determine whether there was an

81. Deaton (1997, chap. 2).
82. Maddala (1983); Deaton (1997, chap. 2).

out-of-court settlement or a decision by a jury or a judge. Recent results in an experimental context indicate that, compared with the decisions of juries, judges' decisions are more in line with the law when science, costs, and benefits come into play.[83] In lead paint litigation, does the party whose side is based more strongly on technical details than on emotions strive to have the case decided by a judge?

Policy

As the authors argue convincingly, lead paint lawsuits produce wrongly targeted incentives, especially because house resale values are unaffected by cleanup of the paint and because landlords' risks from lawsuits are low. To me the most important unresolved issue relevant to policy is, why are there such high award-to-damage ratios? Can the difference between basic economic losses from exposure to lead paint by children and award size be explained by empirical research on pain and suffering awards?[84] Need public policy experts worry about awards that are twenty times damages? My concern over the high ratio stems from a desire not to encourage lawsuits. I am not unsympathetic to the view that U.S. society is too litigious and that less confrontational ways to reach decisions are more desirable than tort suits, especially if there is valid concern that contentious litigation weakens the so-called social glue that binds our society together.[85]

References

Anderson, Eugene R., and Joan L. Lewis. 1997. "Abate, Don't Wait: New Lead Paint Disclosure Rules Point to Insurance Coverage." *Tennessee Bar Journal* (March-April):19–23.

Battelle Memorial Institute. 1998. *Risk Analysis to Support Standards for Lead in Paint, Dust, and Soil*, prepared by Battelle Memorial Institute for Office of Pollution Prevention and Toxics. EPA 747-R-97-006. Washington: U.S. Environmental Protection Agency.

Box, G. E. P., and D. R. Cox. 1964 "An Analysis of Transformations." *Journal of the Royal Statistical Society.* Series B (26): 211–43.

Berney, Barbara. 1993. "Round and Round it Goes: The Epidemiology of Childhood Lead Poisoning, 1950-1990." *Milbank Quarterly* 71 (1): 3–39.

Buzby, Jean C., Paul D. Frenzen, and Barbara Rasco. 2001. *Product Liability and Microbial Foodborne Illness*. Agricultural Economic Report Number 799. U.S. Department of Agriculture, Economic Research Service.

83. Viscusi (2001).
84. Viscusi (1988).
85. Putnam (2000).

Campbell, J. R., S. J. Schaffer, P. G. Szilagyi, K. G. O'Connor, P. Briss, and M. Weitzman. 1996. "Blood Lead Screening Practices among U.S. Pediatricians." *Pediatrics* 98 (3, part 1): 372–77.

City of Philadelphia. 2001. *Five-Year Financial Plan (FY 2002–FY2006)*. Presented by Mayor Street.

Deaton, Angus 1997. *The Analysis of Household Surveys: A Microeconometric Approach to Development Policy.* Johns Hopkins University Press.

Farquhar, Doug, J. D., Cathy Atkins, J.D., and Carla Kohler J.D. 2001. *State Lead Poisoning Prevention Statutes.* Denver: National Conference of State Legislatures.

Fraas, Arthur, and Randall Lutter. 1996. "Abandonment of Residential Housing and the Abatement of Lead-based Paint Hazards." *Journal of Policy Analysis and Management* 15 (3): 424–29.

Heckman, James. 1976. "The Common Structure of Statistical Models Of Truncation, Sample Selection, and Limited Dependent Variables and a Simple Estimator for Such Models." *Annals of Economic and Social Measurement* 5 (4): 475–92.

Hunt, Tanner. 2000. "Memo: Lead-based Paint Products Litigation." Beaumont, Texas: Law Offices of Wells, Peyton, Greenberg and Hunt, L.L.P (August).

Jacobson, Peter, and Kenneth Warner. 1999. "Litigation and Public Health Policy-Making: The Case of Tobacco Control." *Journal of Health Politics, Policy and Law* 24 (4): 769–804.

Kaminsky, Alan, ed., Paul Bottari, and Michael Boulhosa, co-authors. 1998. *A Complete Guide to Lead Poisoning Litigation.* American Bar Association. Chicago.

Konigsberg, Alan U. 1996. *Proving and Defending: Lead-Based Paint Poisoning Cases.* New York: Practising Law Institute.

Lutter, Randall. 2001. "Getting the Lead Out Cheaply: A Review of the EPA's Proposed Residential Lead Hazard Standards." *Environmental Science and Policy* 4: 13–23.

Maddala, G. S. 1983. *Limited-Dependent and Qualitative Variables in Econometrics.* Cambridge, UK: Cambridge University Press.

New York Independent Budget Office. 1999. "Preventing Lead Poisoning in Children: Fiscal Impact of Intro. 205, A Legislative Alternative to Local Law 1."

Pirckle, James, Debra Brody, Elaine Gunter, Rachel Kramer, Daniel Paschal, Katherine Flegal, and Thomas Matte. 1994. "Decline in Blood Lead Levels in the United States: The National Health and Nutrition Examination Surveys (NHANES)." *Journal of the American Medical Association* 272 (4): 284–91.

Putnam, Robert 2000. *Bowling Alone: The Collapse and Revival of American Community.* Simon and Schuster.

Sargent, James D., Madeline Dalton, Eugene Demidenko, Peter Simon, and Robert Klein. 1999. "The Association between State Housing Policy and Lead Poisoning in Children." *American Journal of Public Health* 89 (11): 1690–95.

Schonbrun, Lawrence. 1997. "The Class Action Con Game." *Regulation* 20 (4): 50–55.

Schwartz, J. 1994. "Low-level Lead Exposure and Children's IQ: A Meta-Analysis and Search for a Threshold." *Environmental Research* 65: 42–55.

Sunstein, Cass, Daniel Kahneman, and David Schkade. 1998. "Assessing Punitive Damages (with Notes on Cognition and Valuation in Law)." *Yale Law Journal* 107 (7): 2071–2153.

University of Rochester School of Medicine, Departments of Pediatrics, Biostatistics, and Environmental Medicine, and the National Center for Lead-Safe Housing. 1995. *The Relation of Lead-Contaminated House Dust and Blood Lead Levels Among Urban Children: Final Report.* MLDP T0001-93. Rochester, N.Y., and Columbia, Md.

U.S. Agency for Toxic Substances and Disease Registry. 1992. *Analysis Paper: Impact of Lead Contaminated Soil on Public Health.* Atlanta: U.S. Department of Health and Human Services, Public Health Service.

U.S. Centers for Disease Control and Prevention (CDC). 1997. "Update: Blood Lead Levels—United States, 1991–1994." *Mortality and Morbidity Weekly Review* 46 (7): 141–46.

———. 2000. "Blood Lead Levels in Young Children—United States and Selected States, 1996–1999." *Mortality and Morbidity Weekly Review* 149 (50): 1133–37.

U.S. Department of Housing and Urban Development (HUD). 1999. "Requirements for Notification, Evaluation, and Reduction of Lead-based Paint Hazards in Federally Owned Residential Property and Housing Receiving Federal Assistance; Final Rule." *Federal Register* 64 (178): 50140–231.

———. 2001. *National Survey of Lead and Allergens in Housing,* Final Report, Volume I: Analysis of Lead Hazards. Revision 6.0. Office of Lead Hazard Control (April).

U.S. Environmental Protection Agency (EPA). 1998a. *Economic Analysis of Toxic Substances Control Act Section 403: Hazard Standards.* Washington.

———. 1998b. "Lead; Identification of Dangerous Levels of Lead; Proposed Rule." *Federal Register* 63 (106): 30302–55.

———. 1998c. "National Primary Drinking Water Regulations: Disinfectants and Disinfection Byproducts; Final Rule." *Federal Register* 63 (241): 69389–476.

———. 2000. *Economic Analysis of Toxic Substances Control Act Section 403: Lead-based Paint Hazard Standards.* Washington.: Economic and Policy Analysis Branch Economics, Exposure and Technology Division, Office of Pollution Prevention and Toxics.

———. 2001. "Lead; Identification of Dangerous Levels of Lead; Final Rule." *Federal Register* 64 (4): 1205–40.

U. S. General Accounting Office (GAO). 1998. *Medicaid: Elevated Blood Lead Levels in Children.* Washington.

Viscusi, W. Kip 1988. "Pain and Suffering in Product Liability Cases: Systematic Compensation or Capricious Awards?" *International Review of Law and Economics* 8: 203–20.

———. 2001. "Jurors, Judges, and the Mistreatment of Risk by the Courts." *Journal of Legal Studies* 30 (1): 107–42.

York, Louis B. 2000. *Opinion: In the Matter of the Application of New York City Coalition to End Lead Poisoning, Inc., et al. v. Peter Vallone, et al.* 120911/99 (N.Y. Sup, N.Y. Co).

JONI HERSCH

5 | Breast Implants: Regulation, Litigation, and Science

Silicone-gel-filled breast implants have been available in the United States since 1962. Yet until 1992, when the Food and Drug Administration (FDA) imposed a ban on silicone breast implants, sparking the largest class action settlement in history as well as widespread concern about health risks, no scientifically valid studies of the long-term health effects of breast implants had even begun. Although manufacturers knew since 1976 with the passage of the Medical Devices Amendments that the FDA could call on them to provide safety information at any time, the track record clearly shows they did only minimal research before 1992. It was not until 1994 that the first important epidemiological study providing evidence that silicone gel does not cause serious systemic health problems was published, and not until 1999 that the Institute of Medicine of the National Academy of Science analyzed all of the evidence and concurred.

Although current scientific evidence consistently and convincingly indicates that silicone breast implants do not cause serious systemic health problems, evidence produced during litigation suggested otherwise, leading to numerous multimillion dollar awards to individual plaintiffs, an FDA-imposed ban in 1992 on silicone breast implants, a multibillion dollar class action settlement, and the bankruptcy reorganization of the largest silicone

The author thanks Jessica Pishko and Jonathan Patchen for excellent research assistance.

manufacturer, Dow Corning. Because these outcomes now seem inconsistent with the scientific information indicating that implants are safe, many observers view the breast implant experience as a legendary example of legal and regulatory failure.[1] Statements such as "recall the silicone-implant litigation fiasco" are commonplace.[2] Critics complain that by failing to wait until reliable scientific evidence became available before making decisions, the FDA and the courts made mistakes of catastrophic magnitude.[3]

Whether regulation and litigation erred and how they have erred requires an understanding of the informational context of their actions. In much the same way as the liability of companies should be assessed based on the state of information at the time of corporate decisions, similarly one should base assessments of the courts and regulatory interventions on the state of information at the time. This general principle includes, of course, the role that such institutions can play in generating requisite information, but it also includes recognition of the possibility that companies may withhold or fail to generate the key information. My evaluation based on this state of the information approach yields a quite different perspective than that of the standard critiques of the breast implants experience, many of which have taken advantage of the wisdom afforded by hindsight.

The practical consequence of awaiting the outcome of large-scale, long-term epidemiological studies is that regulatory bodies and the courts will fail to act even if a product is believed to be risky. How the courts and regulators should proceed with imperfect information is a complicated matter. The key concern is whether regulators and the courts acted properly based on the information available. The additional concern about the regulators is whether they exercised their authority to obtain information in a timely fashion.

The breast implants experience demonstrates how manufacturers control the flow of information and how litigation can provide information

1. See, for example, "The $4.3 Billion Mistake," *Wall Street Journal*, June 17, 1994, p. A14; and Denise Grady, "A Conversation with Robert Fenichel: Calculating Safety in Risky World of Drugs," *New York Times*, March 6, 2001, p. D1.

2. This quote appeared in "Unleashing Science: A 21st Century FDA," *Wall Street Journal*, February 2, 2001, p. A10, but this sentiment is expressed frequently throughout the media.

3. Marcia Angell, M.D., a highly vocal critic of the FDA and judicial system during the breast implant experience, summarized this viewpoint on Frontline, February 27, 1996, as "history is replete with instances of health scares based on claims, testimonials, and anecdotes, and we have to wait for the science." Angell was the executive editor of the *New England Journal of Medicine* and is the author of the highly influential book *Science on Trial: The Clash of Medical Evidence and the Law in the Breast Implant Case*. (Video on file at Harvard Law School.)

that stimulates regulation. In the case of breast implants, the FDA did not initially require safety studies. Rather, the key information flow was in the opposite direction, as information revealed in the litigation about corporate behavior and product defects stimulated the FDA to take regulatory action. The possibility that exposure to silicone gel posed more serious risks failed to receive proper scrutiny until litigation pushed this issue to the forefront. Evidence produced during litigation demonstrated that not only did the manufacturers fail to perform safety tests, they also ignored warning alarms raised by their own employees and by surgeons who used the products, suppressed studies that may have indicated problems, and even destroyed evidence from negative studies. From the early days, Dow Corning and the other manufacturers knew of many product problems with breast implants, including bleeding of the silicone gel. Direct silicone injections were regulated as a drug and removed from the market in the early 1960s. Had the FDA known that silicone gel often leaked from the breast implant envelope, it could have classified implants immediately as a drug and so regulated silicone implants.[4]

The breast implants experience also demonstrates the hazards of regulatory agencies failing to exercise their authority in a timely fashion. Whether silicone implants caused systemic diseases was unknown when David Kessler, M.D., called for the moratorium in 1992. The available information mainly consisted of case reports without controls and research undertaken by the manufacturers for compliance purposes that was woefully inadequate by scientific standards. The transparent weaknesses of the studies that were submitted for marketing approval led the FDA to impose a moratorium on implant use while awaiting better information. By shirking its regulatory responsibilities until that time, the FDA set the stage for its authority to be usurped by litigation. Had the FDA exercised its authority in a more timely fashion, it is unlikely that breast implants would have joined the legion of mass toxic torts.

After discussing the history of breast augmentation procedures, I use a unique national survey of medical devices recipients to present new empirical evidence of the probability that a woman would have breast implants. This analysis helps reveal whether implant recipients were likely to be uninformed about the risks of implants. Women with implants tended to be more affluent, and education did not influence the implant decision, indicating that the women who received implants were not especially likely to

4. Indeed, Medical Engineering Corporation's Scientific Affairs Committee speculated in April 1977 that silicone oil bleeding through the shell and to the body tissue might cause the FDA to remove silicone gel implants from the market.

be misinformed or have few viable market alternatives. I also use this data set to provide an analysis of the types of localized defects commonly occurring in implants. The results show that defects and replacements were common. I discuss evidence from the literature on the localized and systemic health risks associated with breast implants. As this section shows, although localized risks were common among those with implants, the combination of relatively low implant usage among the population and low incidence of autoimmune diseases makes it difficult to either find strong evidence of enhanced risk or rule out this possibility, allowing both parties to litigation to use the science to support their position. I then describe the regulatory history of breast implants, followed by a description of the major litigations and the role of litigation in providing safety information. Table 5-1 provides a chronology of the key events in the breast implant experience.

The timeline demonstrates that the breast implant saga is not a tale of a tort system run amok as juries, ignorant of science, fell prey to the manipulations of greedy plaintiffs' lawyers. The courts and regulatory agencies must make decisions at the time based on the available information. The cases presented to the jury had incomplete scientific evidence but did have plaintiffs with significant ailments. Jurors received convincing evidence that the manufacturers were guilty of fraud, negligence, and liability for failing to disclose information about the dangers of implants. There were also numerous case reports in the medical literature of serious autoimmune diseases occurring in women who had breast implants. Only in retrospect does the epidemiological evidence on longer-term hazards such as connective tissue disease exonerate the manufacturers.

History of Breast Augmentation Procedures

Efforts to enlarge breasts, either by surgically transferring fat to the breast from another part of the body or by injecting foreign substances into the breast area, began at least one hundred years ago. Some early examples include paraffin injections reported as early as 1889, followed by injection of other substances such as ivory, glass balls, ground rubber, and foam sponges. The Ivalon polyvinyl sponge was used in the early 1950s to enlarge breasts, although eventually this method was discontinued as the prosthesis tended to crush, reducing breast size and causing the breast to harden.[5]

5. Sarwer and others (2000, p. 845); and Bondurant and others (2000, p. 21).

Table 5-1. *Timeline of Critical Events*

Year	Event
1962	Silicone-gel-filled breast implants first used.
1965	Silicone injections classified as a drug and not approved for human use.
1976	Medical Devices Amendments give FDA authority to regulate breast implants. Implants grandfathered in.
1977	*Mueller* v. *Corley*. Plaintiff is awarded $170,000 due to rupture.
1978	FDA General and Plastic Surgery Devices Panel recommends Class II status. FDA concerns in 1978 include gel leakage in intact implants.
1982	FDA proposes Class III status.
1984	*Stern* v. *Dow Corning*. Plaintiff is awarded over $1.7 million for claim that ruptured implants caused connective tissue disease. Internal Dow Corning documents showed Dow had suppressed risk information. These documents were then sealed by court order.
1988	Silicone implants are classified as Class III requiring manufacturers to submit safety information. FDA concerns in 1988 include capsular contracture, breakage, bleeding outside the shell, migration of silicone to organs, interference with the accuracy of mammogram, calcification of the fibrous capsule, immune disorders, and cancer.
Nov. 1991	Manufacturers' safety information deemed inadequate by FDA.
Dec. 1991	*Hopkins* v. *Dow Corning*. Plaintiff is awarded $840,000 in compensatory damages and $6.5 million in punitive damages for claim that ruptured implants caused her connective tissue disease.
Jan. 1992	FDA imposes a moratorium on silicone implants.
Feb. 1992	First class action filed in wake of FDA moratorium. Eventually 440,000 women join.
April 1992	Silicone implants withdrawn from market except in limited cases.
1994	Mayo clinic study shows systemic health risks not likely.
1995	Federal settlement approved with Dow dropping out.
1995	Dow Corning files for Chapter 11 bankruptcy reorganization, citing 19,000 individual implant lawsuits and at least 45 putative class actions.
1996–98	Courts appoint science panels. All panels conclude implants do not cause systemic diseases. Various courts do not allow plaintiffs' experts to testify under Daubert.
1999	Institute of Medicine concludes only localized risks of silicone implants including "overall reoperations, ruptures or deflations, contractures, infections, hematomas, and pain."[a]

a. Bondurant and others (2000, p. 5).

Silicone was an attractive alternative to such materials. Transformed from the natural element silicon, silicone is truly one of the most versatile and useful manmade materials. Developed in the 1930s by Dow Chemical, silicone is used as an insulator, coolant, and lubricator, and also is widely used in products inserted in the body such as joint replacements and pacemaker covers. Jack W. Snyder surveys the use of silicone in medical products and the scientific evidence on safety.[6] More than 500 medical products contain measurable amounts of silicone. The biologic effects of silicone have been tested in animals dating back at least to 1950. All scientific evidence indicates the substance is inert. The only adverse effect that has been detected in reaction to silicone implantation in animals is a tumor of soft tissue known as sarcomas or solid-state carcinogenesis. Animals who are implanted with any smooth object, including silicone, nylon, glass, and metals, are known to develop solid-state carcinogenesis. This is not a reaction to the chemical involved. This effect seems to be restricted to animals: there is no evidence that solid-state carcinogenesis also occurs in humans.

Silicone has been used to enlarge breasts since at least the 1940s. Initially, silicone oil was directly injected into the breasts. To prevent the silicone gel from migrating to other parts of the body, the silicone gel would be deliberately adulterated with other oils or other substances such as petroleum jelly, beeswax, or shellac to cause scarring in the breast area. Japanese prostitutes used silicone to enlarge their breasts, believing that American servicemen preferred large breasts. Direct injections were also widely used by showgirls in Las Vegas, where as many as 40,000 women had silicone injections by 1976.[7] These direct injections of adulterated silicone caused serious medical problems as well as deaths. In 1965 the FDA classified silicone injections as a drug regulated under the Food, Drug and Cosmetic Act, and the FDA has not approved silicone injections for human use or any cosmetic purpose.[8]

The modern era of breast implants began in the 1960s. Two plastic surgeons from Texas, Frank Gerow and Thomas Cronin, replaced direct injections with silicone gel inserted into a silicone envelope. In 1962 Timmie Jean Lindsey entered a hospital to have tattoos removed and became the first woman to receive silicone breast implants. Dow Corning began marketing these implants under the trade name "Silastic" in 1963. As the silicone was encased in an envelope, these implants were classified as a medical device rather than as a drug and so did not at that time fall under the FDA auspices. Saline-filled implants, in which saline is placed in the

6. Snyder (1997).
7. Bondurant and others (2000, p. 23).
8. U.S. House Committee on Human Resources (1992, pp. 3–4).

envelope instead of silicone gel, have also been available since the late
1960s but are widely considered to produce an inferior cosmetic effect.

Dow Corning was the only supplier of silicone implants from 1962 to
1968, and remained the largest producer of implants through 1992 when
the company opted to withdraw from the market rather than continue to
seek FDA approval. A number of companies entered the market after 1968,
with four manufacturers comprising 80 percent of the implant market:
Dow Corning, Bristol-Myers Squibb, Mentor Corporation, and McGhan
Medical Corporation.[9] Although Dow Corning was the largest producer of
implants at the time it withdrew from the market, the total value of its
implants operations amounted to less than 1 percent of its business.[10]

There are no exact data on the number of silicone implant procedures
conducted before 1992. The most commonly cited value as of 1992 is that
about 1 million American women had silicone breast implants, with most
sold between 1980 and 1990. It was estimated that about 20 percent were
for reconstruction after breast cancer or to correct abnormalities.[11] The
FDA revised its estimate of the number of implant patients in 1992, halv-
ing it to 1 million from 2 million, because the original estimate of 2 million seemed to be based on the number of implants sold.

Two national surveys that allow estimates of the number of implant
recipients were conducted in the late 1980s. The Medical Device Implant
Supplement to the 1988 National Health Interview Survey (NHIS) provided data on medical implants.[12] The National Center for Health Statistics
analysis of the data reports that 143 women within the sample had silicone
breast implants, implying that as of 1988 there were an estimated 620,000
implants in 381,000 women.[13] The second national survey was sponsored
by Dow Corning. This mail survey of 40,000 households in 1989 reported
227 women with implants out of 27,538 women sampled. Extrapolated to
the entire population, these values implied that an estimated 815,700
women in the United States had breast implants as of 1989.[14] The Dow
Corning survey did not limit their definition of breast implants to silicone
only, which may in part account for the larger estimated number of

9. U.S. House Committee on Human Resources (1992, p. 5).
10. *In re Dow Corning Corp.*, 211 B.R. 545 (Bankr. E.D. Mich. 1997).
11. U.S. House Committee on Human Resources (1992, p. 3).
12. As this survey provides the primary data for my analysis, I discuss these data in detail in the next
section.
13. Moss and others (1991). An analysis of the same data by Bright and others (1993) yielded an
estimate of 304,000 women with silicone breast implants.
14. Cook and others (1995).

implants. However, since the vast majority of implants through this period were silicone, only a small component of this disparity is likely to be accounted for by the difference in the types of breast implants reported in the respective surveys. The users of the NHIS data note that other sources suggest that their estimate may be an underestimate of the actual number.

The American Society of Plastic Surgeons (ASPS) has kept data on the number of plastic surgeries performed by member plastic surgeons since 1992.[15] Their trend data show that cosmetic surgery procedures in general, and breast augmentation in particular, have increased dramatically through this decade. Overall, cosmetic surgery procedures increased by 175 percent between 1992 and 1999, with women far more likely to undertake cosmetic surgery than men. Of approximately 1 million cosmetic surgery procedures performed in 1999, 89 percent of the patients were women.

Despite the fallout over silicone implants beginning in 1992, breast augmentation procedures have become even more popular, increasing by 413 percent over the 1992–99 period. Breast augmentation is second only to liposuction, with 167,318 breast augmentations performed in 1999 alone. But breast surgery is not limited to augmentation procedures: another 82,975 patients had surgery for breast reconstruction, and almost as many—78,169—had breast reduction surgery. Of those with implants for reconstructive purposes, 13,009 had them removed, with about 73 percent replacing their implants.

Empirical Profile

To examine who gets breast implants and the characteristics of implants, I use data from the Medical Device Implant Supplement to the 1988 National Health Interview Survey. The National Health Interview Survey (NHIS) is an annual survey containing demographic and socioeconomic questions asked of all respondents in each year, such as sex, age, race, marital status, veteran status, education, family income, industry and occupation, limitations on activities, hospital stays, and doctor visits. Besides the annual core questions, the survey requests information on special topics that vary annually. To provide information for the FDA's regulation of medical devices, the FDA's Center for Devices and Radiological Health collaborated

15. "Statistics and Costs." www.plasticsurgery.org [March 2001]. These numbers represent a lower bound since some nonmember surgeons also perform these procedures.

with the National Center for Health Statistics to include questions about medical device implants in the 1988 NHIS. The Medical Device Implant Survey was the first nationally representative, population-based survey of prevalence and utilization experience of implanted medical devices.

All respondents to the NHIS (122,310 observations) were asked to report whether they had an implant of any kind. There were 5,592 sample respondents reporting a total of 7,600 implanted medical devices. (One reason that many respondents had more than one implant was that the survey would report breast implants in both breasts, or lenses implants in both eyes, as two devices.) The survey requested specific information for five of the more common implant types: artificial joints, fixation devices, artificial heart valves, intraocular lenses, and pacemakers. Respondents were not asked whether they had a breast implant. The survey also included a catch-all category for any other implanted medical device, and this information is used to perform the following analyses of breast implant usage and characteristics.

For each medical device, the respondent (or proxy) was asked a series of questions, including the number, type, and body part in which the implant was located, dates of insertion of original device and any replacements, frequency of replacement and reasons for the most recent replacement, length of time with the device, and any adverse effects or complications such as healing problems, pain, infections, or defect.

As I discussed earlier, two early analyses of these data reported that there were 143 women in the sample with silicone breast implants, based on the number of women who reported a silicone implant inserted into the breast. Since other types of implants were in use as of 1988, including saline and polyurethane implants, I performed an independent analysis of the NHIS data and determined the number of breast implants more broadly. First, one survey question asked the part of the body where the device is located. There were 170 women who responded that the device was located in the breast. Of these 170 women, one respondent reported that the implant in her breast was an infusion pump, and one respondent was an improbable seven years old. After eliminating these two observations, the sample is composed of 168 respondents with breast implants that are a silicone implant (143 respondents), other device (10 respondents), or unknown (15 respondents). Although there is some chance that my measure of implants is overinclusive, I note that other devices inserted in the chest or breast area such as heart valves, pacemakers, some fixation devices, infusion pumps, shunts, or catheters, and so forth, are asked about separately and are therefore unlikely to be erroneously identified by my method as a breast implant.

Silicone implants accounted for the majority of implants during the pre-1992 period. Of the 168 women with implants, 143 (85.1 percent) reported silicone implants. The age of the implant recipients ranged from twenty-one to seventy-seven. The survey did not request information on the reason for implantation, so there is no way to know which of these individuals received implants for medical reasons (for example, reconstruction after mastectomy or prophylaxis) and how many received them for cosmetic reasons. To get a sense of the implant rate implied by this sample, there were 42,378 female respondents from twenty-one to seventy-seven years old to the full NHIS survey, indicating a breast implant rate of 0.40 percent.

To assess the probability that a woman has breast implants, I estimated a probit equation for the women in the NHIS sample. The results are presented in table 5-2. Breast implant use increases with age, but at a diminishing rate, peaking at age forty-one. In terms of the demographic profile, breast implant users are more likely to be white, divorced, and affluent. Breast implant use is more common in the South and the West, which reflects the historical origins of breast implant surgery in Texas and is consistent with the known high usage of silicone injections in California and Nevada.

A useful question to ask for any risky product is whether only groups who are likely to be misinformed or with few viable market alternatives will purchase it. There is no evidence of this form of market failure for breast implants. Education is not a significant determinant of implant status, and more affluent women with a greater choice of medical treatments are the ones most likely to obtain breast implants.

The NHIS data also illuminate the extent to which patients with breast implants report problems with the device. The survey requested information only on product defects and localized characteristics such as pain and bleeding. The survey did not elicit information on any long-term or systemic health effects such as connective tissue disease (CTD) that have been the focus of litigation. The first columns of table 5-3 provide statistics on the problems recipients have with their current implants, and the second column reports statistics on the problems users had with their initial implant that led to a replacement. Of the women with breast implants, 22 percent reported problems with their current implants. The most frequently cited difficulties are pain, defects or malfunction, and infections.

Table 5-2. *Probit Analysis of Breast Implant Use*

Explanatory variable	Coefficient (standard error in parentheses)
Age	0.057**
	(0.016)
Age squared x 100	−0.069**
	(0.017)
Education	0.012
	(0.011)
White race	0.924**
	(0.203)
Married	0.230
	(0.141)
Previously married	0.600**
	(0.147)
Family income	0.010**
	(0.002)
Family income missing	0.269*
	(0.114)
Employed	0.047
	(0.064)
South	0.288**
	(0.077)
West	0.278**
	(0.083)
Northeast	−0.250*
	(0.115)
MSA over 1 million	−0.028
	(0.070)
MSA 0.25–1 million	0.036
	(0.074)
Constant	−5.550**
	(0.417)
Observations	42,399

Source: Author's calculations from the Medical Device Implant Supplement to the 1988 National Health Interview Survey.

a. Dependent variable: has breast implant. *Significant at 5 percent; **significant at 1 percent

More noteworthy is that 15 percent of the women with breast implants had their original implants replaced at least once. The reason for replacement resulted primarily from defects or malfunction, infections, and pain. The information from this survey on the high replacement rate was available by 1989, thus predating David Kessler's moratorium and the extensive breast implant publicity.

Localized Breast Implant Risks

It has long been known that silicone breast implants may cause localized problems, such as hardening of the breast tissue. They have a high rate of rupture, releasing silicone gel into the body. Even without rupture, silicone gel can bleed outside the shells. They are not lifetime devices. Replacement involves additional surgery risk.

In humans, insertion of any foreign object into the body's tissue leads to an inflammatory response. Scar tissue or a capsule frequently forms around all types of implants, squeezing the implant and making the breasts hard and painful. This effect is called capsular contracture. Studies indicate that capsular contracture is common. The degree of capsular contracture is graded by the Baker grading scale, where grade III indicates the breast is firm and looks abnormal, with visible distortion, and grade IV is more severe, with painful breasts and greater distortion. A 1984 study found a capsular contracture rate of grade III or grade IV of 54 percent among patients with silicone implants for reconstruction. Recent studies by Mentor and McGhan of the rate of capsular contracture of saline-filled breast implants of grade III or IV indicate a rate of 9 percent among augmentation patients and 25 or 30 percent among reconstruction patients.[16]

One treatment option for capsular contracture is to surgically remove the tissue capsule or replace the implant. The alternative is a technique called closed capsulotomy. In this procedure, the surgeon would break the protective layer of scar tissue by hand. Not surprisingly, closed capsulotomy often caused the implant to rupture, as it involved manipulation of the breast tissue sufficiently forceful to break down scar tissue. Manufacturers recommended against using this procedure; despite their warnings, this technique was commonly used.

Implants also frequently ruptured for other reasons including damage

16. U.S. Food and Drug Administration (2000a, pp.18–19).

Table 5-3. *Complications with Breast Implants, U.S. Women, 1988*

Complications[a]	Characteristics of current implant (N = 168)	Characteristics of original implant leading to replacement (N = 25)
		Percentage of devices
Defect or malfunction	5.5	32.0
Infection	3.6	16.0
Pain	6.1	16.0
Healing problem	2.4	4.0
Blood clots	Not asked	4.0
Bleeding	Not asked	4.0
Injury	Not asked	0.0
Other	11.6	52.0
No complications	77.9	0.0

Source: Author's calculations from the Medical Device Implant Supplement to the 1988 National Health Interview Survey.

a. Complications are not mutually exclusive.

by surgical instruments during surgery, injury, or aging of the implant. A retrospective study performed by the FDA found that 69 percent of 344 women who had silicone implants inserted before 1988 had at least one ruptured implant, where the rupture was detected by an MRI examination.[17] Of the total sample of 344 women, 21 percent had gel leakage in one or both breasts.

The earlier implants used a thick envelope and a thick gel. Their advantage was that they were probably less prone to rupture and gel bleed, and if ruptured, the silicone was less likely to disperse through the body.[18] In an effort to reduce the extent of capsular contracture and to make the implants feel more natural, manufacturers switched to a thinner envelope and more fluid gel. The thinner envelopes seemed more prone to rupture, and even if intact, silicone leaked from the envelope and apparently migrated throughout the body. This phenomenon seemed to trigger the broad concern over health risks.

17. U.S. Food and Drug Administration (2000b).

18. Indeed, Frank Gerow M.D., one of the inventors of the silicone gel implant, testified that he and other surgeons would purposely rupture the envelope after the implant was in place, as the gel in use before the mid-1970s was extremely cohesive and would stay as a gel mass within the pocket. See *Henderson* v. *Heyer-Schulte Corp.* Court of Civil Appeals of Texas, Houston (1st Dist.), No. 17627, March 27, 1980.

Besides the localized problems, implants or silicone gel outside the implant can interfere with mammography, making breast cancers more difficult to detect. As the silicone migrates to other parts of the body, granulomas (lumps) may also form around the free silicone. Other localized problems include infections and hematoma.

The Même implant, sold by Surgitek, a subsidiary of Bristol-Myers Squibb, was covered with polyurethane foam similar to that used for chair cushions or filters for air conditioners. This foam was known to break down into TDA, considered a known cancer risk. The polyurethane-covered breast implant was intended to reduce capsular contracture; however, when the polyurethane did break down, surgeons reported that it could not be removed without disfiguring surgery. Approximately 200,000 to 400,000 American women had polyurethane-covered implants, mostly inserted between 1985 and 1990. These implants were removed from the market in April 1991 by Bristol-Myers Squibb as a consequence of FDA pressure. Recent evidence indicates unambiguously that the cancer risk from these implants is trivial, and that women with such implants should not have them removed because of feared cancer risks.

Systemic Problems and Epidemiological Evidence

Although localized problems such as capsular contracture are certainly undesirable side effects of implantation, these localized problems alone did not lead to the FDA ban on silicone implants. The concern of the FDA and the contentious issue in the courts was that leakage of gel from silicone implants causes more debilitating systemic diseases.

The possibility that silicone gel outside the implant envelope causes serious systemic health problems gained momentum in the 1980s, with connective tissue diseases (CTD) and other diseases attributed to the presence of silicone outside of the implant. CTDs and related disorders pertain to the connective tissues of the body such as fibrous tissues and cartilage. The posited mechanism is that exposure to silicone causes the woman's immune system to attack her own cells (that is, an autoimmune reaction.) Defined autoimmune diseases include rheumatoid arthritis, systemic lupus erythematosus, scleroderma, Sjogren's syndrome, polymyositis, and dermatomyositis. A variety of other signs and symptoms that have been linked to silicone implants include joint pain, headaches, chronic fatigue, dizziness, memory loss or problems with concentration, and so forth. Since the array of symptoms does not meet the criteria for a recognized disease, it has been proposed that exposure to silicone causes a new disease called by various names including "human adjuvant diseases," "silicone related syndrome," or "atypical disease."

All of these conditions attributed to silicone occur to some proportion of the population without silicone implants. Table 5-4 presents estimates of the background risks of these diseases. As the table demonstrates, the background risk for the various connective tissue diseases that formed the focal point of the breast implant litigation, such as systemic lupus erythematosus and scleroderma, are quite small, ranging from incidence of 1 per 100,000 or less for dermatomyositis and an upper bound of the estimated range of 38 per 100,000 for rheumatoid arthritis.

The task for litigation is to distinguish whether breast implants significantly increased the risk. The key statistic in epidemiology is the measure of relative risk and the corresponding confidence interval. A relative risk of 1.0 indicates no increased risk. If the value of 1.0 is included in the confidence interval, breast implants do not cause a statistically significant change in risk. Some courts require a doubling of the risks, corresponding to a relative risk of 2.0, which is then interpreted by courts as making it more probable than not that breast implants caused the disease. When dealing with such low-probability events, it is difficult to distinguish whether such a doubling of a risk has occurred, even if an effect of that magnitude was present.

To provide information on the risks of implants as well as to demonstrate the difficulty in assessing risks of breast implants, it is useful to discuss three epidemiological studies using data from the Mayo Clinic Study, the Nurses Health Study, and the Harvard Women's Health Cohort Study that received a great deal of media and legal attention. The study by Sherine E. Gabriel and others used medical records from the Mayo Clinic and affiliated hospitals in Olmstead County, Minnesota.[19] The study compared the incidence of CTDs in 749 women with breast implants to a comparison group of 1,498 women without implants. Within this sample, five implanted women and ten comparison women had any CTD as determined by review of the medical records, which yielded an adjusted relative risk of 1.10 with a 95 percent confidence interval of (0.37, 3.23). This study thereby demonstrates no increased risk from implants; however, given the sample size, the test had little power to detect an effect for any rare

19. Gabriel and others (1994).

Table 5-4. *Background Risk of Connective Tissue Diseases (CTD) in Women*

Disease	Incidence per 100,000 women
Rheumatoid arthritis	27.9–38.0
Systemic lupus erythematosus	2.5–11.4
Systemic sclerosis/scleroderma	1.2–2.0
Sjögren's syndrome	4.0
Dermatomyositis/polymyosisitis	0.3–1.0

Source: Adapted from table 1, III-34, Submission of Rule 706 National Science Panel Report, *In re* Silicone Gel Breast Implant Products Liability Litigation (MDL 926), 174 F. Supp.2d 1242 (N.D. Ala. 2001) (No. CV 92 N-10000-S).

disease. The authors note that assuming a background risk of 1.6 per 100,000 women of scleroderma, they would require a sample of 62,000 women with implants, and 124,000 without implants, followed for an average of ten years each, for a doubling of the relative risk to be detectable.

Jorge Sanchez-Guerrero and others used data from the Nurses Health Study.[20] The Nurses Health Study is a large cohort study started in 1976 with data on more than 120,000 individuals. The 1992 biennial questionnaires requested information on breast implants and injections. Based on self-reported prior information from the biennial questionnaires through 1990 about physician-diagnosed definite CTDs, rheumatic conditions, or other CTD, the authors calculated an adjusted relative risk for a definite CTD of 0.6 (95 percent confidence interval 0.2–2.0). Despite the large cohort, with 88,377 respondents in 1992, only 1,183 respondents had a breast implant of any type, and only 876 had silicone-gel-filled implants. By using medical information on CTDs reported only up to 1990, the authors avoided possible response bias arising from the vast media coverage that started in 1990. However, the study has been criticized for failing to capture other nonspecific complaints such as those arising in the litigation.

The largest study of the health risks of breast implants is based on data from the Harvard Women's Health Cohort Study. This is a retrospective cohort study of female health professionals conducted by Charles H. Hennekens and others.[21] The authors mailed a questionnaire to 1.75 million female health professionals between September 1992 and May 1995. This survey yielded 395,543 respondents who reported information on breast

20. Sanchez-Guerrero and others (1995).
21. Hennekens and others (1996).

implant status and year of implantation, and self-reported information on a diagnosis of five definite CTDs and any other CTD. The authors found statistically significant increases in the risk of "any CTD" and "other CTD" with relative risk values of 1.24 (95 percent confidence interval 1.08–1.41) and 1.30 (95 percent confidence interval 1.05–1.62) respectively. The relative risk for the individual CTDs were all above 1.0 but did not demonstrate a statistically significant increase in risk as the confidence intervals included 1.0. For example, the relative risk of rheumatoid arthritis was 1.18 (95 percent confidence interval 0.97–1.43). As the only major study to find an increase in relative risk, the results of this study have been widely used by plaintiffs to demonstrate the enhanced risk of breast implants. However, given the study design, the authors themselves interpret the study as demonstrating that any enhanced risks, if they exist, will be minor. Since the data were self-reported during a time of highly visible attention in the media, it is possible that women with implants and perceived illnesses were more likely to respond. Supporting this premise is the high reported implant rate that was at least twice the size reported elsewhere, as well as unusually high incidence rates of CTDs.

On balance, the science indicates that there are real and substantial localized problems with many implants, including rupture and capsular contracture. However, based on evidence that for the most part has been developed after the litigation emerged, there is little or no evidence of statistically significant increased risks of autoimmune diseases, and no evidence of risks sufficiently great to make it more probable than not that ailments such as CTDs are attributable to breast implants.

Yet despite the scientific consensus, those claiming that implants are indeed responsible for systemic diseases criticize these studies on two distinct grounds.[22] One criticism that has some merit is that the sample sizes in existing epidemiological studies are too small to detect rarely occurring diseases—that is, the power of the tests is low. Judge Sam C. Pointer, who was appointed to oversee the consolidated federal class action cases, commissioned a Rule 706 National Science Panel to synthesize the emerging literature on breast implant risks.[23] The panel performed a meta-analysis using the reliable available studies at the time, which allowed them to pool information from various smaller studies. Table 5-5 summarizes the

---

22. Another criticism, that as directly or indirectly the studies have largely been funded by the manufacturers, they are automatically suspect, will not be discussed here.

23. Submission of Rule 706 National Science Panel Report, *In re Silicone Gel Breast Implant Products Liability Litigation* (MDL 926), 174 F. Supp.2d 1242 (N.D. Ala. 2001) (No. CV 92 N-10000-S).

estimates of the relative risks of breast implants for various CTD categories. The vast size of the Hennekens study means that it will be accorded great weight in a meta-analysis; for this reason the Rule 706 National Science Panel provided relative risk estimates calculated with and without the Hennekens study. For all of the studies excluding the Hennekens study, the 95 percent confidence intervals include 1.0. When the Hennekens study is included in the meta-analysis, breast implants appear to statistically increase the risk of CTD, but with a risk level far short of the 2.0 standard.

The other major criticism is that silicone implants cause a new disease. Proponents of this view have criticized the epidemiological studies for examining only recognized diseases, therefore failing to uncover evidence of a new condition. In cases involving new diseases, the epidemiological studies will be attacked for not asking the right questions. However, the Sanchez-Guerrero study based on the Nurses Health Study was careful to check not only for existing diseases but also to note any signs or symptoms of these diseases. This study again failed to detect any relation between implants and systemic diseases.

The Institute of Medicine report explains the circularity of any reasoning that generates the existence of a new disease: "The disease definition includes, as a precondition, the presence of silicone breast implants, so it cannot be studied as an independent health problem. The committee finds that the diagnosis of this condition could depend on the presence of a number of symptoms that are nonspecific and common in the general population. Thus there does not appear to be even suggestive evidence for the existence of a novel syndrome in women with breast implants."[24]

There is no evidence that implants cause lupus, scleroderma, or rheumatoid arthritis. Implants are not associated with recognized diseases, and there is no reliable scientific evidence that silicone gel leakage causes a new disease. The Institute of Medicine report stated that the primary safety issue with silicone breast implants is local and perioperative complications,

24. The quotation appears in Bondurant and others (2000, p. 7). The problem with defining the disease by the presence of implants was eloquently expressed in *Kelley* v. *American Heyer-Schulte*, 957 F.Supp. 873, March 11, 1997: "Dr. Espinoza has found that the Plaintiff possesses anomalous antibody levels in her blood chemistry; this anomaly leads him, based upon his observations with other women, to conclude that the Plaintiff's condition is implant-related. However, the witness admits that if the Plaintiff did not have breast implants but had the exact same symptoms and blood chemistry, then his diagnosis would have been non-implant-caused Sjogren's Syndrome. Essentially, this is a bit like saying that if a person has a scratchy throat, runny nose, and a nasty cough, that person has a cold; if, on the other hand, that person has scratchy throat, runny nose, nasty cough, and wears a watch, they have a watch-induced cold."

Table 5-5. *Relative Risks of Connective Tissue Diseases (CTD) in Women Obtained from Adjusted Meta-Analysis*

Disease	Excluding Hennekens	Including Hennekens
	Relative risks (95% confidence interval)	
Definite CTD combined	0.80 (0.62, 1.04)	1.14 (1.01, 1.28)
Rheumatoid arthritis	1.04 (0.72, 1.51)	1.15 (0.97, 1.36)
Systemic lupus erythematosus	0.65 (0.35, 1.23)	1.01 (0.74, 1.37)
Systemic sclerosis/scleroderma	1.01 (0.59, 1.73)	1.30 (0.86, 1.96)
Sjögren's syndrome	1.42 (0.65, 3.11)	1.47 (1.01, 2.14)
Dermatomyositis/polymyosisitis	. . .	1.52 (0.97, 2.37)
Other autoimmune/rheumatic conditions	0.96 (0.74, 1.25)	1.15 (0.97, 1.36)

Source: Adapted from table 6, III-42, Submission of Rule 706 National Science Panel Report.

including "overall reoperations, ruptures or deflations, contractures, infections, hematomas, and pain."[25]

The epidemiological evidence of the 1990s uniformly fails to find evidence supporting a causal link between implants and defined diseases. It is, however, difficult to estimate low-probability events such as these, so that these results should be viewed with caution. Clearly, there are no apparent large risks from breast implants. However, the inclusion of the Hennekens study indicates an increased risk of CTD in some categories. The plaintiffs' successes in numerous cases do not imply that jurors overrode overwhelming epidemiological evidence. Rather, the weight given to scientific testimony, observable product defects, and identified plaintiffs with serious ailments is often greater than the weight given to epidemiology studies that are hampered by small sample sizes in comparison to the risk levels.

FDA Regulation of Drugs and Medical Devices

Understanding the failure of the FDA to ensure that breast implants were safe and to develop the informational base needed to assess breast implant risks requires an understanding of how the government regulates medical devices. Moreover, because silicone gel breast implants have been

25. Bondurant and others (2000, p. 5).

in use since 1962, one must also understand how the different eras of regulation since the advent of breast implants affected the FDA's authority over the product. This regulatory effort also established the backdrop for litigation in that it indicates the extent to which the government has or has not certified the product as having met regulatory standards for safety.

The first legislation giving the FDA authority over safety testing was the Food, Drug, and Cosmetic Act (FDC Act), which was signed into law in 1938. The FDC Act of 1938 gave the FDA the power to require premarket approval (PMA) of new drugs. The PMA process obligated companies to prove to the FDA that new drugs were safe before they were allowed to be marketed, although proof of efficacy was not required until 1962 under the Kefauver-Harris Drug Amendments.

However, premarket approval of medical devices, including breast implants, was not required. Manufacturers could introduce medical devices such as breast implants at their discretion. The FDA did have some authority over medical devices, but the mechanism of enforcement was litigation, not regulation. The FDA had the authority to ask the courts to discontinue sales or halt production of devices introduced into interstate commerce that were adulterated (contaminated by filth) or misbranded (falsely or misleadingly labeled.) In earlier years, this authority was broadly exercised, with 3,848 separate court actions in 1945. However, use of litigation dropped to 843 such actions in 1971.[26]

The failure to require premarket approval of medical devices in the legislation enacted in 1938 was in part related to the state of medical science at the time. Although many medical devices, such as tongue depressors, bandages, and bed pans, were in wide use, the more complex devices that worked by insertion into the body were still to come. Manufacturers began to introduce increasingly complex medical devices after World War II, such as cardiac pacemakers, renal catheters, surgical implants, artificial vessels and heart valves, intrauterine contraception devices, and replacement joints. However, extensions of the FDA's regulatory authority to address such products lagged behind their market role.

As more devices became marketed, the FDA sought expanded regulatory authority of medical devices commensurate with that provided for new drugs. One method the FDA used to expand its authority in the absence of new legislation was to use a broad definition of a drug. For example, the FDA regulated interocular lenses, soft contact lenses, weight-reducing kits,

26. Hutt (1995).

certain intrauterine devices, and some in vitro diagnostic products by classifying them as drugs.

Lacking direct authority to regulate, the FDA continued to use litigation to halt sales of adulterated or misbranded medical devices. Unsurprisingly, this was an expensive and inefficient process. Furthermore, simply removing from the market adulterated or misbranded devices did not touch the salient issue of safety, which is the concern with breast implants. Although hearings were held on the desirability of increasing FDA oversight on medical devices since the late 1960s, it took the Dalkon Shield intrauterine device catastrophe to push through legislation.[27] The new Medical Device Amendments to the Food, Drug, and Cosmetic Act of 1938 were signed into law on May 28, 1976, giving the FDA authority to regulate medical devices fourteen years after silicone breast implants had been introduced.[28] Responsibility for regulation of medical devices was assigned to the FDA Center for Devices and Radiological Health.

The objective of the MDA was to "provide reasonable assurance of the safety and effectiveness of the new device" while "weighing any probable benefit to health from the use of the device against any probable risk of injury or illness from such use."[29] The FDA's authority was expanded to allow it to ban a device and require manufacturers to notify users of risks, repair or replace products, or give refunds. The FDA no longer had to pursue its mission through the courts.

The MDA required the FDA to classify all new medical devices into one of three classes: Class I (such as tongue depressors and elastic bandages), Class II (such as hearing aids), and Class III (such as heart valves and prosthetic hips). Class I devices are subject only to general controls on manufacturing. The MDA subjects Class II devices to performance standards, postmarket surveillance, guidelines for use, and other appropriate controls. Only Class III devices are required to submit proof of safety and effectiveness, and such devices cannot be marketed or sold until approved.

To obtain premarket approval for new devices, manufacturers are required to submit test data, including clinical studies showing that the

27. The Dalkon Shield intrauterine device, manufactured by A. H. Robins, was introduced in the United States in 1971. This unregulated device frequently caused pelvic inflammatory infections, which often caused infertility, spontaneous septic abortion, and other problems. Under pressure from the FDA, the manufacturer reluctantly removed this device from the market in 1974. But by then the damage was done. More than 3.6 million units had been sold, and the ensuing litigation resulted in 400,000 claimants, who received nearly $3 billion from the Dalkon Shield Claimants Trust.

28. 21 USC, sec. 360(c).

29. 90 U.S. Stat., p. 541.

device is safe and effective. When the MDA was passed in 1976, devices deemed "substantially equivalent" to a preamendment device already on the market were grandfathered in to the market, implying that they could remain on the market without further review. As silicone breast implants had been in use since 1962, they were grandfathered in. Nevertheless, breast implants were not explicitly guaranteed an exemption from such regulatory scrutiny. The FDA could also require that preamendment device manufacturers submit PMA applications. However, this authority was rarely used, with makers of only 9 percent of preamendment Class III devices required to submit PMA applications through 1991.[30]

The Regulatory History of Breast Implants

Following the enactment of the Medical Devices Amendments in 1976, the FDA had the authority to classify breast implants, and if they were classified as Class III, to require that manufacturers submit safety information in their premarket approval (PMA) applications. Classification of implants was slow.[31] The FDA General and Plastic Surgery Devices Panel recommended Class II status in 1978, despite evidence presented at the meeting that even intact implants might leak.[32] Ignoring this recommendation, in 1982 the FDA published in the *Federal Register* its proposed rule to classify implants as Class III devices. This classification was finally attained in June 1988.

The impetus for finally classifying implants as Class III devices largely arose from medical concerns. An increasing number of complications such as rupture, gel bleed, and capsular contracture were reported in the medical literature as well as to the FDA through the 1980s. Several concerns about risks were raised during the FDA's General and Plastic Surgery Devices Advisory Committee meeting in November 1988. The committee listed eight potential risks associated with breast implants: capsular contracture, breakage, bleeding outside the shell, migration of silicone to organs, interference with the accuracy of mammograms, calcification of the fibrous capsule, immune disorders, and cancer. The last two risks have not been borne out by the evidence, but the fact that the FDA noted these

30. U.S. House Committee on Energy and Commerce (1993, pp. 7–9).
31. The regulatory history is described in detail in U.S. House Committee on Human Resources (1992).
32. U.S. House Committee on Human Resources (1992, p. 5).

conditions as potential risks as recently as 1988 attests to the void in scientific information at the time.

With the Class III assignment, the FDA could now require PMA applications for all breast implants. But assigning Class III status is only the beginning of a long process. After issuing this final classification regulation, the manufacturers had thirty months to submit their PMA application, to allow time for research and data analysis.

But before requiring the PMA, the FDA had to first publish a 515(b) regulation in the *Federal Register,* which would describe known risks as well as the type of data required to demonstrate that the benefits exceed the risks. This final rule had to be available to the manufacturers at least ninety days before the deadline for their PMA. However, this final rule had not been written by December 1990, the end of the thirty-month period. The proposed regulations were issued in May 1990, the comment period ended in August 1990, and the final regulations were finally published in April 1991.

At this point, the manufacturers were given at least ninety days to respond. The due date was July 9, 1991. The FDA then had forty-five days after the submission to evaluate the applications to determine whether they should be granted a full review.

After evaluating the data submitted in July 1991, the FDA's General and Plastic Surgery Devices Panel concluded in November 1991 that the manufacturers' PMA applications did not adequately address the safety of implants. Three applications were rejected at this point, and these manufacturers were notified that they could no longer sell their products. Despite the recommendation of the FDA scientists to reject the seven remaining applications, the FDA informed the manufacturers that their applications were seriously flawed, and they were required to provide additional information by January 6, 1992. Their products could stay on the market until then but would have to be taken off the market on January 6, 1992, until the FDA completed its full review.

The subcommittee review of the PMAs documented certain shortcomings in all seven remaining applications. Criticisms of the applications were that most studied women for two years or less, so that information on long-term risks was not assessed; various biases owing to reporting and study design; inadequate pre-implant assessment; the majority of women were lost to the study after a few months; the samples of reconstruction patients were too small to allow separate reliable analysis; certain models of implants produced by manufacturers were not studied, as manufacturers assumed that safety was the same among models; and in several studies women were not asked about symptoms of connective tissue or autoimmune disorders, cancer, or other medical problems. Medical records of plastic surgeons would not reveal these conditions as women would consult other physicians for these conditions. The women returned to their plastic surgeon for complications directly related to their surgery, so information on such risks generally, if present, could not be assessed.

For example, the reviewer of Dow Corning's application noted that physicians were instructed to note only complications at the implant site, thereby ignoring any potential systemic adverse effects and underestimating the types and rates of complications. The McGhan study had limited and incomplete follow-up of implant patients and studied only two of its four implants models listed in its PMA. The Bioplasty study assessed only 6 percent of its 860 patients with its MISTI implants at the two-year follow-up, yet the company reported safety and efficacy as though a larger sample had been used.

Although Dow submitted information on animal studies, none of these studies examined silicone placed in or beneath the breast tissue. There were no studies of what "energy" would be required to rupture an implant.

Citing inadequate information, on January 6, 1992, FDA Commissioner David Kessler called for a voluntary moratorium on sales of silicone breast implants until the FDA and the advisory panel were able to review newly available information. The moratorium rested on two bases. First, the manufacturers' safety data were deemed inadequate, for reasons including those just noted. Second, the FDA wanted time to review new information. This included internal Dow documents that the FDA saw for the first time in December 1991, as well as new information from rheumatologists on a possible link between breast implants and connective tissue diseases.

Reconvening in February 1992 to review the new information, the General and Plastic Surgery Devices Panel concluded that no causal link had been established between implants and autoimmune diseases. Nonetheless, the panel recommended restricted use until more safety information was available, including information from epidemiology studies.

Kessler announced in April 1992 that the moratorium was lifted for women in urgent need of implants, which included women in three categories: replacement for rupture or contracture, reconstruction patients who had started the reconstructive process, and reconstruction patients who were not suited for saline implants. Until additional information on safety was available, silicone implants would not be available for purely cosmetic purposes. By this point, only two manufacturers, McGhan and Mentor, remained on the market, as Dow Corning, Bristol-Myers Squibb, and Bioplasty withdrew from the market in March 1992.

Although silicone implants were withdrawn from the market in 1992, saline-filled implants remained available. Like silicone implants, saline implants had been grandfathered in 1976, and the FDA had not required manufacturers to go through the PMA process. The FDA started the PMA regulatory process for saline implants shortly after silicone implants were removed from the market, and both Mentor Corporation and McGhan Medical Corporation were granted approval to market their saline-filled breast implants by the FDA in May 2000. These implants were approved for reconstruction and for augmentation in patients age eighteen and older.

The Environment Leading to the 1992 FDA Ban

Kessler's decision to withdraw silicone implants from the market occurred in the context of active lobbying efforts and widespread media attention, for and against implants. Pressure for enhanced regulatory controls came from the Public Citizen's Health Research Group, the Boston Woman's Health Book Cooperative, the Command Trust Network, and the National Woman's Health Network.[33] In contrast, other groups such as the Breast Implant Information Foundation and the National Organization of Women with Implants lobbied for continued availability of implants after mastectomy.

Ralph Nader's Public Citizen Health Research Group, under the leadership of Sidney Wolfe, began raising alarms over a possible connection of silicone breast implants to cancer in the 1980s. Wolfe's and Public Citizen's interest in breast implants was fairly obvious. Implants had not been regulated for years after the FDA had the authority to do so; if implants were indeed a public health problem, Public Citizen would have additional evidence to support a more activist regulatory regime.

There was a flurry of activity, with questions raised about the safety of

33. Palley and Palley (1999, p. 12).

silicone implants on several fronts in December 1990. The television program "Face to Face with Connie Chung" featured an episode in which women claimed that their various health conditions, such as dizziness, swollen glands, fatigue, and so forth, were caused by their implants.[34] Chung began this episode with the dramatic statement: "For almost 30 years, American women have been getting breast implants, [with] an astounding average of 350 implant operations each day. But what is shocking is that these devices haven't been approved by the federal government. Only now is the government looking at the dangers. But, for some women, it may be too late." Sybil Goldrich, co-founder of Command Trust Network, dramatically exposed her scarred and disfigured chest from operations to remove implants to Chung's audience.

A week after Chung's show aired in December 1990, Representative Ted Weiss headed a congressional hearing on implant safety. Weiss was highly critical of "the anti-regulatory attitude of the Reagan administration." Only three scientific experts testified, and all were employed by plaintiffs in litigation.[35] Among the concerns raised in this hearing was the unavailability of various Dow Corning documents that were sealed by court order in consequence of the Stern verdict in 1984 (discussed in the following pages).

As an example of efforts on the other side, in 1991 the American Society of Plastic and Reconstructive Surgeons (ASPRS) actively lobbied to keep breast implants on the market. An example of their efforts included paying for almost 400 women to fly to Washington to lobby about the importance of implants to their self-esteem. Their pro-breast implant arguments included the scare tactic that women would be less likely to seek medical attention for lumps if silicone implants were not an option.[36]

Besides manufacturers' information, other interest groups weighed in on the safety of implants. Much of the available information was misinformation or even intentionally misleading. For example, the American Society of Plastic and Reconstructive Surgeons (ASPRS) distributed information brochures on safety that were inconsistent with scientific research. They emphasized the low rate of capsular contracture, indicating it was 10 percent, rather than the 30–40 percent rate reported in the literature

---

34. This program was broadcast on December 10, 1990.

35. Nir Kossovsky and Frank Vasey testified in the 1991 Hopkins case; Pierre Blais in the Johnson trial as well as other consulting for plaintiffs.

36. U.S. House Committee on Human Resources (1992, p. 26).

of the time, and that implants are lifetime devices, again ignoring the high rate at which they were replaced.[37] In retrospect, their statement that "loose silicone does not appear to be a health risk" has been confirmed, although at the time of their writing the validity of this assertion simply was not known.

Similarly misleading information was provided by Dow Corning. In response to the widespread negative media attention, Dow Corning initiated an 800 telephone hotline in late 1991 to answer questions. FDA staffers who called the hotline were told that "scientific data and research show that they are 100 percent safe. . . . We have done lengthy studies as have thousands of plastic surgeons to show they are safe." Other callers were told on December 30, 1991, that "there has been significant testing on arthritis, scleroderma, lupus, and other problems with the immune system. There is no link between this or cancer or silicone problems" and that "there is no detrimental effect to having silicone in the body."[38] At the end of 1991, there simply were no lengthy studies or scientific evidence to support the claims of proven safety.

Opponents of breast implants also provided misleading information. Evidence that silicone gel caused cancer in rats and that it might do so in humans was discussed in the 1988 meeting, but FDA officials emphasized that the results were inconclusive. The impetus was internal documents from Dow describing rat studies and provided by Public Citizen, in which Dow Corning scientists had implanted a blob of silicone gel under the skin of 200 rats in 1985–87. Twenty to 25 percent of the rats developed fibrosarcoma. However, as discussed earlier, it was well known among scientists that rats often developed fibrosarcoma if any large smooth object was implanted under their skin, and that there was simply no evidence that this result also occurs in humans. Despite the known lack of cancer risk of this sort to humans, Sidney Wolfe, M.D., president of Public Citizen, made public statements, picked up by the media, that implants were dangerous and should be banned.

Litigation and Safety Information

The court system began to take action against breast implants long before serious FDA scrutiny began. Although there were a few isolated

37. U.S. House Committee on Human Resources (1992, p. 35).
38. U.S. House Committee on Human Resources (1992, pp. 36–37).

suits in the 1970s based on ruptures, the real action in litigation did not begin until reports surfaced in the 1980s that silicone gel causes systemic diseases in humans. The first successful lawsuit against Dow occurred in 1977, awarding the plaintiff $170,000 for complications related to rupture.[39] Richard Mithoff, a Houston attorney, successfully argued that his client's ruptured implants and subsequent operations had caused pain and suffering. Patient information at the time claimed that leaks could occur only as a result of trauma. Although this case received little publicity, Dow then changed its package insert in 1978 to warn of potential nonpathogenic side effects such as rupture and scar tissue. The warnings about these potential side effects seemed to effectively prevent lawsuits against Dow on these grounds.

A turning point in litigation occurred with *Stern* v. *Dow Corning*.[40] In 1984, after a month-long jury trial, the jury awarded Maria Stern $211,000 for compensatory damages and $1.5 million for punitive damages. For the first time, the silicone-immune disorder connection was introduced by experts into court. Attorney Dan Bolton successfully argued that her connective tissue disease was attributed to silicone implants. The case turned on many internal Dow Corning documents discovered by Bolton in a Dow storage area discussed in the following paragraphs. The punitive damages were imposed because Dow Corning was found guilty of fraud in misrepresenting animal studies. The Dow documents produced in trial were then sealed by court order. The success of this case turned not on the strength of the scientific evidence that implants caused Stern's disease—there was none—but instead on the issues of corporate irresponsibility and fraud, including the jury's belief that Dow had doctored a dog study.

Dow's product warnings were changed in 1984 after this successful suit to acknowledge that there were "reports of suspected immunological responses to silicone mammary implants" but also that "convincing evidence does not exist to support a causal relationship between exposure to silicone materials and the acquisition or exacerbation of a variety of rheumatic and connective tissue disorders."[41]

In July 1991, Brenda Toole was awarded $5.4 million in her suit against Baxter/Heyer-Shulte.[42] The jury found that although Toole had

---

39. *V. Mueller & Co.* v. *Corley*, 570 S.W.2d 140 (Tex. Civ. App. 1978).

40. *Stern* v. *Dow Corning Corp.*, No. C-83-2348-MHP (N.D. Cal. Nov. 5, 1984).

41. Cited in Angell (1996, p. 57).

42. See chronology on *Frontline* (www. pbs.org/wgbh/pages/frontline/implants/cron.html [April 24, 2002]).

only preliminary symptoms of systemic autoimmune problems, she faced an increased risk of an autoimmune disease according to the plaintiff's experts, owing to the presence of silicone in her lymphatic system.

The trial of *Mariann Hopkins* v. *Dow Corning Corporation* is notable in that it brought to light the Dow Corning memos that had been sealed after the Stern trial.[43] Mariann Hopkins was awarded $7.3 million in December 1991, of which $6.5 million was for punitive damages, in her suit in California against Dow Corning. Hopkins claimed that her ruptured silicone implants had caused connective tissue disease. The suit alleged fraud, negligence, and product liability for Dow's failure to disclose information about the dangers of implants, with many of the memos presented initially at the Stern trial also presented as evidence in the Hopkins trial.

This trial raised two important issues that were influential in shaping future regulation and litigation outcomes. Although the severity of Hopkins's connective tissue disease was not disputed, Dow Corning denied that a causal link between silicone breast implants and CTD had not been established, and Hopkins's expert testimony was not admissible. However, as of 1991 (and indeed until 1994) there simply was no epidemiological evidence that could provide such information. The court noted that "the record reflects that Hopkins's experts based their opinions on the types of scientific data and utilized the types of scientific techniques relied upon by medical experts in making determinations regarding toxic causation when there is no solid body of epidemiological data to review."[44]

In affirming the punitive damages award, the court noted that "given the facts that Dow was aware of possible defects in its implants, that Dow knew long-term studies of the implants' safety were needed, that Dow concealed this information as well as the negative results of the few short-term laboratory tests performed, and that Dow continued for several years to market its implants as safe despite this knowledge, a substantial punitive damages award is justified."[45]

What was in these incriminating memos that had such influence at trial? The memos included such information as the following.

A February 1975 memo noted concern about inflammatory reaction to implants in Dow Corning's animal studies. Tom Talcott, a Dow engineer,

43. *Hopkins* v. *Dow Corning Corp.*, 1991 WL 328043 (N. D. Cal. Jan. 9, 1991).
44. Indeed, as part of its defense, Dow Corning claimed that "a simple investigation would have revealed to Hopkins the possible connection between implants and MCTD [multiple connective tissue disease]" —a connection that Dow Corning denied existed! *Hopkins* v. *Dow Corning Corp.*
45. *Hopkins* v. *Dow Corning Corp.*, 33 F.3d 1116 (9th Cir. 1994).

wrote a memo in May 1975 that in part reads, "We are hearing complaints from the field about the demonstration samples they are receiving. The general claim is that the units bleed profusely after they have been flexed vigorously. . . . Please run appropriate testing when you receive these samples to determine if a bleed rate problem exists."[46]

Dow senior clinical research specialist Art Rathjen wrote in a June 1976 memo, "I have proposed again and again that we must begin an in depth study of our gel, envelope, and bleed phenomenon. Capsule contracture isn't the only problem. Time is going to run out for us if we don't get underway."

Plastic surgeons had also contacted the company over concerns about gel bleed and rupture. For example, plastic surgeon Charles Vinnik wrote to a Dow vice president in September 1981 about "considerable silicone reaction to the extruded material" to an implant that was "totally disrupted with the implant shell incorporated within the gel mass" and the presence of "an obvious siliconoma." Emphasizing the limited information made available to surgeons, Vinnik continued to voice his concerns about the high rupture rate and silicone gel bleed reaching the tissues. His September 1985 letter reads in part, "Inasmuch as this is not generally known by my colleagues, I feel that your company has both a moral and legal obligation to make this information available through your representatives and in your literature."

A 1983 Dow Corning memo presented by Dan Bolton at the Stern trial stated, "I want to emphasize that to my knowledge, we have no valid long-term implant data to substantiate the safety of gels for long-term implant use."

One of the memos that continued to haunt Dow Corning was directed to the salespeople:

> It has been observed that the new mammaries with responsive gel have a tendency to appear oily after being manipulated. This could prove to be a problem with your daily detailing activity where mammary manipulation is a must. Keep in mind that this is not a product problem; our technical people assure us that the doctor in the O.R. will not see any appreciable oiling on the product removed from the package. The oily phenomenon seems to appear the day following manipulation. You should make plans to change demonstration samples often. Also, be sure samples are clean and dry

46. The memos quoted in this section were publicly released by Dow Corning on February 10, 1992. These memos have been widely quoted in numerous sources including Angell (1996) and U.S. House Committee on Human Resources (1992).

before customer detailing. Two easy ways to clean demonstration samples while trav-
eling, 1) wash with soap and water in nearest washroom, dry with hand towels, 2)
carry a small bottle of IPA and rag. I have used both methods and the first is my
choice. I will be interested to hear if any of you are seeing the oiling.

Memos produced in *Johnson* v. *Medical Engineering Corporation*
(MEC) also showed that safety information had been suppressed or
destroyed. MEC's Scientific Affairs Committee speculated in April 1977
that silicone oil bleeding through the shell and to the body tissue might
cause the FDA to remove silicone gel implants from the market. A 1978
document reported beagle studies demonstrating adverse reactions such as
hemorrhage, possible pneumonia of the lung, and hyperplasia of lymphoid
tissue in the large intestines. The company president said to "sacrifice dogs
ASAP" and to keep "no organs of dogs in freezer." In responding a year
later to a letter about animal maintenance costs, this president wrote, "I
thought we wiped out all dogs and had parts sent to W. L. [a company
vice president]. My rec[commendation]—kill dogs; forget organs; just dis-
pose of them."[47]

Given what is now known about the safety of silicone implants, the
memos serve not to provide evidence that implants are indeed risky but
instead to demonstrate that the manufacturers had suppressed warning
signs along the way and had not resolved or even researched the safety issue
despite litigation that highlighted potential areas of concern. Keep in mind
that to date there were no epidemiological studies that may have demonstrated the safety of implants. Thus these memos provide the informational context in which juries had to make decisions. They could not defer
judgment to wait for more scientific evidence.

The most notable outcome of the Stern and Hopkins trials is that
although the court records were sealed in the Stern case, the information
revealed at trial eventually made its way to the FDA and was ultimately
influential in shaping regulation. Notably, much of the information on
what manufacturers knew or suspected about health risks before 1991
became available only as a result of litigation. At the November 1988 FDA
meeting, a lawyer, a former Dow engineer, and other experts testified that
they had seen information indicating that Dow Corning and other manufacturers had concealed safety information and verbally described this

47. U.S. House Committee on Human Resources (1992, p. 35).

information. The documents they described had been produced in the 1984 case of *Stern* v. *Dow Corning*. Dow Corning released these internal documents to the FDA in February 1992 as a result of the Hopkins trial.

Litigation after the FDA Moratorium

The public concern generated by these cases and the information that was obtained as part of the litigation contributed to the regulatory interest in breast implants. The moratorium announced by Kessler in 1992 on the distribution or implantation of implants in turn opened the floodgates for new litigation. There were thousands of lawsuits after the FDA required that silicone implants be removed from the market. For example, by December 1991, there were 137 individual lawsuits filed against Dow Corning. The number of suits surged after that, as more than 3,000 lawsuits were filed against Dow Corning in 1992, increasing to more than 8,000 new cases in 1993 and close to 7,000 new cases in 1994. The other manufacturers were also hit with lawsuits.

Perhaps the most consequential litigation outcome of the FDA's moratorium imposed in January 1992 was a class action suit filed in February 1992 by Cincinnati lawyer Stan Chesley. Eventually all federal cases were transferred to Alabama federal judge the Honorable Sam C. Pointer. After two years of negotiation, a class action settlement was approved in which the four major breast implant manufacturers—Dow Corning, Baxter, Bristol-Myers Squibb/MEC, and 3M—would contribute $4.25 billion, with Dow Corning responsible for nearly half of the total. Women who presented medical evidence of a connective tissue disease or of symptoms of such diseases that began or worsened after their breast implants were inserted would receive payments based on age and type of disease. Potential class members were told they would each receive between $200,000 and $2 million, later reduced to $105,000 to $1.4 million. Class members would be able to opt out if the number of claims filed reduced the settlement amount below the original estimate.

The large number of claims filed—more than 440,000 women filed claims by spring of 1995— would result in individual claimants receiving only a small percentage of the original offer. More than 15,000 class members opted out of the proposed settlement, and the settlement fell apart by May 1995. By this time, Dow Corning was a defendant in more than 19,000 individual breast implants suits and at least forty-five class actions, as well as in 470 more suits involving nonbreast implant medical products. Dow Corning filed for bankruptcy reorganization in 1995 in reaction to the flood of suits.[48] The global settlement was reconfigured without Dow Corning, and Dow Corning also crafted its own settlement.

Juries awarded plaintiffs large damages throughout the early 1990s, as no new information on safety was yet available. In December 1992, Texas attorney John O'Quinn successfully argued that Pamela Jean Johnson's ruptured implants were linked to her mixed connective tissue disease, autoimmune responses, chronic fatigue, muscle pain, joint pain, headaches, and dizziness. Even though her expert witnesses and lawyers described her symptoms as amounting to a bad flu, Pamela Jean Johnson was awarded $25 million in her Texas suit against Bristol-Myers Squibb, of which $20 million was for punitive damages.

In March 1994, a Houston jury awarded three women $27.9 million in a case against 3M. Once again John O'Quinn represented the plaintiffs. Of the total award, $15 million represented punitive damages, with the remainder compensation for illnesses identified as atypical lupus, neurological impairment, and a "silicone induced" autoimmune problem.

Gladys Laas v. *Dow Corning*, February 1995, was the first major trial after the Mayo Clinic study failed to show any causal effect of implants on systemic health conditions.[49] This case indicated that the early scientific evidence apparently carried little weight in jury decisionmaking. Laas received implants for reconstruction. She claimed her surgeon told her the implants were harmless and would last a lifetime, and she was happy with her implants for thirteen years. Her health problems started around 1990. She reported that her shoulders would freeze up, her face would sting, and she had double vision, numbness in the tip of her tongue, memory loss, and spasms. When her suit against Dow Corning went to trial in 1995, the jury awarded her $5.2 million in compensation. Two jurors interviewed by Frontline after the trial stated that they gave little weight to the Mayo study. As my earlier discussion indicated, this study involved a small sample and had low power to detect an increase in risk. The jurors did not think silicone caused Laas's disease, and that while there was no evidence that silicone was harmful, there was also no evidence that it was safe. They

48. *In re Dow Corning Corp.*, 187 B.R. 919, 922 (E.D. Mich. 1995).
49. *Gladys J. Laas*, et al. v. *Dow Corning Corp.*, et al., No. 93-04266, 157th Judicial District (Harris County, Tex., Dist. Ct. 1995).

stated that they awarded so much money because Laas was sick and needed money for housework help and medical bills.[50]

With Dow Corning under bankruptcy reorganization, the question arose whether Dow Chemical, the parent company, could be held liable. This question was answered affirmatively in *Mahlum* v. *Dow Chemical* in Reno, October 1995.[51] Charlotte Mahlum was awarded $3.9 million in compensatory damages and $10 million in punitive damages. In 1998 the Nevada Supreme Court upheld the compensatory damages but set aside the punitive damages award.[52] At this time, there were about 13,000 pending implants suits against Dow Chemical. State appellate courts varied in whether they held Dow Chemical liable.

Plaintiffs have recently received large damages awards in breast implant cases, although some are overturned. Some recent examples are *Meister* v. *MEC* in which a DC jury awarded $10 million in compensatory damages in 1999, and *Barrow* v. *Bristol-Myers*, a 1998 nonjury case in Florida in which the plaintiff was awarded $357,000 in compensatory damages and $400,000 in punitive damages.[53]

Litigation continues among the opt-out cases despite the scientific evidence, although it appears that the dramatic damages awards of the early 1990s are becoming more rare, and judges seem to be more inclined to dismiss cases for lack of scientific evidence of causality. For example, Oregon Federal Judge Robert E. Jones appointed a panel of masters similar to that appointed by Judge Sam Pointer and, based on their report determining that silicone breast implants did not cause the alleged diseases, declined to allow the plaintiffs' experts to testify.[54]

Concluding Remarks

All of the attention directed to the safety of implants was not in vain. Moving on beyond the undeniably weak studies submitted by the manufacturers as part of the PMA process, society has had the benefit of rigorously

50. *Frontline*, February 27, 1996.

51. *Mahlum* v. *Dow Chemical Co.*, No. CV-9305941, 1995 WL 725642 (Nev. Dist. Ct. Nov. 7, 1995).

52. *Dow Chemical Co.* v. *Mahlum*, 970 P.2d 98 (Nev. 1998).

53. *Meister* v. *Medical Engineering Corp.*, No. 92-CV-02660-WBB (D.D.C. Aug. 29, 1999) aff'd 267 F.3d 1123 (D.C. Cir. 2001); *Barrow* v. *Bristol-Myers Squibb*, 1998 WL 812318 (M.D. Fla. Oct. 29, 1998), aff'd 190 F.3d 541 (11th Cir. 1999).

54. *Hall* v. *Baxter Healthcare Corp.*, 947 F. Supp. 1387 (D. Or. 1996).

conducted studies that were scrutinized not only through the journal peer review process but also subjected to rigorous scrutiny by several appointed science advisory panels.

The story of breast implants is like a roller coaster ride. After emergence of substantial and increasing fears of health risks, concerns tied to scientific evidence have subsided. In the simplest terms, breast implants were faulty products, as they often ruptured and hardened, causing breasts to be painful or even unsightly. The manufacturers knew of these product problems from at least the early 1970s—indeed the problem of capsular contracture prompted most of the product innovations. As a result of litigation that found companies liable for such problems, manufacturers provided hazard warnings to alert physicians and consumers to these risks. Whether implants caused only localized problems or also caused serious systemic health problems was unknown until recently. The manufacturers clearly had information from the early 1970s that raised alarms over health risks, but they suppressed such information. However, with the new scientific studies that followed the litigation explosion, we know that the unique risks of silicone implants are restricted to localized problems.

In the breast implant situation, litigation did not lead to new regulations. The regulations granting the FDA authority to regulate implants as a medical device were passed in 1976. However, as implants had been in use since 1962, they were grandfathered in, and the FDA did not require the manufacturers to go through the premarket approval process for another fifteen years, until murmurs of possibly serious health problems caused by implants turned into shouts.

Litigation played an important role in spurring FDA action. Information about suppressed safety information discovered in the 1984 Stern trial was reported at the FDA advisory meeting in 1988. This information, which was new to the FDA, generated the impetus for the FDA to require that the manufacturers submit information on safety and efficacy. When the manufacturers ultimately submitted information, their submitted information was too inadequate to meet scientific standards, and the FDA reacted by imposing a moratorium on silicone implants. In turn, the FDA ban on implants sparked large-scale litigation beginning in 1992.

As a consequence of the costly litigation, Dow Corning and other manufacturers withdrew from the implant market entirely rather than continue to seek FDA approval to market implants. Also in consequence of the litigation, judges convened scientific panels to study the health risks of silicone implants. Together with the study by the Institute of Medicine, the conclusion of this careful scrutiny is a consensus that silicone breast implants do not cause systemic or autoimmune diseases.

The message of the breast implant story is that the FDA dropped the ball and then overreacted when rejoining the game. Had the FDA requested information from the manufacturers in a more timely fashion, the risks, or lack of risks, would have been known, and the litigation crisis would have been avoided. Breast augmentation is a highly popular cosmetic surgery, as saline-filled implants remained on the market while going through the premarket approval process after silicone implants were banned. Silicone implants had been overwhelmingly preferred to saline when both types were marketed. In the light of the increasingly compelling scientific information, perhaps silicone implants will be granted broad marketing approval.

The principal lesson of the breast implant experience is that the FDA has the power to create substantial public alarm and drive mass litigation. Obtaining scientific information in a timely manner, and giving appropriate weight to the scientific evidence as opposed to worst-case fears, would have eliminated the breast implant debacle. Whether the FDA has learned this lesson is unclear. The current experience with phenylpropanolamine (PPA) is so far following the breast implant paradigm. PPA was grandfathered in when the Food, Drug, and Cosmetic Act was passed in 1938, and it was used annually by millions of Americans in popular over-the-counter cold remedies and appetite suppressants. Only one epidemiological study demonstrates an increased risk of hemorrhagic stroke and then only among women using appetite suppressants.[55] Legitimate questions exist about whether these results would be replicated in a larger study. Nevertheless, the FDA successfully requested a voluntary recall of products containing PPA. Fortunately, it is much easier for people to give up their favorite cold remedy than to have breast implants removed out of fear of life-threatening illnesses. However, the FDA's action has launched a deluge of class action and individual lawsuits that have yet to be resolved.

55. Kernan and others (2000, p. 1830). The relative risk is 16.58, with the 95 percent confidence interval of (1.51- 182.21). These values are based on six cases with stroke and one control. Statistically significant effects were not present for any men or any other subgroup of women.

COMMENT BY
Peter Schuck

I would like to comment on Joni Hersch's interesting chapter by identifying some facts in it and then giving them a somewhat different interpretation than Hersch did.

The first is that a breast implant is a very valuable product. One million women purchased these implants. Hersch says that she thinks it costs about $2,000 to do so, so that's a $2 billion value that women evidently placed on this product. I also understand from Hersch that the breast implants have been restored to the market in most or all European countries. So the demand is there, and this demand must be weighed in the balance.

Second, by 1992, when the Food and Drug Administration imposed this ban, the product had been on the market for thirty years. That is a long time. That is a very large body of data on the effectiveness and safety of the product. Now, it is not clear to me from the science whether long-term, latent effects are alleged to result from exposure to this product, or whether, if the causal pattern is as alleged, the damage happens quickly. My understanding is that damage is evident more quickly. We are not dealing with a latency period of thirty or forty years, as happens with exposure to asbestos.

A third fact is that very little systematic, long-term research had been conducted by 1992. Again, this product had been on the market for thirty years, so a very large number of women had used the product and quite satisfactorily so.

Four, the FDA had grandfathered this product until 1988. The manufacturers believed this product was going to be regulated on a Class II basis, which meant that they would not have to conduct the kinds of studies for which they were subsequently criticized as not having conducted. And manufacturers only learned in 1988 that the implants were going to be classified as a Class III device, and therefore the companies had to conduct these studies. Hersch also tells us that the FDA's advisory panel recommended that the product be classified as a Class II device, not a Class III device, thereby fortifying any belief that the companies might have had that they would not be required to produce this kind of research.

A fifth fact that certainly is incontrovertible is that plaintiffs won huge compensatory awards by any standards. The plaintiffs did not die because of these products. They suffered terribly, no question about that. But given the norms of personal injury verdicts, the compensatory awards mentioned in this chapter, at least, were very high. And these awards were rendered, in some cases, even after the epidemiological evidence had, as far as such evidence can, exonerated the product.

It seems to me that silicone gel breast implants have a good deal in common with Bendectin, in which, again, juries rendered very large verdicts even after the epidemiological evidence, virtually unanimously, had exonerated the product. Hersch mentions a trial court in Washington, D.C., that rendered one of these large verdicts after data failing to show causation had come in. The same thing happened to Bendectin, in the Oxendine case (*Oxendine* v. *Merrill Dow Pharmaceuticals*). Well after Bendectin had been proved a very useful product and one that created no untoward effects, the jury gave the plaintiff a large award.

These punitive damage awards, which by Hersch's account seem to have been routine in these cases, were also enormous, presumably because of the perception by the juries of corporate wrongdoing. Recall that these punitive damage awards were rendered even though the product had been grandfathered until 1988. As I understand the regulatory scheme, therefore, the manufacturers were under no obligation to have conducted systematic, long-term research. Again, the product had been in use, at that point, for twenty-six years, without any evidence that it caused systemic harms of the kinds alleged by the plaintiffs.

Now, maybe there was evidence of a cover-up by companies. But the evidence presented in the chapter of a cover-up does not seem very clear-cut. There are two examples. Perhaps if one looked at them closely, they would constitute a cover-up, but one of them is based on a memorandum to the sales force urging salespeople to move oil before showing the product to potential buyers, which seems to me an innocuous and perhaps even sensible precaution. I do not know the context well enough to judge for sure. And the second is a memo connected with the sacrificing of dogs that apparently had evidence of some pathological symptoms. Again, it is hard to know, without knowing more about the context, whether or not sacrificing the dogs was a cost-saving move. Something in Hersch's account suggests that this decision was part of an effort by the management to reduce the cost of animal maintenance. This may have been a pretext. I have absolutely no idea. But the evidence of a cover-up is at least ambiguous.

The last interesting fact, which Richard A. Epstein and David Rosenberg will certainly debate, is that the class action courts in Alabama and

Oregon handled these disputes in a much more systematic way than other courts. In Alabama and Oregon, courts kept complex scientific disputes away from the jury until the scientific disputes were resolved in the sense that, according to the courts, no reasonable juror could find causation.

Given the nature of epidemiological evidence, which deals with large populations, and given that the class contained 400,000 or more women—maybe it was even the more than one million women who had purchased implants—the isomorphism between the size of the class and the size of the population studied epidemiologically strengthens the no-causation inference that the court could draw from this evidence. A class action facilitates this inference.

I am left with a few broader questions that grow out of this episode. The first—and I really am agnostic about the answer—is whether the industry's initial decision not to conduct long-term research before the late 1980s was a prudent one. Certainly, given what we know now, it was a sensible decision.

But given the facts I've emphasized from Hersch's account—that is, the long period of usage without much evidence of harm, a disease pattern without long latency periods, and that the product had been grandfathered until the late 1980s—it is plausible to think that the industry's decision not to conduct the research for which they are now being faulted was, at least at the time, a prudent one.

Another question is, what incentives does this create for the FDA? The FDA banned a product, which sparked massive litigation that brought the manufacturer into bankruptcy and produced claims and large judgments that were based on spurious scientific claims. I think that the FDA, in retrospect, would conclude that it ought not to have acted decisively in the way that it did. In the future the FDA may, other things being equal, be somewhat less energetic in pursuit of its statutory responsibilities.

Another question is whether punitive damages are appropriate when an agency regulates an industry closely, and the industry complies with the agency's orders. I raise this question even though there is evidence from Hersch's account, which I am prepared to believe, that the FDA did not regulate and monitor implants as vigilantly as it should have, particularly after the public commitment it made in 1992.

I am also concerned about the perversity of public policy that allows twelve people, or maybe it was six people, selected at random to impose huge punitive damage awards. These juries had no legal guidance about which criteria, other than their own sense of indignation, to apply to their judgments. After all, in the case of breast implants, the industry was regulated, compensatory damages were substantial, the reputational costs imposed on drug companies were enormous, and a number of other important factors came into play.

Finally, Hersch says that the lesson she draws from this episode is that the FDA should have acted sooner. She may be right, but I want to know what the regulatory opportunity costs of the FDA would have been. The FDA is a fairly small agency monitoring a very large set of industries. If the FDA had acted more vigilantly and vigorously, there are presumably other regulatory activities that it could not have conducted. I think that regulatory trade-off is especially poignant in the case of the FDA, because it is egregiously underfunded in light of its responsibilities. Until we know what the opportunity costs of the agency were, it is difficult to say, even in retrospect, that the agency should have acted sooner.

References

Angell, Marcia. 1996. *Science on Trial: The Clash of Medical Evidence and the Law in the Breast Implant Case.* W. W. Norton.

Bondurant, Stuart, Virginia Ernster, and Roger Herdman, eds. 2000. *Safety of Silicone Breast Implants.* Washington: National Academy Press, Institute of Medicine.

Bright, Rosalie A., Lana L. Jeng, and Roscoe M. Moore, Jr. 1993. "National Survey of Self-Reported Breast Implants: 1988 Estimates." *Journal of Long-Term Effects of Medical Implants* 3 (1): 81–89.

Cook, Ralph R., Robert R. Delongchamp, Maryann Woodbury, Laura L. Perkins, and Myron C. Harrison. 1995. "The Prevalence of Women with Breast Implants in the United States—1989." *Journal of Clinical Epidemiology* 48 (4): 519–25.

Gabriel, Sherine E., W. Michael O'Fallon, Leonard T. Kurland, C. Mary Beard, John E. Woods, and L. Joseph Melton III. 1994. "Risk of Connective-Tissue Diseases and Other Disorders After Breast Implantation." *New England Journal of Medicine* 330 (24): 1697–1702.

Hennekens, Charles H., S. E. I-Min Lee, Nancy R. Cook, Patricia R. Hebert, Elizabeth W. Karlson, Fran LaMotte, JoAnn E. Manson, and Julie E. Buring. 1996. "Self-Reported Breast Implants and Connective Tissue Diseases in Female Health Professionals." *Journal of the American Medical Association* 275 (8): 616–21.

Hutt, Peter Barton. 1995. "Philosophy of Regulation Under the Federal Food, Drug and Cosmetic Act." *Food and Drug Law Journal* 50: 101–09.

Kernan, Walter N., Catherine M. Viscoli, Lawrence M. Brass, Joseph P. Broderick, Thomas Brott, Edward Feldmann, Lewis B. Morgenstern, Janet Lee Wilterdink, and Ralph I. Horwitz. 2000. "Phenylpropanolamine and the Risk of Hemorrhagic Stroke." *New England Journal of Medicine* 343 (25): 1826–32.

Moss, Abigail J., Stanford Hamburger, Roscoe M. Moore, Lana L. Jeng, and L. Jean Howie. 1991. "Use of Selected Medical Device Implants in the United States, 1988." *Advance Data from Vital and Health Statistics of the National Center for Health Statistics* 191 (February 26).

Palley, Howard A., and Marian Lief Palley. 1999. "The Regulatory Process, the Food and Drug Administration, and the Silicone Breast Implant Controversy." *Journal of Health and Social Policy* 11 (1): 1–20.

Sanchez-Guerrero, Jorge, Graham A. Colditz, Elizabeth W. Karlson, David J. Hunter, Frank E. Speizer, and Matthew H. Liang. 1995. "Silicone Breast Implants and the Risk of Connective-Tissue Diseases and Symptoms." *New England Journal of Medicine* 332 (25): 1666–70.

Sarwer, David B., Jodi E. Nordmann, and James D. Herbert. 2000. "Cosmetic Breast Augmentation Surgery: A Critical Overview." *Journal of Women's Health and Gender-Based Medicine* 9 (8): 843–56.

Snyder, Jack W. 1997. "Silicone Breast Implants: Can Emerging Medical, Legal, and Scientific Concepts be Reconciled?" *Journal of Legal Medicine* 18 (2): 133–219.

U.S. Food and Drug Administration. 2000a. *Breast Implants: An Information Update.*

———. 2000b. *Study of Rupture of Silicone Gel-Filled Breast Implants.*

U.S. House Committee on Human Resources and Intergovernmental Relations, Subcommittee on Government Operations. 1992. *The FDA's Regulation of Silicone Breast Implants: A Staff Report.* 102 Cong. 2 sess. Government Printing Office (December).

U.S. House Committee on Energy and Commerce, Subcommittee on Oversight and Investigations. 1993. *Less Than the Sum of Its Parts: Reforms Needed in the Organization, Management, and Resources of the Food and Drug Administration's Center for Devices and Radiological Health.* Committee Print 103-N. 103 Cong. 1 sess. Government Printing Office.

DANIEL P. KESSLER
MARK B. MCCLELLAN

6 Malpractice Pressure, Managed Care, and Physician Behavior

Because of the complexity of medical care, the scope of coverage of managed care plans cannot be specified fully in contracts with providers or consumers. A medical treatment (or provider behavior) might be appropriate in some circumstances but inappropriate in others. For this reason, people, upon signing up for managed care, agree to give plans discretion in this dimension in exchange for the cost savings that this discretion may provide.

Inevitably, the same factors that create demand for the services of plans also create demand for regulation. Just as consumers find it difficult to evaluate the appropriateness of a physician's decisions about treatment, so do they find it difficult to evaluate whether the coverage decisions of their plan conform to the letter or spirit of their insurance contract. Regulation of plans, then, involves a fundamental trade-off. On one hand, limitations on discretion to manage utilization can protect patients from opportunistic behavior and the risk of mistakes by plans. (Even if coverage decisions by plans comply on average with the initial agreements with consumers, because individuals want to avoid the risk of a possible denial of coverage, even rare random mistakes by plan officials making decisions

The authors thank Laurence Baker, David Emmons, and Sara Thran for assistance and helpful discussions, and participants in the Brookings/AEI Joint Center for Regulatory Studies Conference on Regulation through Litigation for helpful comments. Funding from the Agency for Health Care Research and Quality through a grant to the National Bureau of Economic Research is greatly appreciated.

about coverage may be socially costly.) On the other hand, limitations on plans make them less valuable to consumers precisely because such limitations narrow the scope of the management services that consumers sought in the first place.

Because the social costs and benefits of restrictions on plans depend on the behavior of doctors and hospitals, appropriate managed care regulatory policy depends on the other incentives facing health care providers and on how managed care and these incentives interact to affect decisions about medical treatment. In particular, the incentives provided by the medical liability system and managed care are likely to interact. Moral hazard from health insurance means that physicians, hospitals, and patients may bear only a small fraction of the true costs of precautionary care. For this reason, as long as conventional liability law imposes penalties of the same magnitude as the costs of injuries, it would be expected to encourage defensive medicine—precautionary medical treatments that have minimal expected medical benefit but are administered because of fear of legal liability. The regulation of managed care may affect the costs to providers of precautionary care—and thus not only the effectiveness of managed care but also the prevalence of defensive medicine.

Unfortunately, because most of the regulatory policy options currently under discussion have no direct precedent, definitive evidence about their likely effects, and how they will interact with the existing liability system, is difficult to obtain.[1] To provide insight into the likely effects of these regulatory reforms, this chapter identifies empirically how the incentives provided by managed care and the malpractice system affect physicians' decisions about treatment. We analyze responses by physicians to several survey questions designed exclusively for this project, administered as part of the 1998 AMA Socioeconomic Monitoring Survey of physicians (AMA SMS). We match these survey responses with data on the characteristics of individual physicians and with state-level data on malpractice claims and managed care enrollment rates to measure differences across states in the importance of the malpractice system and managed care organizations to physicians' behavior.

---

1. State-law expansions of plans' liability for medical malpractice, such as those adopted by California, Georgia, Missouri, and Texas, are likely to have less dramatic consequences than the changes to federal law being proposed. The scope of the state-law expansions (in contrast to the proposed changes to federal law) is limited by the Employee Retirement Income Security Act (ERISA) of 1974, which has been interpreted as preempting most suits based on state law against health plans to recover damages for medical injuries.

First, we study how state indexes of managed care enrollment, physician characteristics, and what we call "malpractice pressure," that is, the incentives provided by the liability system to undertake precautionary care affect treatment decisions specific to five different medical specialties. We examine the use of treatments likely to have questionable indications in marginal patients, because it is in these patients that nonmedical factors are likely to have the greatest effects. For example, for obstetrician-gynecologists, we identify the determinants of the proportion of patients receiving a hysterectomy and the proportion of pregnant patients receiving at least one ultrasound. Second, we study how these same factors affect average time spent per patient office visit because the average number of minutes spent on an office visit is a measure of precautionary care that is valid across specialties. Third, we analyze detailed responses about physicians' experiences with the liability system for those physicians who experienced a malpractice claim in the past three years. We identify how the characteristics of the regulatory environment, and of physicians and their patients, affect physicians' self-reported description of the incident underlying the claim. We also identify which aspects of the malpractice system the respondent found most unpleasant.

Empirical Literature

Previous empirical work has shown that the incentives provided by the malpractice liability system and by managed care organizations have important effects on medical care. At the most basic level, this work shows that doctors and hospitals in areas with greater malpractice pressure practice more defensive medicine,[2] and that increasing penetration of managed care in the 1990s has reduced the use of some treatments that are likely to have little medical benefit.[3] One extension assesses empirically the extent to which managed care and "tort reform" that reduces liability interact to influence the cost of care and health outcomes of elderly Medicare beneficiaries with heart disease.[4] That work presents two main findings. First, although reforms that directly reduce liability (such as caps on damages)

2. See, for example, Rock (1988); Harvard Medical Practice Study (1990); Localio and others (1993); Kessler and McClellan (1996, 1997, 2000a); Dubay and others (1999); but see Baldwin and others (1995) for an alternative view.
3. See, for example, Baker (1999); Cutler and Sheiner (1998); Kessler and McClellan (2000b; forthcoming); Heidenreich and others (2001).
4. Kessler and McClellan (forthcoming).

reduce defensive practices in areas with low and high levels of managed care enrollment, managed care and direct reforms are substitutes, so the reduction in defensive practices that can be achieved with direct reforms is smaller in areas with high enrollment in managed care. Second, managed care and direct reforms do not interact over the long run in ways that are harmful to patients' health.

Other work has explored how aspects of hospital care are affected by managed care and malpractice pressure. For example, based on an analysis of Medicare beneficiaries hospitalized with heart disease, matched with data on malpractice claims and claims rates, we estimate the effect of financial and nonfinancial measures of malpractice pressure on diagnostic and therapeutic medical expenditures and in turn on patient health outcomes.[5] Although we found that malpractice claims rates and compensation conditional on a claim had the most important impact on medical expenditures (especially diagnostic expenditures), our results suggest that other policies that reduce the time spent and the conflict involved in defending against a claim can also reduce defensive practices substantially. Based on analysis of detailed clinical data from the Cooperative Cardiovascular Project, Paul A. Heidenreich and others investigate whether higher levels of overall managed care market share are associated with greater use of recommended therapies for Medicare fee-for-service patients with acute myocardial infarction.[6] After adjustment for patient characteristics, severity of illness, characteristics of the hospital of admission, specialty of treating physicians, and other area characteristics, patients treated in areas with high levels of managed care had greater relative use of beta blockers during hospitalization and at discharge and aspirin during hospitalization and at discharge, consistent with more appropriate care. Patients from areas with high enrollment in managed care may be less likely to receive angiography when compared with patients from areas with low levels of managed care, although this result was only marginally significant. Laurence C. Baker and others have focused on the related question of how managed care affects hospitals' decisions to make costly investments in high-technology equipment.[7]

Less attention has been given to how these incentives affect individual physicians' decisionmaking. This gap is important, especially because

5. Kessler and McClellan (2000a).
6. Heidenreich and others (2001).
7. See, for example, Baker and Brown (1999); Baker and Wheeler (1998).

many of the policy options under consideration have never been implemented. Understanding which signals to physicians lead them to change their behavior, and which aspects of their behavior are most responsive to changes in incentives, is necessary to simulate accurately the likely effects of proposed policies.

In previous work we examined how tort reforms altered physicians' perceptions of the appropriateness of medical care.[8] That work found that physicians from states adopting tort reforms that reduced liability reported significant relative declines in the perceived impact of malpractice pressure on practice patterns. However, this work did not measure actual physician behavior and did not attempt to assess the value of care induced or forgone by the change in malpractice-based incentives. This chapter extends this work by identifying how malpractice pressure and managed care affect five well-defined treatment decisions. It estimates the extent to which the characteristics of physicians affect their responses to the incentives provided by managed care and the liability system. Finally, it investigates how managed care and other factors affect the qualitative nature of physicians' encounters with the liability system.

Data and Models

We analyze responses to several questions on the physician survey designed exclusively for this project, administered as part of the 1998 AMA SMS.[9] The 1998 survey responses fall into two categories. First, we analyze responses to questions on practice patterns that are specific to five different medical specialties. We asked about the following decisions:

—For general practice-family practitioners and internal medicine physicians, the fraction of their patients in the past month with headaches and without known cancers who were referred for MRI or CT scans;

—For general practice-family practitioners and internal medicine physicians, the fraction of their patients in the past month with lower back pain who were referred to an orthopedic surgeon;

8. Kessler and McClellan (1997).

9. The SMS was administered during March through August 1998. We appreciate the efforts of David Emmons and Sara Thran at the American Medical Association for their help with the design of the following survey questions and their advice and assistance with the SMS survey more generally.

—For obstetrician-gynecologists, the fraction of completed pregnancies in the past year that received more than one ultrasound.

—For obstetrician-gynecologists, the fraction of patients in the past month receiving a hysterectomy;[10] and

—For urological surgeons, the fraction of surgeries in the past month that were radical prostatectomies.[11]

Finally, for all physicians (except psychiatrists, radiologists, anesthesiologists, and pathologists), we investigate the determinants of the average number of minutes per patient spent on an office visit in the most recent week of practice.

Second, we analyze detailed responses about physicians' experiences with the liability system for those physicians who experienced a malpractice claim in the past three years. We asked physicians which of the seven following types of alleged errors were most causally related to his or her most recent malpractice claim:

—The procedure in question was improperly performed;

—There was a failure to perform or delay in performing a necessary procedure;

—There was a diagnosis error;

—There was a failure or delay in referral, obtaining consultation, or hospital admission;

—There was a failure to supervise or monitor the case, including any failure to recognize a complication of treatment;

—There was some other medical error; or

—There was no medical error.

We also asked physicians which of the five following aspects of their experience with the liability system was most unpleasant:

—Damage to reputation;

—The expenditure of uncompensated, personal time;

—The delay and uncertainty in resolving the claim;

—The monetary costs of the claim; or

—Something else.

---

10. We proxy for the number of patients with the number of office visits and the number of hysterectomies.

11. We proxy for the number of surgeries with the number of radical prostatectomies and the number of transurethral resections of the prostate.

We match these survey responses with data on characteristics of individual physicians and with state-level data on malpractice claims and managed care enrollment rates. Information on physician characteristics from the SMS includes the fraction of a physician's patients covered by Medicare and Medicaid; whether the physician was a solo practitioner and/or an owner of his or her practice; and the number of years of the physician's experience (measured as years since first year of practice, excluding residency). We calculate a state-level index of managed care enrollment as the average enrollment per capita in managed care plans in January 1997 and July 1998, based on data from InterStudy.[12] We calculate a state-level index of malpractice pressure as the fraction of physicians in each state in the SMS sample experiencing a malpractice claim in the past three years.

Appendix tables 6A-1 and 6A-2 summarize the SMS and InterStudy data. Table 6A-1 shows, for example, that the average physician refers approximately 13 percent of patients with headache without known cancers for an MRI or CT scan; 10 percent of patients with back pain to an orthopedic surgeon; and more than one-third of completed pregnancies for more than one ultrasound over the course of the pregnancy. Table 6A-2 presents each state's rank in managed care enrollment and malpractice pressure for the study period, where higher ranks represent higher enrollment and claims rates. California, Oregon, and Massachusetts rank as the states with the greatest managed care enrollment per capita; New Jersey, Louisiana, and Utah rank as states with the most intensive malpractice pressure.

We use three types of models to estimate the effect of managed care, malpractice pressure, and physician characteristics on physicians' decisionmaking. First, we use grouped logit to model each of the specific treatment decisionmaking processes because our data take the form of the proportion of a physician's patients receiving or not receiving a treatment. Under the assumption that the underlying model of the probability of patient i of physician j in state s receiving a treatment T is

$$(1) \qquad \Pr\!\left(T_{ijs}=1\right)=\frac{e^{\alpha_r + w_s\beta + x_j^\gamma + z_i\delta}}{1+e^{\alpha_r + w_s\beta + x_j^\gamma + z_i\delta}},$$

where α_r denotes a region-specific constant term, w_s is a vector describing the managed care enrollment and malpractice pressure in state s, x_j is a

12. We appreciate Laurence Baker's assistance in obtaining and using the InterStudy HMO enrollment data.

vector describing the physician's characteristics, and z_i is a vector describing the patient's characteristics, the parameters (β, γ, δ) can be obtained from the weighted-least-squares regression

$$(2) \qquad \ln\left(\frac{P_{js}}{1-P_{js}}\right) = \alpha_r + w_s\beta + x_j\gamma + \bar{z}_j\delta + \eta_{js}$$

with weights $\eta_{js}p_{js}(1 - p_{js})$, where $p_{js} = T_{js} / \eta_{js}$, T_{js} is the number of physician j's patients receiving treatment T, $\bar{z}_j$ is the average for physician j of z_i, and η_{js} is the total number of physician j's patients.[13]

Second, we use linear weighted least squares to model the process determining the time spent per patient,

$$(3) \qquad \ln(m_{js}) = \alpha_r + w_s\beta + x_j\gamma + \bar{z}_j\delta + \eta_{js},$$

where m_{js} is minutes per patient, with weights η_{js}, representing the total number of physician j's office visits.

Third, we use multinomial logit to model the process underlying the types of alleged medical errors and other physician experiences with the liability system, defining the probability that physician j reports a medical error or other experience of type E = 1, . . . , 7 (types of medical errors) or E = 1, . . . , 5 (types of other experiences with the liability system) as

$$(4) \qquad \Pr(E_{ijs} = k) = \frac{\exp\left(\alpha^{(k)} + w_s\beta^{(k)} + x_j\gamma^{(k)} + \bar{z}_j\delta^{(k)}\right)}{\sum_K \exp\left(\alpha^{(k)} + w_s\beta^{(k)} + x_j\gamma^{(k)} + \bar{z}_j\delta^{(k)}\right)}.$$

Results

Tables 6-1 and 6-2 present the estimated effects of state, patient, and physician/practice characteristics on the six treatment decisions we study without and with controls for region effects, respectively. The tables show that both malpractice pressure and state managed care enrollment affect physicians' decisionmaking, although malpractice pressure affects a broader range of the treatment decisions that we examine than does state

13. Greene (1997, chap. 19).

average managed care enrollment. Patients from states with high levels of managed care enrollment are less likely to receive a hysterectomy (although these results become statistically insignificant when we include eight indicator variables to control for the census region of physician practice). In contrast, malpractice pressure significantly increases the usage of diagnostics such as an MRI or CT scan for patients with a headache, and the usage of intensive therapeutic procedures such as hysterectomy and radical prostatectomy. Physicians from areas with high levels of enrollment in managed care plans spend statistically significantly more time per patient office visit, and physicians from areas with high malpractice pressure spend statistically significantly less time per patient office visit. Patients from states with above-median managed care enrollment experience office visits that are approximately 7 percent longer, and patients from states with above-median malpractice pressure have office visits that are approximately 7 percent shorter.

Characteristics of physicians and their patient populations also affect physicians' use of the treatments we study. Not surprisingly, physicians with high proportions of elderly patients are more likely to refer patients with headache for imaging and more likely to order hysterectomies. The less experienced general practice-family practice and internal medicine physicians are more likely to refer patients for testing or treatment, although less experienced obstetrician-gynecologists are less likely to order multiple ultrasounds during a pregnancy.[14] Solo practitioners (who are by definition owners of their practice) spend more time with their patients than do physicians in group practice who own their practice but approximately the same amount of time as do nonowner physicians in group practice.

Table 6-3 presents estimates from variants of models 2 and 3 that allow the effects of malpractice pressure and managed care enrollment to vary for physicians with less versus more than ten years of experience, that is, estimates from variants of 2 and 3 that include an interaction term between w_s and the element of x_j that denotes whether a physician has less than ten years of experience. Table 6-3 shows that the regulatory environment has important differential effects by years of experience on the five treatment decisions studied. Managed care enrollment is more likely to lead less experienced physicians to decrease referrals for imaging, referrals for back surgery, and the use of hysterectomy and radical prostatectomy, compared with its effects on their counterparts who had been in practice longer. Taken

14. Interpreting the estimated effects of physician characteristics as causal is complicated by the fact that physicians with different amounts of experience may have unobservably different populations of patients; for example, younger physicians may see more or less complicated patients on average.

Table 6-1. *Effects of State, Patient, and Physician/Practice Characteristics on Selected Treatment Decisions*

Variable	Headaches referred for MRI/CT (%)	Back pain referred to orthopedic surgeon (%)	Pregnancies receiving >1 ultrasound (%)	Patients with hysterectomies (%)	Radical prostatectomies (%)	ln (minutes spent per patient office visit)
High managed care enrollment state	-0.055 (0.128)	0.078 (0.121)	-0.008 (0.269)	-0.262* (0.137)	-0.272 (0.204)	0.072** (0.022)
High malpractice pressure state	0.273** (0.136)	0.170 (0.138)	-0.209 (0.311)	0.561** (0.164)	0.554** (0.265)	-0.070** (0.024)
Percent of patients covered by Medicare	0.008** (0.003)	0.003 (0.003)	0.020 (0.021)	0.026** (0.007)	-0.005 (0.009)	0.001 (0.001)
Percent of patients covered by Medicaid	-0.004 (0.004)	-0.000 (0.004)	0.012* (0.007)	0.002 (0.003)	-0.016 (0.027)	0.001 (0.001)
Solo practitioner	-0.079 (0.156)	0.140 (0.150)	0.226 (0.307)	-0.322** (0.161)	-2.276** (0.606)	0.143** (0.026)
Owner of practice	0.051 (0.159)	-0.165 (0.141)	-0.388 (0.340)	-0.132 (0.177)	-1.213** (0.277)	-0.125** (0.028)
Less than 10 years' experience	0.320** (0.163)	0.472** (0.143)	-0.763** (0.342)	0.135 (0.184)	-0.136 (0.250)	0.038 (0.027)

10-20 years' experience	-0.125	0.782**	-0.532	0.167	1.749**	-0.025
	(0.156)	(0.143)	(0.361)	(0.174)	(0.233)	(0.026)
N	531	580	97	201	40	1,735
Specialties included	GP/FP, Internal medicine	GP/FP, Internal medicine	OB/Gyn	OB/Gyn	Urological surgery	All

Note: Grouped logit parameter estimates obtained by running weighted least-squares regressions of $\ln(p/(1-p))$ on X, where p is the proportion of a physician's patients receiving the treatment in question, with weights $np(1-p)$, with n representing the number of patients. High managed care enrollment states and high malpractice pressure states are those ranked twenty-sixth or higher. Years of experience measured as years since first year of practice, excluding residency. "All specialties" excludes psychiatry, radiology, anesthesiology, and pathology. Estimates of effects on minutes per patient visit obtained with weighted least squares, weights equal to the number of office visits in the most recent complete week of practice.

*Significantly different from zero at the 10 percent level.

**Significantly different from zero at the 5 percent level.

Table 6-2. *Effects of State, Patient, and Physician/Practice Characteristics on Selected Treatment Decisions, with Region Effects*

Variable	Headaches referred for MRI/CT (%)	Back pain referred to orthopedic surgeon (%)	Pregnancies receiving >1 ultrasound (%)	Patients with hysterectomies (%)	Radical prostatectomies (%)	ln (minutes spent per patient office visit)
High managed care enrollment state	0.113	0.012	0.277	-0.341	1.554	0.075**
	(0.185)	(0.193)	(0.650)	(0.218)	(1.093)	(0.032)
High malpractice pressure state	-0.048	0.109	-0.421	0.468**	1.399**	-0.076**
	(0.170)	(0.174)	(0.589)	(0.207)	(0.552)	(0.029)
Percent of patients covered by Medicare	0.008**	0.003	0.024	0.027**	0.030	0.001
	(0.003)	(0.003)	(0.025)	(0.007)	(0.020)	(0.001)
Percent of patients covered by Medicaid	-0.001	-0.000	0.013*	0.002	-0.069	0.001
	(0.004)	(0.004)	(0.007)	(0.003)	(0.052)	(0.001)
Solo practitioner	0.057	0.194	0.119	-0.307*	-0.928	0.142**
	(0.160)	(0.154)	(0.336)	(0.166)	(1.633)	(0.026)
Owner of practice	-0.002	-0.243*	-0.127	-0.130	-0.604	-0.123**
	(0.160)	(0.142)	(0.390)	(0.187)	(0.425)	(0.028)
Less than 10 years' experience	0.337**	0.442**	-0.758**	0.187	0.353	0.041
	(0.162)	(0.143)	(0.378)	(0.190)	(0.314)	(0.027)
10-20 years' experience	-0.135	0.721**	-0.506	0.219	1.986**	-0.022
	(0.158)	(0.147)	(0.376)	(0.184)	(0.284)	(0.026)
N	531	580	97	201	40	1,735
Specialties included	GP/FP, Internal medicine	GP/FP, Internal medicine	OB/Gyn	OB/Gyn	Urological surgery	All

Note: See note to table 6-1.
*Significantly different from zero at the 10 percent level.
**Significantly different from zero at the 5 percent level.

with the result from tables 6-1 and 6-2 that less experienced physicians generally refer a greater fraction of patients for testing and treatment, table 6-3 implies that the treatment behavior of less experienced physicians from areas with high enrollment in managed care more closely resembles that of their more experienced counterparts. This is consistent with the hypothesis that managed care reduces the extent of practice variation among physicians. However, neither managed care nor malpractice pressure has a differential effect by years of experience on time spent per office visit.

Table 6-4 presents multinomial logit estimates of the effect of state, patient, and physician/practice characteristics on the type of alleged medical error for those physicians reporting a malpractice claim in the last three years. Table 6-4 shows that physicians from states with high enrollment in managed care are far less likely to report an error arising from a failure to supervise or monitor the case, including any failure to recognize a complication of treatment; this is consistent with plans providing improved care coordination to patients and physicians. Table 6-4 also shows that physicians from states with high enrollment in managed care are significantly less likely (at the 10 percent level) to report an error arising from a failure or delay in referral, obtaining consultation, or hospital admission.

Table 6-5 presents multinomial logit estimates of the determinants of physicians' qualitative experiences with the liability system, for those physicians with a malpractice claim in the past three years. Physicians from states with high malpractice pressure are less likely to report that delay and uncertainty in claim resolution was the most unpleasant aspect of their experience with the liability system; managed care enrollment and malpractice pressure do not have other significant effects on physicians' experiences. Physicians in solo practice are more likely to report that harm to reputation and monetary costs were the part of their encounter with the malpractice system they disliked most.

Conclusion

Previous research has shown that optimal regulation of managed care plans depends not only on the effects of managed care on treatment decisions but also on the interaction between managed care and the existing liability system. Regulation of managed care may affect not only plans' ability to manage utilization, but also the prevalence of defensive medicine, by

Table 6-3. Effects of State, Patient, and Physician/Practice Characteristics on Selected Treatment Decisions, by Number of Years of Physician Experience

Variable	Headaches referred for MRI/CT (%)	Back pain referred to orthopedic surgeon (%)	Pregnancies receiving >1 ultrasound (%)	Patients with hysterectomies (%)	Radical prostatectomies (%)	ln (minutes spent per patient office visit)
High managed care enrollment state	0.406*	0.256	0.023	-0.029	3.106**	0.081**
	(0.220)	(0.214)	(0.736)	(0.244)	(1.343)	(0.036)
High malpractice pressure state	-0.026	-0.171	-0.784	0.329	1.311	-0.089**
	(0.202)	(0.206)	(0.598)	(0.238)	(0.898)	(0.033)
Less than 10 years' experience* high managed care	-0.607**	-0.633**	-0.220	-0.841**	-1.655*	-0.026
	(0.270)	(0.247)	(0.663)	(0.285)	(0.921)	(0.048)
Less than 10 years' experience* high malpractice pressure	-0.270	0.656**	1.401**	0.432	0.679	0.046
	(0.287)	(0.286)	(0.621)	(0.343)	(1.106)	(0.053)
Less than 10 years' experience	0.839**	0.316	-1.656**	0.255	0.500	0.023
	(0.279)	(0.270)	(0.666)	(0.313)	(0.710)	(0.047)
10-20 years' experience	-0.091	0.748**	-0.710*	0.208	1.903**	-0.022
	(0.159)	(0.147)	(0.384)	(0.181)	(0.292)	(0.026)
N	531	580	97	201	40	1,735
Specialties included	GP/FP, Internal medicine	GP/FP, Internal medicine	OB/Gyn	OB/Gyn	Urological surgery	All

Note: Models estimated with controls for region effects. See note to table 6-1.
*Significantly different from zero at the 10 percent level.
**Significantly different from zero at the 5 percent level.

Table 6-4. *Effects of State, Patient, and Physician/Practice Characteristics on Types of Alleged Medical Errors, Physicians with a Malpractice Claim in the Past Three Years*

	Type of alleged medical error (omitted group = no medical error, N = 99)					
Variable	Improper performance (N = 53)	Fail to perform (N = 64)	Diagnosis error (N = 54)	Failure (N = 50)	Failure to supervise (N = 52)	Other error (N = 65)
High managed care enrollment state	−0.193 (0.374)	−0.161 (0.354)	−0.079 (0.373)	−0.679* (0.372)	−0.919** (0.364)	−0.042 (0.361)
High malpractice pressure state	0.233 (0.507)	−0.181 (0.430)	−0.373 (0.444)	−0.227 (0.454)	0.498 (0.509)	0.878 (0.554)
Percent of patients covered by Medicare	−0.011 (0.009)	−0.003 (0.008)	−0.006 (0.009)	−0.005 (0.009)	0.001 (0.009)	−0.007 (0.008)
Percent of patients covered by Medicaid	−0.012 (0.014)	−0.003 (0.013)	0.018* (0.011)	−0.022 (0.016)	0.006 (0.013)	−0.017 (0.014)
Solo practitioner	0.425 (0.396)	−0.277 (0.372)	−0.235 (0.414)	0.036 (0.431)	0.148 (0.395)	−0.042 (0.372)
Owner of practice	0.003 (0.473)	1.092** (0.519)	0.101 (0.444)	−0.487 (0.443)	0.461 (0.503)	0.492 (0.470)
Less than 10 years' experience	0.068 (0.441)	−0.388 (0.405)	−0.042 (0.421)	−0.758 (0.481)	−0.519 (0.435)	−0.395 (0.425)
10–20 years' experience	0.868** (0.427)	0.302 (0.396)	0.461 (0.426)	0.490 (0.418)	0.208 (0.424)	0.747* (0.393)

Note: N = 437. Estimates from multinomial logit model.
*Significantly different from zero at the 10 percent level.
** Significantly different from zero at the 5 percent level.

Table 6-5. *Effects of State, Patient, and Physician/Practice Characteristics on Physicians' Experiences with the Liability System, Physicians with a Malpractice Claim in the Past Three Years*

	Most unpleasant aspect of experience with the liability system (omitted group = other, N = 108)			
Variable	Harm to reputation (N = 74)	Uncompensated time (N = 94)	Delay/uncertainty in claim resolution (N = 85)	Monetary costs (N = 82)
High managed care enrollment state	-0.201	-0.230	-0.376	-0.389
	(0.329)	(0.307)	(0.314)	(0.318)
High malpractice pressure state	-0.183	0.207	-0.876**	-0.681
	(0.464)	(0.457)	(0.399)	(0.418)
Percent of patients covered by Medicare	-0.002	-0.003	-0.007	-0.005
	(0.008)	(0.007)	(0.008)	(0.008)
Percent of patients covered by Medicaid	-0.006	0.013	-0.003	0.017
	(0.013)	(0.011)	(0.013)	(0.011)
Solo practitioner	0.700*	0.199	0.203	0.782**
	(0.360)	(0.341)	(0.350)	(0.353)
Owner of practice	0.036	0.281	0.620	0.195
	(0.409)	(0.379)	(0.414)	(0.406)
Less than 10 years' experience	0.205	-0.315	-0.141	0.375
	(0.395)	(0.375)	(0.375)	(0.380)
10-20 years' experience	0.512	0.351	0.021	0.459
	(0.368)	(0.336)	(0.354)	(0.364)

Note: N = 443. Estimates from multinomial logit model.
*Significant at 10 percent level.
**Significant at 5 percent level.

altering the costs to providers and patients of precautionary medical care. Increasing penetration of managed care in the 1990s has reduced the use of some treatments that are likely to have little medical benefit and increased the use of other beneficial, more cost-effective therapies. But previous work has also found that managed care and liability-reducing tort reforms are substitutes for each other. Fewer reductions in low-benefit care can be achieved in areas with liability reforms in place.

For this reason, understanding how managed care and liability reforms interact to affect physicians' decisionmaking is important. Based on analysis of physicians' responses to several survey questions designed exclusively for this project, we present three main findings. First, malpractice pressure and state managed care enrollment affect physicians' use of one or more treatments likely to have questionable medical benefits. Malpractice pressure, however, affects a broader range of treatments than does managed care enrollment. Patients from states with high levels of managed care are less likely to receive a hysterectomy (although this result is only marginally statistically significant in some specifications); patients from states with high levels of malpractice pressure are more likely to receive several of the study treatments. Malpractice pressure and managed care enrollment also affect time spent per patient office visit. In contrast to the five treatment decisions we studied, patients from states with high levels of malpractice pressure have significantly shorter office visits, and patients from states with high levels of managed care enrollment have significantly longer office visits, controlling for the characteristics of physicians and patient populations and for region effects.

Second, the effects of managed care enrollment vary with physician characteristics. Physicians with fewer than ten years of experience are more responsive (in absolute value terms) to managed care plans' incentives than are physicians with ten years or more of experience. Third, physicians from states with high enrollment in managed care are significantly less likely (at the 5 percent level) to report an error arising from a failure to supervise or monitor the case, and significantly less likely (at the 10 percent level) to report an error arising from a failure or delay in referral, obtaining consultation, or hospital admission.

Taken together, these findings are consistent with the hypotheses that increases in managed care enrollment lead to more efficient treatment and that increases in malpractice pressure lead to less efficient treatment. (Because we only observe area average rather than physician-specific managed care enrollment rates, we cannot identify whether the effects of managed care we observe are because of the direct effects of managed care on patients enrolled in managed care plans or the spillover effects of managed care on patients enrolled in fee-for-service plans.) Increases (reductions) in managed care enrollment (malpractice pressure) lead to lower rates of use of treatments with marginal indications but greater time spent per patient office visit. If the five specific treatment decisions we study have lower benefit-cost ratios on the margin than does additional time spent per patient, then managed care (malpractice pressure) leads to allocation of resources from less (more) to more (less) socially valuable patterns of care. Managed care also leads to reduced variation in practice patterns among physicians. The generally greater propensity of less experienced physicians to order imaging for patients with headache and to refer patients with back pain to an orthopedic surgeon is lower in areas with high levels of managed care. This reduction is efficiency enhancing to the extent that the additional services ordered by less experienced physicians are socially wasteful.[15] Physicians from areas with higher rates of managed care enrollment report fewer errors arising from failure to supervise or monitor, suggesting that managed care plans provide improved care coordination to patients and physicians.

Our findings do not provide clear support for conventional theories underlying some forms of proposed managed care regulation. For example, although we find evidence that managed care reduces the rate of hysterectomy and reduces less experienced physicians' rate of referrals for imaging and back surgery relative to more experienced physicians, we do not find any evidence of increased patient injuries from failure to refer in areas with high enrollment in managed care. Indeed physicians from areas with high enrollment in managed care are less likely to report a medical error due to a failure or delay in obtaining referral. We find no evidence that managed care leads to uniform reductions in services to patients. Rather managed care leads to a reallocation of resources from relatively more to less intensive forms of medical care.

These conclusions are qualified by several important limitations of our study. Most important, the efficiency implications of our results

---

15. Of course, if the additional services ordered by less experienced physicians are socially constructive—for example, if referral for additional tests or procedures serves as a substitute for experience—then the reduction in practice pattern variation associated with managed care enrollment in an area would be socially harmful. However, in multinomial logit results not reported in table 6-4, we find no statistically significant interaction effects between physician experience and managed care on type of alleged medical error.

depend on assumptions about the marginal cost-benefit ratios of the five specific treatment decisions we study and of additional time spent on patient office visits. In addition, interpreting our estimated effects as causal depends on the absence of unobserved physician- and area-level determinants of treatment decisions that are correlated with but not caused by managed care and malpractice pressure. For example, to the extent that differences in managed care enrollment rates across states are correlated with unobserved area characteristics that affect treatment decisions, the estimated effect of managed care will represent a combination of the true effect and the effect of the omitted factor(s). Finally, the applicability of our findings about the effects of managed care on medical errors is limited because we do not observe information on medical errors that did not lead to a malpractice claim. We also do not observe an independent assessment of the source of medical errors but rather only have individual physicians' retrospective self-assessment.

Our results also suggest an important avenue for further study: the differential effects of managed care regulation on key subgroups of physicians. Our results suggest that the behavior of less experienced physicians would be more affected by managed care regulation than the behavior of their more experienced counterparts. Our study does not identify if this differential effect is because less experienced physicians are more likely to contract with managed care plans (and therefore more likely to be affected directly by increases in area managed care enrollment) or because less experienced physicians are more susceptible to the spillover effects of managed care on practice patterns in an area. And without important assumptions, we cannot conclude whether the differential effects of managed care on less versus more experienced physicians are efficiency enhancing or efficiency reducing. Future research might focus on how managed care and regulation of managed care would affect these physicians' incentives and behavior.

Table 6A-1. *Descriptive Statistics*

Variable	Total number of observations	Mean	Standard deviation
Percent headaches referred for MRI/CT	583	12.80	22.74
Percent back pain referred to orthopedic surgeon	637	10.43	17.64
Percent of pregnancies receiving >1 ultrasound	104	36.77	36.29
Percent of patients with hysterectomies	224	1.45	6.85
Percent of radical prostatectomies	40	26.21	29.29
Minutes spent per patient	2,121	27.17	19.45
Type of alleged medical errors:	437		
Improper performance		12.13	
Failure to perform		14.65	
Diagnosis error		12.36	
Failure to refer		11.44	
Failure to supervise		11.90	
Other error		14.87	
No medical error		22.65	
Most unpleasant aspect of experience w/liability system:	443		
Harm to reputation		16.70	
Uncompensated time		21.22	
Delay/uncertainty in claim resolution		19.19	
Monetary costs		18.51	
Other		24.38	
Percent of patients covered by Medicare	3,120	34.69	21.67
Percent of patients covered by Medicaid	3,434	14.72	17.37
Solo practitioner (1=yes)	3,808	0.258	
Owner of practice (1=yes)	3,800	0.634	
Less than 10 years' experience (1=yes)	3,808	0.366	
10-20 years' experience (1=yes)	3,808	0.312	

Table 6A-2. *Classification of States*

State	Managed care enrollment rate-rank	Malpractice claims rate-rank
Alabama	13	20
Alaska	1	3
Arizona	36	35
Arkansas	11	31
California	48	36
Colorado	42	15
Connecticut	43	11
Delaware	47	9
Florida	37	27
Georgia	17	16
Hawaii	34	28
Idaho	9	24
Illinois	24	46
Indiana	14	26
Iowa	8	19
Kansas	16	43
Kentucky	40	34
Louisiana	22	49
Maine	23	14
Maryland	46	29
Massachusetts	50	13
Michigan	29	41
Minnesota	41	21
Mississippi	5	10
Missouri	39	47
Montana	6	33
Nebraska	20	6
Nevada	28	5
New Hampshire	35	38
New Jersey	32	48
New Mexico	33	45
New York	44	42
North Carolina	18	8
North Dakota	4	1
Ohio	25	44
Oklahoma	15	12
Oregon	49	17
Pennsylvania	38	40

Table 6A-2. *(continued)*

State	Managed care enrollment rate-rank	Malpractice claims rate-rank
Rhode Island	26	37
South Carolina	10	22
South Dakota	7	2
Tennessee	30	39
Texas	19	32
Utah	45	50
Vermont	2	18
Virginia	21	25
Washington	27	23
West Virginia	12	30
Wisconsin	31	7
Wyoming	3	4

Note: Managed care enrollment rate calculated as the average of enrollment per capita in January 1997 and July 1998, based on data from Interstudy. Malpractice claims rate-rank calculated based on the number of physicians in the Socioeconomic Monitoring System survey reporting a malpractice claim in the past three years. Higher ranks represent higher enrollment and claims rates.

COMMENT BY
Patricia Danzon

This is an interesting study that extends previous work that Daniel P. Kessler and Mark B. McClellan have done on the effect of tort reform and managed care on defensive medicine. Their study tends to confirm the evidence from their previous work, that tort reform and managed care function as substitute ways of controlling defensive medicine. What is new in this study is that they have a new data set that has more detailed information on physicians' practice patterns and on the types of claims that physicians have experienced. The study uses this new data set to present more evidence on the theme of their earlier work.

In this comment, I briefly focus on their results, then discuss "errors of commission," and then turn to what I think is a rather major error of omission in the study, although Kessler did address this omission somewhat in his presentation at the conference.

First, a few remarks on the actual analysis. The main value of this study is that it uses a new data set. But a significant disadvantage of this new data set is that it has a relatively small sample of physicians, and this sample is not necessarily representative by specialty. Not having a representative sample is particularly problematic when the authors create their measure of malpractice pressure in each state by using the number of claims in the previous three years as reported by the physicians in the sample for each state. Imagine that you have only four or five physicians in each specialty in each state. Recall that the frequency of claims per physicians varies enormously by specialty, with roughly an 8-to-1 ratio of claims per physician in the highest-risk specialties (say, orthopedics and neurosurgery) compared with low-risk specialties (such as general and family practice). The average number of claims per physician could vary greatly across states owing to variation in the mix of specialties that happen to be in the sample in a particular state, which may confound measurement of the overall malpractice climate in the state.

This sampling variability may explain why Kessler and McClellan have a rather unexpected ranking of states when ordered by malpractice pressure. For example, I was surprised to see Utah ranked as having the highest malpractice pressure, Louisiana as number two, and Florida as number 23. I would have expected the reverse ordering, based on previous evidence I have seen of claim frequency by state.

I recommend that rather than using the actual average claims measure in their sample, the authors use a measure of malpractice pressure that a number of previous researchers, including myself, have used in previous studies. This is the premium rate for malpractice insurance for a given level of coverage for a given specialty, in other words, the price of insurance for, say, $100,000 limits of coverage per occurrence, $300,000 total per policy year. This approach would be a more accurate measure of the expected claims cost for each state and could be obtained on a specialty-specific basis. This would be a much more reliable measure of their key explanatory variable.

In fact, perhaps because the authors mistrust their measure of pressure, they do not actually use the full variation that they have. Instead, they use a dichotomous measure to classify a state as either in the bottom half or the top half of the "pressure" distribution. This dichotomous variable throws away a lot of potential information about true variation. Consequently, I do not think that Kessler and McClellan have an accurate measure of malpractice pressure. Serious measurement error is potentially a major problem with their key explanatory variable.

The second problem with this variable is endogeneity. In fact, their results may be contaminated by reverse causation. One of the most interesting findings was the finding that areas with high malpractice pressure seem to be associated with less time per visit, whereas if one believes that there is a deterrence effect, then high malpractice pressure should be associated with more physician time per visit. I suspect that one possible explanation for this unexpected finding is simply reverse causation, that the physicians who are not spending much time per visit are being careless and are getting sued a lot.

Using the claims rate reported by the physicians in this survey as a measure of malpractice pressure greatly increases the risk of endogeneity or reverse causality, whereas if malpractice pressure were measured as the cost of malpractice insurance coverage for physicians in a given specialty in a state, there would be much less risk of bias from reverse causation. So endogeneity of the claims reported by these physician respondents is one possible reason for the rather surprising result, that high malpractice pressure is associated with a short time per visit.

Another possible factor contributing to this result is that in this particular equation—and only in this equation—all the specialties are pooled together and observations are weighted by the number of visits per physician. My guess is that the estimates are dominated by the general practitioners, who would probably be more numerous and have more patient visits than other medical specialists. It seems likely that one possible explanation for the unexpected positive association between managed care penetration and length of visit—we normally think of managed care penetration as reducing length of visit—may simply be that areas of high managed care penetration have relatively more GPs. This relationship assumes that GPs on average spend more time per office visit, because office visits are their major business, whereas the specialists may spend very little time per office visit, because most of their time is spent in hospital visits and procedures.

In summary, in order to really trust these results, the estimates need to be disaggregated by specialty, with use of an exogenous, specialty-specific measure of malpractice pressure such as the malpractice premium for specified limits of coverage. It would also be useful to look carefully at the correlation between the malpractice measure and the managed care measure. The coefficients for these two variables are of almost identical magnitude but opposite sign. Such a result often reflects a high correlation between two explanatory variables. Since these variables are critical to the analysis, more careful attention is needed to determine their separate, marginal effects.

Let me turn now to errors of omission, which were partly remedied in the authors' oral presentation. This study focuses on the effect of malpractice pressure on the behavior of physicians. The empirical measure of malpractice is intended to measure the direct malpractice liability of physicians. The study largely ignores the main current trend in litigation and regulation, which involves litigation against and regulation of managed care organizations (MCOs). Managed care organizations, such as health maintenance organizations (HMOs), are insurance organizations that manage health care by contracting with networks of preferred providers, who agree on measure to contain expenditures. I am much more skeptical than is Kessler that one can draw inferences from these results, which pertain to physician liability, for what might be the effects of holding MCOs liable.

On the likely effects of managed care liability, I have no empirical results, but I would like to make some comments based on simple theory. These arguments are laid out in full in an article of mine published a few years ago.[16] Richard A. Epstein has also written on this topic and fortunately reaches a similar conclusion, so it must be right.[17] Basically, MCOs

16. Danzon (1997).
17. Epstein and Sykes (forthcoming).

are being sued mainly on two issues. One is liability for denial of coverage. Second, MCOs are being held vicariously liable for the negligence of the physicians in their networks. To get to the bottom line, Epstein and I argue that MCOs should be responsible in contract, not in tort, for denials of coverage, but they should not be vicariously liable for the negligent practice of their physicians.

Let me briefly outline the logic leading to this conclusion. The MCOs are basically insurance entities that have developed innovative strategies to control moral hazard. Traditional indemnity insurance only had one way of controlling moral hazard; that was copayment. Copayment is often an inefficient way to control moral hazard because it undermines the insurance protection. If the insured is paying a lot out of pocket, that reduces the value of the insurance coverage. So what managed care offers is another set of strategies for controlling moral hazard. These strategies include putting incentives on the physicians and other providers to charge lower fees and be cost conscious, and use of some direct controls by the insurance entity such as utilization review. The basic strategy was to shift from patient-targeted cost sharing to provider-targeted incentives. But the role of an MCO is still ultimately that of an insuring entity. The managed care organization sets the premiums, defines the terms of coverage, and ultimately is the residual claimant to profit and loss.

Any claim that alleges improper denial of coverage is an insurance claim that should appropriately be against the MCO as the insurer; however, it should be a claim in contract, not a claim in tort. Tort liability presupposes some standard of "due care." But what is the standard of care, what is "due care" on an issue of insurance coverage? The coverage associated with a particular insurance product, implicitly or explicitly, depends largely on what coverage the consumer chose and paid for. It therefore depends on the specific details of the insurance contract. But the way the courts are handling these claims in practice is to fall back on the notion of "customary medical care." In other words, they may hold a managed care entity liable for denial of coverage if it denies something the court deems customary medical care. But what has become customary medical care evolved under the incentives of the old indemnity form of insurance coverage, which was subject to severe moral hazard, because of the limitations of copayment. The whole purpose of managed care was to change the incentives and reduce the excesses of that traditional indemnity insurance regime. Thus to use a standard of "customary care" in a tort action for denial of coverage is to undermine the fundamental purpose of managed care.

There are other issues of detail, about whether a managed care organization could be held liable for punitive damages, if the case is handled as a breach of contract case and, if so, what criteria and limits on awards are appropriate. On this issue too I think Epstein and I agree. Punitive damages may make sense in contexts in which consumers misperceive risks and markets alone result in suboptimal quality. However, in the case of health insurance coverage, specifically the coverage provided by managed care organizations, it seems likely that market forces work reasonably well. If consumers feel that they are not getting appropriate care, they can vote with their feet, they can switch plans, or they can lobby their employer to switch plans. So it is not obvious that this market is subject to serious failure. Moreover, in deciding whether or not to permit punitive damages, one has to consider potential costs as well as potential benefits, particularly if the system works imperfectly. In these coverage cases, the jury would need to understand the problem of insurance-induced moral hazard and the advantages of physician incentives compared with patient cost sharing as strategies to control overuse. It seems likely that these issues would be hard to convey, particularly the need to evaluate the optimal insurance contract from the standpoint of the group as a whole, or the consumer before he or she gets sick, not just from the ex post perspective of the individual who happens to get sick. Given the risk that these issues will not be well understood by courts, combined with the lack of evidence of serious market failure on average, I favor holding MCOs responsible in contract for delivering the coverage implied by their contract, but I believe punitive damages should not be permitted except perhaps in the most egregious circumstances.

The second category of claims against MCOs involves claims alleging the vicarious liability of managed care organizations for the negligence of their physicians. Vicarious liability might make sense if MCOs really had good information on what constitutes appropriate care for a specific patient and if they could monitor the practice of physicians to enforce compliance. The reality, unfortunately, is far from that. The predominant and growing forms of managed care organization are independent practice associations and point-of-service plans, where the physicians practice in their own offices, loosely linked by an administrative network. There is no way that the managed care plan could determine appropriate care or enforce it on a patient-specific, case-by-case basis.

If one follows the principle that liability for negligence should be placed on the person who is in the best position to determine and implement appropriate care, in the case of most MCOs, that person surely is the physician. If the managed care entity is held jointly and severally liable for the physician's negligence, together with the physician, the likely effect is simply to add another deep pocket. Adding MCO liability creates incentives for the physician defendant to attempt to switch the liability to the MCO, and juries may be biased against MCOs as faceless and often unpopular organizations. Even without MCO vicarious liability, there is already a risk that disputes about the quality of care may be turned into disputes over coverage, that is, defendants may argue that they could not have provided better care because the MCO would not have paid for it, making a negligence issue into a coverage decision. This tendency to shift liability from physicians to MCOs would be reinforced if MCOs can also be held vicariously liable for the negligence of their contracted physicians. Potential adverse consequences of such a trend would be to dilute the negligence liability and hence the deterrence effect of liability on physicians, in addition to adding costs of litigation and possibly inappropriate care.

In conclusion, the optimal liability rule would certainly hold managed care companies liable for negligence in selecting the physicians in their network. Thus MCOs could be liable in negligence for contracting with physicians who have a bad record of prior claims, since this is an action within their control and should be done with care. But if an MCO has exercised appropriate care in selecting its physicians, then responsibility for negligent practice should be placed only on the physicians, not on the MCOs. Neither the current trends in MCO liability nor an evaluation of their effects are addressed in the chapter. I hope that Kessler and McClellan will be able to extend their empirical work in the future to examine the effects of MCO liability as opposed to physician liability. I believe that this subject is where the action currently is, and that there is potential for serious harm if current trends in MCO liability continue.

References

Baker, Laurence C. 1999. "Association of Managed Care Market Share and Health Expenditures for Fee-for-Service Medicare Patients." *Journal of the American Medical Association* 281 (5): 432–37.

Baker, Laurence C., and M. L. Brown. 1999. "Managed Care, Consoldiation among Health Care Providers, and Health Care: Evidence from Mammography." *RAND Journal of Economics* 30 (2): 351–74.

Baker, Laurence C., and S. K. Wheeler. 1998. "Managed Care and Technology Diffusion: The Case of MRI." *Health Affairs* 17 (5): 195–207.

Baldwin, L. M., and others. 1995. "Defensive Medicine and Obstetrics." *Journal of the American Medical Association* 274 (20): 1606–10.

Cutler, David M., and Louise Sheiner. 1998. "Managed Care and the Growth of Medical Expenditures." In *Frontiers in Health Policy Research: Volume 1,* edited by Alan Garber, 77–115. MIT Press.

Danzon, Patricia. 1997. "Tort Liability: A Minefield for Managed Care?" *Journal of Legal Studies* 27 (2), part 2: 491–519.

Dubay, Lisa, Robert Kaestner, and Timothy Waidmann. 1999. "The Impact of Malpractice Fears on Cesarian Section Rates." *Journal of Health Economics* 18 (4): 491–522.

Epstein, Richard, and Alan Sykes. Forthcoming. "The Assault on Managed Care: Vicarious Liability, ERISA Preemption, and Class Actions." *Journal of Legal Studies.*

Greene, William H. 1997. *Econometric Analysis.* Prentice Hall.

Harvard Medical Practice Study. 1990. *Patients, Doctors, and Lawyers: Medical Injury, Malpractice Litigation, and Patient Compensation in New York,* a report of the Harvard Medical Practice Study to the state of New York. Cambridge, Mass.: The President and Fellows of Harvard College.

Heidenreich, Paul A., Mark McClellan, Craig Frances, and Laurence C. Baker. 2001. "The Relation between Managed Care Market Share and the Treatment of Elderly Fee-for-Service Patients with Myocardial Infarction." Working Paper 8065. Cambridge, Mass.: National Bureau of Economic Research (January).

Kessler, Daniel P., and Mark B. McClellan. 1996. "Do Doctors Practice Defensive Medicine?" *Quarterly Journal of Economics* 111: 353–90.

———. 1997. "The Effects of Malpractice Pressure and Liability Reforms on Physicians' Perceptions of Medical Care." *Law and Contemporary Problems* 60: 81–106.

———. 2000a. "How Liability Law Affects Medical Productivity." Working Paper 7533. Cambridge, Mass.: National Bureau of Economic Research (February).

———. 2000b. "Is Hospital Competition Socially Wasteful?" *Quarterly Journal of Economics* 115 (2): 577–615.

———. Forthcoming. "Malpractice Law and Health Care Reform: Optimal Liability Policy in an Era of Managed Care." *Journal of Public Economics.*

Localio, A. R., and others. 1993. "Relationship between Malpractice Claims and Cesarean Delivery." *Journal of the American Medical Association* 269 (3): 366–73.

Rock, S. M. 1988. "Malpractice Premiums and Primary Caesarian Section Rates in New York and Illinois." *Public Health Reporter* 108: 459–68.

KENNETH S. ABRAHAM

7 | *The Insurance Effects of Regulation by Litigation*

Mass tort and similar major lawsuits have been a fixture in the courts of this country for more than twenty-five years. Toward the end of this chapter I discuss whether all or only a portion of this litigation should be defined as "regulation by litigation." For insurance purposes, however, the motive behind a lawsuit is largely irrelevant. Insurance is most affected when liability is potentially sizable and unpredicted, regardless of what plaintiffs intend to achieve through their lawsuits. Thus I concentrate on a general class of major lawsuits whose effects on insurance are significant.

Since mass tort and other major civil liability suits first appeared on the legal scene, there have been two liability insurance "crises." The first, in 1975 and 1976, was largely limited to medical malpractice liability and insurance.[1] The second, however, in 1985 and 1986, was far more widespread and severe, affecting business liability and insurance generally.[2] Yet liability insurance is now and for more than a decade has been widely available; until recently, price increases for liability insurance during this period, to the extent that they have occurred at all, have been

---

1. For accounts, see generally Symposium (1977); Feagles and others (1975), proposing tort law modifications to counter the rising cost of medical malpractice insurance.
2. Priest (1987); Abraham (1987).

unremarkable.[3] The two temporary crises in the availability and afford-
ability of liability insurance are now but distant memories. To the outside observer, the current insurance climate probably seems untroubled.
Given this peaceful market picture, is regulation by litigation really a
problem for insurance?

To paraphrase a famous deponent, it depends on the meaning of
"problem." The liability insurance market has not fallen apart at the
prospect that regulation by litigation seems here to stay. For more than fifteen years there have been no acute, systemic effects of regulation by litigation on liability insurance. However, regulation by litigation has
produced, or at least contributed to, significant chronic effects that undermine the optimal functioning of liability insurance.

First, at the point of sale, wholesale uncertainty generated by the ever-
present threat of regulation by litigation inevitably raises the cost of insurance, in some settings virtually indiscriminately. This results in what I call
an "uncertainty tax" and tends to promote the shift from broadly protective "occurrence" coverage to less desirable "claims-made" coverage.

Second, at the point of claim, the enormous sums at stake have transformed some ordinary insurance claims into protracted mega-coverage
disputes, and extreme cases into desperate, bet-the-company litigation.
Policyholders sometimes pursue claims with a very low probability of success, and insurers undoubtedly deny some claims that should be paid.
Nearly a century ago, after the 1906 San Francisco earthquake spawned
an avalanche of fire and property insurance claims, the Lloyds underwriter
Cuthbert Heath is said to have cabled his agents, "Pay all our policyholders in full irrespective of the terms of their policies."[4] In contrast,
today a de facto "big-claim" exclusion has found its way into business liability insurance policies, although naive policyholders may not discover
this exclusion until they make a big claim.

The liability insurance system has endured in the face of these challenges, but it has not thrived. To analyze the developments that have lead
to the current state of affairs, I briefly sketch the history and nature of
Comprehensive General Liability (CGL) insurance—the principal source
of general liability insurance for American business. I separately address

---

3. See, for example, Mooney (2000) (commercial lines price index was negative every year for the
period January 1988 to January 2000); Ruquet (2000, p. 1) (since 1998, average renewal prices for
general business liability insurance had either declined or risen less than 4 percent until latest
renewals).

4. Raphael (1994).

the effects of regulation by litigation on CGL and allied forms of business liability insurance, such as Professional Liability and Errors and Omissions insurance, at the two points I have just identified: uncertainty effects at the point of sale and litigation effects at the point of claim. I then address the special considerations connected with lawsuits pertaining to guns or health maintenance organizations (HMOs) and conclude with some thoughts about the relation between civil liability, health and safety regulation, and the regulation of liability insurance.

A Primer on CGL Insurance

The antecedents of commercial insurance against civil liability reach back to the late nineteenth century, when Employers Liability insurance—the first real form of liability insurance—emerged in response to the growth of tort liability on the part of employers to employees.[5] But the modern history of business liability insurance begins in 1941, when the standard-form CGL insurance policy was first marketed. Until this time, different policies covered different "hazards," or causes of loss. Premises, Elevator, and Manufacturers' liability, for example, often were covered under separate policies.[6] The contribution of the new CGL insurance instrument was to provide all available coverage against liability for bodily injury and property damage in a single policy, regardless of the nature of the policyholder's business or the character of the legal hazards the business posed.[7]

The coverage afforded by the original CGL insurance policy was comprehensive and general in this sense, but this coverage was not unlimited. First, the policy only covered liability incurred because of physical damage. It insured against liability for bodily injury or property damage, not against all forms of tort liability. There was no coverage of liability for pure economic loss, for example.

Second, the policy required that the injury or damage in question be "caused by accident." Insurers took the position that this phrase not only precluded coverage of liability for injury that the insured expected or intended. They also contended that the term "accident" had a temporal

5. Kulp (1928); Caverly (1939).
6. Malecki and others (1986).
7. Abraham (2001).

component and therefore covered liability for harm arising out of abrupt, but not gradual, events. Though policyholders frequently disagreed, coverage of liability for continuous or long-term exposure to hazardous conditions or substances was often denied. The London market eventually began offering an "occurrence" policy that expressly covered both, and American insurers felt market pressure to respond. It was not until a 1966 revision of the standard-form American CGL policy explicitly added "occurrence" coverage of liability for injury or damage resulting from continuous or long-term hazardous exposures, however, that this uncertainty was definitely resolved.

Third, the coverage afforded by the CGL insurance policy has always been limited by a number of exclusions from coverage. Originally there were five exclusions: against liability assumed under contract; arising out of aircraft, watercraft, or motor vehicle operation; statutory liability to employees; damage to property owned or occupied by the insured; and water damage liability.[8] These exclusions set in motion a dynamic that continues to this day. To combat adverse selection, any insurer must take into account the existence of risks that are likely to vary substantially from policyholder to policyholder. Certain such variations are reflected in the classifications that CGL insurers employ in charging premiums that are proportional to the risk posed by each policyholder. Chemical manufacturers are likely to pay more for CGL insurance than pillow makers. Other risks, however, are excluded from the coverage afforded by CGL policies and left to be covered separately, if at all, by specific-purpose policies tailored to cover these risks alone. The current state of the market reflects this historically chosen division of labor among policies, and the efficiencies available are now at least partly a function of that choice.

During the decades it has been in use the CGL policy has been revised periodically. Policy language has been fine tuned, minimal coverage against liability for certain forms of intangible loss has been added,[9] and (as noted) since 1966 the standard-form policy has made it clear that injuring-causing events need not be temporally abrupt. But aside from these expansions of coverage, the major changes in the CGL policy from its origin up until the present time have involved the contraction of coverage. The policy has been getting less comprehensive and less general over time.

8. Malecki and others (1986).

9. This coverage has varied over the years, but at present principally includes false arrest and imprisonment, product disparagement, malicious prosecution, wrongful eviction, certain forms of invasion of privacy, and infringement of copyright through advertising. See Abraham (2000).

Probably the most noteworthy example of the progressive limitation of the coverage provided by the CGL policy involves pollution. In 1973 the standard-form policy was revised to limit coverage to liability for injury or damage resulting from the "sudden and accidental" discharge of pollutants or contaminants. In 1986 this "qualified" pollution exclusion was broadened, and coverage was thereby further limited by what the insurance industry called the "absolute" pollution exclusion. Although the title "absolute" has proved to be wishful thinking by the industry, the 1986 exclusion certainly limits coverage far more effectively than the qualified exclusion.[10] For example, claims for coverage of liability for harm associated with lead paint have often hinged on whether the exclusion is applicable to this form of harm. Not surprisingly, there is a severe split of authority on the issue.[11]

The evolution of other areas of excluded liability has followed a similar pattern. For example, a series of "business risk" exclusions has long precluded most coverage of liability for damage to the policyholder's own products or work. But as product recalls became more common, a "sistership" exclusion limiting coverage of the costs of recall was added to this series of coverage-limiting provisions.

The usefulness of the CGL policy has been reduced not only by the continuing accretion of exclusions from and limitations on coverage but also by the growth of new forms of liability that fall outside the scope of affirmatively provided coverage. The CGL policy once covered most of the major forms of tort and tort-like liability that the typical business could expect to encounter. The development of liabilities that did not exist or existed only minimally in the past, however, has rendered the CGL policy an uncertain, and in many respects wholly inadequate, vehicle for general protection against civil liability. For example, because of the uncertain

10. See, for example, *American States Ins. Co.* v. *Koloms*, 177 Ill.2d 473, 687 NE.2d 72 (Ill. 1997) (absolute exclusion does not preclude coverage of liability for injuries resulting from emissions of carbon monoxide from a defective furnace); *West American Insurance Co.* v. *Tufco Flooring East, Inc.*, 104 N.C. App. 312, 409 S.E.2d 692 (1991) (absolute exclusion does not preclude coverage of liability for food contamination resulting from emission of vapors during floor resurfacing).

11. *Compare Lefrak Organization, Inc.* v. *Chubb Custom Insurance Co.*, 942 F. Supp. 949 (S.D. N.Y. 1996) (whether lead paint chips and dust are a pollutant within the meaning of the absolute pollution exclusion is ambiguous) and *Insurance Co. of Illinois* v. *Stringfield*, 685 N.E.2d 980 (Ill. App. 1997) (lead is not pollutant within meaning of absolute pollution exclusion) with *U.S. Liability Insurance Co.* v. *Bourbeau*, 49 F.3d 786 (1st Cir. 1995) (lead paint chips are pollutant within meaning of absolute pollution exclusion) and *Auto-Owners Insurnace Co.* v. *Hanson*, 588 N.W.2d 777 (Minn. Ct. App. 1999) (absolute pollution clause precludes coverage because chipping and flaking of lead paint is a "discharge, dispersal or release" within meaning of exclusion).

scope of coverage afforded by the CGL policy, for businesses whose activities risk liability related to the Comprehensive Environmental Response, Compensation, and Liability Act (CERCLA), employment discrimination, intellectual property, or the Internet, it is prudent to attempt to obtain endorsements to their CGL policies that confirm coverage of these liabilities or purchase special purpose coverage. Such specialty coverage, however, is often far less easily available or affordable than CGL insurance.

The Definitional Challenge

Since its inception, two problems have plagued CGL insurance, each in essence concerned with the definition of what is and is not covered. The first is the endemic tension between the goals of providing general coverage and drafting clear borderlines between covered and excluded liabilities. The second is the problem of the long-tail liability.

General Coverage and the Borderline Problem

From the beginning, the general, ostensibly "comprehensive" coverage language of the CGL policy has posed a critical problem for insurers. They have never been able to craft coverage language that defines the scope of affirmative coverage with sufficient precision. The CGL policy always has been essentially an "all-risks" or "open-peril" policy, to use the language of property insurance. The policy covers all risks of liability falling within the terms of its broadly worded "Insuring Agreement," or affirmative grant of coverage, except those specifically excluded elsewhere in the policy. Under the current policy language, there is coverage of sums that the insured is "legally obligated to pay as damages" because of "bodily injury or property damage" that takes place "during the policy period," caused by an "occurrence."

Over time, this insuring language and its predecessors have prompted a variety of disputes regarding scope and proper application. One such long-running dispute, just noted, was whether injury or damage resulting from gradual or long-term events such as exposure to hazardous substances was "caused by accident" under pre-1966 policies.[12] That issue was litigated

12. See, for example, *Beryllium Corp.* v. *American Mutual Liability Insurance Co.*, 223 F.2d 71 (3d Cir. 1955); *Canadian Radium and Uranium Corp.* v. *Indemnity Insurance Co. of North America*, 411 Ill. 325, 104 N.E.2d 250 (1952).

but never definitively resolved. Rather, the 1966 revision of the standard-form CGL policy substituted the term "occurrence" for "accident" and defined "occurrence" to include events that were not abrupt.

A second continuing dispute has involved the "trigger" of coverage, or event that activates insurance under the policy, which requires that injury or damage occur "during the policy period." More than twenty years ago, in suits over coverage of liability for long-latent harms such as contamination of water supplies by hazardous waste and personal injury resulting from exposure to asbestos, proper application of this trigger became important. The issue now figures in claims for coverage of a number of the liabilities addressed in this volume, including breast implants and exposure to lead paint.[13] Policyholders have tended to argue for multiyear triggers based on the years of actual injury or damage, whereas insurers have usually contended that only the policy on the risk during the year when damage manifested is triggered. Despite this long-standing disagreement, a series of revisions of the CGL policy has never addressed the issue but instead has always retained essentially the same operative language, which makes coverage hinge on whether there was bodily injury or property damage "during the policy period."[14]

A third issue has been less prominent but may well more frequently find its way into future disputes over coverage of new forms of regulation by litigation. Like virtually all liability insurance policies, the CGL policy affords coverage only for what the insured is "legally obligated to pay."[15] In the ordinary case this phrase means that the insured must suffer a judgment or enter into a settlement to which the insurer agrees. There may well be situations, however, in which the insured party determines that preemptive remedial action, or monetary settlement of potential claims or suits, are in its best interest. Indeed, one can easily imagine a future in which preemptive action is often employed to minimize exposure to massive possible liability at the hands of various new forms of regulation by litigation.

Does the CGL policy afford coverage of the cost of such remedial action or settlement, if the insured was in fact "legally obligated" to take these actions? For example, a statute, ordinance, or regulation might make it unlawful to lease premises that pose a danger of lead paint contamina-

13. See, for example, *In re Dow Corning Corp.*, 198 B.R. 214, 224-25 (Bankr. E.D. Mich. 1996); *U.S. Liability Insurance Co. v. Selman*, 70 F.3d 684 (1st Cir. 1995). See also Fischer (1997).

14. Abraham (2000).

15. Abraham (2000).

tion to tenants. If the other prerequisites to coverage are satisfied, a claim for coverage of the cost of remedying such conditions may turn on whether the insured was "legally obligated" under these sources of law to take remedial action. A few analogous cases involving remediation of environmental risks posed by hazardous waste have ruled on the issue,[16] but it is far from definitively resolved in other contexts.[17]

Finally, as seemingly fundamental a matter as what constitutes "property damage" for coverage purposes may be disputed. Does the mere incorporation of asbestos, plastic pipe, or lead-based paint into a building constitute property damage, or must some of the hazardous substance first migrate from the particular site of installation to a place in the building where it can cause harm?[18]

These definitional concerns, and a number of others related to the Insuring Agreement in the CGL policy, have been continuing problems.[19] But they may be problems for policyholders as much as insurers. The CGL definitional difficulties are such that, once an insurer decides to contest a coverage claim, there are any number of possible arguments it may raise in defense of its position.

Problems in the interpretation of the Insuring Agreement, however, are by no means the end of the matter. Application of the exclusions from coverage has been at least an equal, and arguably greater, source of trouble. Because of the broad and general scope of the CGL Insuring Agreement, the exclusions from coverage must do substantial work in defining the risks covered. When a general Insuring Agreement cannot define the line between what is and is not covered with sufficient precision, express exclusions from and limitations on the coverage otherwise affirmatively

16. See, for example, *Weyerhaeuser Co.* v. *Aetna Casualty and Surety Co.*, 874 P.2d 142 (Wash. 1994); *Metex Corp.* v. *Federal Insurance Co.*, 675 A.2d 220 (N. J. Super. 1996).

17. See, for example, *San Diego Housing Commission* v. *Industrial Indemnity Co.*, 68 Cal. App.4th 526, 540-44 (1998) (compliance by landlord with contractual duties under a lease and statutes does not qualify as being "legally obligated").

18. See, for example, *Eljer Manufacturing, Inc.* v. *Liberty Mutual Insurance Co.*, 972 F.2d 805 (7th Cir. 1992); *Hoechst Celanese Corp.* v. *Certain Underwriters at Lloyd's of London*, 673 A.2d 164 (Del. 1996); *Maryland Casualty Co.* v. *W. R. Grace and Co.*, 23 F.3d 617 (2d Cir. 1993).

19. For example, when an insurer provides coverage on a per occurrence basis, the number of occurrences that are considered to have given rise to a particular liability may be critical; when policies covering different years are triggered, determining how to allocate coverage responsibility among triggered policies may have a substantial impact on recovery; and whether liability for the cost of medical monitoring or for fear of contracting a disease is incurred "because of bodily injury" may determine whether there is any coverage at all in certain classes of cases.

provided under the Insuring Agreement are the means by which this line must be defined.

As new forms of liability have emerged and fallen within the terms of the Insuring Agreement, however, the exclusions have often been asked to deal with unanticipated issues. From the pollution exclusion, the owned-property exclusion, the business-risk exclusions, and the conditions requiring notice to the insurer, to the limitation of coverage to liability for harm that is neither "expected nor intended," there has consistently been protracted litigation over the border between covered and excluded risks.[20] As new forms of liability or other unanticipated claims are brought, the policy has sometimes been redrafted in an effort to deal with certain of these issues. But decades after policy language has been incorporated in the CGL policy, often there still is debate, not merely over application of this language to particular sets of facts, but over the scope of fundamental concepts. The nature of general coverage will inevitably generate further litigation regarding the borderlines of coverage in a number of areas of liability.

The Love-Hate Relationship with the Long Tail

Although insurers continually face the twin threats of adverse selection and moral hazard, setting insurance premiums that are proportional to the level of risk that each insured poses can help to combat these threats. The CGL insurer's ability to employ this tool, however, is undermined as the difficulty of assessing risk levels increases. Ironically, the trigger of coverage under CGL policies itself contributes to this difficulty.

Because this trigger of coverage is the occurrence of injury or damage "during the policy period," CGL policies cover liability for long-latent injury or damage imposed many years after a policy is issued. In a real sense, a CGL policy provides coverage from the date it is issued until the end of time, as long as the injury or damage for which liability ultimately is imposed occurred during this policy year.[21] When the occurrence of injury or damage as a result of a policyholder's actions is immediate and obvious, ordinarily the statute of limitations on the right to bring an action seeking to impose liability for this injury or damage begins to run immediately. In

20. For detailed discussion of the law governing application of these exclusions to hazardous waste and toxic tort coverage claims, see Abraham (1991, pp.129–93).
21. Abraham (1997, pp. 2103–05).

this situation, a coverage claim typically is made and resolved within a few years. But if the injury or damage resulting from a policyholder's activities is latent, under the law of most states the period during which a suit may be brought does not begin to run until this harm is discovered, or in the exercise of reasonable care should have been discovered. Consequently, it is not only possible but common to find claims made against CGL policies issued many decades earlier. Many claims for coverage of liability for harm caused by tobacco, lead paint, or breast implants, for example, have been or would likely be made against CGL policies issued years ago, among others.

The great problem for CGL insurers under these circumstances is how to set an accurate price for coverage. To the extent that a policyholder is vulnerable to long-tail liability, its CGL insurer is exposed to potential claims for coverage of that liability. Setting a price for coverage therefore requires predicting the frequency and severity of the policyholder's liability, long into the future. To make such predictions the insurer must anticipate changes in scientific and medical knowledge, estimate future legal change, and anticipate economic inflation, since each of these factors will affect the scope of the policyholder's future liability. In the seemingly stable decades between 1945 and 1970, the pace of legal and economic change that had occurred in the immediate or recent past seemed to insurers to be a reasonably reliable predictor of the pace of future change. In that setting, reliably predicting increased risk levels and setting premiums accordingly seemed mainly to be a matter of extrapolating from the past.

During the three decades that followed, however, CGL insurers have learned that this is no longer true, and that pricing their product is a much less reliable exercise than it seemed to be in the past. Without a reliable base of data on which to make long-term predictions, CGL insurers have for some time faced the prospect that writing this form of coverage may prove to be as much an exercise in speculation as in prediction. The problem of the long tail on claims thus goes to the heart of CGL insurance enterprise.

At the same time that insurers hate the long tail on CGL occurrence policies, however, they love the investment income that can be earned on the portion of premiums that are held as loss reserves for many years. In a period of booming stock markets or high interest rates, the tendency for an insurer to engage in cash-flow underwriting to capture premiums for long-term investment may be extremely tempting. But of course investment income cannot be earned on reserves that have been paid for underwriting losses: "If the original business is too severely underpriced, no

investment wizardry or daisy chain of reinsurance can keep the game looking profitable unless more and more cash keeps coming in. Growth must
not stop, just as there must never be final delivery of a chain letter."[22] For
this reason, what might otherwise seem to be the puzzling persistence of
occurrence-based coverage turns out to be a product not only of policyholder demand but also of the investment advantages of this instrument
to the insurer.

Point-of-Sale Effects

Two major effects of regulation by litigation on insurance at the point
of sale deserve attention. The first is the wholesale upward pressure on premiums that I call the "uncertainty tax"; the second is the tendency for
insurance to shift from occurrence-based to claims-made coverage in order
to limit exposure to long-tail liabilities.

The Uncertainty Tax

A key characteristic of regulation by litigation is that the nature of this
litigation makes it extremely difficult for insurers to predict the subject
matter that will next be the focus of a lawsuit seeking to impose massive
liability, whether in the name of promoting future safety or affecting some
other change in the behavior of the defendant. A chain-saw manufacturer
may be a somewhat more likely target of such litigation than a maker of
lollipops. But even this is only a matter of speculative probability. And
which chain-saw manufacturer or lollipop maker is the most likely target
is often impossible to say. In any event, class actions against an entire
industry are common. Within broad bounds, regulation by litigation may
strike like lightning, almost randomly.

There is often little a CGL insurer can do under these circumstances to
differentiate among its policyholders. The ordinary incentive effects of differential pricing based on predicted differences in loss experience are likely
to be minimal or completely absent. Nevertheless, the insurer must anticipate the possibility—and at some points, the probability—that a subset
of all its policyholders will face substantial costs because of regulation by
litigation. The insurer's only choice is to attempt to collect sufficient

22. Stewart (1980).

additional premiums to cover the increased costs that it will eventually incur because of such regulation by litigation.

In the extreme case the insurer cannot in any way predict the incidence of this liability, and the additional premiums it attempts to collect are a mere guestimate of the costs it may face in the future. In the face of such complete uncertainty, the additional premium charge is for each policyholder the equivalent of a tax assessed on premium payments. Since each insurer's predicament is identical, this "uncertainty tax" is unavoidable. It is simply a cost of doing business.

The ultimate incidence of this uncertainty tax will of course vary, depending on many factors. The tax may be passed on, in whole or in part, to a policyholder's customers or employees, or shouldered by shareholders. Or it may be paid by decreasing the amount of insurance coverage purchased. Under certain conditions, however, the elasticity of demand for liability insurance may preclude insurers from assessing the uncertainty tax at the point of sale at all. I suspect that this may more nearly account for what has occurred during the past decade, when premiums for CGL insurance have remained relatively flat. The matter does not necessarily end, however, with the insurer's shareholders bearing the uncertainty tax. On the contrary, as I suggest later, the battleground may shift to the point of claim, where the insurer may attempt to recapture all or part of the cost of regulation by litigation.

The Shift to Claims-Made Coverage

Whereas occurrence-based CGL insurance covers long-tail liabilities, the "claims-made" form of CGL insurance has the potential to vastly limit this form of exposure. The trigger of coverage under claims-made policies is a claim first made during the policy period. Like occurrence policies, claims-made policies may also cover long-latent injury or damage—if a claim alleging liability for such damage is first made during the policy period. But claims-made policies typically preclude coverage of liability for injury or damage that occurred before a specified "retroactive date," even if a claim made during the policy year for such injury or damage would otherwise be covered. The most common retroactive date is the day the claims-made insurer sold its first policy to the insured. Consequently, unless the insured has been covered by claims-made policies issued by the same insurer for many years, most claims-made policies are unlikely to cover liability for long-latent injury or damage.

Claims-made coverage requires only comparatively short-term prediction by the insurer. The question for the occurrence insurer is how much liability will be imposed on the policyholder, between today and the end of time, for injury or damage that occurred this year. In contrast, the question for the claims-made insurer is how much liability will be imposed on the policyholder for claims made during the next year, arising out of injury or damage that has occurred subsequent to the retroactive date specified in the policy. The answer that the claims-made insurer must give in order to set a reliable price for coverage involves a much simpler predictive task. Moreover, if it turns out that there is a steep and unpredicted rise in claims arising out of a particular activity during a claims-made policy year, the insurer may choose not to renew, and thereby limit the losses it will suffer to those arising out of this year's claims. No such cutoff is possible under an occurrence policy.

Of course, the shift to claims-coverage does not eliminate the uncertainty that plagues occurrence coverage. That shift simply transfers the risk of an uncertain liability future from the insurer to the policyholder, which may not have the insurer's risk-diversification capacity. Given the proclivity of modern business enterprises to favor short-term over long-term gains, the tendency to shift toward claims-made coverage is likely to dominate insurers' superior risk diversification capacities, since the nominal price of claims-made coverage (because the self-insurance component associated with claims-made coverage is not included in its nominal price) will be lower than the price of occurrence coverage. In effect, claims-made coverage permits the insured enterprise to put off paying for long-tail liabilities—or for insurance against them—until they are a more concrete threat.

During the period in which regulation by litigation has come to prominence, there has been a tendency for insurers to shift from occurrence to claims-made coverage. This shift has been most noticeable in specialty forms of insurance that cover discrete forms of liability: Directors and Officers Liability insurance, Employment Liability insurance, and Pollution Liability insurance, for example. But the shift has been evident, though probably less extensive, in CGL insurance as well.

Over time, the shift to claims-made coverage may help to solve the challenge that regulation by litigation poses for CGL insurers. But CGL insurers will nevertheless remain exposed under prior occurrence policies for many years to come. Three areas of litigation that are the subject of this volume—breast implants, lead, and tobacco—involve liability for what typically are long-latent injuries. For this reason, the principal targets for coverage claims made by the defendants in these three areas are likely to be their comparatively older CGL insurance policies. Whether and under what circumstances they may find coverage depends on several complex variables.[23] Some of these defendants' insurers may even have included express exclusions of liability for lead-related or tobacco-related injury, for example, in their policies. But whatever the character of these actual or potential coverage claims, the important point is that the merits of these claims are fixed, because the claims are against occurrence-based CGL policies for injuries that have for the most part already occurred. We may not yet know how these coverage claims will be resolved on the merits, but the ingredients of decision are dependent on past facts. Even if more lead or breast implant lawsuits are brought in the future, as long as they are based on long-latent (even though recently manifested) injury, older CGL policies will be the source of coverage for these liabilities. And neither the insurers who issued these policies nor the policyholders who purchased them can any longer do anything to affect what the policies do or do not cover.

One possible qualification is that, to the extent that suits seek damages for injuries that have occurred more recently, older CGL policies are not the proper target of claims for coverage. One can easily imagine that there are tobacco, lead, or breast implant suits filed last year (or that will be filed next year), alleging liability for injury that did not begin occurring until, for example, 1995. Insurers and their policyholders will have effectively had it within their power to cover or exclude such liabilities from recent CGL policies, because by 1995 the risk that more lead or breast implant suits would be instituted was well known to both parties. But the percentage of claims against the lead, breast implant, and tobacco defendants that fall into this category is probably comparatively small. As a consequence, neither the placement of lead, breast implant, or tobacco liability exclusions in current CGL policies, nor a shift by the insurers of these defendants from occurrence to claims-made coverage, nor even the discontinuation of coverage altogether—can have much impact on the proportion of liability that will be shouldered by the insurers of these defendants. For these insurers, for the most part, the cat is already out of the bag.[24]

23. For example, claims for coverage of breast implant liability must avoid the defense that the insured "expected or intended" harm; and claims for coverage of lead liability must avoid the defense that harm falls within the qualified or absolute pollution exclusions. Although tobacco defendants have not litigated any insurance claims, they would undoubtedly encounter their insurers' expected-or-intended defense, among others, if such claims were made.

24. The only possible exception may be tobacco lawsuits, which conceivably could continue to be brought for many years to come, for example, by those who have only recently begun smoking. Whether such suits would be successful, given contemporary warnings and consumer risk awareness, is of course a separate question.

In contrast to lead, breast implant, and tobacco litigation, auto-related and handgun-related products liability and HMO claims involve comparatively short-tail liabilities. In between the long-tail and short-tail extremes probably fall suits by municipalities for recovery of costs associated with handgun injuries, such as additional ambulance and police services, for example. Insurers covering the short-tail liabilities—whether under occurrence or claims-made policies—can avoid insuring various such liabilities in the future by policy revision. For example, if carmaker X begins in the year 2002 to receive claims for injuries arising out of the defective design of the steering wheel in its year 2002 vehicles, its occurrence insurer can add a year 2002 vehicle steering wheel exclusion to its 2003 policy, shift to claims-made coverage with a 2003 retroactive date, or refuse to renew on any basis. Carmaker X will then have coverage only under its 2002 policy and then only for injuries that occurred during 2002. There will be no coverage of liability for injuries occurring in 2003 and thereafter, even though the year 2002 vehicles were sold in 2002.

To address this coverage gap, some manufacturers purchase what is known as "batch" coverage, under which notice of a "batch" occurrence in year 2001, for example, will bring within the scope of the 2001 policy all future injuries associated with a particular product defect. But batch coverage of this sort is not standard and tends to be sold mainly as excess or umbrella coverage subject to a lower layer or deductible of at least $20 million.[25]

The predicament of an HMO would be similar. Suppose that Congress enacted an amendment to the Employment Retirement Income Security Act (ERISA), authorizing suits against otherwise exempt HMOs for wrongful denial of medical care, and permitting the recovery of extra-contractual damages resulting from such denial of care.[26] An HMO's past occurrence-based Errors and Omissions or Professional Liability policies would potentially cover its liability in such suits for injuries that had occurred in the past. And current claims-made policies would cover such suits during the current year. But for all future injuries or claims resulting

25. See Dolan and Posner (1998, pp. 68, 69–72).

26. The law regarding the circumstances under which such an action may be brought is in flux. Compare *Pilot Life Insurance Co. v. Dedeaux*, 481 U.S. 41 (1987) and *Thompson v. Gencare Health Systems, Inc.*, 202 F.3d 1072 (8th Cir. 2000) (both courts holding that actions for recovery of bad faith denial of insurance benefits subject to ERISA are pre-empted) with *In re U.S. Healthcare, Inc.*, 193 F.3d 151 (3rd Cir. 1999) and *Herrera v. Lovelace Health Systems, Inc.*, 35 F.Supp.2d 1327 (D.N.M. 1999) (both courts holding that extracontractual damages are available for improper provision of health care but not for improper denial of benefits).

from the denial of care, insurers could add exclusionary endorsements to occurrence policies or shift to claims-made policies with a current retroactive date and thereby completely avoid providing coverage. Alternatively, future policies could be priced to take account of the HMO's newly increased liability exposure.

Point-of-Claim Effects

If the persistence of occurrence-based CGL insurance in the face of regulation by litigation needs explaining, the addition of what might be called "point-of-claim underwriting" to the underwriting that conventionally takes place at the point of sale may be the answer. Anyone involved in a sizable mass tort insurance claim during the past ten to fifteen years has experienced this process. Typically, insurers do not readily acknowledge coverage of such claims. Rather, many such claims are more likely to occasion litigation than willing payment or quickly negotiated compromise and settlement.

This phenomenon has become so familiar that the policyholder side of the market has given it the facetious title of the "big-claim exclusion." No doubt insurers see things differently, perhaps perceiving many claims for coverage as extravagant and preposterous. But whether the truth lies somewhere in the middle or at one of the two extremes is beside the point. When an individual policyholder makes a claim against its insurers for coverage of a massive liability—the sort of liability that characterizes regulation by litigation—these insurers face the prospect of suffering a massive loss under their policies. If the claims are made under CGL policies written decades ago, then any small "contingency factors" built into the premiums for these policies cannot begin to cover the losses. And even if the claims are made against more recently issued CGL policies, the payoff to the insurer from declining the claim and litigating that denial may be substantial. Conversely, when a policyholder faces an enormous potential civil liability, it may be worthwhile to invest in the litigation of insurance claims with a very low probability of success, since the reward available for success may be high.

The result, as the judicial dockets of the past two decades reveal, is the proliferation of lawsuits over insurance coverage of major liabilities, including those falling into the general category of regulation by litigation.

The policy issued at the point of sale is the legal reference point for the rights and obligations of the parties. When a big claim is at stake, however, in practice the policy often merely provides the policyholder with the authority to seek judicial intervention in the process of claim making and resolution.[27]

The interaction of tort and insurance coverage litigation can affect each form of litigation in other ways. From the tort defendant–policyholder's standpoint, the ideal is to know as the underlying tort litigation proceeds whether and to what extent any liability that may be imposed in that litigation would be covered. In practice, however, the availability of insurance in the event that liability is imposed is uncertain. In fact, it is common for the underlying liability actions and claims for insurance coverage to proceed simultaneously, though on different tracks. Policyholders must then take care that developments on one track do not adversely affect the other. The most salient risk is that facts developed or rulings made in one will be used to disadvantage the policyholder in the other. For example, probably the most common insurer defense to claims for coverage of major tort liabilities is that the insured "expected or intended" harm, in violation of an exclusion employing that phrase.

Under one scenario, if the claim for a declaratory judgment as to insurance coverage proceeds ahead of the underlying tort claim, then discovery by the insurer may reveal facts that the plaintiffs in the tort case can use to their advantage. A tort defendant who is proved to have expected or intended harm is obviously more vulnerable than one proved to have been merely negligent. To deal with this risk, the insured may choose to place its insurance litigation on hold until the tort case has been resolved or to seek a protective order making discovery in the insurance litigation confidential. The former approach sacrifices the opportunity to secure early confirmation of coverage; but the latter approach may solve the problem only temporarily, since holding an entirely confidential trial of a major insurance coverage case is almost certainly infeasible.

Since we are talking about facts, it may seem odd to take a critical point of view about procedures (such as a coverage trial addressing whether the policyholder expected or intended injury or damage to result from its activities) that help to uncover the truth. In the ordinary case, however, a liability insurer has a duty to its insured that precludes taking action to the insured's prejudice. The standard primary CGL insurance policy imposes

27. For further discussion, see Abraham (2001).

an obligation on the insurer to provide the insured with a defense whose costs do not deplete the insurer's indemnity obligations. Measures taken by an insurer to resist a coverage claim that result in the revelation of facts undermining the insured's defense against the underlying tort claim are certainly inconsistent with the spirit, and arguably with the letter, of the insurer's duty to defend. Such measures will aid the plaintiff in the underlying action and thereby undermine the very defense that the insurer is supposed to provide.

Conversely, under a second scenario, if the tort case proceeds ahead of the insurance claim, facts developed in the tort case may prejudice the insurance claim. The defendant/insured can have no valid complaint that this gives an unfair advantage to the insurer, since the right to coverage depends on the actual facts. And in any event, one of the two cases must go first. But the fact that the insured's right to coverage of major tort liabilities is so often in dispute means that an important ingredient in potential settlement—knowledge of the scope of insurance coverage available to help fund settlement—will not necessarily be available at the time when that knowledge could be of most use.

One of the secondary effects of regulation by litigation is that minor players are sometimes swept into the current of this litigation. Because of the threat that a single co-defendant may be held jointly and severally liable for indivisible injury or damage caused by other defendants, the threat of liability may be out of all proportion to a minor player's actual contribution overall. Thus operators of vending machines may be joined as defendants and threatened with significant liability in tobacco litigation, makers of breast implants may seek contribution from suppliers of silicon, retail dry cleaning establishments may be notified that they are potentially responsible partners in CERCLA cases, and so forth. These secondary effects may in turn have insurance impacts. Minor players may be placed in the same position as major players vis-à-vis their insurers, in the manner I described above, when they are named as defendants in major litigation. In addition, the prospect that this may occur sometimes prompts the addition of exclusions from or limitations on coverage in the insurance policies of the minor players. When these exclusions are not carefully targeted but prophylactic —the absolute pollution exclusion is an example—the result is that small enterprises lose entire categories of coverage.

Of course, the loss of insurance coverage against a major potential liability is an occasion for concern even for a sizable business. But when a smaller enterprise is met with a new exclusion from coverage—especially if that exclusion addresses a principal source of potential liability—then the ability of that enterprise to continue safely in operation may be threatened. A substantial uninsured liability can be a bet-the-company proposition. Along with the impact of insurance disputes on the major players, therefore, we must also count the ripple effects on minor players as one of the costs of regulation by litigation.

Lawsuits Pertaining to Guns and HMOs

With a couple of exceptions, the gun suits seek recovery for economic losses suffered by municipalities in dealing with gun-related injuries, not damages for bodily injury.[28] When they are permissible at all, suits against HMOs seek contractual and extracontractual damages. Contractual damages are simply the cost of medical services that the plaintiffs allege were the HMO's obligation to pay. Extracontractual damages, by contrast, consist principally of general or punitive damages for wrongful or bad-faith breach of the HMO's obligations to the plaintiff.

Suits of this sort have even more obvious regulatory objectives than toxic tort and product liability actions. The municipalities' gun suits seem directed mainly at threatening sufficient monetary liability to induce the defendants into some kind of acceptable nonmonetary settlement that will involve the promise of behavioral change by the gun makers. Similarly, proponents of legislative authorization of suits against HMOs for extracontractual damages seem to view the *in terrorem* effect such a cause of action might have on HMO behavior as its principal benefit.

The insurance implications of these types of suits are somewhat different from those involving toxic torts and product liability, precisely because gun and HMO suits are so much less concerned with obtaining compensation for injury and so much more concerned with behavioral effects. Although some of the costs that municipalities seek to recover from gun makers are incurred "because of" bodily injury, as required by standard CGL policies, other costs sought in these suits probably are not. And it remains to be seen what coverage, if any, will be afforded HMOs under

28. See, for example, *Archer* v. *Arms Technology, Inc.*, 725 F.Supp. 2d 784 (E.D. Mich. 1999); *City of Bridgeport* v. *Smith & Wesson, Inc.*, No. CV-99-036-1279 (Conn. Super. Ct., filed January 27, 1999); *City of Chicago* v. *Beretta U.S.A. Corp.*, No. 99-2518 Ill. Cir. Ct. Cook County, filed November 12, 1998). The most prominent case seeking damages for personal injury is *Hamilton* v. *Accu-Tek*, 62 F. Supp. 2d 802 (E.D. N.Y. 1999). See also Lytton (2000).

Professional Liability or Errors and Omissions policies issued once suits against HMOs are generally authorized. Liability insurers have sometimes been reluctant to insure against the consequences of another insurer's failure to comply with its obligations under a contract of insurance. Consequently, whether there will be any substantial insurance available to cover gun and HMO liabilities is uncertain at this point.

The Hydraulics of Regulation

One of the messages of the preceding pages is that liability insurance pricing is wholly unconcerned with the motive for imposing civil liability. What matters is not why liability is imposed but what the incidence of liability will be and how much it will cost. Predicted frequency and severity rule the calculation of liability insurance premiums.

Nevertheless, although all tort litigation is ostensibly concerned with what occurred in the past, the difference between litigation over forms of activity that have ceased to occur and those that continue may have different insurance impacts. Some litigation addresses injuries resulting from activities that have ceased altogether by the time a suit ends up in court. Suits alleging liability for injury or damage associated with lead-based pigment fits in this category. In contrast, other kinds of litigation are concerned with activities that not only have caused (or are alleged to have caused) injuries in the past but that continue to occur. Tobacco lawsuits are a prime example.

In one sense, the predominately backward-looking litigation in the first category is nonregulatory, whereas the forward-looking litigation in the second category often has an explicit regulatory aim. Lead-pigment suits can no longer have a regulatory impact on the manufacture of lead pigment, because lead pigment is no longer put to the uses that generated this litigation. Tobacco, however, continues in use, and tobacco lawsuits suits might well have an impact on the tobacco industry. Indeed, achieving such an impact is the avowed aim of at least some of the parties involved in the tobacco litigation.

The frequency and severity of civil liability for injury or damage associated even with obsolete, discontinued activities, however, is bound to influence current decisions about what activities to engage in and how to engage in them, and in turn what to charge for insurance against liability damage arising from a policyholder's activities. In this sense, every lawsuit is potentially regulation by litigation. Ideally, the threat of civil liability has a regulatory effect by promoting optimal deterrence—the taking of precautions and selection of activities that minimize the sum of accident costs and accident avoidance costs. To make good on this threat, liability must actually be imposed. But this conception of regulation by litigation aims to achieve deterrence by leaving the actors threatened with liability to decide whether to take additional precautions in response to the threat of liability or simply to incur liability instead. Under this conception, the choice between accidents and accident avoidance is made by potential injurers, in part because the legal system is less than fully confident of the optimal mix of these options.

A narrower conception of regulation by litigation might be limited to cases in which the explicit motive of the plaintiffs is in fact to change defendants' behavior, rather than merely to create an incentive on the part of the defendant to consider whether to change. Of course, because actors are still permitted to continue their activity as long as they pay the requisite price in liability, this form of regulation by litigation is by no means certain to achieve its objectives. Moreover, because these different conceptions of regulation by litigation have no doctrinal significance, they are not always recognizable or distinguishable.

Interestingly, however, whether the subject is such "backward-looking" litigation as lead paint, breast implant, and auto litigation, or such "forward-looking" suits as gun and tobacco litigation, the uncertainty effects on liability insurance are likely to be similar. The insurance analytics, and as nearly as I can tell the insurance empirics, are virtually identical whether one considers backward-looking or forward-looking litigation. It seems likely, however, that the incidence of forward-looking litigation— the core of regulation by litigation—is at least partly influenced by the extent of administrative regulation of the same subject matter. Administrative regulation enhances public trust of the safety of an activity. And public distrust of an activity is an important predicate for regulation by litigation, since distrust makes successful litigation results more likely. Thus, other things being equal, we should expect to see more regulation by litigation focused on activities that receive relatively soft administrative regulation than activities that are heavily regulated. The rise of gun and tobacco litigation provides at least some confirmation of this observation.

What is true of personal injury suits is probably also true of insurance. Softening insurance regulation without full public confidence in the wisdom of deregulation is likely to lead to greater distrust of insurers and thereby to encourage more insurance coverage litigation. Other factors will of course also be influential, and in particular cases, dominant. But it is worth considering the possibility that regulation may have a tendency to seek its own level. We may well have the option of choosing the mix of litigation and administrative regulation we prefer, even while the body politic, in the end, determines the total quantum of regulation that our system requires.

COMMENT BY
J. David Cummins

Kenneth S. Abraham has written an insightful chapter on the insurance effects of regulation by litigation. My commentary first provides an overview of the effects of regulation by litigation on insurance markets and then discusses two issues involving liability insurance—claims-made versus occurrence policies and multiple-year occurrences (MYOs).

Insurance Effects of Regulation by Litigation

Insurance tends to work best when coverage is provided for a large number of exposure units experiencing losses that are relatively small, frequent, and statistically independent. Under these conditions, insurers with large pools of units exposed to risk can take advantage of the law of large numbers to estimate future losses, and the average expected loss of the pool converges to the true expected value of loss. Insurers can guarantee their promise to pay claims even if losses are larger than expected with a relatively low-risk charge or loading.

Regulation through litigation and other mass torts cause problems in insurance markets because they create claiming environments that are inconsistent with the fundamental principles of insurance. Mass torts violate the statistical independence assumption by affecting many policies and claimants simultaneously. With correlated losses, the diversification that can be achieved in an insurance risk pool is significantly reduced. Instead of the risk charge converging toward zero as the number of exposure units in the pool increases as in the case of independent risks, the risk charge in a pool of correlated risks converges to a positive value that can be large relative to the expected value of loss, increasing the price of insurance to pay for the additional capital needed to bond the promise to pay claims.[29] Taken to the limit, covariability can lead to market failure, such that insurance becomes excessively expensive or simply unavailable.

As Abraham points out, regulation by litigation also increases the difficulty faced by insurers in estimating the expected costs of coverage. Estimating expected claims costs requires insurers to forecast the frequency and severity of claims some distance into the future. This is a difficult problem even for relatively predictable coverages such as automobile liability insurance, where disputes about contract coverage are relatively rare. Regulation through litigation exacerbates the frequency and severity forecasting problem by exposing insurers to liability for events that could not be foreseen when the insurance contracts were executed. As Abraham points out, "A chain-saw manufacturer may be a somewhat more likely target of such litigation than a maker of lolly pops. But even this is only a matter of speculative probability. . . .Within broad bounds, regulation-by-litigation may strike like lightning, almost randomly." In effect, with regulation by litigation, insurers are required to bear not only the inherent stochastic risk of claim frequency and severity, which would be present even if loss probability distributions were known with certainty, but also the risk that judicial decisions will shift the underlying probability distributions in ways that increase expected losses and loss volatility.

In the presence of extreme difficulties in predicting loss frequency and severity, it is not surprising that insurers have taken measures to protect themselves against the additional uncertainty created by regulation through litigation. These measures fall into two primary categories: point-of-sale effects and point-of-claim effects. The point-of-sale and the point-of-claim effects represent attempts to shift a significant share of the risk of unpredictable claims from the insurer to the insured. Given that insurers arguably have a superior ability to diversify risk by covering multiple firms, industries, and geographical regions, the allocation of more risk to the buyer is unlikely to be Pareto optimal from a risk-sharing perspective but may be viewed as a necessity by insurers in order to preserve their financial stability.

The point-of-sale impact of mass torts can take several forms. In Abraham's terminology, insurers seek to increase premiums by levying an "uncertainty tax" to guard against unpredictable increases in loss frequency

29. Cummins (1991).

and severity. Insurers also attempt to restrict coverage by offering lower policy limits and requiring higher deductibles. Coverage also can be restricted by writing exclusions into liability contracts, such as the "absolute" pollution exclusion, and by redefining coverage triggers to shift liability "payout tail risk" from the insurer to the insured. The latter type of risk shifting is exemplified by the insurance industry's attempt to shift from traditional "occurrence-based" liability triggers to "claims-made" triggers in commercial and professional liability insurance policies.

Occurrence policies cover the insured for any injury or damage "during the policy period," for which the insured becomes legally obligated to pay. As Abraham points out, occurrence liability policies provide coverage from the date the policy is issued *"until the end of time"* (emphasis added) and hence are particularly risky for insurers in terms of the potential for unforeseen future liabilities. Claims-made policies attempt to shift the "tail risk," that is, the risk of unforeseen claims arising in the future, from the insurer to the insured by providing coverage only for claims made during the policy period rather than claims arising from actions taken by the insured during the policy period, as in occurrence policies. As discussed in the following paragraphs, however, the operation of competitive liability insurance markets has resulted in less risk shifting through claims-made policies than might have been anticipated when the policies were introduced.

As mentioned, insurers also attempt to shift risk to the buyer at the "point of claim." As Abraham points out, mass torts provide an incentive for claimants to pursue lawsuits that have low probabilities of recovery because of the possibility of receiving very large liability judgments if the claims are successful. However, the potential magnitude of the award in lawsuits affecting multiple claimants also gives insurers the incentive to resist claims, even for damages that were contemplated when the policy was written. This has given rise to a de facto "big-claim exclusion" in liability coverage, whereby the insurers tend to automatically resist large claims, regardless of their merit.

The big-claim exclusion and insurer resistance to mass torts in general produces a "whipsaw effect." The effect occurs because the policyholder is simultaneously defending itself against liability suits from claimants and pursuing coverage litigation against the insurer. This not only weakens the promise of the insurer to provide a legal defense to the policyholder but also creates the risk that information leakage from one of the legal actions (that is, the claimants' actions against the policyholder and policyholder's dispute with the insurer) will adversely affect the outcome of the other. These effects represent inefficiencies in the insurance market created by mass torts that reduce the beneficial effects of insurance on economic welfare and lead to suboptimal risk-sharing outcomes.

Claims-Made Policies and "Tail Risk"

Claims-made policies were introduced in an attempt by insurers to shift to policyholders much of the risk of the liability insurance claims payout tail previously covered under occurrence-based policies. By limiting coverage to claims filed during the policy period, insurers hoped to shed their liability for unexpected events resulting from regulation through litigation and other mass torts. However, occurrence-based liability insurance policies emerged through the interaction of supply and demand in competitive insurance markets, revealing that buyers have a preference for transferring tail risk to insurers. Thus it could be expected that claims-made policies would not be universally appreciated among buyers of liability insurance and that competitive pressures would develop to blunt the transfer of tail risk to policyholders.

The prediction that claims-made policies have been less than totally successful in shifting risk to the buyers is supported by figure 7-1, which shows the market penetration of claims-made policies in general liability insurance over the period 1987–2000.[30] The percentage of premiums accounted for by claims-made policies increased steadily during the period but still represented only 37 percent of total liability insurance premiums by 2000. Thus the market outcome still favors occurrence-based policies.

Buyer demand for coverage of the liability payout tail also has resulted in the convergence of coverage in claims-made policy forms toward the type of coverage traditionally provided under occurrence-based policies. Contractual provisions have been introduced into claims-made policies that reduce the differences between claims-made coverage and occurrence coverage. The most important contractual modification is the "extended reporting period" or "tail coverage" provision included in most claims-

30. Figure 7-1 and the other figures included in this commentary are based on industrywide data on the "other liability" line of insurance as reported in insurance company regulatory annual statements. This category includes general liability insurance but excludes medical malpractice. The market penetration of claims-made policies in the medical malpractice market is much greater than in general liability insurance. See A. M. Best Company (2001). The results shown in all figures are based on premiums and losses net of reinsurance.

Figure 7-1. *General Liability Insurance Claims-Made Premiums/*
Total Premiums

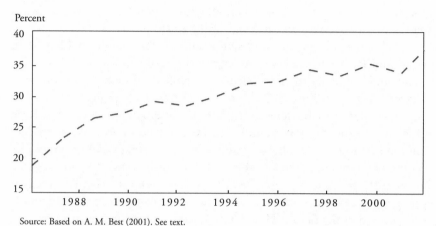

Percent

Source: Based on A. M. Best (2001). See text.

made policies. The standard extended reporting period clause provides a
five-year coverage extension, whereby claims made during a five-year
period following the coverage year are covered under the policy as long as
the events generating the claims were reported to the insurer during a
sixty-day period following the end of the coverage year. It is also possible
and common for policyholders to purchase "supplemental extended
reporting period" coverage that extends the standard tail-coverage period
beyond five years or lengthens the reporting period for events that generate covered claims. Thus claims-made policies are available that offer coverage similar to that provided by occurrence-based liability policies.
Coverage extensions are particularly prevalent during "soft market" phases
of the insurance underwriting cycle, when coverage is widely available and
prices are relatively low. During such periods, it is very difficult for insurers to enforce contractual restrictions that impose unwanted risk on policyholders.

Evidence that claims-made general liability insurance policies do not
have significantly different tail behavior than occurrence policies is presented in figure 7-2, which shows the payout tails for the occurrence and
claims-made coverages. For the purposes of this discussion, the payout tail
is defined as the ratio of paid losses to incurred losses as a function of the
number of years after policy issue, where incurred losses represent insurers' best estimate of the total losses that will eventually be paid for any

given coverage year. For example, the figure shows that the ratio of paid to incurred losses for both occurrence and claims-made policies is about 36 percent at the end of the policy period, with the balance of incurred losses representing reserves for claims that will be paid in the future.

If claims-made policies shift significant tail risk to policyholders, then we would expect to observe higher ratios of paid to incurred losses for claims-made policies than for occurrence policies in each year of the payout tail. Although figure 7-2 shows that claims-made policies do tend to pay claims faster than occurrence policies, the differences are not as large as might be expected. For example, the ratio of paid to incurred losses during the first four years following policy issue is virtually indistinguishable for the two types of coverage. The paid to incurred ratios begin to diverge in the fifth coverage year, but the difference between the claims made and the occurrence paid to incurred ratio never exceeds 5 percent for the runoff years shown in the figure. Thus claims-made policies do not seem to have shifted a substantial amount of tail risk from insurers to policyholders.

Further information on the payout tail of claims-made and occurrence policies is provided in figure 7-3, which shows the ratio of the incurred but not reported (IBNR) reserve to the total reserve for claims-made and occurrence policies, again as a function of the number of years since policy inception. The IBNR reserves are estimated liabilities for losses the insurer believes it will eventually have to pay for claims that have not yet been reported to the insurer. Claims-made policies were supposed to drastically reduce the IBNR reserve by shortening the period during which insured events and the resulting claims could be reported to the insurer. However, because of market demand for tail coverage, the claims-made policies that have actually been issued have not had as large an effect on IBNR as might have been expected. Although the IBNR is significantly lower for claims-made policies during the runoff years shown in figure 7-3, the ratio of IBNR to total reserves for claims-made policies is equal to or greater than 45 percent for nine of the ten runoff years. In years 4 through 7, the IBNR reserve-to-total reserves ratio for claims-made policies is only slightly lower than for occurrence policies, and claims-made policies still have substantial IBNR reserves in the tenth runoff year. This provides further evidence that claims-made policies have not resulted in the substantial elimination of event risk uncertainty resulting from an IBNR claim.

To summarize, the convergence of claims-made policy coverage toward occurrence policy coverage is attributable to competitive conditions in the general liability insurance market, whereby buyers demand

Figure 7-2. *General Liability Insurance Payout Tails Paid Losses/ Incurred Losses, Reported in 2000*

Percent

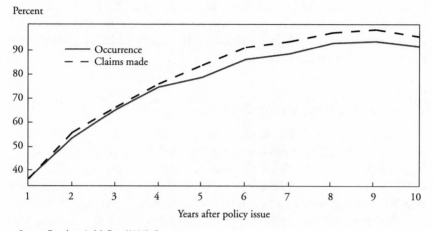

Years after policy issue

Source: Based on A. M. Best (2001). See text.

Figure 7-3. *General Liability: IBNR Reserve/Total Reserve Occurrence versus Claims Made*

Percent IBNR

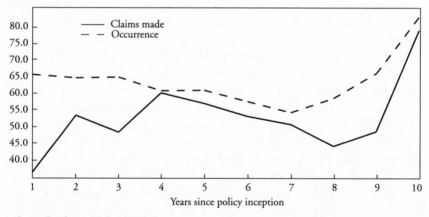

Years since policy inception

Source: Based on A. M. Best (2001). See text.

and insurers supply coverage that shifts significant tail risk from the policyholder to the insurer. Even though insurers would prefer to shift more of the tail risk to the policyholder, buyer demand for tail coverage has resulted in relatively low market penetration for claims-made policies, and the use of extended reporting periods results in insurers bearing significant tail risk, even in claims-made policies.

Multiple-Year Occurrences (MYOs)

Point-of-claim inefficiencies relating to regulation by litigation and mass torts also can be created when courts seek "deep pockets" to pay for large liability claims. Such inefficiencies arise when courts expand coverage of liability policies to include events, insured amounts, and time periods that were not intended to be covered when policies were issued. Judicial expansiveness results in insurers paying claims for which no premium was collected and exacerbates the problem of forecasting claim frequency and severity. An especially troublesome instance of this type of point-of-claim inefficiency is provided by multiple-year occurrences (MYOs). MYOs result from behavior that causes damage over a significant period such as the exposure of workers to asbestos or harmful chemicals over several years.

A major coverage issue confronted in settling MYOs arises from the presence of multiple insurers that were on the risk for some subset of the period during which the occurrence took place.[31] The multiple insurance policies covering the risk during the occurrence period often have deductibles and policy limits that differ across years. Excess coverage policies for claims larger than covered by primary policies may be present in some years but not others and may have different attachment points and coverage limits. There also may be gaps in coverage, that is, years when no coverage was purchased, the insurer later became insolvent, or the insurer cannot be identified because the policy has been lost.

In awarding judgments under MYOs, courts may ignore policy exclusions and deductibles or adopt a "pick and choose" strategy that arbitrarily allocates losses to years with low deductibles and high policy limits. Solvent insurers may be required to pay claims that should be covered by insurers that are now insolvent, and coverage under policies from solvent insurers may be extended to years when no coverage was in effect or the insurer cannot be identified.

31. Cummins and Doherty (1996).

Because insurers price liability insurance on the assumption that the policies will cover claims falling within the insuring agreement of the policy and arising during specified exposure periods, the judicial extension of coverage to other events and time periods puts insurers in the position of paying claims for which no premium was collected. Such unanticipated extensions of coverage tend to increase the uncertainty tax for policies issued in the future and provide incentives for insurers to invoke the big-claim exclusion.

Conclusion

Regulation by litigation has the potential to generate suits against entire industries, resulting in damages for unforeseeable events and massive loss liabilities. Such suits are difficult to handle in insurance markets because they violate the underlying theory of insurance, which relies on the law of large numbers and statistical independence across insured exposure units to enable the insurer to estimate premiums and diversify risk. Mass torts create correlations among insured exposure units, reducing the efficiency of risk pooling. In the extreme, such events can result in market failure, such that insurance is unavailable or excessively priced.

The emergence of large, unanticipated losses leads insurers to attempt to shift payout tail risk to policyholders and leads policyholders and courts to attempt to shift risk to insurers. Risk shifting can occur at the point of sale or the point of claim. Insurers can shift risk to buyers at the point of sale by adding policy exclusions, increasing deductibles, decreasing policy limits, and levying an "uncertainty tax" in the premium. Insurers also have attempted to reduce tail risk by introducing claims-made policies to replace traditional occurrence-based policies. However, competition in insurance markets limits the extent to which insurers are able to exploit these measures to reduce their risk. As a result of extended reporting periods, for example, the payout tail of claims-made general liability policies is not much different from that of occurrence policies.

At the point of claim, policyholders and courts often are successful in shifting the risk of unforeseen occurrences to insurers. This is done by ignoring exclusions and deductibles and extending policy coverage to events and periods of time not contemplated when the contracts were issued. Thus insurers are required to cover unforeseen events for which no premium was collected.

Regulation through litigation and other types of mass torts misuse the liability insurance market, in effect breaking the linkage among premiums, covered events, and liability for payment. This result is not only detrimental to insurers but also leads to resource misallocation to the extent that those causing losses are not charged for the expected value of the damages. As Abraham points out, "Regulation by litigation has produced, or at least contributed to, significant chronic effects that undermine the optimal functioning of liability insurance markets." Economic efficiency could be improved by bringing judicial interpretations of liability insurance policy provisions more into line with the intent of the parties when the policies were issued.

References

Abraham, Kenneth S. 1987. "Making Sense of the Liability Insurance Crisis." *Ohio State Law Journal* 48 (2): 399–411.

———. 1991. *Environmental Liability Insurance Law: An Analysis of Toxic Tort and Hazardous Waste Insurance Coverage Issues.* Prentice Hall Law and Business.

———. 1997. "The Maze of Mega-Coverage Litigation." *Columbia Law Review* 97 (November): 2101–16.

———. 2000. *Insurance Law and Regulation: Cases and Materials.* 3d ed. New York: Foundation Press.

———. 2001. "The Rise and Fall of Commercial Liability Insurance." *Virginia Law Review 87* (March): 85–109.

A.M. Best Company. 2001. *Best's Aggregates and Averages: 2001 Edition.* Oldwick, N. J.

Caverly, Raymond, M. 1939. "The Background of the Casualty and Bonding Business in the United States." *Insurance Counsel Journal* 6 (October): 62–63.

Cummins, J. David. 1991. "Statistical and Financial Models of Insurance Pricing and the Insurance Firm." *Journal of Risk and Insurance* 58 (2): 261–302.

Cummins, J. David, and Neil A. Doherty. 1996. "Allocating Continuous Occurrence Losses Across Multiple Insurance Policies." *Environmental Claims Journal* 8 (Spring): 5–42.

Dolan, Mitchell F., and Ethan M. Posner. 1998. "Understanding the Bermuda Excess Liability Form." *Journal of Insurance Coverage* 1 (Autumn): 68–84.

Feagles, Prentiss E., and others. 1975. "Comment: An Analysis of State Legislative Responses to Medical Malpractice Crisis." *Duke Law Journal* 1975 (6): 1417–68.

Fischer, James M. 1997. "Insurance Coverage for Mass Exposure Claims: The Debate over the Appropriate Trigger Rule." *Drake Law Review* 45 (3): 625–96.

Kulp, C. A. 1928. *Casualty Insurance.* Roland Press Company.

Lytton, Timothy D. 2000. "Tort Claims against Gun Manufacturers for Crime-Related Injuries: Defining a Suitable Role for the Tort System in Regulating the Firearms Industry." *Missouri Law Review* 65 (Winter): 1–81.

Malecki, Donald S., and others. 1986. *Commercial Liability Risk Management and Insurance.* Vol. 1, 2d ed. Malvern, Pa.: American Institute for Property and Liability Underwriters.

Mooney, Sean F. 2000. "Commercial Lines Ride Rougher Profit Road." *National Underwriter* (November 6): 1.

Priest, George L. 1987. "The Current Insurance Crisis and Modern Tort Law." *Yale Law Journal* 96 (June): 1521–90.

Raphael, Adam. 1994. *Ultimate Risk: The Inside Story of the Lloyds Catastrophe.* Bantam Press.

Ruquet, Mark E. 2000. "Market Hardening Speeds Up, Surveys Say." *National Underwriter* (December 4): 1.

Stewart, Richard E. 1980. "The Risk Money Game." Address to the American Farm Bureau Federation (January).

Symposium. 1977. "The Medical Malpractice Crisis: Managing the Costs." *Maryland Law Review* 36 (3): 489–585.

DAVID ROSENBERG

8 | *The Regulatory Advantage of Class Action*

T his chapter explains the principal and generally unrecognized regulatory advantage of adjudicating mass production tort cases by class action rather than in the standard process of separate actions.[1] My analysis is premised upon and measures regulatory advantage by the social objective of mass production tort liability: to minimize the sum of accident costs. In particular, the aim is to minimize the costs of precautions against accident, plus the costs of unavoided harm, plus the costs of adjudication, including expense incurred to administer the tort system and litigate claims. (This social goal is also referred to as "optimal tort deterrence.") This regulatory objective does not include compensation of those injured by tortious activity; the injured would replace their losses through standard commercial and governmental insurance as they would the losses from natural and other nontortious risks that account for most of the annual national toll in death, disability, and property damage.[2]

The author thanks Michael Allen, Norina Edelman, Trevor Livingston, Catherine Rosenberg, Wesley Shih, and Michael Zarren for substantive comments and editorial assistance that were very helpful in preparing this chapter.

1. The thesis I advance draws and builds on my prior work and that of others, most importantly Calabresi (1970); Shavell (1987); and Kaplow and Shavell (2001).

2. For documentation of the widespread availability of government and commercial sources of first-party insurance, see Kaplow and Shavell (2001, p.1097). See also Priest (1987, pp. 1586—87), noting that those who lack direct insurance coverage, generally individuals from lower-income groups,

Normally, and for purposes of my analysis, the deterrence goal of min-imizing the sum of costs for precautions and from unavoided harm (exclu-sive of costs of adjudication) entails imposing liability for damages equal to total tortious harm (defined strictly, by the negligence standard, or oth-erwise). Threatening monetary sanction in this degree provides would-be tortfeasors with financial incentive to invest optimally in precautions that prevent unreasonable risk of accident. In the mass production tort context, which involves business activity that exposes some population to risk of accident, deterrence requires enforcing claims by all tort victims to impose liability for the total *aggregate* tortious harm ("aggregate liability"). For example, if factory pollution would cause each of one hundred people tor-tious loss of $1,000 unless the firm takes cost-effective precautions, such as installing a filtering device, then to achieve the appropriate deterrent effect courts must enforce all one hundred claims to confront the firm with the prospect of bearing aggregate liability of $100,000.

Consequently, the choice between using separate actions or class action to achieve optimal tort deterrence resolves to the question of which mode of adjudication best, most cost effectively, ensures the enforcement of all claims arising from a mass production tort event to establish aggre-gate liability. Refining the issue further, the choice is between two means of allocating law enforcement resources. The standard process of separate actions relies on a competitive market in tort suits in which the profit-maximizing motive of plaintiffs' attorneys serves to select the most eco-nomically promising ("marketable") claims arising from a mass production tort event for investments of time, money, and effort by courts as well as by lawyers. The attorneys compete in acquiring shares of marketable claims, in effect fractionally aggregating adjudication as well as represen-tation of these claims. Fractional aggregation will likely involve multiple courts exercising more or less independent adjudicative authority to resolve claims in separate groups. In the factory pollution example, several law firms would divide up the one hundred claims (assuming all are marketable) and prosecute the fractional shares, say 20 percent each,

---

qualify for public assistance when they suffer loss from serious harm. Because first-party insurance is generally less risky and costly than tort insurance, tort law makes "tort insureds" worse off to the extent that it prohibits them from contracting out of some or all of its inefficient insurance coverage. For an example of general prohibition of contract disclaimer relating to insurance under product liability law, see Restatement (Third) of Torts: Products Liability, sec. 18 (1977). The case against relying on tort to supply accident insurance or to effect progressive redistribution of wealth is developed in Fried and Rosenberg (forthcoming).

coordinating their efforts to some degree, but largely acting independently, litigating before different courts and investing generally to maximize their own profit from their respective holdings of twenty claims. Class action, in contrast, is a form of regulation that overrides the market-based process to aggregate all claims for collective litigation as a single claim for aggregate liability. By comparison to the fractional aggregation of the standard market-based process, class action would collectively aggregate all one hundred pollution claims, marketable or not in the separate action process, for prosecution by a single profit-maximizing attorney (or firm of attorneys) and for adjudicative management by a single court.

I show that class action provides the more cost-effective means of adjudicating mass production torts. Only class action aggregates all mass production tort claims to provide the opportunity for fully exploiting economies of litigation scale that ensure maximum regulatory, optimal deterrence benefit from mass production tort liability. The standard, market-based process of separate actions suffers from collective action and other fundamental defects that undermine the regulatory objective by precluding universal aggregation and resulting enforcement benefits from litigation scale economies. The basic problem is that the market-based process operates ex post, after tortious harm occurs, and therefore aggregates mass production tort claims only to the limited extent consistent with interests and strategies of maximizing individual wealth for some, heedless of the ex ante value of optimal deterrence from universal aggregation that maximizes individual welfare for everyone. The class action design that solves this problem would immediately and automatically aggregate all potential mass production tort claims for collective resolution, on a mandatory no-exit (opt-out) basis. A single court would assume exclusive, centralized managerial control over the entire litigation from start to finish. Of greatest significance, class action would vest one plaintiff's lawyer or firm of lawyers ("class counsel") with a proprietary monopoly over the prosecution of all claims. (As discussed later, class counsel would be selected by auctioning "ownership" of the entire class action to the highest bidder.)

My analysis has import for how courts should manage a major portion of civil actions currently prosecuted against business defendants. Conventional associations of "mass production torts" with the gargantuan asbestos and tobacco litigations, each comprising millions of temporally and territorially dispersed claims, create the misimpression that regulatory concerns only relate to aberrant phenomena. These litigations, however, are merely extreme versions of the multiclaim product liability or other business-risk case that pervades court dockets today. All arise from the mass production processes and goods (products and services) of business enterprise that often, as an unavoidable cost of their benefits, systematically place some population of workers, consumers, and others at risk of incurring personal injury and property damage ("mass production torts"). Because of the potential for serious harm, the legal system assiduously regulates business risk taking to keep it within socially acceptable bounds, usually specified by the mandate to minimize the sum of accident costs.[3] Despite increasing reliance on the comprehensive, expert, and publicly financed authority of independent and executive administrative agencies, tort law continues to serve a significant and (I assume for present purposes) needed enforcement role, especially as a check against administrative capture and slack, in optimally deterring unreasonable risk-taking by business.[4] Thus, while using the term "mass production tort" and focusing on suits for damages for convenience, I regard the following analysis of the regulatory advantage of class action (or its functional equivalent) as fully applicable to any multiclaim case of civil liability against a common business defendant, whatever the cause of action or remedy involved (including suits charging environmental degradation, invidious employment discrimination, contract breach, securities and other consumer fraud, antitrust violations, nuisance, and corporate mismanagement).

From the regulatory perspective, mass production torts are inherently suited to class action aggregation that maximizes enforcement benefits from litigation scale economies. Indeed, all else being equal, the benefits from "class action scale economies" continue to increase, albeit at a diminishing rate, as claim aggregation increases, reaching maximum level only when all claims are aggregated for collective resolution. The key feature of regulatory relevance is that the target of mass production tort liability is the mass production decision, which generates the systematic risk that gives

3. To this end, the legal system employs a wide variety of enforcement options ranging from focused oversight by specialized expert bureaucracies to the more or less roving commission exercised by a generalist judiciary under the law of torts. Thus a vast array of state and federal independent and executive agencies now police business risk taking not only by levying taxes and monetary (and prison) sanctions in response to actualized risk or harm but also by intervening preemptively to command and control the terms for permitting dangerous activity, if any. For discussion of the appropriate allocation of legislative and judicial roles in tort law reform, see Fried and Rosenberg (Forthcoming).

4. That the social regulatory objecive requires tort liability and a system of nonexpert policymakers can realistically achieve results approximating optimal tort deterrence are pivotal and contested assumptions. See Schwartz (1994).

rise to all claims. Focused on determining the tortious character and consequences of the core mass production decision, all mass production tort
claims necessarily present basic common questions of law (for example,
whether state-of-the-art qualifies liability), fact (for example, causation),
and law-fact (for example, negligence), generalizable methods and applications of proof, and other significant opportunities to exploit economies of
litigation scale (for convenience, "common questions"). More significantly,
because of the statistical and unitary nature of mass production decisions,
for deterrence purposes all claims can be resolved in the aggregate and, for
the most part, on the basis of statistical analysis and projections. Determination of aggregate liability does not entail resolution of noncommon questions or consideration of claim-specific variables beyond conducting
statistical sampling for purposes of formulating estimates of probablility.

   In the factory pollution example, estimates on the margin of the indivisible aggregate cost of installing the filtering device for the related indivisible aggregate benefit in reduced liability determines that some
population known to the firm solely in terms of a weighted average of relevant demographical characteristics will incur an indivisible aggregate risk
of accident. If the firm recognizes that courts will seek to further the goal
of optimal tort deterrence, its calculation should anticipate that pollution
accident would be followed by enforcement of all claims resulting on average in total aggregate liability of $100,000. Since the firm's initial mass
production decision is based on its calculation of total aggregate costs and
benefits that maximize net return in lower liability from investing in precautions, and is unaffected by any set of specific accident conditions later
on, courts need only estimate total aggregate tortious harm statistically and
impose total aggregate liability for that amount, in this case $100,000, to
achieve optimal deterrence.

   My argument for regulatory class action goes beyond suitability to
necessity. In sum, only scale efficiencies of class action maximize the regulatory benefits of mass production tort liability. All else being equal, to
achieve optimal deterrence, mass production tort liability must threaten
damages equal to the total aggregate tortious harm. As an abstract matter,
nothing less than universal aggregation of all claims can provide the incentives for courts and parties not only to avoid duplicative effort, but, most
important, to make the respective and joint optimal investments that maximize the deterrence value of judgment or settlement. In reality, however,
mass producers litigate in the standard separate action process from the
posture of a de facto class action, and thus automatically reap scale

economies as if all the claims have been aggregated in a mandatory non-opt-out class action. By contrast, plaintiffs litigating in the separate action process rarely can voluntarily aggregate their claims to a degree approaching the universal aggregation achieved automatically by defendant. Collective action problems, notably free riding, and high costs of organizing and monitoring all stymie coordination by plaintiffs. For similar reasons, courts lack scale-based incentives to invest optimally in policing a defendant's use of its edge in litigation power and in acquiring the expertise needed for effective regulatory decisionmaking. Only class action aggregation of all claims can correct the litigation advantage of defendant over plaintiffs and courts, which skews outcomes and, consequently, undermines optimal tort deterrence.

Part one develops the normative foundation for the regulatory objective of optimal tort deterrence. I show that optimal deterrence represents the rational preference of the individual seeking maximum well-being. Prefaced by a brief extension of the normative thesis, part two explains class action scale economies and the regulatory value of harnessing that mode of enforcing mass production tort liability. Part three addresses the asymmetry in litigation power favoring defendants that arises from their ability to exploit de facto class action scale economies in the standard separate action process. I show that affording defendants, but not plaintiffs and courts, the advantage of class action scale economies undermines the regulatory objective of optimal tort deterrence. I then turn in part four to demonstrate the regulatory need for, and efficacy of, using mandatory class action to correct the systemic bias favoring defendants.

Mass Production Tort Liability for the Individual Good

It is useful to work out the individual welfare argument for optimal deterrence because legal literature does not simply leave the individualist premise unstated, it generally misses the point entirely. Furthermore, showing that an individual rationally prefers committing legal resources to optimal deterrence provides a normative baseline for testing and improving the utility of systems and rules, and even for breaking away from ingrained conventions. In particular, that baseline implies the use of mandatory collectivization (in practical design, mandatory class action or functional equivalent) to adjudicate mass production tort cases.

My argument starts from a more fundamental, but nonetheless assumed premise that the legal system should aim to improve the well-being of individuals and that individuals seek their maximum welfare. The appropriate objective of the legal system, and indeed the propriety of every feature of its structure and operation, depends ultimately on the consequences for maximizing individual welfare. What the legal system should do about accident risk, in short, equates with what an individual seeking maximum welfare would prefer a legal system to do.

To discern this preference, I adopt and justify the "ex ante" perspective of placing individuals "behind a veil of ignorance," without information about their situation in the "ex post" world-to-come of accident risk and scarce resources. Reasoning from that perspective, I conclude that any given individual would rationally choose a legal system that minimizes the sum of accident costs—of particular concern here, the cost of precautions, plus cost of unavoided injury; plus cost of administering the system and litigating claims. This preference implies the basic regulatory objective: to ensure optimal precautions.

Ex Ante versus Ex Post Perspective

The mode of rational choice analysis I employ recognizes that individual preferences are relative to whether the choice is made under conditions of uncertainty or conditions of certainty about the event or matter in question—here, the person's relevant economic, accident, and legal fates. Ex ante, the individual's preference is determined under conditions of uncertainty, at a point in time before the person knows which of possible alternative fates will come to pass. Ex post, the individual's preference is determined after knowing which of these alternatives has (or will) come to pass. Individuals give different answers about what they want the legal system to do about accident risk, depending on whether the question is put ex ante or ex post. Only the answer given ex ante ensures maximum individual welfare regardless of what fate has in store.

The critical point to recognize is that ex ante and ex post preferences are mutually exclusive concerning the fundamental purpose of mass production tort liability in preventing unreasonable risk. Ex ante, before knowing the relevant accident and legal fates, an individual would rationally prefer a legal system that promotes the collective interest in minimizing the sum of accident costs, particularly through optimal precautions. In contrast, ex post, after knowing the "luck of the draw," individuals rationally prefer a legal system that promotes their separate interests regardless of the consequences for accident costs—the attitude epitomized by an insured party who, having suffered no insured loss during the policy period, demands that the insurer return the premium.

This relativity of rational preference requires favoring the ex ante over the ex post perspective. This priority maximizes the individual's total expected welfare, because the ex ante perspective accounts for ex post preferences, while the ex post perspective disregards ex ante preferences. Only the ex ante perspective coheres with the premise that the legal system should promote individual welfare and that individuals seek their maximum well-being. The ex post perspective, in which the individual knows his or her accident fate and related advantages in the existing legal system, effectively conflicts with preferences for optimal precautions, leading the individual to make choices that seem good at the time but that would have the effect of lowering overall expected welfare. Consequently, the individual cannot choose a legal system to manage accident risk in a fashion that maximizes total net expected welfare unless the ex ante preference is given exclusive effect. As I explain more fully below, the individual can maximize expected net welfare through the legal system's management of risk only if the rational preferences honored are those expressed ex ante and, indeed, only if those preferences are understood as implying a "mast-tying" agreement that precludes giving effect to conflicting ex post preferences.[5]

More generally, there is distinctive normative appeal to the ex ante perspective in eliciting individuals' "impartial" preference. Standing in the shoes of all others, the individual ex ante rationally prefers what everyone rationally prefers. In particular, the preference for a legal system that minimizes the sum of accident costs is universally shared. In contrast, ex post individuals treat their respective self-interest as superior to the interests of others. Indeed, the "lucky" act as if they were on separate, well-stocked

5. My conception of rationality consists of the three simple axioms that compose the foundation of rational choice theory—the study of individual choice under conditions of uncertainty and risk that undergirds the basic theories of law enforcement (including general deterrence). See Harsanyi (1977). First, I assume that individuals compare all alternatives consistently, meaning that if A is preferred to B and B is preferred to C, then A is preferred to C. Second, I assume that individuals prefer a lottery with more valuable prizes to a lottery with the same probabilities but in which one or more of the prizes is less valuable. Third, I assume that individuals have continuous preferences, so that a small shift in the value of an outcome would not produce a drastic shift in individuals' valuation of that outcome. These axioms supply the complete basis for proving that individuals will maximize the expectation of their utility—that is, the sum of the utilities corresponding to each outcome weighted by the probability that each outcome will be realized.

islands, while the "unlucky" would save themselves at all cost. The ex ante
perspective, then, compels attention not only because it is the only standpoint in theory and practice that enables the individual to choose a legal
system that maximizes net expected welfare across all states of the world
but also because of its moral appeal in expressing common, unprejudiced
interests. One would expect such preferences to have sufficient persuasive
("legitimating") power to win acceptance ex post.

Some deny the importance, and even relevance, of the ex ante perspective and defend its general neglect by lawmakers and legal academics.
These critics do not deny that ex ante preferences are relatively impartial,
or that crediting individuals' ex post preferences recreates a Hobbesian
state of nature of all-against-all (more accurately, "lucky" against
"unlucky") and makes everyone worse off ex ante. Rather, critics object
that the ex ante perspective is too hypothetical and unrealistic, that it purchases objectivity at the price of determinacy. This objection is not well
founded. The ex ante perspective is the best available method for analyzing legal policy. Like the model of a perfect market, the ex ante perspective on individuals' rational preference for a legal system that minimizes
the sum of accident costs provides analysts a robust critical benchmark.
Undoubtedly, we can never attain a perfect ex ante perspective, one in
which analysts as well as the individual subjects of inquiry lack all knowledge of their respective traits and the prospects that affect their fates in the
ex post world. Also, the world to come is far too complex to be perfectly
represented in the ex ante model. Careful analysis, however, can recognize
the theoretical difficulties with the ex ante approach and do the best it can
to adjust estimates appropriately. Adding dimensions of accident cost,
such as risk aversion, surely complicates analysis of policy options and
related experience, but it does not change—and, so long as individual well-
being is the test, cannot change—the individual's ex ante rational preference for the legal system to minimize the sum of accident costs.

Nor can anyone credibly deny the realistic usefulness of the ex ante
perspective. Plainly, it is indispensable in making and interpreting contracts and in organizing economic and social enterprise generally. The ex
ante perspective is the natural, legislative vantage that affords individuals the most comprehensive view of preferences and set of options to
advance them. This perspective is precisely the one people adopt every
day in evaluating the relative costs and benefits of an undertaking, especially in considering the safety of a product they might buy or their long-
term needs for insurance. The reality of the ex ante perspective is

confirmed by the evidence of how the world actually works, including the net expenditure of trillions of dollars on precautions and insurance against accident risk. There is bountiful real-world information about how individuals behave in these relatively ex ante postures, which analysts can use in determining necessary adjustments to pure theory. The disregard of the ex ante perspective by most of the legal profession is not as astonishing—in view of standard legal education and practice—as it is socially irresponsible.

Minimizing the Sum of Accident Costs

The ex ante perspective I adopt posits a single individual who anticipates living in a world characterized by scarce resources and accident risks that are distributed variously among the people who inhabit it. The individual is given the opportunity of choosing the legal system for managing accident risk, before knowing his or her own prospects in that world regarding accident, access to resources, and advantage in the chosen legal system. Essentially, each individual internalizes all possible fates of all possible people. Seeking maximum well-being regardless of what fate has in store, each individual would rationally choose a legal system that minimized the sum of accident costs by employing optimal tort deterrence to prevent unreasonable risk.

This conclusion follows from the straightforward logic that efficient reduction of accident costs increases the individual's total expected net welfare across all possible states of the world. In other words, in order to maximize the net welfare derived from the total amount of goods he or she expects to have across all possible states of the world, the individual spends resources on precautions to avoid greater accident costs. Indeed, efficient reduction of accident costs means more social welfare to distribute in any given state of the world to make everyone better off not only ex ante but ex post as well. If an individual ex ante expects a certain share of total social benefit, the individual would want a legal system that maximized aggregate social benefit in order to maximize his or her individual share.

A simple example illustrates the general significance of the argument. Suppose an individual ex ante confronts two equally probable fates of being either party in an accident in which driver A hits driver B in an intersection. Assume that both drivers have equivalent wealth of $10,000 and that driver B will lose $1,000 in the event of accident. (I treat the individual ex ante as risk neutral, so that wealth correlates directly with welfare derived from wealth.) Now consider the individual's rational preference as between three otherwise identical legal systems. Regime I would spend nothing to reduce accident risk and, consequently, imposes no tax on the drivers. Regime II would avoid all accidents by posting a police officer at the intersection at a cost of $500 in increased taxes evenly divided between the drivers. Regime III would post a stop sign to avoid 75 percent of the accidents at a cost of $50, again borne evenly by the drivers. Plainly, seeking maximum expected net welfare, the individual ex ante would choose Regime III, even though it allows a substantial risk of accident. Under Regime I, the individual's total expected net welfare is $9,500, equaling the average of both parties' net wealth after an accident in which one will lose $1,000. Under Regime II, the individual's total expected net welfare is $9,750, equaling the average of both parties' net wealth given that each pays $250 for a police officer. By comparison, Regime III promises the greatest net welfare by minimizing the sum of accident costs (here limited for convenience to the costs of precautions plus costs of injury). The individual's total net expected welfare is $9,850, given that each party pays $25 in taxes for the stop sign, and in addition has a 50 percent chance of bearing $250 in expected injury costs (25 percent chance of $1,000 loss). Another way to put the point is that ex ante, the individual rationally prefers the legal system, here Regime III, that maximizes total net social welfare, and therefore average net individual welfare, by minimizing the sum of accident costs.

This preference for minimizing the sum of accident costs to prevent unreasonable risks through optimal deterrence implies the regulatory objective for mass production tort liability as well as for the basic case of reciprocal risk. Individuals ex ante rationally prefer investing social resources to reduce accident risk up to the point on the margin that the cost of further investment in precautions is greater than the cost of the risk that the further investment could avert. Optimal precautions, in other words, prevent unreasonable risk—risk that costs society more to incur than to avoid—and, all else being equal, minimize the sum of accident costs and hence maximize the individuals' expected net welfare. Risk aversion magnifies but does not motivate this result; even assuming risk neutrality, individuals ex ante are made better off by eliminating the deadweight cost of accident.

On the rare occasion when academics, and the still rarer occasion when lawyers, judges, and other lawmakers consider committing the legal system to optimal precautions, most treat the benefits as accruing to society as a whole rather than to the individuals comprising it and hardly ever to a given individual ex ante. This disjuncture in thought may explain the apparent readiness of many to overinvest social resources in precautions. This way of thinking makes everyone worse off ex ante when it is put in practice.

Consider a slightly more complex example to illustrate the significance of optimal deterrence to the maximization of individual welfare ex ante. Assume an individual who is seeking maximum well-being and has an equal chance of being the owner of a firm worth $100,000 that manufactures a product that places consumers at risk of accident and of being a consumer who, in the event of an accident, would lose total wealth of $50,000. (Treating the individual as risk neutral, I equate wealth with welfare derived from wealth.) Suppose the firm could invest in precautions at three levels that affect the chance of accident according to table 8-1:

The optimal investment in precautions is $10,000 because that expenditure minimizes the sum of accident costs (costs of precautions plus residual accident risk) at $15,000. Investing less results in total accident costs of $50,000; investing more results in total accident costs of $30,000. From the ex ante perspective, the individual rationally prefers the optimal investment because it maximizes his or her net expected welfare regardless of whether the individual turns out to be the factory owner or the accident victim ex post. If the optimal investment is made, the individual's total net expected welfare is $67,500, calculated as the sum of a 50 percent chance of having the firm's net wealth of $90,000 ($100,000 minus the $10,000 investment for precautions) and a 50 percent chance of having consumer's net wealth of $45,000 ($50,000 minus the $5,000 expected loss from accident).[6] The individual ex ante would not want a liability rule that results in suboptimal deterrence and an investment of zero in precautions. Such a rule would yield total net expected welfare of only $50,000, calculated as the sum of a 50 percent chance of having the firm's wealth of $100,000 and a 50 percent chance of having the consumer's net wealth of zero. Nor would the individual ex ante want a liability rule inducing an excessive

---

6. Courts can use either of two liability rules to achieve the appropriate investment in precautions and thus optimal tort deterrence. The first is strict liability, which compels the firm to internalize all of the costs of tortious harm. The second is a negligence standard, which penalizes the creation of unreasonable risk by holding the firm liable for all accident costs if it takes less than "reasonable precautions," zero in this example. These rules are theoretically equivalent when the mandate for reasonable precautions under the negligence standard accounts for both care and activity levels, though in reality it rarely does. See Shavell (1987, pp. 24–25).

Table 8-1. *Investment Schedule for Firm Seeking to Avoid Accident*

Investment in precautions ($)	Probability of accident (%)	Expected loss (probability of accident × $50,000)	Total cost of accident ($)
0	100	$50,000	50,000
10,000	10	$5,000	15,000
30,000	0	0	30,000

investment of $30,000 in precautions. Such a rule would yield total net expected welfare of only $60,000, calculated as the sum of a 50 percent chance of having the firm's net wealth of $70,000 and a 50 percent chance of having the consumer's net wealth of $50,000.

Collective Interest in Optimal Deterrence

There are many elements that compose the collective interest in optimal deterrence that everyone individually shares ex ante. Most indicative of all is that ex ante individuals rationally prefer progressive redistribution of wealth to fund precautions and, as I discuss later, litigation to ensure optimal deterrence against unreasonable risk. Anticipating a real world in which wealth will be distributed unequally among the people, a risk-averse individual ex ante would recognize that he or she might not be able to afford basic goods; of particular relevance here are optimal precautions. Investments in optimal precautions consume enormous quantities of social resources that beneficiaries pay in market prices for products, services, and labor, and in taxes for government programs. Consequently, the individual's ex ante preference includes a legal system that mandates funding the provision of these goods for those unable to afford them, primarily because of genetic, social, and other dictates of circumstance beyond their practical control. Such a system will necessarily involve some degree of redistribution to the less well off.

Because such redistribution may depress incentives for productive enterprise and thus the availability of the goods at any level, the individual ex ante rationally prefers that the system optimize the trade-off between wealth variation to motivate work on the one hand and wealth invariance to insure against the adversities of fate. There are, of course, many difficult design questions in determining the optimal level of redistribution. Most daunting are those posed by strong ex post incentives that threaten to destroy redistributive programs. Thus the program requires effective safeguards against fraud and other forms of "moral hazard." Equally apparent, such programs must be designed to navigate between two conflicting sets of ex post incentives to exploit political power in democratic institutions. On the one side, there will be the lucky with incentives to exit or underfund an arrangement they have no ex post personal interest in supporting. And, on the other, there will be the unlucky with motive to pressure for redistribution above the optimal level. However, I can bypass these difficulties since my point is simply that the individual ex ante rationally prefers some level of what I call progressive funding of optimal precautions to prevent unreasonable risk, consistent with whatever level of wealth redistribution optimizes the trade-off between social security and productivity.

To illustrate this preference, I modify the preceding example simply by assuming that the firm produces and sells electric power and poses a pollution risk to the neighbor. The firm passes through all costs of production to the neighbor-customer, including the cost of supplying optimal precautions and liability insurance against loss from accident. In particular, the firm charges the customer-neighbor $15,000, representing $10,000 for optimal precautions and $5,000 as the actuarially fair premium (equal to risk of accident) for optimal insurance. Compare the rational preference of the individual ex ante between two legal systems. Regime I does not progressively fund the supply of optimal precautions and liability insurance, so that the customer-neighbor bears the full cost. Regime II progressively funds by requiring the firm's owner to absorb one-third of the cost, so that the customer-neighbor bears two-thirds of the cost.

To depict the individual's diminishing marginal utility (welfare) from money, which implies risk aversion, I equate the square root of a given amount of wealth with the welfare the individual would derive from that wealth. Using square roots to translate money into utility provides a graphical curve that is sensitive to marginal changes in wealth and derivative utility.[7] Thus, under Regime I, the individual has total net expected welfare of 251.66, calculated as the sum of a 50 percent chance of owning the

---

7. Gradually increasing wealth by the same dollar increment thus results in a smaller increment to utility as the base level of wealth rises. If wealth increases from 0 to 5, from 5 to 10, and from 10 to 15, utility rises, but at a decreasing marginal rate: 0 to 5 yields 2.2; 5 to 10 yields 1 (3.2−2.2); and 10 to 15 yields 0.7 (3.9−3.2). For a more technically sophisticated formula, see Shavell (1987, pp. 199–202).

firm and having 316.23 in welfare from $100,000, plus a 50 percent
chance of being the neighbor-customer and having 187.08 in welfare from
$35,000 (given deduction for optimal precautions and liability insurance).
Under progressive redistribution of Regime II, the individual ex ante
expects greater total net welfare of 354.11, calculated as the sum of a 50
percent chance of owning the firm with 308.22 in welfare from $95,000
(after absorbing one-third of the cost of optimal precautions and insurance), plus a 50 percent chance of being the customer-neighbor with 200
in welfare from $40,000 (after paying two-thirds of the cost). Regime II
makes the individual better off ex ante, because it distributes an amount
of wealth to a less wealthy state of the world in which he or she would
derive greater marginal utility from the money than he or she would in the
alternative, wealthier state of the world.

Mast Tying

After the veil of ignorance lifts, revealing the actual distribution of
accidents and wealth among the population, individuals rationally prefer
a legal system that allocates resources in ways that are antithetical to the
system they preferred ex ante. Ex post, few will be motivated to have the
system invest in optimal precautions to prevent accidents, since the accidents have already occurred; the lucky who escaped accident have no
incentive to compensate those who suffered loss, and, similarly, the
wealthy have no desire to fund benefits for the less wealthy. Therefore, if
the legal system is to make individuals as well off as possible, ex ante preferences should prevail. Indeed, this is precisely what the individual ex ante
would rationally prefer. The individual would choose a legal system that
minimized the sum of accident costs through progressively funded optimal precautions and that precluded individuals ex post from opting out of
that mandate or otherwise acting in conflict with it. Individuals wish to
precommit themselves—"tie themselves to the mast"—to ensure that the
socially optimal and individually beneficial preferences they chose ex ante
will be carried out in the ex post world despite the siren call to maximize
wealth instead.

The need for mast tying to solve collective action problems that prevent the legal system from effecting the ex ante mandate is nowhere more
evident and pressing than in the context of tort law. The special predicament for tort law arises from its general reliance on the market to screen
for claims and defenses that are cost effective to litigate. The parties (on

plaintiffs' side, the lawyers) who finance the litigation select among competing claims according to their relative expected net return: to plaintiffs in recovering and to defendants in avoiding damages. Assuming the parties' net return, in particular the plaintiffs' net return, serves as a close proxy for net social welfare from litigation, then there are evident efficiencies in employing a claims market system to perform this "gate-keeping" function. Assigning the task to courts or other government authorities would entail higher information and transaction costs. But while the assumption might be true for tort compensation, it does not hold for tort deterrence.[8] Plaintiffs' investments in litigation after accident necessarily discount the deterrence value of the claims to an excessive degree and depend on rewards in recovered damages that foreclose progressive funding to achieve deterrence goals.

To illustrate the point in terms of deterrence, assume that as in the above example the optimal level of precaution for the firm is $10,000, and that without the precaution an accident will occur in which ten neighbors would each lose $5,000. Assume, for simplicity, that strict liability would govern the ensuing tort claims and that each claim would cost $6,000 to litigate. It is apparent that judged by their market value ex post, none of the claims is worth prosecuting. If the firm anticipates this result, it will lack legal incentives to take optimal precautions, with the consequence that all of the neighbors will suffer $5,000 loss with certainty. Ex ante, the individual rationally prefers a mast-tying agreement that would compel suit by at least two (and no more than three) of the neighbors in the event of accident.[9] Threatening liability from three claims totaling $15,000 would create sufficient incentive for the firm to make the optimal investment of $10,000 in precautions. Although litigation costs for three claims would exceed damages by $3,000, the ex ante benefit in reduced accident risk of $45,000 makes that ex post investment worthwhile. Given the optimal investment in precautions, more than three claims would be unnecessary and, therefore, a waste of social resources, diminishing the individual's net expected welfare ex ante. Indeed, assuming that the neighbors have similar levels of wealth, the individual ex ante would rationally prefer allocating the net litigation burden equally among all of the neighbors so that none suffers a distributive disadvantage.

8. See Rosenberg (1984, pp. 849, 901). For my argument that the assumption fails for tort compensation or insurance, see Rosenberg (2002, p. 831).

9. If negligence is the governing liability rule, then ex ante mast tying would simply guarantee suit by the appropriate number of victims in the event the accident results from negligence.

Effect of Litigation Scale Economies on Deterrence

Given the widespread availability of commercial and government-supplied first-party insurance for serious harm, the basic, if not singular, function of tort law is to create incentives for avoiding unreasonable risk of accident. Optimally, tort deterrence achieves this goal by threatening potential injurers with liability for all losses their tortious conduct may cause, compelling them to internalize the costs of tortious harm before they take risky action. Mass production tort cases, involving businesses that usually react quickly and rationally to cost factors, present the most advantageous opportunity for tort law to effect optimal deterrence.

The conventional understanding of the relationship between class action and optimal tort deterrence is that the need for aggregation arises only in two situations. First, class action aggregation is justified when claims involve amounts of loss too "small" to be marketable to plaintiffs' lawyers ("uneconomical" to prosecute) as separate actions. Second, courts employ class action aggregation in the event some fraction of claims is economically attractive to plaintiffs' attorneys. Ignoring deterrence objectives, courts and commentators take the need for class action in these cases as strictly limited to avoiding duplicative litigation, though it is often deemed too costly even for this use and rarely employed for claims involving serious personal injury.

Prevailing consensus and practice misconceives the essential dependence of optimal deterrence in mass production tort cases and the scale economies of class action. Scale economies from aggregating all mass production tort claims improve adjudicative efficiency at two levels:

AVOIDING DUPLICATIVE LITIGATION.   Class action produces the well-known benefit of avoiding the waste of duplicative litigation. For example, if A sues defendant firm Z on a claim that B, C, and others also independently have against Z, then courts can class (aggregate) all such similar claims, pending or not, for resolution in a single proceeding. Separate, simultaneous, or subsequent actions by B, C, and so on are thus precluded (if necessary enjoined), and final judgment based on trial or settlement between A as class representative and Z binds all "absentee" class members as well as defendant Z, barring them from relitigating any common question in a subsequent phase of the class action or a separate action. Thus the legal system could achieve substantial economy by avoiding litigation of "common questions" more than once, and instead adjudicate them once and for all. Although other means exist to avoid wasteful repetitive litigation, notably a "two-way" form of collateral estoppel (under which the first claim to reach final judgment determines the outcome for all pending and subsequently filed similar claims) and encouraging free riding, none also includes regulatory advantage from the two other, unique efficiencies of the scale economies of class action.[10]

MOTIVATING OPTIMAL INVESTMENT.   Far more important, but generally unrecognized, are the benefits of class action in motivating the court as well as parties to make the optimal investment that maximizes the regulatory value from mass production tort liability. Optimal aggregate investment in litigating common questions represents the special and generally overlooked benefit of scale economies that result from aggregating 100 percent of the classable claims. Essentially, the higher the stakes, the more mass production tort litigants invest in developing the merits of their respective sides on the common questions. Because this higher, cost-effective investment on the common questions promotes success at trial on all claims, classable claims as a whole are worth far more than the sum of their separate parts.

More precisely, like any business investing in a potentially profitable opportunity, litigants invest in developing their respective sides of a claim to the extent that net return on investment is maximized—plaintiffs seeking the greatest recovery of damages and defendants seeking the greatest reduction in damages paid. Because a party usually has the option of making continuously varying investments of resources, and because increasing investment increases returns but at a diminishing rate, the party will cease investing when the additional unit of time, money, and effort yields an equal or lower unit in benefit. Crucially, compared with the limited return from investing in any fraction of the classable claims, classwide aggregation ensures the opportunity for optimally investing to the point of diminishing marginal returns, which maximizes the enforcement value from all claims in the aggregate ("optimal aggregate investment"). With more at stake, the party invests more and with greater effect, not only to reap maximum net aggregate benefit but also to raise the value of each classable claim. Indeed, investment cost per claim will rise in absolute terms, relative to the commitment of resources for a separate action, but the added expense will be more than made up by the higher return per claim. Significantly, neither claim preclusion, free-riding, nor any other disaggregative mode of litigation would generate optimal incentives for investing to maximize the aggregate deterrence value of classable claims.

Optimal investment in all classable claims produces either of two efficiencies: decreased average per claim cost or increased average per claim

10. For development of this point, see Rosenberg (2001).

productivity. Thus aggregating claims might make worthwhile a higher investment that reduces per claim costs, for example, by purchasing specialized computer software to replace a less efficient generic program for handling voluminous discovery material. Alternatively, aggregation might warrant a considerably broader discovery campaign, the higher cost of which would be more than offset by higher expected recovery at trial. Of course, aggregation motivates both types of investments, but the total net effect will more than offset the expense of higher investment either by reducing costs overall or by producing greater positive benefit (for example, increased probability of success at trial, correlating with increased regulatory effectiveness).

For a simple illustration of the point, return to the example of factory pollution that subjects one hundred individuals each to tortious loss of $1,000. Assume that among other common questions, all claims center on whether the firm's mass production choice of antipollution technology was reasonable. Suppose further that a litigant (either defendant or plaintiff) sees advantage in acquiring an expert scientific assessment of the issue. Assume that the litigant could obtain a reliable study for $10,000. All else being equal, if a litigant's stake is bounded by the $1,000 value of a single claim, no scientific study would be commissioned. Plainly, the $10,000 investment would swamp even the highest possible benefit in recovered or avoided damages for one individual claim ($1,000). Even if the study would provide a 100 percent chance of success at trial, it would be a waste of money for any party to make the investment. By contrast, if the litigant could aggregate the one hundred classable claims to capture the potential benefit of $100,000 in recovered or avoided damages, the party would be much more likely to make the investment. From that perspective, the litigant would rationally make the investment as long as the resulting study more than "paid for itself" by either increasing or decreasing the probability of the technology being found reasonable at trial. In this example, if such a study increases the litigant's chance of success at trial by more than 10 percent on every claim, it would be worth commissioning since its aggregate expected value of $10,000 covers its cost. If we assume that the study is dispositive of the reasonableness question, it is easy to see how the presence or absence of scale economies by classwide aggregation determines the enforcement benefit from mass production tort litigation. It also should be emphasized that raising the stakes of decision to classwide level provides courts with greater incentive to invest judicial resources in managing litigation, marshaling evidence, and otherwise exercising informed, independent judgment to increase the effectiveness of its regulatory decision.

Optimal Deterrence Requires Optimal Litigation Investment

Conventional analysis fails to recognize that optimal deterrence requires not only the enforcement of all claims arising from a mass production tort event *but also* their joint prosecution on the basis of the optimal investment that maximizes aggregate value from litigation, which only scale economies effected by class action can ensure. The following argument makes this point first. I then show that everyone's interest in that investment is collective, indeed, unitary, thus demonstrating that everyone's rational preference is for class action that effects mandatory (no opt-out) collective aggregation.

"SMALL" CLAIMS. There is no empirical let alone analytical basis for distinguishing "small" from "high-stake" claims. Only class action aggregation ensures the opportunity for fully exploiting scale economies to motivate the optimal investment that maximizes net return—for the parties and society—from the adjudication of mass production tort cases.

The crudity of commentary and judicial opinion making this distinction is underscored by the failure to consider institutional aggregators of "small" claims, such as wholesalers in price-fixing cases, mutual funds harmed by securities frauds, banks suffering damage to collateral from consumer frauds, and subrogated insurers generally. Even in the absence of institutional litigation, innovations in law firm organization and in locating and soliciting clients enable plaintiffs' attorneys to consolidate a sufficient number of "small" claims to warrant litigation. Other plaintiffs' attorneys will often prosecute "small" claims by free riding on the work product of institutional and consolidated litigation.[11] More broadly, this distinction is also pressed without regard to substantial litigation costs that render "high-stake" claims "small," and often uneconomical in the separate action marketplace. These costs include not only the burden and risk in prosecuting claims that present an enormously complex mix of fact, law, technology, and public policy questions but also the expense of search,

---

11. To avoid misunderstanding, I emphasize that in noting the possibility of aggregating "small" or otherwise separately uneconomical mass production tort claims for profitable litigation in the absence of class action, I am in no way suggesting that the market process suffices for deterrence purposes. On the contrary, I am making the point to demonstrate the impoverished understanding of deterrence exhibited by the conventional view that the need for class action lapses when some percentage of mass production tort claims is marketable. Fractional aggregation in the standard market process may result in the prosecution of some, or even all, claims, but generally it fails to provide the opportunity of fully exploiting litigation scale economies that ensures maximum enforcement benefit from mass production tort litigation. Only collective aggregation through mandatory class action provides such scale economies and assurance of regulatory effectiveness.

assessment, and competition in acquiring claims, especially when claims are widely dispersed over time and territory. In part because of the litigation cost barriers in high-stake cases, plaintiffs' attorneys "voluntarily" aggregate claims for en masse development to spread the burden and risk. More generally, it never profits a plaintiff's attorney to prosecute any number of mass production tort claims short of the maximum he or she can acquire to further spread the cost of litigation, that is, to exploit scale economies more fully. Rarely, if ever, does an attorney prosecute a claim by separate action, completely independent of benefit from scale economies afforded by some present and anticipated holding of a number of similar claims, except when there is a possibility of free riding on some other attorney's work product. Indeed, judging from the market demand for aggregation, the professed value of litigant "autonomy" borders on the fictitious if not fraudulent; but for collective action problems and costs, the market would supply only universal, mandatory aggregation. Advocates for "plaintiff autonomy" assume that an individualized "right-duty" relationship exists between the parties in mass production tort cases and that litigants prefer to control and prosecute their claims separately from one another rather than exploit scale economies from collective action. I challenge these suppositions, the first on grounds of intellectual incoherence and the second as lacking reality.[12]

However, it is important to recognize the prevalence of the problem that unmarketable separate actions pose for the regulatory objective. That problem, of course, is evident when minimally competent plaintiffs' attorneys refuse to "buy" (typically, trading legal services for a "contingent" interest in the outcome) any claim on any terms. But consider the more realistic case in which some claims are marketable—precisely the case, according to conventional analysis, that has no need of class action for deterrence purposes. Assume that in the event of a mass production tort, one hundred consumers will suffer aggregate harm of $100,000 and that the mass producer can increase safety through investments that reduce risk but at a diminishing rate. Also, assume that the probability of accident and costs of safety are distributed uniformly among the one hundred consumers, but that accidents will cause each of fifty to lose $1,500 and the other fifty to lose $500. Finally, assume that litigation costs per claim equal $750 and that courts employ strict liability. Now compare the fractionally aggregated market process with collective aggregation effected by mandatory class action.

12. Rosenberg (2002, pp. 857–66).

The contrast in supply of deterrence benefits is striking. The market-oriented system of voluntary adjudication, responding to plaintiffs' demand for maximum individual recovery from their respective claims, threatens liability for $75,000 (50 × $1,500), only three-quarters of the amount required to deter the firm from taking an unreasonable risk rather than precautions against it. (The other fifty potential plaintiffs will not find it worthwhile to sue.) Mandatory class action, vesting sole ownership of all claims in a single investor, provides the aggregate incentive sufficient to seek the maximum aggregate recovery of $100,000, which would achieve optimal deterrence. Even if plaintiffs recover nothing personally, mandatory collectivization makes *everyone* better off by minimizing the sum of accident costs, thereby maximizing individual net expected benefit from the mass production good and the legal system.

"HIGH-STAKES" CLAIMS.   It should be evident that "small" claims represent the problems of collective action at the limit. Ex post no one has any incentive to "subsidize" and make the optimal investment to litigate separately unmarketable claims for optimal deterrence purposes, despite everyone's ex ante preference for precisely that to occur. At the limit, class action prosecutes all claims, both at the level of number and investment that maximizes the aggregate value of litigation. But number and investment are not necessarily linked when mass production tort claims are separately marketable—that is, economical to prosecute based on "voluntary" joinder or fractional aggregation.

In making this point, it is useful (though not analytically necessary) to emphasize the more realistic conditions that govern investment, both in litigation and precautions. Investors (plaintiffs, or more accurately, plaintiffs' lawyers and mass producers) have virtually continuous investment levels and options. Plaintiffs, for instance, could invest in any number of studies, experts, and tests to prepare their side of the common scientific questions presented by the case. Plaintiffs, moreover, have almost limitless choices in the amount of time, effort, and money to commit for research, discovery, other trial preparation, and so forth. Similarly, mass producers usually choose among a boundless range of devices, methods, designs, rates of production, and other incremental adjustments in fine tuning levels of care and activity (frequency and intensity of risky behavior) to avoid unreasonable risk. Of course, the point of negative diminishing marginal return sets the boundary of efficient investment by both parties. Given continuous investment options, that point is marked by the maximum aggregate expected value from all classable claims in damages recovered or avoided. This leads to an important conclusion: *incentives for optimizing investments in both litigation and precautions derive from the same source: maximum aggregate expected value from enforcing 100 percent of the classable claims. The greatest net regulatory return from mass production tort liability is ensured only when both parties internalize the maximum aggregate expected value of 100 percent of the classable claims.*

With that reality in mind, consider an example illustrating the dependence of optimal deterrence on the efficient level of both the number of claims and the investment in their litigation. Thus assume that a business activity poses a danger of causing $1,000 harm to each of one hundred individuals and that the firm would invest $100,000 in precautions to avoid the accident risk were it threatened with tort liability equal to the aggregate harm of $100,000. Suppose that plaintiffs can incrementally raise investment of litigation resources, say time, in equal units to effect a corresponding increase in the probability of recovery but at a diminishing rate. Representing the probability of recovery at any level of investment as the square root of the number of units of time invested produces a curve depicting declining marginal returns. Thus the investment schedule for any given plaintiff seeking recovery of $1,000 in individual harm includes the options shown in table 8-2 (for simplicity, valuing each unit of time as equal to $1).

All else being equal, it is possible that every plaintiff would separately sue defendant to recover $1,000. Separate suit by each is economical because even the minimum investment of $1 yields a positive return. Driven to maximize net recovery, a single plaintiff would invest to the point of diminishing marginal return. Here that point is reached at $25. Despite the prospect of all claims being prosecuted, the regulatory result is deficient. Internalizing aggregate expected liability of $,5000 (=5% × $1,000 × 100 claims), defendant lacks the incentive to invest optimally in precautions against accident.

Now, compare the schedule of selected investment options for a plaintiff given the prospect of recovering aggregate tortious damages of $100,000 (table 8-3).

Optimal deterrence is achieved by the optimal litigation investment of $10,000 that maximizes net recovery of the aggregate damages of $100,000. Only the reward of aggregate damages from 100 percent of the claims ensures that investment.

Similarly, on the realistic assumption that the firm also had continuous opportunities to invest in precautions, nothing less than the threat of aggre-

Table 8-2. *Investment Schedule for Plaintiff Seeking $1,000*

| Investment in time (unit = $1) | Expected individual recovery | | |
	Probability of recovery (%)	Gross	Net (minus time value) ($)
1	1 (square root of 1)	10	9
4	2 (square root of 4)	20	16
25	5 (square root of 25)	50	25
64	8 (square root of 64)	80	16
81	9 (square root of 81)	90	9

Table 8-3. *Investment Schedule for Plaintiff Seeking $100,000*

| Investment in | | Probability of recovery (%) | Expected aggregate recovery ($) | |
Time	Value		Gross	Net (minus time value)
100	$121 ($1 × 1.21)	10	10,000	9,879
400	$488 ($1 × 1.22)	20	20,000	19,512
900	$1,107 ($1 × 1.23)	30	30,000	28,893
1,600	$,1984 ($1 × 1.24)	40	40,000	38,016
2,500	$3,125 ($1 × 1.25)	50	50,000	46,875
3,600	$5,400 ($1 × 1.5)	60	60,000	54,600
4,900	$8,575 ($1 × 1.75)	70	70,000	61,425
6,400	$12,800 ($1 × 2)	80	80,000	67,200
8,100	$20,250 ($1 × 2.5)	90	90,000	69,750
10,000	$30,000 ($1 × 3)	100	100,000	70,000

Note: To add a further note of reality, each additional unit of time has greater value than the preceding unit. This modification removes discontinuities at the higher levels of investment.

gate damages would serve the goal of optimal deterrence. Thus, supposing the firm has the same investment-return schedule as plaintiff's, except that each $10 expenditure on precautions reduces the probability of accident (equal to the square root of 10% × amount invested) but at a diminishing rate, then it would make the $100,000 investment in precautions to avoid accident only if plaintiff musters a threat of enforcing all claims. Should plaintiff aggregate fewer than all claims, then defendant would fail to take optimal precautions, thereby exposing plaintiff to unreasonable risk of accident. For example, if defendant anticipated enforcement of ninety-nine

rather than one hundred claims, it would internalize expected liability of
$99,000. Lacking incentive to invest more, the firm would take precau-
tions worth $99,000, unreasonably subjecting plaintiffs to a .5 percent risk
(= square root of $99,000 / 100) of losing roughly $501 (or $5 each).

Ex Ante versus Ex Post Preference for Deterrence

It should be apparent from the immediately preceding example that
individuals ex ante have a collective interest in all claims being prosecuted
collectively to secure enforcement of all claims not only in number but also
on the basis of the optimal investment that maximizes aggregate value
from litigation. Realistically, any shortfall in incentive to invest, meaning,
in turn, any less than 100 percent return investing in the litigation of all
claims, makes everyone ex ante worse off. By definition, everyone suffers
a loss of expected welfare relative to the situation in which the optimal
investment effects the regulatory objective, because the expense of avoiding unreasonable risk is always less than the costs of bearing the resulting
harm (or insuring against it). Yet, ex post rational preferences to maximize
wealth, especially relating to collective action problems and costs, are likely
to frustrate that ex ante collective interest.

As noted, a principal barrier to 100 percent voluntary joinder consists
of costs, for instance, to acquire the marginal claim. Thus, in the preceding example, consider the effect of increasing the search costs by $2,000
for the holder of the ninety other claims to find, assess, and join the last
ten claims. It is doubtful that plaintiffs seeking to maximize recovery from
mass production tort liability would incur the marginal expenditure of
$2,000, given that the ten claims yield marginal net return on their litiga-
tion investment of only $250 (= $70,000 − $69,750). Yet acquiring the
ten marginal, profit-reducing claims for prosecution by the ninety-claim
holder would make everyone ex ante decidedly better off. Each would
expect to bear an additional cost of $20 (=$2000 / 100), and thus total
litigation cost of $120, to create the necessary incentive for defendants to
take precautions that avoid harm of $1,000. In the absence of those claims,
plaintiffs' attorney holding ninety claims maximizes net return by investing 8,100 rather than 10,000 units of time; at 8,100 units, expected net
return equals $60,750 (= 90% × $90,000 − $20,250), while 10,000
units yield $60,000 (100% × $90,000 − $30,000). Note that even if the
ten marginal claims sued jointly on their own (assume no costs for their
separate aggregation), the plaintiff's attorney operating under the further

constrained scale economies maximizes net return by investing only 900—1,600 units for a probability of success just below 40 percent. Consequently, instead of internalizing the full tortious loss, defendant could expect total damages of roughly $85,000, too low to motivate optimal precautions against accident.

Exit and Deterrence

Class action or some other formal device might be used to aggregate all claims, but there is little chance of accomplishing the regulatory objective unless collectivization is mandatory. Given an opportunity to exit, the collective would unravel. The extent of dissolution would depend on degree of competition, bargaining strategy, litigation-related discontinuities (such as a rule of repose or requirement for preponderant proof) and a range of cost variables, including free-riding, litigation, organization, monitoring, and information. Exit in any substantial degree realistically threatens the regulatory objective in many cases.

Return to the immediately preceding example for an illustration of the exit effects of collectivization. Suppose a class action is certified to aggregate all claims that would entail an additional $10,000 in search and assessment costs for the marginal ten claims. Allowing exit, however, motivates another lawyer to set up a competing organization against class counsel, offering representation to all except the marginal ten claims. In theory, the competing offer might succeed in inducing all of the "infra-marginal" claims to exit, leaving only the marginal ten in the class action. While the competing attorney would maximize net return from ninety claims, as above, investing 8,100 units for 90 percent probability of success, class counsel would find the residual holding of the ten marginal claims uneconomical to prosecute despite the opportunity, albeit constrained, of exploiting scale economies. The threat of liability is thus further diluted, though that effect has no bearing in this case, as defendant already lacked sufficient incentive to take optimal precautions.

Depending on the circumstances, however, class counsel might retain a number of inframarginal claims as well as find it worthwhile to search for the marginal ten. Because benefit from litigation scale economies corresponds inversely with the number of claims, as the class shrinks, the investment value of an additional claim increases, enabling class counsel to spend more for the additional claim—inframarginal and marginal—than the competitor. But greater parity in the number of claims held by class counsel and competing counsel may further undermine deterrence relative to a scenario in which all inframarginal claims exit. Thus suppose that the equilibrium from competition between class and competitor counsel results in each holding fifty claims. In that situation, each would separately invest approximately 6,400 units, yielding an 80 percent probability of success, to maximize net return at $27,200 (= 80% × $50,000 − $12,800). Investing for a 90 percent success rate would diminish net returns to $24,750 (= 90% × $50,000 − $20,250). The combined effort confronts defendant with total expected aggregate liability of $80,000. This result is inferior to the deterrence benefit produced when a single lawyer (the competitor) holds all of the inframarginal claims, and the marginal claims go by default. Based on total expected aggregate return from the ninety inframarginal claims, the competitor would invest 8,100 units for a 90 percent probability of success or total expected aggregate liability of $81,000. Collective aggregation of fewer claims may prove more important for deterrence purposes than fractional aggregation of more claims, further illustrating the crucial enforcement role of litigation scale economies.

Systemic Bias and Class Action

Class action scale economies produce a further and crucial adjudicative efficiency by eliminating the systemic bias favoring defendants. Class action scale economies benefit defendants far less than plaintiffs and courts, because defendants litigate mass production tort claims in the standard separate action process from the posture of a *de facto* class action. Faced with numerous actual and potential claims presenting common questions of liability and damages, a defendant always naturally and necessarily prepares one defense for all of those claims. Because it "owns" the defense interest in the classable claims that constitute a given mass production tort case, the defendant litigates as if all the claims have been aggregated in a mandatory non-opt-out class action. In contrast, plaintiffs litigating in the separate action process rarely can voluntarily aggregate their claims to a degree approaching the universal aggregation achieved automatically by defendant. Collective action problems, notably free riding, and high costs of organizing and monitoring, all stymie coordination by plaintiffs. With classwide aggregation of the defense interest, the defendant exploits economies of litigation scale to invest far more cost effectively in preparing than plaintiffs. For similar reasons, courts lack scale-based incentives to invest optimally in policing defendant's use of its edge in litigation power as well as in acquiring the expertise and other information for effective regulatory decisionmaking. The essential consequence of mass production tort class action is to ensure that plaintiffs and courts have an opportunity to exploit scale economies as fully as that afforded to defendant.

Defendants' De Facto Class Action Edge

In mass production tort cases, defendants naturally collectivize the common defense to any given set of classable claims and thus exploit the scale economies of a de facto class action. Defendants face none of the organizing costs and free-rider obstacles to classwide aggregation that plaintiffs confront in litigating without the benefit of class action.[13] Since the defendant automatically aggregates all classable claims, it has optimal investment incentives, which create a built-in advantage over plaintiffs. Litigating in the separate action process, they generally can aggregate only a fraction of the claims on a voluntary basis, and then only at substantial costs in overcoming collective action problems and costs. As the single owner of the total potential benefit gained by avoiding damages on all claims, the defendant will be able to spread costs and reap return from its investment on the common questions over the claims of all the plaintiffs. In contrast, on the plaintiff's side, different plaintiffs are likely to be represented by different lawyers, no one lawyer handling—owning beneficial interest in—all the claims. Therefore, no plaintiff's lawyer is able to spread costs and reap the return gained by investing to maximize the aggregate value from litigating the questions common to all claims.

Because of this asymmetry, the defendant will make investments in the litigation that no plaintiff's attorney can match economically. The defendant will invest up to the point at which the cost of additional investment

13. This is not to deny that the standard market process takes a toll on defendants. Needless redundancy taxes their resources. For example, even though the defendant can invest once and for all in developing the documentary and empirical bases for an expert scientific opinion, the potential for numerous, overlapping, or widely separated actions may require hiring and preparing more than one expert. Similarly, the defendant will hire attorneys and other personnel to perform purely duplicative work. Defendants may also bear substantial coordination costs in cases that involve multiple named or potential defendants. Courts can mandate defendants' class action to overcome collective action problems and costs that prevent multiple defendants from fully exploiting scale economies; courts can thereby promote defendants' optimal investment in developing shared positions on common questions.

exceeds the gain from additional investment, relative to the aggregate value from 100 percent of the classable claims. All else being equal, a given plaintiff's attorney (handling only a fraction of the classable claims) will reach that point before the defendant does.

In general, the unequal investment incentives for defendants and plaintiffs in mass production tort cases translates into a much greater chance that in litigating the common questions the defendant, who aggregates all classable claims automatically, will prevail over the plaintiffs' attorney, who acquires fewer than all claims. This analysis holds true for virtually any type of investment in the litigation of questions common to classable claims, be it discovery, expert witnesses, legal research, or any of numerous other investments of time, effort, and money. It holds true, indeed, for the total investment in litigating those questions. Because the investment bears on an issue common to all the claims, the defendant always exploits the scale economies of investing to maximize the aggregate return from all classable claims, confronting an adversary who, as a practical matter, lacks comparable litigation opportunities.

The differential access to scale economies from classwide aggregation undermines the regulatory objective of effective and administratively efficient tort deterrence. Thus the argument for parity of litigation power is grounded on the theoretically and empirically demonstrable benefits for everyone from removing artificial constraints on the provision of needed tort deterrence. Moreover, affording plaintiffs equal opportunity with defendants to exploit class action scale economies promises to improve the working of a generalist system of lawmaking and policymaking that relies heavily on aggressive competition between adversaries to generate needed information and advice.

Social Costs of Systemic Bias

This systemic bias undermines the regulatory objective of optimal tort deterrence. It would be an error for policymakers to ignore these effects in determining whether correcting the bias would enhance or diminish social welfare. Legal process serves substantive ends, not itself. Mass production tort litigation, like any other public enterprise that consumes social resources, must, therefore, find justification in its overall social benefit. Mass production tort debates and decisions unfortunately have focused almost exclusively on questions of process, rarely considering questions of tort law and policy beyond superficial asides. This mistake corrupts analysis of the subject on every dimension, beginning, of course, with the basic structure and incentives of the system addressed here.

LITIGATION. Systemic bias prevents plaintiffs from investing optimally in developing the aggregate value of their claims while the defendant engages in precisely that investment strategy to strengthen its case on the common questions and further drive down its adversary's expected benefit. Because the investment required by plaintiffs would outweigh the potential damages, claims of injury for which the defendant should pay are not brought or prosecuted vigorously enough (in part, because defendant's greater litigation power enables it to spend simply to increase plaintiffs' litigation costs). The systemic bias favoring the defendant subverts the goal of fully internalizing the costs of tortious harm in order to prevent it from occurring in the first place.

The general point is readily shown in the context of judgment based on trial. Assume that of one hundred individuals each will suffer a $60,000 loss—$6 million in the aggregate—from ground-water pollution by the defendant, a hazard that it reasonably could reduce to zero at a cost of $4 million. Further, assume that a plaintiff has the schedule shown in table 8-4 of possible (and, for simplicity, discontinuous) common question investments and related probabilities of recovery.

From the deterrence perspective, the only effective investment is $2.5 million. This investment alone generates a threat of liability sufficient to provide the prospective defendant with needed incentive to take reasonable precautions, namely, the threat of $6 million in damages if the firm fails to spend $4 million to prevent harm. Investing less lowers the probability of success and correspondingly reduces the threat of liability below the threshold required for optimal deterrence. But the fact that the investment serves deterrence goals does not guarantee that it will be made. Because tort, like other common law systems, relies on "private" investors—here a plaintiff's attorney—the value of an investment depends on its "private" returns, specifically the aggregate recovery of damages over and above the cost of investment.[14] In the example, the optimal aggregate investment given 100 percent participation among potential plaintiffs is $2.5 million, not

---

14. Plaintiffs' attorneys gauge the worth of an investment in the hard currency of recovered damages, not by its deterrence value. They rationally treat deterrence as a public good because its production and benefits are not within the attorneys' proprietary control and because these factors do not affect the magnitude of return on their investment.

Table 8-4. *Investment Schedule for Attorney Depending on Claim Market Share*

Common question investment ($)	Probability of success at trial (%)	Expected aggregate recovery		Expected per claim recovery ($)	
		Gross	Net	Gross	Net
250,000	40	$2,400,000 (= 40% × $60,000 × 100 claims)	$2,150,000 (= gross − $250,000 cost)	24,000	21,500
600,000	60	$3,600,000 (= 60% × $60,000 × 100 claims)	$3,000,000 (= gross − $600,000 cost)	36,000	30,000
2,500,000	100	$6,000,000 (= 100% × $60,000 × 100 claims)	$3,500,000 (= gross − $2,500,000 cost)	60,000	35,000

because it is highest, but because it results in the highest (or maximum) net return from litigating all classable claims.[15] Relative to investing at $600,000, for example, it is economical to raise the common question investment to $2.5 million, because the marginal investment of $1.9 million (= $2.5 million − $600,000) increases the aggregate marginal expected return by even more, here $2.4 million (from $3.6 million to $6 million). That investment yields an aggregate net expected return of $3.5 million, more than the next best return of $3 million from the $600,000 investment.

Despite the evident deterrence value of the $2.5 million investment, no plaintiff prosecuting a lone claim would make it or even the minimum investment of $250,000. It would require joinder of at least eleven claims to make the minimum investment worthwhile and thirty claims to

15. To a plaintiff's attorney, there are two key variables in the potential investment: first, the amount of money to spend; and second, the number of plaintiffs' claims to join. The former determines the probability of winning and recovering full losses. The latter determines how many damage awards will be aggregated. Together they determine the expected aggregate winnings and hence the expected aggregate returns on the investment in preparing the common questions for trial. Plaintiffs' incentives are to exploit scale economies to the hilt and thus to aggregate 100 percent of the classable claims to maximize net benefits from investment. That is, they want to approximate the monolithic defendant as nearly as possible, investing to the point that marginal cost equals marginal return.

economically justify investing $600,000.[16] To warrant making the optimal aggregate investment, an attorney must own the beneficial interest in eighty of the one hundred claims; anything less and the attorney is better off investing only $600,000.[17] For the plaintiffs to choose the aggregate optimal investment—by reaching 80 percent participation—is critical to deterrence. If the defendant believed that an 80 percent rate of claims-joinder was highly improbable, then it could realistically discount potential liability by at least 40 percent, since joinder of 30 to 79 percent of the claims motivates only a $600,000 investment and corresponding 60 percent probability of the plaintiffs' succeeding at trial. The defendant facing at most $2.84 million (= $3.6 million $\times$ 79%) in damages would lack the necessary legal incentive to invest $4 million for reasonable precautions.[18]

Until now, I have ignored the defendant's investment and its effects. Defendant, of course, can fully exploit scale economies to make any investment that maximizes aggregate net value in terms of reducing its liability and other cost exposure from litigation. Defendant, thus, has greater litigation power than a plaintiff's attorney holding fewer than all

16. In determining the minimum degree of claim-joinder to warrant an investment, the attorney makes a marginal assessment comparing the aggregate net expected return from the investment alternatives. Marginal analysis shows that zero investment is preferable to investing $250,000 on a single claim, because recovering $60,000 with 40 percent probability of success does not come close to paying for the investment. To warrant the investment, an attorney must acquire the beneficial interest in a minimum of eleven claims, promising aggregate net return of $14,000 (= 11 $\times$ $60,000 $\times$ 40% − $250,000); joining only ten results in a $10,000 loss. The degree of claim-joinder necessary to support higher investments is not simply a multiple of the number of claims needed for the $250,000, because incremental investments yield diminishing marginal returns. Thus nothing less than a beneficial interest in thirty of the one hundred claims would motivate an attorney to make the $600,000 investment. With thirty claims, the attorney expects an aggregate net return of $480,000 (= 30 $\times$ $60,000 $\times$ 60% − $600,000), which is just enough to surpass the aggregate net return of $470,000 from the alternative of investing $250,000 on thirty claims.

17. Again, the attorney seeks to maximize aggregate net expected return from the marginal investment. Holding eighty claims, the attorney calculates that investing $600,000 for expected profit of $2.28 million (= 80 $\times$ $60,000 $\times$ 60% − $600,000) is inferior to spending $1.9 million more on the margin for a total investment of $2.5 million. The latter optimal aggregate investment on all claims promises a $2.3 million return (= 80 $\times$ $60,000 $\times$ 100% − $2,500,000).

18. The numerical example could easily be adjusted so that only a fully collectivized group of one hundred would prefer the high level of investment and thus provide adequate deterrence for the firm. We can also generalize to a more realistic scenario in which the investment levels are continuous rather than at only the three discrete levels assumed for purposes of example. Given a few real world assumptions about how the probability of success continuously rises with investment in discovery, for example, at a diminishing rate, the minimum number of joined plaintiffs required in order to prefer the highest rational level of investment would need to be the full one hundred.

claims, that is, possessing only a fractional aggregate stake. Consequently, defendant will make investment on the merits, or even abusively, that the plaintiffs' attorney cannot match or counter. In an adversarial process, asymmetry in litigation power exacts social cost by skewing outcomes—here in defendants' favor—and thus undermining the regulatory objective of optimal tort deterrence.

The following exemplifies the effect of asymmetrical scale economies in skewing the parties' investment equilibrium, but I emphasize that this scenario illustrates but one of the many ways defendants' superior litigation power distorts outcomes. Suppose that if plaintiffs fractionally aggregate eighty claims to invest $2.5 million, defendant could respond by investing $1.5 million to cut plaintiffs' probability of success from 100 percent to 90 percent. On its face, defendant's investment seems wholly uneconomical. Even with $6 million at stake, the marginal gain from the $1.5 million investment is only $600,000 in reduced liability exposure (=10% × $6,000,000). From the regulatory perspective (that neither party considers), the 90 percent probability of success yields expected liability of $4.32 million, which is enough to provide an optimal incentive for precautions. But by reducing the expected net return on plaintiffs' $1.9 million marginal investment from $2.3 million to $1.82 million (= 90% × 80 × $60,000 − $2,500,000), defendant effectively discourages plaintiffs' attorney from making the $2.5 million investment. Given defendant's investment of (or credible threat to invest) $1.5 million, plaintiffs' attorney will invest only $600,000, which maximizes net return at $2.28 million but produces suboptimal deterrent effects by subjecting defendant to total expected liability of $2.88 million (= 80 × $60,000 × 60%). Defendant's "gain" of $1.92 million on an investment of $1.5 million is society's loss. Instead of minimizing the sum of total accident costs at $4 million in precautions, which would have avoided all harm including litigation cost, the asymmetrically structured separate action process results in total accident costs of $8.1 million ($6,000,000 harm, plus $2.1 million invested in litigation).

Given the privately financed mode of tort law enforcement, the solution to this problem and more generally to the distortions from asymmetrical scale economies is a mandatory class action. Whatever the resulting investment equilibrium, when both parties have an equal opportunity to exploit economies of litigation scale, mass production tort liability best achieves the regulatory objective. In the example, with $6 million in stakes, class counsel would persist in making the optimal investment that maximizes aggregate net regulatory value from litigation. Even if defendant invested $1.5 million to reduce the probability of success by 10 percent, class counsel would still clear $2.9 million, more than enough to warrant the optimizing investment. Society too (and consequently every individual ex ante) is better off. Recognizing that class counsel would make that investment in any event, defendant would not waste the effort of a fruitless expenditure. Indeed, anticipating class action, defendant would internalize the expected tortious harm from deficient precautions, and thus the appropriate incentives to take measures that would avoid an accident in the first place.

A settlement example offers a more general view of the distortions worked by defendants' superior litigation power in the separate action process and the corrective powers of mandatory class action. Assume that a firm's activity poses a risk to one hundred individuals, that each will suffer tortious loss of $500,000 in the event of accident, and that the firm can avoid the risk cost effectively by spending $20 million on precautions. Suppose that the parties can make only two levels of investment on the common questions: $100,000 or $5 million. Further, should both sides invest $5 million, each will have a 50 percent probability of recovering or avoiding total damages at trial, but if not, then the party investing $5 million will gain the advantage of a 70 percent probability of success against the party investing $100,000.[19] Since most cases settle, consider the parties' relative bargaining positions if plaintiffs prosecute their claims through either of two "market" modes: (a) a series of separate actions or (b) a joint venture comprising a sufficient number of claims to make the $5 million investment.

19. For simplicity, I have eliminated the possibility of both parties investing $100,000. As the reader may intuit, providing class action scale economies to plaintiffs may result in both parties reaching a competitive equilibrium on investment that might conflict with the system's informational needs. Thus both parties might be better off spending only $100,000 each in developing their respective positions on the common questions. Yet the court might benefit from the information provided by joint investment of $10 million to formulate a policy that effectively solves problems posed by a broad category of cases that the present litigation merely exemplifies. This divergence between "private" investment incentives and "public" policy needs for developing information in litigation pervades all mass production tort cases and for that matter the entire system of judicial lawmaking. Unless courts receive major infusions of money and expertise to enable them to make public policy more effectively and responsibly, it seems sensible to constrict their jurisdiction over central areas of the nation's economic and social life whenever feasible and substitute more efficient and informed market and regulatory alternatives.

Exploiting scale economies of a de facto class action, the defendant invests $5 million for a 70 percent probability of success at trial because each plaintiff it confronts will have an individual incentive to invest only $100,000 on the common questions. Thus, given a 30 percent probability of success, the expected judgment in any given case equals $150,000 (= 30% × $500,000). Spreading the $5 million cost for its unified defense across all one hundred potential claims, the defendant effectively invests $50,000 per claim and therefore will settle with each plaintiff for no more than $200,000 (= $150,000 + $50,000). Separately bearing the concentrated cost of the $100,000 investment on common questions, each plaintiff will settle for as little as $50,000 (= $150,000 − $100,000). All else being equal, the parties will settle at the mean of their reservation points: $125,000 per claim (= ($200,000 + $50,000) × 50%).

Suppose plaintiffs aggregated 40 percent of the claims, an improbably large-scale joint venture in most mass production tort cases. That level of aggregation, however, would not provide sufficient litigation scale to induce plaintiffs' attorney from making a greater investment than he or she would have made in a single separate action. Despite aggregate stakes of $20 million, plaintiffs' attorney is better off investing $100,000 for a 30 percent probability of success, which yields an expected aggregate net return of $5.9 million. A $5 million investment increases the probability of success to 50 percent, and thus aggregate expected recovery to $10 million, but nonetheless yields the insufficient expected aggregate net return of $5 million.

Indeed, in the example, a minimum of fifty of the one hundred plaintiffs must band together to make the $5 million investment worthwhile.[20] Should the unlikely event occur that 50 percent of the plaintiffs proceed jointly (and ignoring collective action costs), both parties would make equal investments, yielding each a 50 percent probability of success at trial. Nevertheless, while the defendant would spread the cost across all claims, effectively reducing its per claim expense to $50,000, plaintiffs could spread the cost only over fifty claims, equaling $100,000 per claim. Consequently, given consensus on the expected judgment of $12.5 million (= 50 claims × $500,000 loss × 50% probability of success),

20. At forty-nine claims, the joint venture is indifferent because both investments promise net aggregate recovery from trial of $7.25 million.

defendant's maximum settlement offer equals $15 million (= $12.5 million + $2.5 million (half the litigation costs)). Plaintiffs' minimum demand equals $7.5 million (= $12.5 million − $5 million litigation cost). If the parties settle at the mean point, plaintiffs' aggregate recovery would be $11.25 million, or $225,000 per claim. While the 50 percent joint venture represents a regulatory advantage, it does not accomplish the objective of optimal deterrence.

Under these conditions, both parties invest $5 million and spread costs across all claims, effectively reducing per claim expense to $50,000. Given consensus on the expected judgment, and bearing equal costs for trial, the parties would settle at the mean of $25 million. This result increases each plaintiff's net recovery by $25,000, but more important, the class action achieves the regulatory objective of optimal deterrence. Indeed, everyone is better off because the threat of mass production tort liability by class action avoids the accident (and adjudication cost) entirely.

ADJUDICATION.   The effect of class action on adjudication is conventionally measured in terms of lower cost per claim from avoided duplicative litigation. To be sure, class action scale economies lower per claim costs by eliminating duplicative effort, but that "economy" for courts, as for the parties, represents only part of the regulatory story.[21] First, it fails to measure the effect of cost cutting on regulatory benefits; duplicative litigation, as noted below, is not always inefficient or, at least, is not necessarily wasteful. Second, and more generally, it is false economy to deem lowering costs in absolute terms efficient. Because cost reduction generally diminishes benefit, efficiency requires comparison of whether the marginal

21. Class action provides a further advantage. By aggregating all similar claims, class action enables courts to generalize or broaden the scope of common questions subject to final judgment. In contrast, claims in separate action process often involve the same relevant evidence as that admitted in the class action, but because a specific action narrowly focuses on the given plaintiff's claim, the trier of fact may not decide, or at least need not decide, the general question to which the evidence pertains. Consequently, the evidence may be marshaled repeatedly in a number of cases before the general common question is necessarily posed and decided, if ever. Consider the "state-of-the-art" question that governs many design defect cases in which the product is marketed and causes harm over a period of years. Because class action aggregates all claims arising from product sales in the relevant time period, a single determination resolves the state-of-the-art question for all claims. In the separate action process, the parties and courts might repeatedly rehearse the same data, but neither the plaintiffs nor the court would have the optimal incentive to investing in acquiring, evaluating, or using it for maximum regulatory effect.

saving in resources exceeds the marginal sacrifice in adjudicative value. Although it may seem obvious to measure judicial "savings" by the "opportunity costs," emphasis is warranted because courts rarely, and then only superficially, consider deterrence effects in evaluating management and other costs of mass production tort class actions. Indeed, those assessments miss a further dimension of adjudicative benefit from class action scale economies: motive for courts to make the optimal investment that maximizes aggregate value from judicial regulation.

Class action scale economies are essential to motivate courts to make the optimal adjudicative investment, which maximizes the prospect of achieving the social objectives of deterrence from mass tort liability. As mass torts often inflict harm on third parties, courts cannot simply rely on the narrow and generally underinclusive "private" interest of the parties to generate an appropriate informational basis for deciding the "public interest." Nor do the parties fully internalize the benefits or costs of the mass production activities and consequent litigation. Moreover, parties shape their respective positions strategically and opportunistically to gain advantage not only over each other but also over the court.

The adversarial process by its nature presents decisionmakers with a wide spectrum of choices between and possibly beyond the parties' competing positions on the questions presented concerning evidence, policy analyses, liability rules, remedial theories, and a host of other points of controversy. Mistaken decisions by courts in mass tort cases entail potentially high social costs—large-scale, serious injury; substantial gap in needed tort insurance; and distortion of incentives threatening the benefits and even availability of mass production goods and processes on which the lives and livelihoods of most people depend. These costs of error often justify courts' independently developing relevant information, and supplementing and verifying the party-created record, to establish a comprehensive and reliable basis for making regulatory judgments.

Establishing an independent regulatory role, however, is costly for courts, given the complex of multifaceted and highly specialized information they often must acquire, evaluate, and effectively apply to adjudicate mass tort claims. This information includes theoretical and empirical knowledge concerning science, technology, macroeconomics, statistics, regulation and law enforcement, insurance, distributive policy, market conditions, and business organization, finance, and practice. Furthermore, courts must work out an understanding of the facts and policies that relate to the conduct of the particular firm, as well as the risk and accident losses involved.[22]

To the extent courts allocate judicial resources to maximize net adjudicative benefits in mass tort cases, they must have the optimal incentive to acquire, evaluate, and use the relevant information effectively. Courts are apt to invest much less in developing and using information to decide any fraction of classable claims in the standard market process. Similar to free-riding attorneys who create collective action problems in the claims market, courts often merely copy—under rules of *stare decisis*, estoppel, and precedent—what other courts have done or else incorporate other courts' work by reference. Class action scale economies are thus necessary to motivate as well as to warrant the judicial investment that maximizes the social value of mass tort adjudication.

Class Action versus Market Alternatives

In the separate action process, a defendant facing a large number of plaintiffs generally has an enormous and unwarranted upper hand over the plaintiffs. The defendant firm exploits economies of litigation scale more fully than plaintiffs or courts. This edge enables defendant to invest far more cost effectively in the litigation relative to its adversary, plaintiffs, or the decisionmaker, courts. The upshot is that the plaintiffs— precisely because of their large number (and courts for related reasons)— will benefit less from trial or in settlement than they would have if there had been fewer of them. In effect, the defendant is able to use the plaintiffs' numerosity against them, so that the value of their claims is reduced

22. Consider the information demands of the prevailing standard for judging the reasonableness of product design. See Restatement (Third) of Torts: Products Liability, sec. 2 (1997). To judge a product defective, the court and jury must find that "the foreseeable risks of harm posed by the product could have been reduced or avoided by the adoption of a reasonable alternative design by the seller or other distributor, or a predecessor in the commercial chain of distribution, and [that] the omission of the alternative design renders the product not reasonably safe" (Restatement (Third) of Torts, sec. 2). This reasonableness (risk-utility balancing) test governs negligence cases generally. Applying the test requires courts to engage in complicated fact finding and to make debatable policy judgments on the net benefits of competing allocations of scarce social resources. The court's role includes evaluating the distributive consequences for individuals of varying wealth. Each case asks the court and jury to weigh the relative benefits and costs of the product design in question against those of competing designs, whether

for no reason other than that they are in large numbers. This is an arbitrary and, from the standpoint of regulatory policy, undesirable result that makes everyone ex ante worse off.

The potential virtue of a mandatory litigation class action is that it prevents the defendant from using the plaintiffs' numerosity against them (and to constrain judicial overview). Once the plaintiffs' claims are aggregated and the task of representing them assigned to a single group of attorneys, the plaintiffs (and court managing the class action) can exploit the same scale economies as the defendant. Because the plaintiffs' lawyers can spread their investment over all of the claims—just as the defendant does—it becomes possible for them to make investments in the litigation that they could not make if the claims were prosecuted separately. This puts the plaintiffs (and the class action court) in a position of parity with the defendant, who will exploit scale economies whether or not the case is brought as a class action, and achieves the regulatory objective of optimal deterrence, which from the ex ante perspective makes everyone better off.

Yet the reality of mass production tort litigation is that the separate action process generally operates through a fairly competitive claims market in which a relatively few corporately organized firms of lawyers compete against each other for market share of the classable claims. Profit maximizing attorneys will necessarily seek returns from scale economies and are motivated to aggregate and "mass produce" large holdings of claims. Perhaps the most significant development in the mass production tort field has been the transformation of the claims market from one populated by numerous small firms that coordinate their efforts on an ad hoc basis to one dominated by a relatively few large-scale law firms operating through nation- or worldwide networks of cooperating or franchise agents to locate, acquire, and prosecute claims. Given this competitive claims

---

or not these are commercially available at the time of sale. This task entails making a benefit-cost assessment of industry custom versus the most advanced safety technology available or in development and determining whether an alternative design was practicable, that is, whether consumers could afford the costs of additional precautions. Because riskless products are generally unaffordable and often impractical, if not impossible, to use for their intended purposes, judgments in product design cases strike a balance along many dimensions that effectively raises some risks while reducing others—for example, a safety latch on car doors designed to keep them closed in a collision may limit egress in case of fire.

In describing the information costs entailed by the judiciary's regulatory task, I am not suggesting that the benefits are worth the expense. Courts lack the resources to make reliable determinations of the standard, yet crucial, benefit-risk assessments essential to the regulatory enterprise. See Fried and Rosenberg (forthcoming). For a recent judicial concession that benefit-risk decisions are beyond the capacity of courts in the standard civil system, see *Pegram* v. *Herdrich*, 120 S. Ct. 2143, 2150–51 (2000).

market, with each firm seeking to maximize its investment return, it seems natural to ask whether market forces motivating "voluntary joinder" (fractional aggregation) correct the asymmetry in litigation scale more effectively and efficiently than mandatory mass production tort class action. I divide analysis between trial and settlement, in part because of the growing use in recent years of what seems a "middle" ground, the "settlement-only" class action, and in part because litigation class action poses a distinctive problem of nuisance-value settlement. My conclusion is that market forces do not, either by themselves or as enhanced by the settlement-only class action or by more or less compulsory "joinder" devices like consolidation, serve the regulatory objective in correcting systemic bias as well as mandatory litigation class action.

Comparison of the mandatory litigation class action and standard separate action process presents something of an "apples and oranges" dilemma. Whether and how much damages are paid to tort victims generally does not serve the regulatory objective of optimal tort deterrence, outside of motivating their cooperation. Indeed, paying them damages often works to thwart that goal. Removing all but payment for cooperation from the picture makes it quite simple to design a highly streamlined model of mandatory class action to enforce mass production tort liability, which eliminates the need not only for courts to monitor and calculate the fee for class counsel but also for contributory negligence and other rules to deter plaintiffs' from unreasonable risk taking, essentially making it possible to deploy the ideal of "double-edged" strict liability. In contrast, it is difficult to abstract the separate action process from the payment of damages to tort victims, and difficult to readily conceive of that mode of enforcement presenting a cost-effective alternative. To provide a plausible basis for comparison, I assume that the separate action process operates through a well-working ex post claims market, in which plaintiffs' attorneys or other investors purchase outright and total "ownership" interest in mass production tort claims. I put mandatory class action on a similar footing by assuming that courts would auction to the highest bidder outright and total "ownership" interest in the entire class action—not restricted, as is current practice, to a fee for serving as class counsel. The winning bidder pays the amount of the bid to the court, for its regulatory uses (for example, hiring experts and other actions), not to the class members, who look to first-party commercial and governmental insurers for compensation of mass production tort losses as they do for the same type of losses from far more prevalent, nontort sources of accident. Courts would not review the amounts paid to acquire separate or class claims but, instead, would rely on market forces to keep respective prices under each claim-sale regime at competitive levels.[23]

Trial

The following discussion distinguishes between the problems and costs of collective action that primarily affect party incentives to aggregate claims and the burdens that courts incur to manage aggregated claims. Analysis of each set of questions compares the costs and benefits of aggregated litigation in the class and separate action processes.

COLLECTIVE ACTION. There are problems and costs of collective action on two levels: aggregation and litigation. The problems and costs of aggregation arise in acquiring and developing claims and in coordinating their prosecution.

Mandatory class action for regulatory purposes entails far lower costs of acquisition than the separate action process. There is neither need nor incentive for class counsel to conduct any initiatory work, beyond investigating claims for information development purposes and filing a few claims for the representational purpose of informing the court about the contours of the class action to facilitate delimiting its preclusive effect prejudgment. Plaintiffs' attorneys bidding to win exclusive control over the class action need not have filed any claims; they need only demonstrate financial ability to pay the price of the winning bid. Given the regulatory objective, there is no reason for class counsel to identify, enlist, consult, or consider the interests of particular class members beyond, as discussed below, sampling claims to select a statistically reliable set of test cases for probabilistic analysis for purposes of discovery, dispositive motion, and trial.[24]

23. In general, there is little reason for being concerned that the winning bidder paid the "correct" amount, the expected value of the class claim minus costs of prosecuting it. Vested with exclusive proprietary interest in the aggregate return on the class claim, class counsel, like any "monopolist," is motivated to invest optimally in maximizing the expected net recovery and therefor the deterrence benefit from adjudicating mass production tort cases.

24. Indeed, class action effects considerable savings in initiatory work. Except in cases requiring preservation of perishable evidence relating to noncommon questions, the need for initiatory work on the balance of class members' claims arises only if and when class counsel succeeds on the merits of the common questions of aggregate liability and damages.

The separate action process will incur far higher costs for acquisition and development than class action, first and foremost because plaintiff attorneys will compete, from the start, to acquire large claim inventories. Second, in contrast to the mandatory class action, defendant will have an incentive to spend resources at the acquisition stage of the separate action process. It will seek and settle the stronger claims, in particular those acquired by lawyers with greater competence, tolerance for risk, and claim holdings (that determine litigation scale economies and in turn investment incentives), as part of a strategy of maneuvering weaker claims to the front of the queue for trial. This strategy reflects the correlated litigation value of mass production tort claims; litigation of one claim supplies information about claim value as well as work product to lawyers holding other claims. In a market of disparate holdings and relatively high information costs, defendant can depress claim values and rates by a series of early victories that signal the strength of its case and its commitment to litigate.

Coordination costs are also considerably lower in class actions compared with fractional claim aggregations in the market-oriented separate action process. Markets tend toward arrangements that foster and exploit scale economies, and the market for mass production tort representation is no exception. That market, like any that satisfies widespread public demand for mass production goods, has evolved into a cluster of relatively large-scale suppliers of mass production tort representation that compete for market share of classable claims. In particular, large, variously structured organizations of plaintiffs' attorneys vie against one another to acquire market share and represent classable claims en masse. Though conceivable, it is highly unlikely that the competing organizations would form a joint venture to fund the optimal aggregate investment, let alone that a single organization (or otherwise optimally assembled group of lawyers) would acquire beneficial interest in all classable claims. By contrast, because defendants' de facto class action scale economies derive essentially from the market, they are likely to retain decisive litigation superiority over plaintiffs.

Two obvious market defects severely constrain, if not preempt, efforts at collective action by attorneys. First, voluntary joinder entails substantial transaction costs to work out mutually beneficial arrangements designating those in charge of the litigation, distributing financial and other burdens and benefits, and monitoring compliance with the terms of agreement.[25] Indeed, given diminishing marginal benefit from acquiring each additional claim, search costs alone may be prohibitive.[26]

Second, voluntary joinder is beset by free riding. Much of a lawyer's work product in litigation falls into the public domain and creates the incentive for other attorneys holding similar claims to free ride. (At the limit, if it is very likely that one, and only one claim will be prosecuted to final judgment and the underlying work product is costless to copy and use in subsequent cases, then free riding might avoid virtually all duplicative litigation, except the considerable expense of competitive acquisition of claims.)[27] Free riding would seem an even more profitable strategy in a claims market dominated by relatively few firms, in which notwithstanding the incentive for free riding, one firm is likely to invest in litigation, and that investment is easily tracked and likely to be worth copying by other firms.[28] Once joined, the claim owners—plaintiffs and in many situations their preacquisition attorneys—present substantial organization problems for the firm, especially in securing their cooperation in the collective effort.

25. For example, an attorney may consider acquiring an additional claim, the value of which is simply to spread investment costs. Suppose lawyers A and B have similar claims each for $100 and are incurring litigation costs of $10 on the common questions. A and B are both better off merging representation, with A doing the work once for both claims. With no natural basis for splitting the surplus of $10, high bargaining costs will drain value from, and may well preclude, mutually beneficial agreement.

26. Even assuming that the acquiring firm benefits from scale economies, in cases involving similar claims dispersed widely over time and territory, the rising costs of acquiring marginal claims are likely to nullify much if not all of the firm's efficiencies.

Moreover, whenever initial ownership of classable claims is divided among two or more plaintiffs' attorneys, the cost of collective action generally includes "bribes" in the guise of "referral," "finders," and other fees that directly reduce plaintiffs' net recoveries because they pay off attorneys not for value-adding contributions but solely for their relinquishing claims to the joint venture.

27. Uncertainty about which claim will first reach final judgment also generates duplicative initiatory work. In effect, "defensive" multiple filings, discovery, and other aspects of development may result from the recognition of pervasive incentives for free riding that leaves many lawyers uncertain about whether anyone else will file and prosecute a claim to final judgment. Additional factors contributing to uncertainty are the relatively high information costs of tracking claim filings, compounded by defendant's strategy of settling strong claims. Defendant's strategy will hasten and increase filings of strong claims for settlement and weaker claims for trial on the expectancy that the stronger ones will settle. Moreover, much duplication of effort will result from time-bars compelling claim filings, and default and other sanctions that enforce various other more or less mechanical requirements relating to pleading, discovery, and pretrial preparation.

28. The costs of collective action are magnified in toxic substance, product liability, consumer fraud, and other cases of mass exposure torts because of the need to locate and evaluate claims widely dispersed over territory and time. Unless initially assigned to a single owner, the intervention of free-riding attorneys makes it doubtful that the joint venture would acquire all claims.

Indeed, the acquiring firm is apt to incur high monitoring costs to prevent its various stakeholders and agents from defecting or withholding contributions of effort, money, and claims in hopes of benefiting from the collective work product without paying for it. It is difficult for joint venturers to thwart noncontributors from capitalizing on collective legal work product, as it usually enters rather quickly into the public domain through court records and leaks from insiders.

The magnitude of these collective action costs and problems in any particular case is undoubtedly an empirical question. But it would be fanciful to believe that coordination barriers do not prevent a joint venture from acquiring ownership of the beneficial interest in 100 percent (or even the hypothesized 80 percent or 50 percent in the above stylized examples) of the classable claims needed to maximize their aggregate value. In the rare situation in which a joint venture achieves class-wide aggregation, it is doubtful that the organization, search and "payoff" costs make it preferable to the litigation class action.[29]

The collective action costs of the separate action process and the resulting fractionated aggregation of claims may be rationalized as the burden for its special benefits. In particular, the separate action process offers the opportunity for multiple trials and individualized determinations. Neither benefit justifies the added cost of litigating mass production tort claims by separate actions; multiple trials and mandatory class action are not mutually exclusive, and individualized determinations represent a wasteful, indeed, incoherent objective.

Mass production tort litigation often results in repetitive trials as a prelude to defendant's offer or "global settlement." Given the potential savings from global settlement, one needs an explanation for why the parties ever go to trial even once, let alone repeatedly. The standard explanation for the occurrence of trial is that the parties' respective estimates of the expected judgment differ sufficiently to wipe out the potential for joint savings from settlement; in particular, plaintiff's estimate exceeded defen-

---

29. This is not to say it can never happen. For example, a single plaintiff's attorney might directly acquire ownership interest in 100 percent of the classable claims arising from a small-scale pollution event affecting a confined area and limited number of individuals. Given prevailing procedures and practices, a class action might involve more costs than the market alternative, even after taking account of benefits from judicial oversight of class counsel's fee and settlement decisions. Although beyond the scope of this chapter, note that class actions could be reformed to effect a great increase in their efficacy, including use in handling small-scale mass production tort cases.

dant's estimate by more than the joint savings from settlement. Why would the parties in mass production tort cases conduct more than one trial before global settlement? There are two related explanations: accuracy and risk aversion.[30]

Because of the magnitude of aggregate stakes for plaintiff attorneys and defendant, divergence in their estimates of the expected judgment will likely involve a sufficiently large sum to warrant effort in reducing uncertainty. Hence they might find it worth their while to conduct multiple trials to derive a more accurate sense of the average, or weighted average, value of the claims, rather than rely on a single, possibly outlier, basis for projecting these values. It is plausible to understand much of the duplicative litigation in the separate action process as a system (sometimes organized by the parties explicitly) for resolving uncertainty respecting expected judgment by conducting and averaging out the results of a more or less statistically reliable sample of test claim trials.[31]

Risk aversion magnifies the parties' preference to reduce uncertainty and to achieve this through multiple trials rather than a single "coin toss." Obviously, the specific outcome of one trial poses a far greater likelihood of substantial variance from the "true" expected judgment than the average outcome of many trials. In other words, a party's chance of losing every one of a series of trials is far less than the chance of losing a single trial. The party rationally prefers paying for multiple trials, to the extent that the costs of risk bearing exceed the costs of litigation.

This discussion suggests that multiple trials in the separate action process, or more realistically, by fractional aggregation, could represent an efficient level of duplicative litigation. But the parties have other incentives for conducting multiple trials that do not necessarily further the social objectives for civil liability. Defendant could be waging a war of attrition (essentially the reverse of a "strike" or "nuisance-value" litigation) and, given the correlated effects of this type of litigation, could be signaling a "scorched earth" strategy or attempting to mislead marginal plaintiffs' attorneys about the strength of the case against it. Plaintiffs' attorneys with large aggregate holdings may conduct multiple trials rather than settle to further a strategy of seeking a nuisance value settlement by establishing the credibility of their threat of repeatedly going to trial with the possibility of

30. The implicit assumption is that settlement approximating the value of claims at trial ("true" value) better serves the social objective, all else equal, than simply terminating litigation on any terms.
31. See *In re Rhone-Poulenc Rorer Inc.*, 51 F.3d 1293, 1299 (7th Cir. 1995).

verdict and, in any event, generating publicity adverse to the defendant, regardless of the actual lack of merit to their claims.

Yet providing multiple trials to remove information barriers to settlement and burdens on risk-averse parties from a single, class-wide trial is not inconsistent with mandatory class action. Nothing inherent in the separate action process or class action suggests any design constraints. Thus mandatory class action readily accommodates the option for multiple trials, the number and variations being determined either by the court based on expert assessment of the needs for statistically reliable sampling or by the parties exercising much the same discretion as they would in the separate action process. Class-wide liability and recovery of damages would be discounted according to the probability of verdict for defendant revealed by the results of multiple "test" trials. Of course, defendant and class counsel could effect global settlement to avoid the added costs of formalizing the results by comprehensive judgment.[32] The key difference between the two modalities is in the investment incentives of plaintiffs' attorneys and the court that come from having the opportunity comparable to that of the defendant of fully exploiting litigation scale economies. Class action necessarily provides those investment incentives essential to maximizing the prospect of achieving optimal deterrence through mass production tort liability, while the fractionally aggregated process does not.

It might be said in favor of the separate action process that it adjudicates each claim according to its particular factual and legal circumstances, in contrast to the class action that determines liability and damages in the aggregate. For regulatory purposes—and while beyond the scope of this chapter, it should be noted for distributive and insurance purposes as well[33]—such particularization, even if a coherent enterprise, is generally a waste of resources. To achieve optimal deterrence, mass production tort liability need threaten damages equal to total aggregate tortious harm, that is the aggregate, weighted average of tortious harm suffered class-wide. No greater "accuracy" is required. Ex ante, mass producers do not and cannot "particularize" the infinitely variable circumstances of accident; in deciding what, if any, precautions to take, they calculate their profit-maximizing benefit-risk quotients based on the estimated aggregate, weighted average of all

32. Indeed, to save costs, the court could direct the parties to draw up a consent decree or submit counterproposals for comprehensive judgment based on the multiple trial outcomes.

33. For discussion of the insurance and other distributive benefits of "averaging," that is, awarding damages according to the severity of loss rather than fact, law, and other claim-specific variables, see Hay and Rosenberg (2000b); Rosenberg (1987, 1996, 2002).

possible accident/no-accident states of the world. The ex post circumstances of accident are relevant only for purposes of tallying tortious harm to assess damages when statistically estimating risk from ex ante perspective entails greater expense. Even that degree of "accuracy" could be avoided if it were less costly (including costs from defendants' strategic behavior) to calculate and assess damages equal to the activity's aggregate average rather than actual, aggregate tortious harm in the event of accident.[34]

It is important to emphasize that differences in state law are generally irrelevant, because mass producers normally design processes and products not for a particular legal regime but for expected liability under all governing legal regimes on a demographically as well as legally weighted-average basis. A Ford is a Ford in New York and Arizona, or, more precisely, it is the same car in both states, though its design probably reflects the law-related demographics of New York more than those of Arizona. The class action model under study here also has the advantage of eliminating most "non-common" questions, such as those associated with contributory negligence or assumption of the risk. Because class members receive no damages (other than a fee for cooperation), they effectively internalize the residual risk of accident "strictly," regardless of whether the standard governing defendant's conduct is negligence or strict liability. It may or may not serve regulatory purposes to relieve defendant of the costs of class members' unavoided contributory negligence or assumption of the risk. To the extent such relief serves optimal deterrence, it is sufficient to assess the harm attributable to that conduct in the aggregate and apply the fractional share it represents of the tortious harm as a discount on defendant's liability and damages.

The goal of individualization, however, lacks coherence in mass production tort cases arising, as they do, from statistical, unitary, and

34. In light of the legal, factual, and, most significantly, scientific uncertainty (especially about estimates of causation) that often exists in mass production tort cases, it might be thought that the market's supply of disaggregated litigation is a virtue and not a failing. Indeed, many commentators and courts assume that disaggregated litigation is preferable to class actions because it "matures" mass production tort cases by resolving claims through more than one test trial, and often through more than one round of multiple trials. They stress that in conducting multiple test trials and averaging out their variant results, disaggregated litigation avoids the risk of a single, all-or-nothing class-wide trial imposing an outlier award of damages that diverges widely from the mean. There is reason to doubt need for "maturation" on scientific and other issues, which can be resolved by averaging out unbiased decision errors without distorting incentives (as opposed to deciding whether a mass producer in fact acted negligently). But assuming its value for some issues, "maturation" does not require disaggregated litigation. Indeed, the litigation class action can "mature" mass production tort claims more efficiently and effectively. In particular, as I show, class actions can readily accommodate the efficient redundancy of multiple test trials.

systematic business risk taking. Being a pointless regulatory exercise and thus a waste of social resources, pursuit of individualization to the exclusion of mandatory collectivization makes everyone worse off ex ante. Essentially, in mass production tort cases no coherent individualized relationship exists ex ante between "risk" and "expected benefit" or ex post between "wrong" and "harm." Mass production torts arise as an intrinsic byproduct of the means of mass production, which achieves scale economies by standardizing the design of processes and goods. At the core of those designs is a deliberate decision to strike a balance between expected benefit and corresponding risk of injuring members of some potentially affected population of workers, consumers, or non-contractually related or "third" parties. To exploit scale economies, this benefit-risk decision represents a purely statistical average of an infinite range of outcomes for those who will actually constitute the projected population. A mass producer cannot know or predict and, most important, cannot adjust its decision to individual fates—respecting how and in what degree its good will benefit or harm any potential member of the population. In reality, the fixed parameters of that decision incorporate averages of all relevant demographic, legal, and other variables, including price. A Ford is a Ford everywhere, and the core benefit-design decisions that organize its manufacture, marketing, and use are reasonable or not collectively, indivisibly for everyone affected.

But it is important to realize that the ex ante choice for mass production is not a creature of market defects. Even assuming a Coasean world of no transaction costs and perfect information, *no one* ex ante would rationally prefer a system that mandated individually bargained contracts for customized treatment in lieu of the opportunity for scale economy gains in individual welfare derived from the standardized, averaged designs of mass production. Consequently, using voluntary collectivization to force customization makes *everyone* worse off because it undermines the goal of accident-cost minimization.

Pursuing the illusory goal of individualizing a relationship that is inherently collective imposes a wasteful administrative burden on mass producers. Anticipating that burden as an added cost of production, mass producers pass it through in the form of higher prices and lower wages that ripple welfare-depressing effects throughout our interrelated economy and interdependent society. But it also could jeopardize the essential standardized means of mass production—to *everyone's* detriment.

To be concrete, suppose X, who needs a car, has a special preference for the safety features of antilock brakes and would derive sufficient welfare from them to pay \$110 for a car so equipped. But the only cars on the market that generally meet X's needs are mass-produced vehicles costing \$100, and because most buyers prefer normal brakes, the manufacturer offers the antilock version only as a \$25 option. Unwilling to pay \$125 for a car with antilock brakes, X buys one with ordinary brakes for \$100. Subsequently, X has an accident while driving the car that results in some harm that could have been avoided with antilock brakes. Suppose that in a suit against the car's manufacturer, the court—disregarding X's informed choice and contract disclaimers—concludes that because of X's special preference for antilock brakes, their absence rendered the car unreasonably dangerous and justifies awarding damages for the harm that their presence would have avoided. If the manufacturer anticipated this liability rule and knew of X's special preference, it would have charged X a higher price for the car with normal brakes, in all likelihood raising the price by more than \$10 and, thus, to a level higher than X could afford to pay. Such liability makes X and other similarly situated consumers worse off ex post, and all consumers worse off ex ante. If, however, it is impractical for the manufacturer to determine its customers' special preferences and to discriminate in price accordingly, the manufacturer might spread the cost of expected liability thinly enough across all buyers to enable X to afford the car with normal brakes. Nevertheless, because everyone pays extra for no added benefit, all consumers are thus worse off ex post as well as ex ante.

Yet it might be possible for X to afford a car with antilock brakes if the court makes the alternative too costly for the manufacturer. For example, the court might regard the manufacturer's decision to pay damages rather than to supply the antilock brakes as "wanton indifference to X's rights" and then impose punitive damages in an amount that would make it economical to satisfy X's preference for \$10 (or less) by spreading the production cost across all buyers. From the ex post perspective, when consumers have knowledge of whether they have special preferences, those sharing X's preferences benefit at the expense of others. But from the ex ante perspective, before individuals know whether they will have special preferences, compulsory individualization ex post destroys the standardized means of mass production and makes everyone worse off.

COURT MANAGEMENT.   The judicial burden of managing large-scale, multiclaim litigation is usually given as a reason for preferring the separate action process to mass production tort class action. The separate action process is considered superior to class action in requiring less judicial structuring of discovery and trial, and in avoiding the need to monitor agency problems and undertake the related task of setting fees for plaintiffs' attorneys. But the model of mass production tort class action under study poses few if any of the significant manageability difficulties presumed to detract from the relative efficacy of using a more conventional mode of collectivization. Most significantly, auctioning the mass production tort class action eliminates the major, special managerial burden to determine the fee for class counsel.[35]

Class action is often thought to confront courts with difficult problems of structuring discovery and trial for numerous simultaneously prosecuted claims, including variations on common questions. For example, in many product liability cases, the defendant argues that the court must sort out differences in the benefit-risk quotient of various models or brands of a defendant's product, and noncommon questions, such as contributory negligence. These problems are exaggerated in light of special verdicts, phased discovery and trial, and other available management tools, and also because the bulk of noncommon questions usually involves generalizable methods and applications of proof—for example: the objective "reasonable consumer" baseline for determining "unreasonable consumer" behavior, and the economic model for computing past or future reasonable medical expenses and earning capacity. But, more important, these problems largely disappear, given the regulatory object and mass production sources of mass production tort liability. As noted, assessment of the aggregate, weighted average tortious loss (or average, aggregate tortious loss regardless of actual harm) suffices for optimal deterrence. Therefore, no general need exists for courts to subclass, phase, or otherwise particularize evaluation of the reasonableness of the various models (for example, Firestone Tire case) or brands (for example, cigarette litigation) of a defendant's product. Assessment of the overall reasonableness of its product and assessment of aggregate liability and damages provides optimal incentives for a mass producer ex ante to adopt socially appropriate precautions in its

35. The clearest cost advantage for the separate action process over the conventional class action concerns fees for plaintiffs' attorneys. Those fees are set contractually in the normal course of separate action representation. Class action usually affords no practical opportunity for class counsel to negotiate the fee with class members. Consequently, in the conventional class action, the presiding court must set the fee, usually in the form of a contingent reward. This task entails substantial expense for the court to gather the relevant information, including the demands of representation in the particular type of litigation, class counsel's opportunity costs, and the recovery percentage or rate of reimbursement plus multiplier that will lead the lawyer to invest optimally to maximize the probability of success at trial on the common questions. Class action auctions avoid that burden entirely.

designs for all of its various models, brands, and other micromass production and marketing decisions. Carving up the litigation to reflect different models, time periods, and other design features produces no deterrence gain, while it consumes greater adjudicative resources and incurs inefficiency from suboptimal investment.[36]

A pressing problem for courts in conventional class action contexts is ensuring that class counsel adequately represents the class. The cause of inadequacy may result from any combination of factors, including incompetence, risk aversion, collusion with defendant (or some subgroup of class members), and shirking. Of course, while generally ignored, the same problem exists for the separate action process. Competitive market forces of law firms striving to acquire large claim inventories in the separate action process or bidding against one another to acquire the mass production tort class action generally obviate this problem. Indeed, regardless of whether a firm pays too little in the ex post, separate action claims market or in the class action auction, its profit-maximizing incentive will preclude collusion with the defendant. Of course, the acquiring firm in either process may lack a reasonable level of competence and risk tolerance, but given the value of its separate or class-claim holdings, it could hire, merge, or sell out to firms that can maximize the aggregate value of the assets involved.[37] Considering the collective action problems and costs plaguing the separate action process, it is far more likely that regulatory maximizing arrangements will occur in the mandatory class action context that vests "monopoly" control over all classable claims in the winning bidder.[38]

36. In cases involving multiple defendants, courts can use mandatory class action for both sides (similar to the bilateral required coordination in federal, multidistrict consolidation). This procedure is not necessary, however, in the many cases, such as the litigation against Ford and Firestone for tire blowout-related SUV rollover, where the defendant firms have well-working market relationships and thus can employ an ex ante contract to coordinate defense efforts in potential multidefendant cases. Defendant class action would not preclude firms from advancing varying and conflicting defense positions through separate counsel. Variations in defense positions would not require subclassing plaintiffs' side to "balance" litigation, because variations in defense positions would affect plaintiffs' economies of litigation scale.

37. For these reasons, courts have less reason for concern about over- or underinclusive class action certification. Overlapping certifications by different courts pose a problem, but not one that arises frequently or that seems costly to manage. Multiple class actions can be consolidated before a single court under rules that are normally used to centralize judicial administration over multiple similar claims or, better still, rules that would channel class actions to predesignated courts with special expertise, resources, and experience.

38. To minimize these organizational costs, courts probably should prescreen prospectuses from bidders to establish a rough "cut" for firms with minimum experience and financial backing.

Settlement

First, I consider the relative regulatory benefit of fractionally aggregated settlement in the separate action process versus collective settlement in the context of a mandatory litigation class action. Then I address the potential for settlement abuse in the separate action process compared with that in the litigation class action.

SEPARATE VERSUS CLASS ACTION SETTLEMENT. Multiple similar claims have correlated value in the separate action process. The litigation of one claim supplies information about claim value as well as work product to lawyers holding other claims. The overall level of litigation will rise or fall accordingly. Eventually, the accumulated work and results will strongly influence the decision about whether to settle and for how much. In a litigation class action, law correlates the outcome of all claims. Just as in the separate action process, the estimated or actual results of a series of "test" trials in the class action context would have determinate influence over settlement decisions. Thus, all else held constant, the normal incentives to avoid trial costs and risks should, and do, motivate the parties to settle mass production tort claims at roughly the same rate regardless of context. Indeed, defendants will offer "global settlement" on the open market or to resolve the litigation class action when the parties' relative estimates of the expected judgment overlap and stabilize. The only difference is that the former derives from investment incentives skewed by defendant's asymmetric investment advantages, while the latter—formed in the shadow of litigation class action trial—reflects full opportunity to exploit scale economies for both parties, as well as for the court.

The transaction costs of settling separate actions are surely higher than settling in a single, class action proceeding. Indeed, the aggregated character of the separate action process may make global settlement even more costly than it was (or would be) under conditions of less aggregation. In seeking to avoid inefficient customization by proposing relatively standardized terms of settlement, defendant will offer an average return to a middle range of plaintiffs' attorneys. Many of these attorneys will have superior knowledge of the relative strength of their cases—because of the attorneys' above-average competence, the claims' above-average qualities, or both. Consequently, these attorneys have an incentive to make credible threats of rejecting the settlement and going to trial in order to exact some modification or side payment from defendant. Other attorneys have an incentive to masquerade as having above-average claims and appear ready to go to trial unless defendant increases the settlement ante. If any plaintiff's attorney were to win some additional concession from defendant, and the other attorneys learned about the change, then the entire settlement package could unravel.

Although defendant has strong reason to hold fast to its global terms, it lacks the credibility of preclusive effect to deter attempts at strategic bargaining by plaintiff attorneys.[39] This problem of the separate aggregated action process, along with others, explains the use of settlement-only class action. That device provides preclusive effect for the defendant's global settlement offer based on judicial approval. Plaintiffs with above-average claims may opt out, which, because it is irrevocable (unless defendant permits readmission), may signal their relative strength sufficiently to induce a separate, higher payment from defendant. Attorneys holding below-average claims, however, are unlikely to take the chance of opting out, and because defendant is bound by the court-ordered settlement, they are likely to take the settlement terms.[40]

The settlement-only class action is convened for the sole purpose of class-wide settlement. Failure to achieve that result—whether because of a breakdown in bargaining or court disapproval of settlement terms—automatically dissolves the class action and disaggregates the claims, replacing them in the fractionally aggregated separate action process, without any effect on claim values. Litigation class actions are operationally distinctive in the crucial respect that failure to achieve class-wide settlement does not result in disaggregation of litigation. Instead, the case proceeds to trial based on class-wide collective aggregation of all classable claims.

This key difference makes settlement-only class actions inferior to litigation class actions. Plaintiffs' litigation power in settlement-only class actions derives from whatever truncated scale economies they can marshal through disaggregated litigation in the market, which almost always

39. One device commonly used to avoid being whipsawed by plaintiffs' attorneys is to include a "most favored nation" clause in settlements, which provides that any subsequent change increasing the value of relevant settlement terms must also inure to benefit of plaintiffs who settled earlier under less favorable terms.

40. Settlement-only class action may serve other socially useful purposes. This device makes it possible for defendant to offer global settlement terms that have a "public good" character, perhaps doing something symbolic that all in the class would prefer; but because all plaintiffs automatically enjoy the benefit, none has any reason to pay for it.

provides too little incentive for them to optimally invest in maximizing the aggregate expected value of 100 percent of the classable claims. Any resulting class-wide settlement thus reflects claim values not only generated by plaintiffs' suboptimal investment incentive but also depressed by defendant's superior litigation power.

ABUSE. Settlement abuse is assumed to present special problems for class action. Two types of abuse are of particular concern. "Sweetheart" settlements occur when class counsel compromises class members' interests. This complaint arises when class counsel allegedly settles meritorious claims for far less than they are worth. The other complaint concerns the problem of "blackmail" settlements, in which the potential of catastrophic class-wide liability effectively bludgeons defendant into settling cases for more than they are worth. This is the mirror image of the sweetheart settlement: the accusation is that the class recovers more than it should because class counsel is able to threaten the defendant with a costly and risky class-wide trial. Indeed, in extreme cases, the class is positioned to extract a "nuisance-value settlement" despite the clear lack of merit in its claim.

But, again, the supposition of class action deficiency disregards the regulatory objective and mass production source of mass production tort liability, and the substantial, if fragmented, degree of voluntary joinder (aggregation) in that process. The problem of sweetheart settlement virtually disappears when class action has the sole object of deterrence. Blackmail settlement remains a risk for such a class action, but that danger exists in the fractionally aggregated action process, probably to an even greater degree. Yet blackmail settlement is readily avoided by straightforward modification of the rules.

Sweetheart settlement problems arise when plaintiffs' attorney is given special incentive to settle rather than go to trial. This distortion has many sources, including attorneys' risk aversion, side payments by defendant, and court-awarded fees that overestimate the opportunity cost of settlement. None of these sources of abuse represents significant motive for sweetheart settlement in the model of class action under study. Plaintiffs' attorneys, whether serving as class counsel or as representative of a large claim "inventory" in the separate aggregated action process, are capable of acquiring sufficient financial backing and of diversifying their investment portfolios—including by merger with competitors—to minimize the costs of risk bearing in large-scale litigation.[41] Side payments from defendant to class counsel probably pose a very small risk in class action because of judicial oversight.[42] In any event, there are no rational sources of motivation to sell out the class where, as in the model under study, class counsel bids for and receives the entire recovery from trial or settlement. Similarly, judicial error in awarding inflated class counsel fees unrelated to the attorney's opportunity cost of not settling class-wide—the major motivation for class

41. There is warrant for skepticism about suggestions that sweetheart deals stem from class counsel's aversion to placing a substantial pretrial investment at risk by going to trial. Experienced, adequately financed, and competent class counsel would not undertake these burdens unless, judged from the ex ante perspective, the anticipated fee-award exceeds the total expected litigation investment—pre-trial as well as trial—including the costs of bearing the risk of losing. In short, the actual expenditure of resources in preparation for class trial should not affect class counsel's calculation of costs and benefits respecting the choice to settle or go to trial. Indeed, in settlement negotiations on the eve of trial, class counsel would regard pretrial expenditures as irretrievable, sunk costs. Consequently, at this point the hazards of trial should concern the attorney even less than they did originally, before undertaking the case and making those expenditures. Having made the pretrial investment, class counsel rationally compares the expected recovery from class trial to the incremental (even if substantial) costs of proceeding to trial rather than settling. That ratio is likely to yield an expected net return from class trial that is far more favorable than the comparison of the expected trial recovery to total litigation costs that class counsel considered sufficiently profitable to commence the class action in the first place.

Of course, a sweetheart deal might seem attractive to "inadequate" class counsel—too thinly financed and risk averse to bear the expense and uncertainties of a high-stakes class trial. But courts possess ample power and opportunity to scrutinize the adequacy of class counsel. And there is no dearth of adequately prepared lawyers. Whatever may have been true in an earlier period, today, class counsel usually is capable of marshaling the economic wherewithal for effective prosecution of large-scale class actions. These "entrepreneurial lawyers" amass the resources necessary for adequately funding and hedging the risks of litigating a complex class claim through trial in a litigation class action.

42. Risk-neutral class counsel rationally—in unvarnished terms—seeks a kickback to supplement a lower fee-award. Essentially, defendant splits some of its illicit "savings" from avoided liability with class counsel, possibly in the form of a monetary side-payment or, more typically, by supporting or acquiescing in the attorney's effort to mislead the court into making an excessive fee-award. Class counsel profits from delinquency when the combined court-awarded fee from a discounted class settlement *plus* kickback exceeds the court-awarded fee the attorney would otherwise have received by settling the class claim for its true value. Direct side payments of money from defendants to class counsel cannot be ruled out, but the incidence probably is low if not negligible. Class counsel's acceptance of such bribes represents patent violation of professional norms. Courts effectively police this risk, moreover, by requiring defense as well as class counsel to disclose and disavow side payments under penalties for perjury, contempt, and professional dereliction. Also, side payments distributed among many lawyers are quite difficult to conceal. Beyond increasing the likelihood of detection, the large number of participants and others who know of the pay-off raises the possibility that the defendant's as well as class counsel's illicit gains will be appropriated by extortion and blackmail. Class counsel may solicit a kickback in the form of defendant's support or at least silence regarding the attorney's application to the court for an excessive fee-award. Recognizing the potential for abuse, courts seem to attach no formal, and no practical weight to defendant's views (except possibly when negative) on the appropriate fee award.

counsel to settle for too little—is not a factor here. The court does not set fees in the regulatory class action—aggregate class recovery represents class counsel's return on investment, if any.[43]

It is useful to distinguish between two aspects of "bargaining power" that are associated with this problem. The first is risk aversion specifically related to the prospect of a single class-wide trial deciding common questions on an all-or-nothing basis ("single-class trial" blackmail). The second does not hinge on risk aversion but rather stems from the sequential structure of litigation. In this process, the cost for one party to place another in jeopardy is often less than the cost for the other to avoid jeopardy—that is, the party facing jeopardy will settle for something less than the litigation cost of avoiding jeopardy, even when such an investment is certain to succeed ("nuisance-value" blackmail).

Judge Richard Posner recently identified the source of the pressure as the prospect of a single class-wide trial deciding common questions on an all-or-nothing basis. Faced with the significant chance of an outlier judgment awarding catastrophically high damages, a risk-averse firm would rather pay extra in settlement to avoid trial than bet the business on a single flip of the coin. Judge Posner concluded that the only solution was to reject the litigation class action and return plaintiffs to the separate action process. In that process, no single coin toss decides the defendant's fate; rather, it faces its aggregate liability as reflected by the average of outcomes from a series of relatively independent trials—what Judge Posner describes as "a pattern . . . a consensus, or at least a pooling of judgment, of many different tribunals."[44]

There is good reason to doubt that litigation class actions in reality exert systematic blackmail pressure against defendants. First, defendant firms are structured to operate risk neutrally and have many means of hedging against risk, notably derived from laws limiting liability and

43. Class counsel's incentives in settlement depend on the fractional share of a settlement that he or she will receive relative to the lawyer's fractional share of any trial recovery. If the fractional share of a settlement is no greater than the fractional share of the proceeds received from going to trial, then in general—with qualifications to be noted below—class counsel will have no incentive to settle for less than the class members' claims are worth. That is, class counsel should have sufficient motivation to "hold out" for a settlement that gives the class members the full value of their claims. Accordingly, the court can eliminate any incentive to settle for too little by regulating the attorney's fee in such a way as to ensure that the attorney's fractional share of a settlement is no greater than it would have been had the case gone to trial. For elaboration of the appropriate structure for fee awards to class counsel, see Hay and Rosenberg (2000a).

44. *In re Rhone-Poulenc Rorer Inc.*, 51 F.3d 1293, 1299 (7th Cir. 1995).

affording protection in bankruptcy, opportunities for stockholders to diversify their portfolios, and widespread availability of liability insurance. Second, the "blackmail settlement" pressure from a single, class-wide trial is not systematically directed toward defendants alone but rather is directed at both sides of litigation. Risk-averse class members and class counsel are no less likely than a defendant to regard a single class-wide trial with apprehension. In reality, blackmail settlement effects in any given case induce both sides to pay a premium for settlement, which nets out to the disadvantage of the most risk averse.

The solution of consigning mass production tort cases to the separate action process creates the prospect for systematic blackmail effects, directed exclusively against plaintiffs and their attorneys. While defendants spread the risk of adverse judgments across all test trials, each trial decides the fate of each plaintiff party on a single roll of the dice. Moreover, in contrast to the defendant, plaintiffs' attorneys own the beneficial interest in less than 100 percent of the classable claims, and consequently the value of each attorney's claim inventory may be determined by fewer than all test trials.

To the extent that blackmail settlement pressures from class actions undermine tort deterrence objectives, courts have at hand an effective remedy within the framework of a litigation class action. They can conduct multiple class trials, as discussed above, and obtain precisely the "pooling of judgment" that dissipates blackmail pressures on the risk averse. The prospect of multiple class trials would not necessarily increase litigation costs or dull appropriate incentives to settle. The solution does, however, radically change the range of settlement because plaintiffs, not just the defendant, invest optimally in maximizing the aggregate value of 100 percent of the classable claims.

The problem of nuisance-value settlement is quickly grasped from a simple example. Suppose plaintiff can sue the defendant for $500 in damages by spending $10 to prepare and file a complaint. Assume the defendant can either default on the claim and pay $500 in damages or defend, say, by spending $100 to conduct discovery and present the case for summary judgment with 100 percent probability of success. Notwithstanding certain victory, defendant rationally will settle within the range demarcated by their respective reservation points: defendant will not pay more than $100, and plaintiff will not accept less than $10.

But defendant's vulnerability to such nuisance-value blackmail may differ in the separate action process compared with class action. In the separate action process, defendant facing the prospect of many nuisance suits may, in certain circumstances, be able to ward them off. If the issues presented by the suits are related, then the costs of defense could be spread over many plaintiffs, making the costs per plaintiff quite low. Hence a plaintiff would be able to obtain in settlement only this low amount; and if it were less than the costs of filing, plaintiff would be discouraged from filing in the first place. Assume, in the preceding example, that defendant faces one hundred nuisance suits for $500 each, that facts relevant to the defense in all suits would cost $100 to prepare on a once-for-all basis, and that issues specific to the defense in each case would cost only $5 to develop. Then the average cost of defense would be only $6 (= $100 / 100 + $5). Given the $10 cost of filing exceeds this amount, plaintiff would not sue.

Class action alters the parties' relative bargaining power by giving class counsel an "ownership" interest equivalent to defendant's in the aggregate outcome of the multiclaim litigation. Because of the increased opportunity to exploit economies of litigation scale, class counsel may spread the cost of putting defendant in jeopardy across all claims to make nuisance-value suits worthwhile. Thus, in the example, the plaintiffs' costs per claim drop to 10 cents per claim, creating a bargaining range for nuisance-value settlement between a maximum offer on defendant's side of something less than $600 and a minimum demand by class counsel for more than $10.

Nuisance-value blackmail, like single-trial blackmail, has a double edge. The conditions for extorting concession in settlement that exceed the "true" expected judgment are not one sided. Defendant can exploit the sequential structure of litigation to extort nuisance-value settlement from plaintiff. Again, like single-trial blackmail, defendant's advantage arises in the separate action process because of its asymmetric advantage in fully exploiting economies of litigation scale. Thus defendant can wage a "war of attrition" against a plaintiff to discourage meritorious suit even when the claim has 100 percent probability of success. Take the example of the defendant facing one hundred wholly meritorious suits for $500 each, and assume that the cost of filing is only $1 per claim, so all one hundred claims will be filed. But suppose that the defendant could invest $100 per case to force each plaintiff to incur $500 in similar but pointless discovery, say, relating to an expert offering testimony on a common question.

This would discourage filing of all claims because defendant can credibly threaten to spend $100 to avoid 100 percent chance of liability for $500 in each case, and plaintiff would thus have to spend $501 to win $500.

Class action may prevent defendant from engaging in nuisance-value blackmail. In the example, class counsel can spread plaintiffs' $500 expense for discovery, reduced per claim to $5.10 (= $500 / 100 + $1 / 100). Confronted with the 100 percent probability of losing $50,000, despite its strategic expenditure of $10,000 to inflate class counsel's aggregate discovery costs by $500, defendant rationally will choose to settle on the merits.

Thus the choice for rule design is not a clearcut one between safeguarding defendant from nuisance-value blackmail by precluding class action, or subjecting defendant to that abuse by permitting class action. Precluding class action subjects plaintiffs to a mirror image threat of nuisance-value blackmail. The dilemma is avoided, because there is a simple solution to the problem of nuisance-value blackmail from class action. Assuming a sufficiently high risk of class action being prosecuted for nuisance-value settlement, courts could prevent this abuse merely by refusing to accept and enforce class settlement before summary judgment.[45] This rule entails no substantial costs, given that courts review the merits of class settlement anyway, and because only class claims with potential merit will proceed to summary judgment. Given that presummary judgment settlement agreements are unenforceable, no class counsel would have an incentive to prosecute a class action for purposes of nuisance-value blackmail.

---

45. This measure would allow the possibility of the defendant "throwing" summary judgment, but it is doubtful that many would find settling to avoid the costs (plus greater chance) of trial cheaper than the price of ousting the frivolous claim at summary judgment (or even earlier, on the motion to dismiss).

Priest suggests the solution of pre-screening class action on some threshold test of the merits. See Priest (1997, p. 521). See also *Szabo* v. *Bridgeport Machines, Inc.*, 249 F.3d 672 (7th Cir. 2001). Notably, Priest does not acknowledge the threat of nuisance-value blackmail for plaintiffs in the separate action process. In any event, his solution has two flaws. First, a threshold test of the merits reduces the class action threat of nuisance-value blackmail. Some risk remains, and its cost in nuisance-value settlement by defendant depends on the stringency of the threshold test and other empirical questions. Moreover, Priest's proposal adds a layer of substantial administrative and litigation costs for meritorious class actions. These class actions not only incur the costs of initial merits screening but most also foster partially redundant expenditures for subsequent review on motions to dismiss and for summary judgment. Second, a general defect is that a merits test alone, regardless of its stringency, will merely induce nuisance-value settlement on the threat of class action, before suit is filed, with the settlement agreement providing that defendant waives any merits test. Obviously, this last objection falls if courts refuse, as I propose, to enforce settlement before merits review. Summary judgment provides a standard test of the merits, so there is no need to work out some other screening criteria.

Conclusion

Some might criticize my argument for begging an important question. Perhaps, when considered as an integrated whole, taking account of the various problematic features of substantive tort law that distort deterrent effects, the standard fractionally aggregated process best approximates the socially appropriate level of enforcement. There are reasons to doubt that conclusion. First of all, defendants' asymmetric advantage in scale economies wrought by class action systematically skews judgments and settlements and denies courts the incentive to invest optimally in maximizing the regulatory value of mass production tort litigation. Moreover, only sheer coincidence could produce a tort system that best served the regulatory objective, while at the same time is so well adapted to satisfying the parties' ex post, wealth maximizing preferences—including lawyers' rent seeking—that conflict with the ex ante commitment to that objective.

To be sure, tort liability remains problematic. Tort damages are viewed as providing an excessive form of insurance for economic losses, despite an ample supply of far less costly and risky first-party coverage from commercial carriers and government sources, and for nonpecuniary harm, despite the teachings of insurance theory and experience to the contrary. Tort litigation also is criticized for high costs, largely attributed to enormous, possibly excessive, lawyers' fees. Overuse of the tort system is another concern; in many areas litigation costs exceed benefits measured as useful deterrence. Moreover, many believe that mass production tort cases thrust courts into the role of supervising business enterprises and resolving complex questions of science and public policy. The courts lack adequate expertise and resources and sufficiently comprehensive regulatory perspective for these tasks. Indeed, pervasive uncertainty in determining the reasonableness of risk—the central issue in most tort cases—threatens to overdeter firms, pressuring them to take excessive precautions that waste resources, raise prices, and make everyone worse off by shrinking surplus welfare from, and denying access to, goods.

But policymakers should not dodge the problems of substantive tort law by presuming that the system is evolving to the best of all worlds. These problems should be confronted head on. Rather than passing off some intuited balance of "evils" as public policy, we should rebuild the tort system on a foundation of rational, efficient rules and practices, such as mandatory class action. Indeed, correcting a socially detrimental bias in the system provides a theoretically sound and practically workable baseline from which to proceed to design targeted reforms of substantive tort law. Destabilizing effects on other features of the system should be dealt with through targeted, discriminating reforms. Resorting to the indirect and crude approach of offsetting one systemic defect against another—characteristic of much that passes for civil process as well as tort "reform"—is not just intellectually barren, it is socially irresponsible.

COMMENT BY
James Wootton

David Rosenberg advocates formalizing and expanding the quasi-legislative, quasi-executive agency role that the courts have been increasingly assuming. Ten years ago Rosenberg's chapter would have been perceived as radical. Today it is hardly shocking, for it articulates a role for the courts that is only a baby step from the current reality, or at least from the inevitable reality of tomorrow given the current trajectory of change. My comment addresses why his proposal is dangerous and ill-conceived, as a matter of principle and pragmatics.

Rosenberg proposes building on the handiwork of activist judges who aspire to be the architects of social and economic policy in this country. He would give their work the sweep of a legislative action or administrative agency ruling. By bringing massive numbers of citizens under the governance of mandatory class actions, he would advance the efforts of these judges through recreating an elitist form of the agency model within the court system.

This concept is a frightening violation of the doctrine of separation of powers and undermines the checks and balances inherent in our constitutional republican form of government.

The American people have the right of self-governance. They can petition the legislatures, propose new laws, testify at public hearings, and lobby for change. Every federal and state legislator who acts as an agent for this process is elected by the people, directly accountable to the people, and subject to a limited term of office.

Even the administrative agencies in the executive branch are servants of the public in the sense that most of what they do is ultimately open and subject to public comment and petition by the people. And the authority they have is granted by the legislature.

But as Justice Robert Young of the Michigan Supreme Court noted recently at a conference at the U.S. Chamber of Commerce: "In the judiciary, the process, though public in name, is private in essence. The public cannot broadly petition a court to urge the court to reach a particular result, and if the public did, the court is obliged to rebuff such importuning. Further, a court must consider issues largely as they are framed by the litigants, who typically do so only in terms that will serv[e] their vested interests, which is to win that particular case." And . . . "The legislature is free to experiment on policy questions—to try one thing and then another to reach a result satisfactory to the public at large. When the legislature makes a mistake in policy, it simply amends the law. When a court makes a mistake in social policy, and does so on constitutional grounds, its error can persist for generations."[46]

Let me speak for a moment about the people Rosenberg would have preside over the massive economic transfers that would accompany this new world of mandatory class actions.

As we all know, judges are placed on the bench through the involvement of the executive and legislative branches and, in some states, the voting public. However, once there, they serve for life or for terms that often exceed legislative terms in length. And they serve in a system that values judicial "independence" and devalues accountability to the people.

From the bench they wield great power. From the rulings of a few, major social and economic change can be put into effect. As Justice Young has noted, all it takes at the state level is: one trial judge, two judges of the court of appeals, or a majority of justices on the state supreme court. The process is equally efficient at the federal court level.

When one takes the long view and looks at the direction in which U.S. courts are headed, one sees that the Rosenberg proposal takes that trend to one of the furthest extremes. It moves society away from a democratic form of government and toward a new form of oligarchy in which judges increasingly take on attributes of a "ruling class."

Such a movement cannot even be justified by the results it achieves. If evaluated on a purely pragmatic basis, it can only fail to meet the objective of effectively regulating corporate conduct.

Although regulation of corporate conduct can be the product of legislative fiat, I would like to focus on the executive branch agencies that have as their explicit mandate the regulation of business activity. I draw some comparisons between the work of these agencies . . . and class actions.

---

46. "State Judicial Elections: Past, Present, and Future," sponsored by the U.S. Chamber Institute for Legal Reform and the Manhattan Institute, Washington, April 2001.

—First, how does a matter come to the attention of these agencies and enter the agency system as a matter needing attention? For those companies that are regulated, the matter arises as a result of a corporation seeking procedural approval or because of the volume of complaints or comments by the public.

In contrast, the class action is brought to the court by a lawyer with a personal financial stake, often a very large financial stake, in having the suit move forward to a profitable conclusion. Sometimes the lawyers are the original named plaintiffs, at least until it is possible to find others who will lend their names to the action.

—Often the agency review entails careful analysis of massive volumes of data or highly technical information. The information that comes to the courts, however, is often severely limited by the rules of evidence and the legal strategy of counsel.

—Agency evaluation is conducted by people with a high level of expertise in the relevant field. Judges usually have little expertise in the area of scrutiny, and juries have even less expertise.

—Many agencies use cost-benefit analysis. They assess the trade-offs in degrees of risk and the costs associated with eliminating or managing them. This is done in the context of assessing what advances the broad public interest. Courts, however, focus on the facts of a specific case before them and the claims made on behalf of a defined class. The courts do not provide a rational system for evaluating and regulating corporate activities.

To give you a feel for how crude a regulatory instrument we find in the courts, let me tell you about some work W. Kip Viscusi has done on the effectiveness of jurors at the job of risk-cost balancing.

Viscusi conducted an experiment in which he gave a series of cases to 500 mock jurors.[47] He asked them to decide whether punitive damages were warranted in the cases and, if so, how high. The cases they considered were hypothetical but were based on actual scenarios for which companies had done a risk analysis. The imaginary companies assessed the benefits and costs of particular safety innovations and then decided that in some instances the costs exceeded the benefits.

The mock juries were then asked to second guess the analyses the companies had done. These are the results he found based on the feedback from the jurors. If the companies do no analysis at all, the jurors are a lit-

47. Viscusi (2000, 2001).

tle unhappy. If the companies do a full regulatory analysis, assessing benefits and costs, jurors are *very* unhappy. If a company uses a compensatory damage amount of, say, $800,000 to value life, the juries hit the companies harder than if they had done no analysis at all.

The bottom line is that juries are offended by regulatory analysis.

The picture Viscusi's research paints gets worse. One would think that if a company replicated the analysis of a regulatory agency—if it adopted, for example, the procedures and value of life used by the National Highway Transportation Safety Administration—that jurors would be pleased. Actually, Viscusi found that jurors hit the companies harder. Jurors hit companies with a higher punitive damage amount when life was valued at $3 million than when life was valued at $800,000. Jurors sent the message that the higher the monetary valuation of lives, the greater the company's punishment.

The research makes it clear that companies are far better off doing no analysis at all and simply dumping risky products on the market. This is not a good message. And this is no way to regulate industry.

The picture gets even worse when one reviews additional studies done by Viscusi. Mock juries were given a case involving a railroad accident and a choice of whether or not to fix a railroad track in need of repair. Most jurors opted to fix the track later. Then the same case was presented with a scenario in which a serious accident had occurred. Then the jurors wanted to fix the track and punish the railroad company.

Before the fact they said not to fix the track. After the fact, they said to punish the company for not fixing it.

Viscusi's research applies to those cases that would go to trial. It is common knowledge that class actions rarely are tried. They are resolved through settlements that too often are achieved through extortion. Negative media attention to the lawsuit, exorbitant costs of litigating to trial, or the fear of an irrational jury outcome that wipes out the company often pushes that business into a settlement.

The reality is that to advocate using class actions to regulate business conduct is to advocate a system that is indifferent to the facts and merits of the claims.

How should corporate practices be regulated then?

As a person who believes in the free market, I, like many others, think the marketplace does a pretty good job of regulating many forms of business conduct. People do not buy products that are not safe. They do not do business with companies that do not treat them fairly and honestly.

Fortunately for the consumer, the vast amount of information on the Internet makes it increasingly easy to separate the good from the bad, the safe and responsible products and services from those that do not make the grade. There is no more effective regulatory device than the disaffected consumer who takes his or her business elsewhere.

Sometimes regulation is necessary, of course, and the United States has a vast system of regulation of many industries at the federal and the state level. When agency regulation is in play, the rules ought to be clear, understandable, and transparent. Most regulatory agencies work hard to make it apparent to companies what constitutes a transgression, what is unacceptable. For all the reasons I have enumerated in comparing the competence of regulatory agencies and the competence of the courts in these matters, companies that comply with regulatory rules should be shielded from liability. That would be fair, rational, and provide the right incentives for protecting the public rather than enabling lawyers to manipulate the legal system to serve their private interests.

References

Calabresi, Guido. 1970. *The Cost of Accidents: A Legal and Economic Analysis.* Yale University Press

Fried, Charles, and David Rosenberg. Forthcoming. *Making Tort Law: What Should Be Done and Who Should Do It.* AEI Press.

Harsanyi, John C. 1977. "Morality and the Theory of Rational Behavior." *Social Research* 44 (4): 623–56.

Hay, Bruce, and David Rosenberg. 2000a. *The Individual Justice of Averaging.* John M. Olin Discussion Paper Series 285. Harvard University.

———. 2000b. "Sweetheart" and "Blackmail" Settlements in Class Actions: Reality and Remedy. *University of Notre Dame Law Review* 75 (4): 1377–1408.

Kaplow, Louis and Steven Shavell. 2001. "Fairness versus Welfare." *Harvard Law Review* 114 (4): 961–1388.

Priest, George L. 1987. "The Current Insurance Crisis and Modern Tort Law." *Yale Law Journal* 96 (7): 1521–90.

———. 1997. "Procedural Versus Substantive Controls of Mass Tort Class Actions." *Journal of Legal Studies* 26 (2): 521–73.

Rosenberg, David. 1984. "The Casual Connection in Mass Exposure Cases: A 'Public Law' Vision of the Tort System." *Harvard Law Review* 97 (4): 849–929.

———. 1987. "Class Action for Mass Torts: Doing Individual Justice by Collective Means." *Indiana Law Journal* 62 (3): 561–96.

———. 1996. "Individual Justice and Collectivizing Risk-Based Claims in Mass-Exposure Cases." *New York University Law Review* 71 (1-2): 210–56.

————. 2001. "Avoiding Duplicative Litigation between Many Plaintiffs and a Common Defendant: The Superiority of Class Action vs. Collateral Estoppel vs. Nothing." On file at Harvard Law School Library.

————. 2002. "Mandatory-Litigation Class Action: The Only Option for Mass Tort Cases." *Harvard Law Review* 115 (3): 831–98.

Shavell, Steven. 1987. *Economic Analysis of Accident Law.* Harvard University Press.

Schwartz, Gary T. 1994. "Reality in the Economic Analysis of Tort Law: Does Tort Law Really Deter?" *University of California, Los Angeles Law Review* 42 (December): 377–44.

Viscusi, W. Kip. 2000. "Corporate Risk Analysis: A Reckless Act?" *Stanford Law Review* 52 (3): 547–97

————. 2001. "Jurors, Judges, and the Mistreatment of Risk by the Courts." *Journal of Legal Studies* 30 (1): 106–42.

RICHARD A. EPSTEIN

9 | *Implications for Legal Reform*

T his volume addresses the relationship between legislation and litigation as means to control the
untoward consequences of certain key activities, for example, the use of
firearms and tobacco. In truth regulation through litigation does not pertain only to those sinful activities that lie at the edge of the law. Rather any
gainful activity that carries with it the risk of untoward consequences, such
as medical treatment or the use of dangerous products, is a fit subject for
inquiry.

Regulation of such a wide range of activities raises many institutional
and substantive questions. First, what branch of government should make
the rules that determine the rights and duties of individuals and firms
involved in this broad array of activities? Second, should these resulting
obligations be enforced by administrative means on the one hand, or
through the judicial system on the other? There is of course an obvious
potential overlap between these two institutional inquiries: there is nothing that prevents the legislature from imposing requirements on the users
of, say, guns that invoke administrative sanctions on the one hand and private damage actions by aggrieved individuals on the other. Indeed the legislature may authorize private persons to bring tort actions for a breach of
statutory standards,[1] and much authority says that the right to bring these

1. For discussion, see Epstein, (1999, sec. 6.4).

actions will ordinarily be presumed by persons who suffer "special" injury at the hands of a defendant who has acted in violation of the statutory norm.[2]

Preoccupation with these institutional questions should not, however, blind us to the second part of the inquiry: is the combination of administrative and judicial sanctions socially desirable? We cannot rest content with the proposition that the higher enforcement levels perfectly correlate with improved social welfare. Rather, in assessing this and other claims about appropriate regulation, we must begin with the understanding that all human activities are subject to two kinds of error: overbreadth and underbreadth. It is possible to misstep by imposing sanctions on desirable conduct and conversely by *not* imposing sanctions on untoward conduct. Any aggressive effort to limit the adverse consequences of harmful conduct is likely to stifle desirable conduct too. The proper social task is to minimize the sum of errors resulting from over- and underenforcement, not just those shortfalls arising from one side alone. How that is to be done poses major questions that require a solid grasp of the institutional and substantive features of regulation.

This tour of mass torts progresses as follows: an analysis of the situation with respect to gun liability, tobacco liability, and silicon breast implant cases. Next I address medical malpractice questions and insurance issues, and finally I briefly discuss class actions.

Regulation of Guns

What regime of tort liability and legislation should govern the adverse consequences caused by the use of guns and similar weapons?

Personal Liability under Tort Law

I begin with a general tort theory, which remains true to its libertarian origins by holding that the use of force against any other individual constitutes a prima facie wrong for which damages should be awarded. The obvious case of tort liability is one for the deliberate infliction of harm; any alternative to imposing liability in such cases is too horrible to contemplate. Once it is possible for one individual to use force against his

2. *Cort v. Ash*, 422 U.S. 66, 78 (1975).

neighbor, then it becomes impossible to deny that same privilege to all other persons, given their claim to equal rights in (as becomes all too clear) a state of nature. The level of social insecurity that arises from this war of all against all, as Hobbes put it, thus rises to unacceptable levels.[3] In principle it would be possible for individuals who are unhappy about the use of guns to purchase their separate peace from their potential assailants. In a Coasean world of zero-transaction costs, one could easily envision the creation of a huge number of such contracts as people move quickly to eliminate these risks.[4] In some of these cases, we should not even expect the parties to exchange cash or other tangible consideration. In line with the general theory of social contract, there is good reason to believe that the contracting parties would be happy with mutual renunciations of the use of force, even if no cash changed hands. But no matter how clever the contractual approaches, a moment's reflection makes it clear that this ostensible market solution has nothing to commend it once the transaction costs for each separate contract are even weakly positive. Although an individual may be able to buy peace from a single neighbor, he still remains exposed to threats from thousands of other individuals with whom he has not negotiated a similar agreement. Indeed in a society with n individuals, the person who is able to negotiate with only $n-1$ people cannot rest in peace if he knows that the one unaccounted person is stalking him. As is so often the case therefore the entire analysis is in the end driven by a consideration of the anticipated transaction costs of alternative institutional arrangements needed to escape pitfalls of the state of nature. In general, for most individuals the desired resting place is one of mutual security, not one of mutual aggression. We therefore start the social contract analysis with the assumption that all individuals have (tacitly) agreed to the mutual renunciation of force and then (perhaps) allow those individuals who wish to be exposed to aggression (such as participants in a duel) to opt into that system by a side transaction that affects only them, while leaving other individuals undisturbed in the security of their own persons and the possession of their property.

Social contract theory continues to exert such a stronghold on political philosophers for two simple reasons: first, as an empirical matter, the

3. See Hobbes (1985, p. 185) ("Hereby it is manifest, that during the time men live without a common Power to keep them all in awe, they are in that condition which is called Warre; and such a warre, as is of every man, against every man.").

4. The *locus classicus* on this subject is, of course, Coase (1960); for Coase's own regrets about the excessive attention of the zero transaction costs model, see Coase (1988, pp. 14–15).

overall social gains from the mutual renunciation of force far exceed those from the unbridled use of force. Second, no set of voluntary transactions can result in the mutual renunciation of force if we start from the opposite pole because of the aforementioned problems of holdouts and high transaction costs. Hence the state prohibition on the use of force is imposed as a matter of positive law because it best reflects the end state that (virtually) all individuals would choose if faced with the choice between the use of force by all or the use of force by none.

Substantive rules and institutional design, however, are not solved solely by the broad declaration against the intentional use of force. Rather, many institutional choices remain. The early writers on private and international law were largely concerned with filling in the gaps of the system whose central premise was the prohibition against the use of force. Here are some of the questions that they had to face.

First, did the prohibition against the use of force apply only to the intentional use of force against other individuals? Surely the control of that abuse cuts down enormously on the dangers of living in society, but insecurity remains high when the negligent or accidental use of force goes without any form of sanction. It may well be that criminal law should confine attention to the intentional uses of force, but it hardly follows that private persons should be left without a remedy when struck by another individual who acted negligently or even accidentally. There is a huge dispute in the tort law about whether those who suffer harms that are "purely accidental" should be able to recover from the person causally responsible for the infliction of the harm, but there is little dispute that those individuals whose negligent use of firearms causes harm to others could be held liable for what they have done. The argument is simple: do the gains in security from the imposition of liability for accidental harms exceed the costs that this protection imposes, when these costs are measured by the loss of freedom of action that is required and the increased administrative costs of running the overall system? In my view, the movement to a total system of strict liability will do more to increase the overall gain than the more cautious step to a system of negligence liability.[5] The cleaner rules are easier to administer, and each person benefits from the greater freedom of action that is a by-product of the stronger prohibition against the use of force. But no matter which solution is adopted—negligence or strict liability—it is clear that tort liability is not confined to those cases of aggressive actions only.

5. For my early views advocating strict liability, see Epstein (1973).

Second, what ought to be the remedy for the use of force? The most obvious answer is damages for the harm inflicted. Although no one will deny their importance, we should be quick to acknowledge their obvious limitations. Frequently, damages will be hard to recover because the assailant will not be found, or if found she will not have the resources to answer for the harm inflicted. Even if those barriers are overcome, it will often be difficult to assign a monetary value to the harms in question and almost impossible to do so in the cases of death or some serious and irreversible injury. Clearly, the systematic or societal aspiration should be far higher than the use of damages as a remedy after the fact. Accordingly, the appropriate question is how to prevent these losses in the first place.

It is at this point that we come to a dominant theme that has shaped so much of the law of tort and administrative law. Most of the difficulties of this subject arise because of the *imperfections* found in the operation of the obvious tort remedy of damages after the fact. To see why, assume as an abstract proposition that no practical impediments of apprehension or valuation hampered the enforcement of the tort law. In these circumstances, the obvious approach is to set the tort remedy high enough so that no one would engage in harmful activities against another individual unless he were prepared to pay that person enough to leave him at least as well off as he was before the use of force took place. At this point it is difficult to imagine, except perhaps in television specials, any case in which a person would be prepared to pay his potential victim an amount of money that would make him whole. An effective system of deterrence would therefore drive the level of aggression down to zero, so that it would no longer be necessary to cast around for additional remedies to plug up the gaps now found in the law.

Of course, the early history of tort law reveals a different pattern. Although the issue has largely fallen by the wayside in modern tort litigation, the use of force in self-defense was central to the deliberation of the political philosophers of an earlier generation. The obvious point is that self-defense, if properly exercised, will provide an additional deterrent against aggression and also reduce the need for the victims of aggression to seek monetary relief after the fact. It is therefore no accident that the legal writers who first recognized the right to self-defense spent inordinate time trying to figure out the limitations that should be attached to it.

Did one have to wait for an actual assault to use force in self-defense? Here again the question raises the familiar trade-off between two kinds of error. If one waits until the attack, it might be too late. However, if one is allowed to respond in anticipation, then he might, as it were, jump the gun and cause serious harm to individuals who might well have done nothing wrong.

How much force could be used in self-defense? Clearly some prohibition should be imposed on the use of excessive force. After all, it would be most unwise to allow anyone to use a small shove as a pretext to kill his mark. Once again it is trade-off between two kinds of error: allowing the strongest possible response will deter the initial attacks; however this might also encourage some individuals to feign being victims of aggression in order to wreak vengeance on others. As before, there is no easy rule that effectively controls both kinds of error.

Tort Liability for the Wrongs of Others

The unhappiness with these various rules gives rise to another set of complications that inches us toward the modern questions of regulation in connection with the use of guns. In many cases, self-defense does not inject itself into a particular case, but the problem of inadequate remedies for direct assailants remains very much on the table. What then can the common law or a legislature do to overcome this imperfection in terms of broadening the class of individuals or firms who may be made to answer for the infliction of harm by another individual? One way to approach this subject is by asking what kinds of liability should be imposed on individuals who facilitated or did not prevent the deadly attacks by others. Again it is necessary to distinguish a full range of cases. To begin with the easiest case, no one sees much difficulty in imposing liability on a parent who hands a loaded gun to a child with known violent tendencies. The natural assumption of authority by a parent over a child makes it easy to allow an action for the negligent entrustment of a dangerous instrument. Such liability probably induces some modest increases in the care that parents exercise over their children and some modest increases in the compensation paid to innocent victims, but these easiest cases of liability are not likely to induce massive changes in primary behavior. Wholly without liability, the parents and their families stand first in the line of fire and thus have powerful incentives to take care of dangerous weapons or to instruct their children in their proper use. Accordingly, the first and easiest step has but limited consequences.

But what about the next steps? The first transition takes liability outside the family and places it on the retailer who sells a gun to a person who

misuses it. At one level, the requirement of proximate causation blocks liability when the retailer has no reason to believe that the customer will misuse the item sold. As a first approximation, the deliberate wrong of the
user blocks efforts to go back down the chain of causation. Such a limitation seems sensible in the abstract given the number of legitimate purposes, including self-defense, for which weapons can be purchased and
used. Even so, it is not difficult to conceive of circumstances that could
override this bar. Thus the situation is radically changed when the law
makes the sale of guns illegal unless certain conditions are complied with:
guns cannot be sold to persons who do not present proof of age or who
cannot pass certain background checks.[6] The purpose of these specific
legal duties is to lengthen the chain of causation to impose liability on
retailers who do not play by the rules of the newly constituted game. These
explicit statutory commands offer a list of "dos and don'ts" that gives fair
warning of what is expected in the ordinary course of business and thus
prevents the occurrence of rude shocks of liability after the fact. For that
reason we generally prefer statutory grounds for imposing liability on persons whose liability for harm is at best indirect. But even in the absence of
such a scheme, a more limited judicial foray could hold the retailer liable
when he or she has reason to know that the customer is likely to use the
weapon in a dangerous manner, even if the sale offends no specific legal
guideline. Yet by the same token, it becomes indefensible to impose a
regime that holds all retailers responsible for any harms committed with
the guns that they sold, no matter to whom they sell them. That prohibition only makes sense on the assumption that the sale of guns should
be banned, and a judgment of that sort, which goes so heavily against

6. The Brady law requires firearms sellers to obtain applications from purchasers attesting that they
have not been convicted of a crime punishable by more than one year of imprisonment or a domestic violence misdemeanor, that they are not fugitives from justice, that they have not been adjudicated
as mentally defective or institutionalized, that they are legal residents, and that they have not been dis-
honorably discharged from the military. 18 U.S.C, sec. 922(s)(3). But see *Printz* v. *United States*, 521
U.S. 898 (1997) (finding interim provisions of Brady bill unconstitutionally infringed on dual sover-
eignty to the extent that they co-opted state Chief Law Enforcement Officers to conduct federal regulatory background checks). Besides the federal regime, there are state requirements. In Illinois, for
example, to purchase or possess a firearm, an individual must first obtain a Firearm Owner's Identification Card. The application requires the applicants to affirm that they are over twenty-one years of
age (unless they have a parent's signature and have not committed a misdemeanor), that they have not
been convicted of a felony, are not addicted to narcotics, are not mentally retarded, have not spent
time in a mental institution in the past five years, are a legal resident, are not subject to a protective
order prohibiting possession of firearms, and have not committed a domestic battery in the past five
years. 430 Ill. Comp. Stat. 65/4.

established historical practice and constitutional norms, is one that most courts are, properly in my view, loathe to make. The limited form of retailer liability may amount to a sensible first step on a judicial threat of negligent entrustment. But as the scope and completeness of the statutory regime grows, the space left over for any common law liability shrinks: there is just less for judges to do.

Liability against retailers does not radically alter the pattern of gun use and distribution. Most statutory duties are articulated and known in advance. As long as retailers can comply with them, these duties raise the costs of sale but do not become a major source of new unliquidated liabilities. At this point the contention shifts to holding gun manufacturers responsible for the harms that their weapons cause in ordinary use. Some liability for these "remote" sellers (to use the old-fashioned term) surely makes sense under the classical law of product liability. But typically that liability required the proof of a defect in the weapon, existing at the time of initial sale, that made it dangerous in ordinary use. The earliest of these cases, *Langridge* v. *Levy*, held a manufacturer liable to the son of the purchaser of a defective gun whose inferior materials and workmanship made it explode in ordinary use.[7] Since that time, the law has expanded liability to hold the manufacturer strictly liable for such construction and design defects, often when the purchaser has misused the weapon. The defect requirement has remained firmly in place, so that the improved technology of gun production necessarily reduces the number of mishaps and with it the frequency of garden variety product liability cases.

What is needed for these purposes, however, is an expansion of liability that holds the manufacturer responsible for the deliberate misdeeds of the product user with guns made in a fashion that makes them fit for their intended purpose. Once again it is easy to achieve that result by announcing a judicial rule that bans the sale or use of all guns, but this rule would effect such a massive alteration of past practice as to make it highly unlikely that any court would choose to intervene on so broad a ground, no matter what the private predilections of its judges. Accordingly, for liability to succeed on these grounds requires a showing not of product defect but of some culpable misconduct in the marketing or distribution of guns. Theories of this sort, however, are difficult to establish under classical tort principles. The manufacturer is not in direct privity with the purchaser of the gun (or those for whom the purchaser serves as a front). He or she therefore lacks

7. 150 *English Reports* 863 (Ex. 1837).

the ability to make the individualized examination of prospective purchasers that is routinely required of retailers, either by statute or at common
law.[8] On the issue of duty, the hard question is, why impose a second layer
of oversight when the first layer is already in place? There is no easy answer.
As a matter of principle, it seems far simpler and more sensible to boost the
requirements for retailer oversight than to create a whole new apparatus to
deal with liability at the manufacturer's level.

Some sense of the difficulty of these second-tier duties becomes apparent by examining the elements of the proposed cause of action. The threshold question is whether to create this duty through common law litigation
or through statute. As an institutional matter, it seems clear that the statutory route should be preferred—assuming that any liability is created at all.
To see why, note the obstacles that stand in the path of the common law
duty. One possibility easily dismissed is that manufacturers should be held
strictly liable for all harmful activities caused by guns. The burden from
such a system would be so crushing as to drive all firms out of business. It is
one thing to impose a regime of strict liability on the party who uses the
gun to shoot another. It is quite another to impose that same strict liability
on the manufacturer of a gun that is used by another individual whom he
cannot control. This approach would ignore all intervening acts by retailers, parents and users, and would charge gun manufacturers as a group for
all the ills that guns cause but give them no credit for any crimes or violent
activities that guns prevent. The distortion will result in the production of
too few guns—conditional of course on the number of guns already out
there. The strongest advocates of a common law duty therefore shrink from
taking this extreme position.

The question then arises whether some more circumscribed theory can
achieve the same basic result. It is often said that it is highly foreseeable that
some guns sold will be used for criminal activities, or to put it more strongly,
that the market will be "flooded" with guns intended for that purpose. But
it is also known and foreseeable that retailers will conduct individual background checks on their use and that deliberate wrongdoers are subject to
heavy civil and criminal penalties for their misconduct. The question, as
with other forms of liability against remote actors, is not merely whether the
adverse consequences are foreseeable, as they invariably are, but whether the
additional deterrence obtained is worth the heavy administrative costs
imposed in pushing back liability one link in the chain of distribution.

8. See note 6.

In general, the usual arguments made are that the guns can be designed in ways that make them more difficult to be used for illegal purposes. But although it may be possible to add safety locks to prevent accidental discharge, it is difficult to see any safety device that can prevent the deliberate use of these weapons, and the entire question of accidental discharge of guns, although to be deplored, does not seem to be more serious on balance than accidental overdoses of medicine. Accidental discharges therefore cannot be the engine that drives gun control legislation or judicial enforcement. It can be argued, however, that aggressive distribution generates an oversupply of guns, and that some fraction of them fall into illegal hands. To counter the threat, manufacturers could, for example, take steps to cancel the franchises of those distributors that make repeat sales to individuals likely to engage in criminal conduct or that front for people who do.[9]

It is, however, hard to make this theory operational, for no one knows in advance how to set the sales quota for the guns that each and every manufacturer may bring to market in a given community before the flooding takes place. Even if these restrictions were respected, they are likely to prove idle, even when enacted on a national scale, owing to the ability of unlicensed gun entrepreneurs acting on the fringes of the law to smuggle weapons into areas where they are in great demand. Finally, there is a nagging question of causation when the effort is made to link any particular killing to the oversupply of guns. In some cases precise identification can be made, but in others it might be possible to link the gun to a certain subclass of manufacturers (for example, those who made 38-caliber weapons), and in other cases, no identification is possible.

At this point it becomes necessary to move to a "market share" theory of liability, such that each manufacturer held to have engaged in improper marketing practices pays for his proportionate share of the market on the grounds that handguns are essentially fungible once they come into criminal hands.[10] That theory originated in connection with the sale and use of the drug diethylstilbestrol (DES), a generic compound that was never

---

9. For discussion, see *Hamilton* v. *Accu-Tek*, 62 F. Supp.2d 802, 830-832 (E.D.N.Y. 1999).

10. See *Hamilton* v. *Accu-Tek*, pp. 839–46 (applying the market share theory to handgun manufacturer liability). Early application of the market share theory appeared to hold each manufacturer liable for the full amount of any loss, just as in the ordinary case of joint and several liability. See *Sindell* v. *Abbott Laboratories*, 607 P.2d 924 (Cal.1980). But that results in overdeterrence by holding those manufacturers present responsible for losses inflicted by firms that had gone under or were not joined in suit. The subsequent modification of the theory limited liability of each firm to its proportionate share of the market. See *Hymowitz* v. *Eli Lilly & Co.*, 539 N.E.2d 1069 (N.Y. 1989).

under patent, and which was alleged to cause cancer (after a latency period of at least ten years) in daughters of women who ingested the drug during pregnancy.[11] Given the generic composition and long latency period, it was impossible to identify which manufacturer had supplied the DES tablets taken in a particular case. Each seller was therefore held presumptively responsible for that fraction of the plaintiffs' losses equal to its respective percentage of the overall market, such that the liability for any individual firm was identical to that it would have borne if each tablet had been perfectly identified to its seller.[12] That model presupposed not only the fungibility of all DES tablets but also that each tablet from first to last bore its proportionate share of responsibility.

To carry this theory over to guns requires an assumption that the targeted manufacturers would have sold no guns if they followed sound distribution practices, or in the alternative, that none of the guns that they had sold properly would have worked their way into the hands of criminals. The first of these assumptions is little more than a backhanded announcement that the law can make tortious the sale of guns that had formerly been treated as legal. At one time, there was some authority for the proposition that "mere awards" of damages were not inconsistent with a comprehensive legislative scheme that allowed for the sale of certain products once certain conditions were satisfied. The most famous case in this line is *Ferebee* v. *Chevron Chemical Corp.*,[13] which allowed a state-law failure-to-warn claim to be brought against a firm, even though the product's package contained a warning that had been approved by the Environmental Protection Agency pursuant to the Federal Insecticide, Fungicide and Rodenticide Act.[14] That conclusion involved the general doctrine of federal preemption, which would ordinarily prevent the imposition of state law penalties that are inconsistent with a federal law that regulates the same topic.[15] The position in *Ferebee*, which has been widely repudiated, treats the payment of damages as proper simply because it leaves the seller the option of not marketing the product at all.[16] Once it

11. *Sindell* v. *Abbott Laboratories*, p. 925.
12. *Sindell* v. *Abbott Laboratories*, p. 937.
13. 736 F.2d 1529 (D.C. Cir. 1984).
14. 7 U.S.C. sec.136 and following.
15. See generally *San Diego Building Trades Council* v. *Garmon*, 359 U.S. 236 (1959) (finding preemption under the federal labor statutes on grounds that tort liability is directed at deterrence as well as compensation).
16. See, for example, Papas v. Upjohn Co., 926 F.2d 1019 (11th Cir. 1991); *Ferebee* v. *Chevron Chemical Corporation*, 736 F.2d. p. 1543 (suggesting that the manufacturer may opt not to send its product into the state, in this case, Maryland, where it may be subjected to common law damages).

is recognized that any system of warnings is meant to allow the sale of the product, then it becomes evident that the huge unliquidated financial burden is inconsistent with the basic statutory scheme because of its manifest deterrent effect on otherwise lawful activity.

In the gun case, the issues of federal preemption are not present when the state regulation and the possible tort liability are both of state origin, but the implicit tension between the legislative approval on the one hand and the tort liability on the other hand is every bit as jarring. The state court that wishes to be attentive to the purpose of state legislation should read any scheme of licensing and regulation as part of a coherent whole and as such should presume that compliance with state sales requirements precludes imposing tort liability arising from the same transaction. According to this view, any effort to invoke manufacturer liability should be rejected when the source of sale of a nondefective gun is perfectly identified. If we accept this premise, then state courts should reject any effort to impose market share liability on all guns sold from first to last: the market share liability theory simply cannot overcome the fundamental difficulty of having to convert lawful into unlawful gun sales.

A more accurate accounting therefore would hold these manufacturers liable in damages for at most those killings arising from the excess of guns sold under their improper practices relative to the number that would have been sold had they adopted sound practices. In this situation the conflict of interest between the state licensing scheme and the tort system of liability is somewhat attenuated by the argument that the individual seller has somehow abused his right to sell the guns under the system. Abuse, however defined, requires a trier of fact to separate out those sales that were proper under the licensing and regulatory scheme from those that were not—a division that cannot be undertaken in an obvious fashion. The utter uncertainty of that calculation seems to militate strongly against the imposition of any form of ex post liability. Again the institutional concerns should dominate in the absence of some clear and fair notice to manufacturers about which sales, to which retailers, count as excessive or not.

Public Nuisance Law

Another doctrinal path to achieve the same result is to insist that the excessive sale of these guns amounts to a public nuisance owing to the predictable harm that they cause. At this point, at least two complications intrude themselves into the overall analysis. The first question concerns the site for the sale in question. Suppose, as is the case, that the sale of guns is legal in some Chicago suburbs when the guns are alleged to be used to commit crimes in Chicago itself. Should the law of Chicago be able to reach out beyond the city limits and thus have extraterritorial effect? At one level this extraterritorial theory is disclaimed by the proponents of the public nuisance theory, for their argument is that the law reaches outside Chicago only in the case of guns that make their way into the city. Nothing about this public nuisance theory requires imposing liability for guns that are made and used outside city limits. But even that concession to territorial limits does not check the imperial expansion of the local law of one jurisdiction over the activities that take place in another. Guns sold in one location can be used in a thousand different jurisdictions, and it becomes extremely dangerous to argue that each and every one of these remote locales can impose sanctions on individuals outside its jurisdiction who sell guns where such sales are legal under the law of the place of sale. Nor is it necessary to go back so far down the chain of distribution. Even after this form of liability is rejected as duplicative and cumulative, nothing prevents Chicago or any other municipality from imposing liability on the individuals or firms who import these weapons inside city limits or who use them to commit crimes within the city proper. These downstream remedies render questionable the territorial expansion implicit in the upstream regulation of these weapons.

The same point can be made from a more substantive point of view. The definition of a public nuisance is not nearly as open ended as this kind of theory would suggest. The standard account of the law of public nuisance dates back to 1535, when it was articulated in a form that still makes sense today.[17] Suppose that a person digs a hole on a public highway that prevents other people from making safe passage along that road. In principle, each person so delayed could bring a private action for damages, claiming an interference with his or her right of way. But those numerous actions are expensive to bring, and each is for a small level of damages. Think of the consequences that would develop if every rush-hour commuter could sue the driver of the stalled truck that blocked traffic. The imperfections in litigation just noted thus preclude the realization of the principles of corrective justice on a case-by-case basis. Nonetheless the inconvenience caused by that delay should not go unremedied altogether simply because there are too many plaintiffs. Hence one solution is to impose fines meant to deter the defendant from blocking the public road and to defray the costs of removal. The goals of deterrence and compensation are thus severed: the former is preserved while the latter, because of exigent circumstances, is abandoned.

17. Anon. *Year Book Michaelmas*, 27 Hen. 8, f. 27, pl. 10 (1535).

Yet suppose now that the highway blockage causes delay to many people but physical damage to one individual. At this point the trade-offs between the administrative costs and the damage award change. When an identified act of a single individual causes harm to one person, there is no reason to block the unification of the compensatory and deterrent ideals of the tort law. The ordinary cause of action can be allowed. The defendant can be sued for the blockage and can (as is not the case in the administrative proceeding) defend himself by showing the contributory negligence or other misconduct of the plaintiff. In effect, the line between special and general (or background) damages organizes the distinction between a public and a private nuisance on procedure. The line has nothing to do with the substantive conditions of liability, which are identical for public as for private nuisances. Even so the modern definitions that talk about public nuisances emphasize the kinds of conduct that cause offense or interference in themselves.[18] The public nuisance is in principle a subset of the class of nuisances for which administrative action dominates over private lawsuits. For example, the inhalation of fumes is dangerous to health and is thus a private nuisance to the party who breathes enough to become ill but is a public nuisance subject to direct regulation to the extent that it does not cause this particular damage.[19] In operation, however, the public nuisance doctrine is particularly limited, as is illustrated by the constant statutory references to the relatively narrow fields of blocking highways and waterways. In most cases, therefore, the doctrine has been applied to people who have been in possession of property, not to those who have sold products.[20]

18. California's civil code definition is illustrative:

> Nuisance Defined. Anything which is injurious to health, including, but not limited to, the illegal sale of controlled substances, or is indecent or offensive to the senses, or an obstruction to the free use of property, so as to interfere with the comfortable enjoyment of life or property, or unlawfully obstructs the free passage or use, in the customary manner, of any navigable lake, or river, bay, stream, canal, or basin, or any public park, square, street, or highway, is a nuisance. Cal. Civ. Code, sec. 3479 (West 1997). See also Cal. Penal Code § 370 providing a similar definition for public nuisance:

> Anything which is injurious to health, or is indecent, or offensive to the senses, or an obstruction to the free use of property, so as to interfere with the comfortable enjoyment of life or property by an entire community or neighborhood, or by any considerable number of persons, or unlawfully obstructs the free passage or use, in the customary manner, of any navigable lake, or river, bay, stream, canal, or basin, or any public park, square, street, or highway, is a public nuisance.

19. For my discussion of these issues, see Epstein (1979, p.100). For their procedural implications under the law of standing, see Epstein (2001, pp. 17–22).

20. See, for example, *City of Bloomington* v. *Westinghouse Elec. Corp.*, 891 F.2d 611 (7th Cir. 1989) (tying nuisance theories to the use of property only); *Town of Hooksett Sch. Dist.* v. *W.R. Grace and Co.*, 617 F. Supp. 126, 133 (D.N.H.) (refusing to extend law from property owners to manufacturers).

The effort to bring gun litigation under the public nuisance theory is not the first effort of this sort. A similar broad conception of the doctrine was invoked by Frank Michelman in his effort to justify state regulations that suspend the operation of the standard law of trespass in order to allow protesters access to private shopping centers to protest government activities.[21] His basic contention is that the development of the suburbs resulted in the emptying out of the inner city. In the prior state of affairs, when shops lined Main Street, demonstrators had easy access to the public at large by exercising their right, held from time out of mind, to protest in an orderly fashion along the public streets. The competition of the private shopping centers in the suburbs drew away folks from the inner city. It is therefore only a matter of good common sense to allow the demonstrators to follow the shoppers, even if they have to trespass on private property to do so.

Yet this argument extends the law of public nuisance far beyond its traditional confines. Nothing in the extensive list of activities that constitutes a public nuisance includes competitive losses, which is just as it ought to be.[22] Any shift of shoppers from Main Street to the mall represents a clear social gain, especially if customers prefer not to have their shopping disrupted by political demonstrations of any sort. The ability to create a controlled environment effectively limits the unhappy externalities of everyday life. The other lines of communication remain open to anyone who wishes to hear and see protesters, and if their political demonstrations are what is desired, then mall owners can allow them to enter subject to whatever time, place, and manner restrictions they think appropriate. A look at other potential actions for competitive losses emphasizes the absurdity of the broad reading of the public nuisance doctrine: no one would allow the operators of the city stores to sue the mall owners for the creation of a private nuisance that draws away their customers, and there is no apparent reason for the city to sue the malls for drawing away the people who use the public streets.

The notion of public nuisance is no more pliable in the gun context than in the shopping mall context. The public nuisance concept is meant

21. See Michelman (1997). The case that inspired this discussion is *PruneYard Shopping Center* v. *Robins*, 447 U.S. 74 (1980), which held that ordinary conceptions of freedom of speech did not require states to allow protestors onto malls, while ordinary conceptions of private property did not require them to keep the protestors off. For my defense of the property owner in this context, see Epstein (1997).

22. See Keeton and others (1984, p. 643).

to cover those cases of large diffuse harms that meet the ordinary requirements of a nuisance. The lawful sale of a gun does not meet the test. It
could not be the source of liability even if the gun were traced to that seller.
The inability to make that connection does not emancipate one from the
ordinary requirements of the nuisance law, and hence this effort to press
the common law into the service of political action represents an illicit
warping of common law principles, so that it can be properly condemned
as a form of judicial regulation.

The Empirics of Gun Regulation

Even if one recoils, as I do, at the creation of a novel common law liability for improper distribution, legislative restrictions on sale, possession,
and use—no matter how precise—are only justified if the reduction in the
number of guns in circulation reduces the risk of harm. The literature on
this subject is simply enormous, and it is almost fatuous to wade into so
heated a debate in such a short space.[23] But even if the empirical evidence
cannot be exhaustively examined, the theoretical framework for its analysis
can be briefly stated. The increase in the use of guns does not in and of itself
tell us the purposes for which these guns are used. Any restriction on the
sales of guns prevents their illegal use in attack and their legal use in
defense. The overall level of crime therefore becomes a function of two war-
ring tendencies. First, the increase in guns increases the number of individuals who are able to turn them to illegal use, so that it becomes almost
self-evident that the greater availability of guns implies a greater number of
guns in the hands of those who should not use them. Were this all there
were to the situation, then the case for gun control, through liability rules
or through direct legislative restrictions, would be easy. But there is of
course a second complication, often ignored owing to the common psy-
chological trap of overlooking favorable consequences while concentrating
on dramatic but unfavorable outcomes: every restriction on the sale or possession of guns also restricts their lawful use. At this point the number of
crimes is likely to be a function of the number of guns in circulation and the
percentage of guns in the hands of lawful citizens. If that latter percentage
is high, then the returns to a (rational) criminal from the use of guns starts
to fall. He knows that whenever he so much as brandishes a weapon, he

23. See Lott (1998).

exposes himself to the risk of countermeasures from an ever larger number of unknown sources.

At each stage therefore it is necessary to examine the impact that an increase or decrease in the number of guns in circulation exerts on both these critical margins. As an intuitive matter, it seems clear that law-abiding citizens are far more likely to respect legal prohibitions against owning or carrying weapons. Hence it seems likely that any form of gun control will reduce the number of weapons in circulation and increase the percentage of weapons in dangerous hands—individuals who know enough to take advantage of the fact that the government has neatly disarmed many of the individuals who are likely to resist their aggressive activities. Fewer guns in the wrong hands with a higher rate of use can lead to more crimes than the alternative regime. The great vice therefore of imposing, either at common law or by legislation, *any* upstream controls on gun possession is their inevitable overbreadth. It is as though the state decided to enjoin industrial production from all facilities without bothering to check which of them emit pollution and which of those do not. A superior alternative strategy seeks to separate out dangerous from nondangerous users, such that the increase in gun numbers is offset by an increase of the fraction of guns in lawful hands. The trade-off thus seems clear: use anticipatory devices to keep guns out of circulation, and the law sharply restricts the defensive utility of guns. Alternatively, target sanctions—whether through tort liability or through the criminal law—against unlawful users of guns only, and it may be too late to prevent a crime. Which approach promises the greater social return?

To see how the situation plays out, think about standard forms of regulation. First, assume that gun possession is prohibited to all youths under eighteen years of age. Under such a rule, parents who know and like the use of guns are unable to train their children in their use, and reputable schools, whose activities are easy to monitor, can no longer give legal instruction to youngsters who are not allowed to handle guns in the first place. Yet under this rule delinquents can still receive their on-the-job training on the street. The impact is that the majority of guns in the hands of teenagers switches over to unlawful elements. That shift is consistent with an increase in the rate of gun violence. It is hardly a response to say that the level of gun violence would be zero if no youths had possession of guns at all, for the question is the marginal effect of gun regulation in the current situation, not in some pristine state of nature.

Consider, for example, the implications of this model to the claim that gun circulation has to be restricted to prevent mass killings that take place at schools, restaurants, or other public places. A determined fanatic can still gain access to a gun even in the face of strict regulations. Thus any rule against carrying weapons in public places unilaterally disarms potential resistance, particularly in settings where mass killings are possible. The criminal who tracks down a single victim on a lonely street after dark only has to ask whether that one victim is armed, and the chances of that are likely to be small. By contrast, the individual who opens fire in a large public space runs the risk that he will be met by resistance if only one person present is carrying a weapon—a virtual certainty in a room of one hundred people (even if only 10 percent of the population is armed at one time). The empirical evidence tends to line up with the theory. States that have "shall issue" laws (whereby guns may be routinely concealed and carried by individuals who meet certain minimal permit requirements) have lower rates of mass killings than those that do not.[24] It may well be that many mass killers end their crimes by taking their own lives so that conventional deterrence does not work—but even these warped souls do so only after making their parting gesture of inflicting massive harms on others.

The basic theory therefore says much for adopting the strategy that concentrates on the immediate sources of harm—attempts, brandishing weapons—and does less to interfere with the general supply of weapons. The focused effort separates out those individuals whose weapon use is unlawful and thus enlists in the fight against crime all law-abiding individuals in possession of guns. This approach is hardly novel. In dealing with speech meant to incite or cause harm, the Supreme Court's First Amendment jurisprudence accepts the premise that abstract advocacy—analogous to the manufacture, sale, or mere possession of guns—is generally not punishable. Thus only asocial behavior that is intended to, and likely to, produce imminent unlawful action can be regulated.[25] A similar approach, which would reduce the cost of gun regulation, would focus such regulation where it was likely to do the most good and in all likelihood would reduce the number of deaths from violent crime. On this model, the case is for stronger enforcement of those laws that explicitly discriminate between lawful and unlawful uses. The most obvious place to begin is at the street level, in the more effective punishment of the crimes that do take place. If, however, legislators wish to move back on

24. Lott and Landes (1999, p. 9). ("We find that states without shall issue [concealed carry] law had more deaths and injuries from multiple shootings per year both in absolute numbers and on a per capita basis during the 1977 to 1995 period.")

25. See, for example, *Brandenburg* v. *Ohio*, 395 U.S. 444 (1969).

the chain of distribution, they should make some effort to distinguish between those individuals who are likely to engage in the unlawful use of weapons and those who are not. The use of background checks to exclude from purchase and the "shall issue" system persons who have committed violent crimes or who have suffered from mental illness is a better strategy than trigger locks or waiting periods that apply to all users indiscriminately.

In dealing with these issues, Philip J. Cook and Jens Ludwig make all the appropriate theoretical distinctions in chapter 3 when they note that it is an empirical question whether the net effect of gun regulation on homicides (and other violent crimes) is positive or negative. Their test of this effect is one that I find odd, to say the least. They claim that there is a well-validated proxy for gun prevalence, namely "the percentage of adult (twenty-five years old and over) suicides committed with a gun."[26] Once they make the estimation of the level of gun prevalence, they then conclude that the higher the number of guns in any community, the greater the level of homicides. By making certain estimations of the value per life, they conclude that each gun carries with it a $65 negative value, which is not captured in the ordinary price of the weapon.[27] Some form of regulation that counters this negative externality is therefore regarded as appropriate.

To me, this demonstration does not carry the day. First, any system of taxation or regulation that might be imposed will be necessarily focused on the sale of new weapons. There is nothing in these figures that requires us to believe that the sale of new weapons in approved channels carries with it any negative externality. It could well be that a small fraction of guns in the hands of a certain subclass of individuals do all the harm. If so, then the only remedy is to find ways to remove guns from the hands of the individuals who are likely to cause the most harm. It is not clear that any system of bounties or taxation will be able to achieve that goal. A bounty may allow one individual to turn in one gun and to use the proceeds to purchase a better and more modern weapon, adapted for criminal activities. What is needed therefore is not some estimation of the correlation of homicides with gun prevalence but some explanation of how it is that a reduction in sales will improve overall safety. This is not an easy calculation to make given the overall decrease in the U.S. homicide level

26. See chapter 3 in this volume.
27. See chapter 3 in this volume.

in recent years and what appears to be the sharp increase of the total number of guns in private hands during the same period.[28]

I am also troubled by the gap between the proxy and the underlying concern. Most violent crimes are committed by individuals who are under the age of twenty-five. Any reckoning of the suicide rate by individuals over twenty-five offers only an imperfect match between the proxy measured and the phenomenon under study. The high homicide rates could also be consistent with the extensive defensive use of guns in dangerous neighborhoods, which may have prevented the homicide rate from moving even higher. Even if the overall numbers are correct, it hardly follows that a uniform taxation system is appropriate for all new sales, given that the risk of harm will vary strongly from user to user. As such, the ability to move from aggregate to marginal rates is something that is of particular difficulty. In light of the conflicting evidence on the relationship between gun ownership and homicide rates, the empirical question remains troublesome, to say the least. Yet as long as we know that the administrative costs of any scheme of regulation or taxation is likely to be expensive, the case for more gun control still seems to me to be unproved.

Regulation of Tobacco

The situation with tobacco differs in important ways from that found with guns. For tobacco the joint system of regulation and litigation has more or less run its course. The first step in this process was the cigarette labeling acts of the 1960s, which stated that certain disclosures were required on packages of cigarettes and in cigarette advertisements.[29] In one sense, I think that a perfectly respectable case can be made for the statute.

28. Here this argument presupposes that the level of guns in circulation meets these estimates. But these estimations are hard to make. On the one side, it is important to take into account guns that are taken out of circulation, either because they fall into a state of disrepair or are exported from the country for sale elsewhere. But it is also necessary to take into account the clandestine importation and reconditioning of guns. Clearly, if the number of guns has gone down owing to more stringent regulation on their use, then this would count as an argument for maintaining the status quo. But it leaves open the question of whether greater, or fewer, restrictions would have produced a better result.

29. See Federal Cigarette Labeling and Advertising Act of 1965, Pub. L. 89-92, 79 Stat. 282, as amended, 15 U.S.C., sec.1331–40; Health Cigarette Smoking Act of 1969, the key provision of which reads: "No requirement or prohibition based on smoking and health shall be imposed under State law with respect to the advertising or promotion of any cigarettes the packages of which are labeled in conformity with the provisions of this chapter." 15. U.S.C. sec. 1334(b).

Suppose the statutory warnings are largely superfluous because smokers are well aware of the risk of smoking; indeed, suppose that they exaggerate these risks in some significant portion of cases.[30] That scenario could well be accurate because the risks of smoking are common knowledge, obvious to all. The only uncertainty resides in the frequency and severity of adverse consequences. Cases of smokers dying from lung cancer are vivid in the minds of all, but that some smokers live long and happy lives is a fact almost ignored. The salience of the information presented makes it easy for people to overestimate the dangers of smoking. The federal warnings, which make no effort to calibrate the risks, have as their ostensible purpose the reduction of the level of smoking to zero.

Despite its alarmist features, the initial foray into tobacco regulation was in my view on balance well crafted. The basic perception that the risks of smoking are common knowledge does not mean that all individuals are equally aware of the risks. The case for mandatory tobacco warnings is that they inform the laggards without doing much to alter the perceptions of those individuals who already overestimate the risk. Government warnings are numbing at best, and are not likely, in my opinion, to influence behaviors of teenagers who are looking for ways to defy established authority figures. That said, the genius of the original warning strategy is that, properly construed,[31] it obviates the need for individual lawsuits that rely on hard-to-prove theories of misrepresentation, which for the current purpose includes concealment and nondisclosure. Thus in order to succeed under any theory of misrepresentation, a plaintiff must show that the defendant made a false statement of fact, that the plaintiff relied on this false statement to his detriment, and that he suffered damages in consequence.

This proposition rolls easily off the tongue, but it is no small order to prove it in practice. As is the case with public nuisances, it is impossible to understand how the theory of misrepresentation operates in mass tort cases unless and until its operation is well understood in ordinary cases in which a single defendant issues a false statement of fact to a single plaintiff. In the ordinary case of individual misrepresentation, it is not sufficient for the plaintiff to show that the defendant's statements were untruthful or incomplete. Rather, the plaintiff must show that the smoker's behavior would have been altered by the presence of true information, and, further, how the behavioral alteration would have reduced the injury suffered by that party.

30. See chapter 2 in this volume.
31. *Cipollone* v. *Liggett Group, Inc.*, 505 U.S. 504 (1992).

In many representation cases, the defendant's statements supplied the only inducement for action by the targeted plaintiff. This pattern holds, for example, when the representations focus on the operations of a particular firm or business, especially as they relate to a single transaction. Then it is unlikely that the individual plaintiff has independent knowledge of the risks associated with these operations. (Even here, many a plaintiff has stumbled on the obvious riposte that new ventures offering a high rate of return are risky.) Yet the plaintiff in a tobacco case has a hard row to hoe because the dangerous features of tobacco are generic to all cigarettes and thus are not within the exclusive knowledge of the defendant who makes and markets the product. The common knowledge of the tobacco-related risks means that individual plaintiffs are bombarded with information from their family members, doctors, *Reader's Digest*, and public health services, which cumulatively speak endlessly of the risks of smoking—risks that were painfully evident to me as a nine-year-old in 1952 when my father, a physician, quit smoking. Any false statement—even any deliberately false statement—made by tobacco companies is thus countered in a thousand effective ways by other sources of information. Word-of-mouth knowledge that comes from neutral parties carries a lot of punch for most people.

In this situation it becomes dangerous in my view to allow individual cases to reach juries, which could easily ignore the background information that is widely known by individual smokers. Once warnings are placed on the packets, however, it should be possible to make a conclusive presumption that no smokers have been misled by the companies because we now know that they have been exposed to the opposite message in just the form that the government wants to convey it. Hence I would dismiss all suits brought by individual smokers on the ground that common knowledge and statutory warnings take the heart out of any case for misrepresentation, nondisclosure, or concealment. In response it can be said that advertisement and publicity campaigns are designed to alter the perceptions of users. But the appropriate remedy, if any, is to ban fraudulent advertisements, impose fines on companies whose fraudulent ads slip through the net, and change and strengthen (if such is appropriate) the warning placed on cigarette packages and in advertisements. The regulation of the distribution of tobacco-related information should from start to finish be the subject of administrative rules and not of private lawsuits, which should be blocked by government efforts that define what warnings are adequate under the circumstances. If warnings are thought inadequate, then further administrative restrictions can be imposed: sales to minors could be limited, vending machines could be taken out of circulation, and the making of health claims by tobacco companies could be banned. Indeed at the limit, cigarettes could be banned without so much as allowing a single private action.

Nonetheless these actions have succeeded beyond everyone's expectations. The basic strategy has two parts, one of which deals with the tort law, and the other with class actions. Under the tort gambit, the smoker drops all claim for pain and suffering. Next, Medicaid or some other government health care provider asserts that it is bringing an *independent* action for its costs of providing medical care. The claim is so formed to allow the government health care provider to escape any tort law defenses that could otherwise be brought against the smoker who sued in his own right. But this claim for independence should be rejected here, as it is in all other cases in which medical services are provided to injured persons. If a physician renders assistance to an accident victim at the side of the road, he cannot recover from the driver of the other car if the victim himself had no right of action in the first place. He is of course entitled to recover his fees from any tort settlement that the injured party receives and, if unpaid, should be allowed to ask for an assignment of whatever rights the injured party has against the third person, even if the injured party chooses not to go ahead with the suit. Yet when that last maneuver is undertaken, the physician cannot rise above the position of his assignor and claim any money not payable to his patient. The assignment of tort claims is governed by the same principles that govern the assignment of contract claims. In both cases the homely but accurate metaphor is that "the assignee stands in the shoes of the assignor."[32] Two parties by contract cannot increase their rights against a third party without his consent.

The situation hardly changes if the physician had obligated himself by contract to treat his patient under all circumstances before the accident. Here the proper response is for the physician to price his services by taking into account the riskiness of the activities of his patient. Under no circumstances should this contract increase the liabilities that a potential tortfeasor otherwise has to face. The same is true for government agencies that provide their services under some statutory mandate. They too are entitled to reimbursement for medical services supplied to their program beneficiaries, but only when those beneficiaries are entitled to recover from third parties, and not otherwise.

32. See, for example, Farnsworth (1990, p. 809).

The basic situation does not change with smokers. If the patients so covered are smokers, then the government program can easily add a surcharge to the basic fee to cover the additional risk of medical expense. If it chooses not to do this, then it has made a political judgment to introduce a system of cross-subsidies among its insureds and should have no standing to complain that it runs a loss to those individuals who received the preferred rates. The legal principle that gives voice to these concerns is the doctrine of subrogation.[33] Under these rules the third party health care provider is treated as having taken a partial assignment of the injured party's tort claim against the third party. He therefore takes that claim subject to whatever defenses could be raised against the injured party. The assignment of a faction of the basic cause of action does not improve, nor compromise, the validity of the basic claim, which must be resolved as though it were still in the hands of the original plaintiffs.

Second, the insistence on subrogation undercuts the ability of Medicaid or other health care providers to use class actions for the aggregation of individual claims. The class action is for these purposes no different from any suit for public nuisance. Aggregation does not make valid in the aggregate claims that are invalid when standing alone. Hence even if one thought that all these complex representation claims were suitable for class actions under Rule 23 of the Federal Rules of Civil Procedure, they should still be routinely dismissed. In a word, the common law of tort has no part to play in the regulation of cigarettes. It follows that if these suits should not be brought, then the settlements providing large payments to the states (which are a disguised form of taxation from which plaintiff lawyers garnered a disproportionate share of the proceeds) were illegitimate as well. The private tort suit has only a role to play when the tobacco companies

33. Subrogation, which is common in the disposition of insurance lawsuits, occurs when a third party (the subrogee) assumes the legal claim of a potential claimant (the subrogor). The decisions that have allowed recoveries against the tobacco companies have all rejected the proposition that subrogation is the exclusive remedy in these cases. See, for example, *Laborers Local 17 Health and Benefits Fund* v. *Philip Morris, Inc.*, 7 F. Supp.2d 277, 286 (E.D.N.Y. 1998), *rev'd Laborers Local 17 Health and Benefit Fund* v. *Philip Morris, Inc.*, 191 F.3d 229 (2d Cir. 1999). The plaintiffs in *Laborers* urged that the health plan itself was victimized by the wrongful public relations behavior of the tobacco companies and thus could sue for misrepresentations to them. On appeal that theory was rejected on the ground that the health plans' liability all turned on the costs to smokers, who alone had standing to sue for the wrongs created.

The independent cause of action was allowed also in *Iowa* v. *Philip Morris, Inc.*, 577 N.W. 401 (Iowa, 1998). See also *Philip Morris, Inc.* v. *Parris N. Glendening*, 709 A.2d 1230, 1238 (Md. 1998) (outlining the direct actions brought against the tobacco companies, all of which sidestepped defenses available against individual smokers).

do not comply with administrative standards, and that case just does not happen at all.

On this view of the matter, much of what W. Kip Viscusi says about the current levels of taxation imposed on tobacco use is instructive and irrelevant. It is instructive because it indicates that any public cost (that is, cost above and beyond the shortness of life and the pain and suffering borne by the smoker) is more than covered by the elaborate excise and similar taxes that have long been imposed on tobacco firms. But the entire structure of his argument is that even if the companies should be held liable for some common law wrong to the public at large, they have already paid suitable compensation through taxation to the states in question. His evidence does not, however, preclude the argument that I have just made, which is that the entire basis of common lawsuits was misconceived on both the class and individual level. To the extent that there is no liability, there is also no need to find offsets to damages from collateral payments or any other source. It is better to decide the matter on a clear point of principle than on some refined point of damages. The short observation is that the only externalities that are created in connection with tobacco come from the system of cross subsidies that are found under Medicaid and similar programs. Otherwise, the tobacco firms and their customers are in a consensual arrangement in which risk has been assumed, and in which any set of warnings negates the possibility of overriding the defense of assumption of risk on grounds of fraud, misrepresentation, and nondisclosure. Accordingly, one of the great litigation sagas of the late twentieth century should have been a nonevent.

Breast Implant Litigation

Breast implants have been the subject of extensive commentary to which Joni Hersch's analysis is perhaps the latest chapter. The case involves the powerful interaction between administrative action on the one hand, and judicial behavior on the other, for as Hersch notes in chapter 5, there is little doubt that much of the onslaught on breast implant litigation followed on the heels of the decision of then FDA commissioner David Kessler, M.D., to call for a voluntary moratorium on breast implants except when they were required for strong medical reasons. To my mind this entire episode represents one of the most disturbing chapters of administrative action on the one hand and its tort aftermath on the other.

The essential element of any successful tort action is proof of causation. If one goes back to the simple forms of trespass actions brought when plaintiff claimed that he had been struck by defendant, the basic form of the action was defendant hit plaintiff. To that action, it was always possible to raise a large number of nice legal issues—assumption of risk, contributory negligence, and the like—but the case will fail no matter what the theory of liability if the defendant can deny what has been alleged, to wit, can deny that he has hit the plaintiff. The core element of causation does not disappear simply because the causal connections are far more complex in modern cases that involve drugs or medical products. The best defense to a product liability action is the prosaic demonstration that the plaintiff did not take or use the defendant's product. That line of defense is of course not available in the breast implant cases, but it is usually possible to raise a second tier of causal defense, namely, that the product in question was not the cause of the medical condition of which the plaintiff complains. That defense can be raised in two ways. First, it is often possible to show that the product did not cause the type of condition of which the plaintiff complains. If there is no connection between the use of DES and the occurrence of bladder cancer, then this plaintiff's bladder cancer cannot be attributed to her DES. In other cases the causal issue may not be so clear-cut. There is evidence that dioxin in large quantities causes chloracne. But there is no evidence that links it to the host of different conditions for which plaintiffs have sought recovery.

It is at this last level that the silicon implant cases founder. As Hersch reports, ample evidence links silicon implants to localized tenderness and tissue hardening. But "there is no evidence that implants cause lupus, scleroderma, or rheumatoid arthritis. Implants are not associated with recognized diseases, and there is no reliable scientific evidence that silicone gel leakage causes a new disease." To be sure, this conclusion could be attacked by someone who came up with statistical evidence of a strong correlation or with some previously unknown pathway or mechanism by which silicon gel could have caused any or all of these conditions. But the burden of proof is on the plaintiff, and that burden has not been met. At this point all the fine-spun distinctions in product liability cases are beside the point. We do not have to worry about whether the defendants did sufficient tests on the silicon implants, whether their design was state of the art, whether the warnings for use were accurate, whether a doctor's decision counts as an intervening cause, and so on. The simple point is no causation, then no damages, period.

At this point, the unfortunate interaction between the administrative decisions of the FDA and the tort system has produced an avalanche of lawsuits that have resulted in massive liabilities for actual and punitive damages. Clearly, something is amiss, and steps should be taken to make sure that cases of this sort do not reach juries, or if they do, that their verdicts do not stand when they are against the clear weight of the medical evidence. In my view, this cannot be done through any form of case-by-case litigation, which will in all cases suffer from a serious hindsight bias, whereby juries are eager to grasp at straws to find evidence of causal connection because of their antipathy for the implant makers on the one hand or their compassion for injured plaintiffs on the other. And the only way that this result can be achieved is to make it an ironclad rule that in the absence of fraud perpetrated against the FDA, its approval to market the drugs should be conclusive evidence that the product is not defective no matter what future events might prove. The only way to make sure that new products can reach the market without excessive risk is to rely on the FDA to regulate the introduction and use of new drugs to the exclusion of the tort system.

Medical Malpractice

A fourth area this book examines is the familiar tort of medical malpractice. At one level the questions raised in malpractice cases are fundamentally different from those involving firearms or tobacco. Medical malpractice suits are in general not amenable to any easy form of amalgamation. Far from being mass torts, they are expensive torts that take place exclusively on a retail level. The explanation for this critical difference is not hard to see. Tobacco litigation involves a generic product, where differences in toxicity across brands are usually irrelevant to any question of liability. The same is roughly true of firearms, at least when the proposed cause of action concentrates on sales to the wrong person rather than sales of defective products. Neither of these strategies for mounting a class action is available in medical malpractice litigation once we move beyond those ill-conceived lawsuits in which it is claimed that managed care organizations have systematically overcharged their customers for the services they provided.[34] The usual medical malpractice case involves a unique set of patient conditions with a unique set of failures by physicians and hospitals. Although the standards of negligence liability always speak of the failure to exercise reasonable medical judgment and care under the circumstances, each case in litigation tends to stand on its own, with the factually distinct issue taking precedence over any common issues of law or fact that might justify the use of class actions.

That said, it should not be assumed that the outcomes in medical malpractice cases are largely uncorrelated with one another. To the contrary, general shifts in doctrine will exert the parallel influences on decided cases even when these are not amalgamated into a single class action. When a court decides to use the doctrine of *res ipsa loquitur* to allow the jury to draw an inference of negligence from the occurrence of certain unanticipated consequences, that rule will affect everything from the surgical extraction of a tumor to the use of steroids to treat inflammatory diseases. All medical malpractice cases turn on proof of negligence, and any doctrinal change—in, say, the definition of due care—that improves the plaintiff's odds of success in one case will likely have ripple effects. It follows therefore that judicial pronouncements and legislative rules can have a great effect on the overall operation of the medical malpractice system even though malpractice litigation proceeds one hard-fought case at a time.

In light of these general observations, it is possible to understand the source of the uneasiness about medical malpractice from the initial crisis in 1975–76 to the present. The basic judgment of the legal system has long been that medical malpractice cases should be treated as torts governed by the negligence regime, and not as adverse events that arose out of a contractual relationship whose terms then set the conditions for liability, the measure of damages, and the form for decision. The choice of tort over contract carries with it, at least in the eyes of most courts, the conclusion that the patient and health care provider (be it physician or hospital) are not allowed by contract to vary or limit the scope of liability that tort law imposes.[35] The judicial alteration of doctrine creates a common mode risk, making it impossible to adequately diversify liability through the use of insurance. As long as the courts impose by legal rule only those duties that health care providers (or at least most health care providers) wish to provide, then the shift from contract to tort has little

---

34. *Maio* v. *Aetna Inc.*, No Civ. A. 99-1969 (E.D. Penn. 1999) [1999 WL 800315].
35. See *Tunkl* v. *Regents of University of California*, 383 P.2d 441 (Cal. 1963).

operational significance, which is why virtually no health care provider (cases of charitable care excepted) sought to contract out of the rules of the legal system until the first wave of tort system expansion hit in the early 1960s. Once the liability rules shifted on any number of dimensions, then the wedge between the tort standards and the contractual ideal became large enough to provoke a crisis. People were forced to pay ex ante more for protection than it was worth to buy voluntarily.

The question then arose as to the proper form of management of the new dangers posed by medical malpractice liability. The most obvious solution is for individual parties to reverse the changes in legal rule by contract. But that strategy is doomed to fail when judges take as their lodestar the proposition that these exculpatory contracts are infected by imperfect information, inequality of bargaining power, unconscionability, or some other defect in the contract process. The elimination of the direct line of response thus induces health care providers to wander somewhat further afield in their effort to minimize the impact of regulation on their delivery of health care services. Several obvious lines of response suggest themselves. The first is a heavy investment in technology that reduces the level of adverse medical outcomes in the first place. The advances in anesthesiology during the past twenty years have reduced many of the problems associated with keeping individuals under too long or forcing them to have an awkward period of recovery. Once the incidence of adverse occurrences declines, then aggregate malpractice liability goes down as well, no matter what the content of the substantive rule. To be sure, on matters of liability this desirable set of consequences is offset by a contrary factor, namely, that the availability of superior technologies enables physicians to undertake procedures that would have been foolhardy in earlier circumstances. But these exotic and low-frequency advanced procedures are probably in aggregate far less important to the overall level of medical practice than the improvement and simplification in otherwise standard cases. Furthermore, as a general matter bad outcomes for novel procedures are easiest to defend against claims of medical malpractice, except insofar as they fail for truly inexcusable reasons—such as a faulty blood typing—which can occur when one least expects it.

A second margin along which health care providers can move is a change in the system of delivery for health care. It seems as though one of the enduring advantages of the managed care operation is that they are able to pool data across large numbers of patients in order to make much more informed judgments about the efficacy of different approaches and treatment to medical conditions. The gains from these data sets are not confined to potential cases of medical malpractice. Oftentimes the operation simply decides which of two or more accepted courses of treatment seems to produce the better result at a lower cost—it is by no means uncommon for both to happen at the same time. The improved and simplified provision of health care will on average reduce failure rates and with it medical malpractice outcomes. It is for just this reason that Daniel P. Kessler and Mark B. McClellan found in their studies of five key medical procedures that medical care organizations (MCOs) had in general lower rates of utilization without higher rates of failure.[36] The system does make a difference in reducing the cost of providing medical care, once quality is held constant. There is no question that this movement toward aggregated care is in response to cost constraints that have little to do with medical malpractice. But there is no doubt that fear of medical malpractice liability spurs on movements in this direction as well.

The hard question with these developments is whether they would have taken place with equal speed had the specter of medical malpractice not been there in the first place. In part the answer seems to be in the affirmative because there is little doubt that health plans can sell higher rates of safe care to their patients. But what can be said about defensive medicine, which is a third possible response to the increase in tort liability? The theoretical case for positing the use of defensive medicine is easy to state. The tort system holds that the amount of care that is consensually provided is insufficient for the occasion at hand. The physician who is faced with the risk of extensive liability thus tells the patient that he shall have to purchase additional units of care in order to purchase the basic service. That additional care may cost more than it is worth in terms of its direct benefit to the patient. But by the same token it offers some additional insulation from suit. The care will be taken even though it is not indicated for medical reason. The use of defensive medicine thus counts as an inefficiency that permeates the health care delivery system even in those cases that never raise a glimmer of a medical malpractice issue. Yet once again Kessler and McClellan find ample reason in their data to believe that this defensive practice takes place, even though they, like everyone else, are hard-pressed to determine its magnitude or distinguish

36. See chapter 6 in this volume. The practices include the following: resort to MRI or CT scans for headaches; referrals to orthopedic surgeons for lower back pain; multiple ultrasounds; rate of hysterectomies; and rate of radical prostatectomies.

defensive medicine from higher levels of care brought about, say, by increases in wealth or reduction in the costs of technology that also produce demands for additional medical care. But for those of us who think as I do, it is not necessary to sort out the exogenous shifts in demand for health care brought about by market forces from that brought about by fear of tort liability. It is sufficient to allow contracting out of tort liability, at which point the factors will sort themselves painlessly in a voluntary market.

Insurance Complications

This brief overview of the problem of regulation through litigation would not be complete unless I made some observations about the topic of Kenneth S. Abraham's chapter dealing with the stresses that regulation by litigation has on the system of voluntary third-party insurance contracts that have been developed to deal with tort damages.[37] This topic is one that bristles with a set of well-chosen ironies. The original argument for the expansion of tort liability, especially as it developed in product liability cases, was that the manufacturer was the party best able to obtain insurance against what Justice Roger Traynor long ago termed "constant risk" of injury, against which there should be in his view "general and constant protection."[38] The implicit assumption of the Traynor view was that insurance against product-related injuries (and by implication in other contexts) was there for the asking, such that it was simply a matter of adding the small premium for product-related injuries to the purchase price of the product. Ex ante under this model, we could detect no dislocation in initial sales and distribution. Ex post we could insulate individuals against the vagaries of random injury by allowing them a suit under a theory of "absolute liability"—or what we would today call "strict liability"—for the injuries that were so incurred.

At one level, this theory sounds almost too good to be true, for it suggests that the insurance tail can wag the liability dog by ensuring that liability will be imposed for any product-related injury—much as coverage under the workers' compensation law can be imposed for any work-related injury. But the apparent verbal similarity between the two cases conceals

37. See chapter 7 in this volume.
38. *Escola* v. *Coca-Cola Bottling Co.*, 150 P.2d 436, 441 (Cal. 1944).

some vital differences in the calculation of the frequency and severity of the risk. As has been clear from the first, workers' compensation claims involve a statutory bargain in which the expansion of coverage for job-related accidents has as its quid pro quo a limitation on the damages that can be recovered in each individual case.[39] The early workers' compensation statutes were also limited to "personal injuries by accident," thereby excluding from coverage the many cumulative trauma cases (for example, asbestosis) that were later to come back to haunt the product liability and workers' compensation areas. Product liability cases are not subject to such limitations, and to offset that difference, the Traynor formulation of absolute tort liability proved in practice to be far narrower than the subsequent modifications of product liability rules that took place after the adoption of the Second Restatement of Torts in 1965.[40] Under the initial formulations, the product defect (which was meant to include deviations from known and established product standards) had to be present in the product when it left the manufacturer's hands and had to persist in that original condition until it resulted in injury when used in the normal and proper manner by the individual plaintiff or some third party. The net effect of these restrictions was to limit strict liability to random manufacturing errors or to the narrow class of design defects that were serious enough to make a product dangerous when put to its intended use. The former were indeed largely random events that could be counteracted by a sensible system of inspection. The latter design defects were relatively rare occurrences that were typically caught early on in the cycle of production and use and hence did not result in any mass tort litigation.

In this early environment, the liability rules in products and other cases harmonized well with the doctrines of insurance that were designed to regulate their use.[41] Thus the narrow definition of defect meant that the insurer was not likely to be hit with large claims for unknown and unanticipated consequences of standard business practices. The requirement that the product remain in its initial condition when it worked its injury meant that the insurer did not have to anticipate how some downstream user of the product could increase the risk of harm by product modification, and for its part the requirement of normal and proper use meant that the insurer did not have to worry about the moral hazard risks associated

---

39. For a discussion see *New York Central R.R. Co.* v. *White*, 243 U.S. 188, pp. 202–04 (1917).
40. American Law Institute (1965).
41. For my more extensive discussion of this point, see Epstein (1985).

with dangerous uses of a standard product. The early system of tort liability thus worked when dangerous information asymmetries placed innocent consumers at the risk of harms that were more cheaply avoided by manufacturers. In that environment, the happy conclusion that Justice Traynor reached in *Escola* seemed justified, for it ushered in a general age of tort and insurance liability that lasted through the adoption of the Restatement (Second) of Torts until, roughly speaking, the expansion of tort liability that began between 1968 and 1970.[42]

The level of calm inside the insurance industry is well revealed by the debates that took place between 1943 and 1966 on the revisions of the Comprehensive General Liability (CGL) provisions to which Abraham devotes so much attention. This general clause originally covered those cases of accidents during the policy period for which the insured was legally obligated to pay damages. Nothing in the original CGL policy tied coverage to the theory of liability under which recovery was made, except when there was some intentional misconduct by the insured. To cover those cases, the standard policy allows recovery only for losses that are "neither expected nor intended" from the vantage point of the insured. But for such harms, it mattered not one whit whether liability was sought under older theories of negligence or newfangled theories of strict liability. It mattered not whether the plaintiff invoked a theory of *res ipsa loquitur* to establish negligence or a broad or a narrow theory of proximate causation. Simply put, the insurance followed the liability.

One key issue in these early cases was whether the term "accident" should be read as a term of limitation on coverage that excluded liability for "cumulative trauma" cases, defined to include those cases in which a person suffered injury because of repeated exposure to dangerous conditions or substances. This definition stands in contradistinction to the paradigmatic "accident"—a singular sudden event, the focal point of the traditional forms of coverage. The unambiguous decision to extend coverage to cumulative trauma cases raised the obvious question of which insurance policy or policies should be liable in what amount for the new classes of injury. What was so striking about those early debates is that the insurers did not find it

---

42. One convenient point for identification of the new era is *Larsen* v. *General Motors Corporation*, 391 F.2d 495 (8th Cir. 1968), which gave rise to the crashworthiness doctrine, under which automobile manufacturers could be held responsible for injuries to automobile passengers brought about by the driver's own misconduct or that of third parties. A similar landmark development in the duty to warn area is *Davis* v. *Wyeth Laboratories, Inc.*, 399 F.2d 121 (9th Cir. 1968), which introduced liability for a failure to warn to the manufacturers of the Sabin live virus polio vaccine.

necessary to resolve that matter in their collective deliberations over standard policy language. Accordingly, the standard policies allowed for easier comparison of price across firms and the creation of complex insurance structures with multiple policies, often from different carriers. The clear attitude at this time was that the issue of cumulative trauma was so small under the established tort law of the time that each company could be relied on to use its own business judgment in resolving the odd case, which usually arose with a trusted customer with whom the insurer had a long and stable relationship. The firms therefore decided in essence that it was best to "agree to disagree"—a miscalculation that cost the firms billions of dollars a generation later.

To see why this was such a drastic miscalculation, it is necessary to review the theories that could have been explicitly adopted to solve the problem. The first of these is one that telescoped all losses into a single policy year (typically the year the injury became manifest), so that it could then be treated as though it were an ordinary traumatic injury subject to a single policy limit, deductible, and set of exclusions. That position, for which I argued in briefs and academic writings, enjoyed some limited legal success[43] and had the great virtue (or vice) of knocking out policies written years before the dispute arose. Under the first manifestation of this view, policies written in the carefree years before 1960 or 1965 could not be relied on for coverage of losses that began with the onslaught of asbestos claims following the watershed plaintiffs' victory in *Borel* v. *Fibreboard Products Co.*[44]

Yet the history played out in a different fashion. The newer theories of tort liability couple broader definitions of product defect with a narrower set of admissible defenses. Oftentimes the two developments are closely interconnected, for it is impossible to expand the scope of a duty to warn without simultaneously contracting the sphere of the assumption of risk defense.[45] Manufacturers are now subject to a liability regime that was most definitely not in place when the original product was sold. The constant refrain in *Escola* that the tort law should provide constant and

43. Epstein (1984). See *Eagle-Picher Industries, Inc.* v. *Liberty Mutual Insurance Co.*, 682 F.2d 12 (1st Cir. 1982) (adopting theory in case in which it worked for the benefit of the insured).

44. 493 F.2d 1076 (5th Cir. 1973). This decision swept aside the prodefendant law created by decisions that had essentially relegated asbestos victims to recoveries available under the workers' compensation system based on the control that intermediate employers had over the conditions in which asbestos products were used.

45. See, for example, *Bexiga* v. *Havir Mfg. Corp.*, 290 A.2d 281 (N.J. 1962) (rejecting the open and obvious defect defense for machinery).

general protection meant that these new rules were applied without a hitch to products that had been sold in a very different legal climate decades earlier. The next question was whether the losses would remain stranded with the manufacturers or whether they could follow their insurers from the earlier periods. Owing to the effort to secure the largest possible pool of cash for the tort victims, the courts for the most part sided with the insured parties when they insisted that the coverage be extended to the latent phase of injury, which in personal injury cases covered the period that asbestos fibers were found in the lungs,[46] and in property damages covered the periods of apparent latent degeneration of a product (commonly understood to date from the moment of installation).[47] These initial insured victories sought to take into account the peaks and valleys of insurance coverage. Under the standard proration theories, the loss was divided into equal portions over the entire period of exposure. Therefore the insurer took the risk for those periods in which insurance was purchased, and the insured took the risks for those period in which it was not.

That principled compromised position, however, did not last long. Even though there was not a single shred of evidence in support of the proposition, after some initial fumbling the courts adopted the so-called triple trigger theory. According to this idea, the insured, after the injury had manifested itself, could assign arbitrarily all or part of the loss to any particular policy within the broadly defined proration period, even when its sole intention was to maximize the coverage afforded from the full range of primary and excess policies that had been purchased over the years.[48] The net effect of this position was that an insurance company that wrote a no-limits policy for a single day in 1965 could be held responsible in full for all cumulative trauma cases whose initial exposure took place before the coverage as long as the injury manifested itself thereafter. Any connections between the premiums collected and the risk assumed by the insurer disappeared from view. The easy optimism that Justice Traynor had expressed about the ability of the insurance system to fund the new system of strict product liability thus hit the shoals two generations later.

---

46. See *Insurance Co. of North America* v. *Forty-Eight Insulations*, 633 F.2d 1212 (6th Cir. 1980), modified 657 F.2d 814 (6th Cir. 1981).

47. *Eljer Manufacturing, Inc.* v. *Liberty Mutual Insurance Co.*, 972 F.2d 805 (7th Cir. 1992) (rejecting a limited "physicalist" account of property damage that could render coverage "illusory" in an important class of cases).

48. See *Keene Corp.* v. *Insurance Co. of North America*, 667 F.2d 1034 (D.C. 1981).

This clear movement in insurance liability had profound consequences for the structure of the injury. As Abraham makes clear, the die
had already been cast: no changes in any future policies could do anything
to diminish the liabilities that were cast on the insurers by the twin
switches in product liability and insurance coverage rules. Indeed if the
insurance companies got out of business the day the new rules were
announced, they could not have shielded any of their assets from an earlier generation of losses. What they could do was to cut off the possibility
of gaining additional revenues that might help cover the losses that manifested themselves in some future period. Worse still, any change in policy
language would be treated as an implicit concession that the earlier policy
language really did reach as far as the courts said it did. And finally, no one
had any confidence that the next round of policy language would fare any
better at the hands of the court than the earlier language. After all, no one
who worked with the CGL policy had ever contemplated the *Keene* interpretation that in the end came to rule the roost.

Similar forms of legerdemain took place with other policy provisions,
most notably the pollution exclusion, in which the words "sudden and
accidental" were in some but not all cases[49] read in a fashion to allow for
recovery for cases of gradual seepage as long as it was "suddenly" discovered. No insurance company lawyer had any confidence that the limitations that were placed in these policies for the protection of the insured
would survive at the hands of the courts. After all, what is to be expected
when an economics-oriented judge like Richard Posner takes the position
that the purpose of an insurance contract "is to spread risks and by spreading cancel them."[50] There is no doubt that this is one purpose of these contracts, but it is only one. The grand objective for the contract is to provide
gains for both sides of the transaction, and the contract should be read
with that object in view. The inability of the insurer to cancel coverage
once it has learned that something amiss has taken place in a general product line forces it to bear in the future a vast number of common-mode
injuries, for it is commonplace in these cases of regulation through litigation that they involve high-frequency events that gave rise to the term
"mass torts" in the first place. The premiums that were charged in the earlier years were in no sense sufficient to cover a fraction of the losses, and

49. See, for example, *Dimmitt Chevrolet, Inc. v. Southeastern Fidelity Insurance Co.*, 636 So.2d 700
(Fla. 1993).
50. *Eljer Manufacturing*, 972 F.2d, p. 809.

the ability to spread losses is necessarily compromised when all insured parties are subject to the same common-mode risk, as is often the case with standardized products such as guns and tobacco. It seems clear that the one lesson to be learned from the tobacco cases is that it never pays ex ante to insure against these potential catastrophic risks, for it is cheaper to let the firm go bankrupt in the end as long as some dividends can be paid out from profits in the earlier periods. The purchase of insurance would have provided little if any benefit for the tobacco companies, but it would have generated a second round of coverage litigation and complicated the control over the countless lawsuits that were indeed brought. The overall lesson is clear: there is nothing that says insurance markets must remain viable because the courts or legislatures have decided to expand the underlying tort liabilities. The mutual gain condition, which is systematically ignored in the ex post world of insurance coverage disputes, is one that systematically dominates the ex ante calculations of insurers.

The moral should now be clear. Nothing says that any particular insurance market must emerge. In practice, the erratic judicial behavior should lead to a drying up of insurance money for key coverages, as was surely the case with pollution. The one hope for the future that arises out of this checkered past has little to do with the genius of the tort law or the wisdom of the judges, but rather it has to do with the march of technology: to the extent that today's products and services are cleaner and more reliable, we should expect mishaps and trauma cases to shrink to acceptable levels, so that selling insurance once again becomes a viable commercial option. What is striking about the great cumulative trauma cases of the 1970s and 1980s is that they took place in a period of rapid transition. The events that generated the liabilities took place in earlier years only to be judged by the novel rules put in place as much as two generations later. At one time I was prepared to predict that the frequency and severity of asbestos cases, for example, would have to go down if only because the original cohort of exposure victims had already died. But the claims continue to march forward at a record pace.[51] Frequently these claims are brought against what can be described as marginal defendants (for example, health insurers of workers) for relatively low-level injuries. Clearly, the law of mass torts has in some sense diverted from that of the general tort law in product cases. I believe that the breakdown of insurance will not

---

51. See, for example, *Cimono v. Raymark Industries*, 151 F.3d 297 (5th Cir. 1998) (using sampling techniques to handle the onslaught of new claims).

loom as large in the future as it has in the past. But that is little consolation for the tremendous dislocations that the law of mass torts has brought in its wake during the past thirty years.

Class Actions

David Rosenberg, in chapter 8, advances again his well-known and strenuously argued position that a distinctive set of class action rules should be used for dealing with mass torts. In his view, the sole object of the class action should be to force firms to internalize the costs of their misdeeds. To achieve that end, the objective is to make sure that class action lawyers leave no stone unturned to make these defendants pay. Any question of compensation for individual plaintiffs can be handled by a system of first-party insurance calibrated to the needs of the parties in question. The upshot is that the class action lawyers, once selected for the case, should be entitled to 100 percent of the proceeds of recovery.

Most people would find that system a bit grotesque. The reckless bus company that kills innocent passengers will have to pay millions to the lawyers, but not a red cent to the people who suffer serious injuries. The intuitive resistance to Rosenberg's scheme will be so powerful that one can safely say that it will never be adopted. But why not? I wish to offer one brief counterargument to his proposal. What makes class actions so special? Recently, I defended the proposition that the class action is simply a device for aggregation that neither increases nor decreases the substantive rights that class members have against the rest of the world.[52] The logic of the class action is that each member surrenders control of his or her own case to the class in exchange for a share of the recovery in an action that is organized and controlled by others. The class action as a procedural device should neither facilitate nor hamper the rights against possible defendants. It should only be used to overcome administrative obstacles toward suit that otherwise exist.

The Rosenberg proposal has of course very different consequences. As I understand his position, his rule is limited only to class action. But if the basic principle of class action is as Sykes and I describe it, then Rosenberg's position becomes defensible only to the extent that he is prepared to say

52. See, for my views, Epstein (2002); for a recent overview of the entire problem of class actions, see Nagareda (2002) with exhaustive references.

that no individual should have the right to bring a lawsuit for injuries suffered, but that this suit too should be auctioned off to the lawyer who most
aggressively bids for the right to prosecute the case. Any other position creates this awkward discontinuity: as the move takes place from individual
to class suits, far more than amalgamation of individual claims takes place.
One also sees a transfer of the rights of recovery from the individual to the
class action lawyer. In many cases it is a difficult question to decide
whether the common issues of law and fact needed to support a class
action predominate over the separate questions of law and fact raised in
each case. It is hard enough to figure out where to draw this line when all
that is at stake is whether it is permissible to bring together multiple claims
as a class action. In those doubtful cases, however, much more will be at
stake if the consequence of class action certification is to strip individual
plaintiffs of any rights to their claims. The current law allows for these
individuals to opt out from the class to the extent that they think it wise
to maintain their own action. But that feature of control is also necessarily obliterated in Rosenberg's scheme. It is all too Orwellian to see the light
of day.

COMMENT BY
Gary T. Schwartz

I am a discussant on the chapter by Richard A. Epstein, but his chapter
deals with this entire book. Accordingly, by professing to comment on
Epstein, I am really commenting on this book more generally.

What does the title *Regulation through Litigation* mean? This is a question that Kenneth S. Abraham considers in his chapter. Several possible
answers are available. One is quite general. Whenever tort litigation aims
at the goal of efficient deterrence, it aims at a goal that is closely affiliated
with what regulatory agencies such as the Food and Drug Administration
attempt to do (in this regard, Joni Hersch's chapter is also relevant). From
this perspective, all tort litigation can be seen as regulation by way of litigation. But if so, a book on the topic of regulation through litigation turns
out to be a book on tort law as such. Yet it seems unlikely that this was the
original intent entertained by those who devised this book.

Now, regulation through litigation is a notion that seems to have special application to mass torts—which are the subject of Abraham's and

David Rosenberg's chapters. In a mass tort situation, an entire industry, such as asbestos, or an entire product, like the Dalkon Shield, is subject to attack. Steven Shavell has an interesting article, and subsequently an interesting book subchapter, in which he suggests that regulation should focus on larger and more recurring problems, while litigation should focus on problems that are more nearly ad hoc.[53] One problem with Shavell's writings is that they rely on a rather sanitized and depoliticized view of the regulatory process. This reliance perhaps makes those writings not ideal for our present purposes. However, Rosenberg's chapter, in assessing the proper role of tort law, acknowledges that the reality of regulatory performance might be less effective than the regulatory ideal.

But as one thinks further about the topic of regulation through litigation, what is most interesting, and newest on the horizon, is recent tort litigation, in which litigation, besides imposing financial liabilities on companies for past harms, has also sought to impose various kinds of ongoing quasi-regulatory controls on an entire industry. This was what was certainly most remarkable about the proposed 1997 multistate tobacco settlement and the actual 1998 tobacco settlement. Both settlements included various controls on the tobacco industry's advertising and focus on how the industry appeals to teenage smokers. In litigation against the gun industry, plaintiffs have demanded that gun manufacturers install certain safety features that would "personalize" guns, thereby rendering them inoperable in the hands of unauthorized users. The tobacco settlements also shaped their liability provisions in a way that proportioned monetary liability in accordance with the companies' future sales. These provisions seemingly converted the cost of liability into a kind of ongoing future tax.

All of this action really provides dramatic and innovative examples of regulatory results sought or achieved through litigation. W. Kip Viscusi's chapter about tobacco complains about this result in terms of the extent to which regulation by litigation bypasses the procedural protections built into the political process. But the political process that Viscusi has in mind seems to vary from one part of his chapter to another. At times, Viscusi refers to the congressional legislative process, which allows various interest groups to assert their own interests. At other times, Viscusi refers to the regulatory process and all the protections that are built into notice-and-comment rule making; these are the protections included in the Adminis-

53. Shavell (1984; 1987, pp. 277–90).

trative Procedure Act (APA) rule making that can be bypassed when regulations are imposed by way of litigation.

Of course, if one looks at the particular problem of tobacco taxes, the group that is most clearly disadvantaged by the multistate settlement consists of those low-income smokers who can be expected to bear the burden of what certainly seems to be a strongly regressive tax. But if this is the group that is the focus of Viscusi's concern, then it is a little odd that Viscusi does not discuss how well represented low-income smokers would be in either the congressional process or in the notice-and-comment rulemaking process. I am doubtful that this interest group would be able to organize itself to receive effective and vigorous representation. It is also odd that Viscusi, in explaining his concern, fails to refer to J. J. White's long coauthored article published a little while ago, in which White develops the same concern.[54] Another point that should be raised is that in recent years a considerable literature has emerged on a regulatory process that emphasizes regulatory negotiations.[55] For example, the Occupational Safety and Health Administration sometimes allows labor and management to thrash things out through a negotiation process, which is convened and supervised by OSHA. Eventually, OSHA may put its seal of approval on the regulation that has ensued from the process of negotiation.

Indeed, the advocates of "neg reg" often urge that the APA rulemaking process and the judicial review that ensues after the rule has been promulgated should be diminished to take into account the significance of the fact that the regulation has ensued from a process of negotiation. I think that Viscusi's argument and White's argument would be enriched if they took account of the literature on regulatory negotiations and the extent to which such negotiations have been engaged in by OSHA, the Environmental Protection Agency, and other federal agencies. Now the 1997 tobacco settlement, given its terms, did in fact require congressional implementation. That implementation was not provided. The scholarly debate about whether negotiated regulations should be deferred to by the agency can be extended to the question of whether Congress should have given greater deference to the 1997 settlement that had been thrashed out by the states and by the industry.

But there is a further, and somewhat more basic, point that should be made about the 1997 tobacco settlement and the 1998 settlement. It is

54. Dagan and White (2000).
55. Freeman (1997).

common to assess those agreements as involving a liability that—because proportioned in terms of actual future sales—is a kind of de facto tax paid essentially by consumers. However, this assessment holds if, but only if, new entrants into the tobacco market are denied access to consumers. Otherwise, if traditional and older companies are bound by settlements, and accordingly seek to raise their prices substantially, new companies unfettered by past liabilities that are based on past misconduct would be free to come in, charge dramatically lower prices, and take a large share of the market away from the traditional companies. This prospect was handled in the 1997 proposed settlement only because the states agreed in various ways to limit access to state markets to new companies that might seek to come in. I learned of all of this by virtue of a paper that was presented at the Brookings Institution in mid-1998 by Jeremy Bulow, an economist who was then at the Federal Trade Commission and who described those provisions in the 1997 settlement.[56] In a subsequent telephone conversation, Bulow has advised me that the 1998 settlement, which followed the collapse of the 1997 settlement, includes similar provisions, pursuant to which states have agreed to limit access to state consumer tobacco markets by companies that might seek to come in and secure market share by charging lower prices.[57] All of this potential raises serious questions about whether agreements of this sort violate the norms associated with antitrust laws. Granted, it may well be that the settlements cannot be legally challenged under federal antitrust law because of the state-action exemption that has been found implicit in the federal antitrust statutes.[58] But even if state agreements of this sort cannot be overturned as illegal, if they are in violation of important competitive norms, then they certainly should be strongly discouraged by public policy. Similar points can be made about quasi-regulatory restrictions that might be cumbersome, yet might be included in any firearms settlement. Assume, for example, that such a settlement requires "personalized" guns; and assume further that this is a design feature that many consumers would find inconvenient or unsatisfactory. If the settlement is imposed on existing companies, but not on

56. Bulow and Klemperer (1999).

57. For an indication of what smaller companies are now doing even under the terms of the 1998 settlement, see Gordon Fairclogh, "Tobacco Deal Has Unintended Effect, New Discount Smokes," *Wall Street Journal*, May 1, 2001, p. A1.

58. A challenge to the settlement has been rejected, for example, in *A. D. Bedell Wholesale Co. et al. v. Philip Morris, Inc.*, 104 F. Supp. 2d 501 (W.D. Pa. 2000). (This ruling was settled as of June 2001.) 263 F.3d 239 [3d Cir. 2001].) For sharp legal criticism of the settlement, see O'Brien (2000).

new companies, then the settlement might prove workable only if the settlement is structured so that state or local governments agree to deny new
companies access to consumer markets. But if the settlements are so structured, then they would raise serious questions about the compliance of the
settlements with U.S. basic antitrust norms.

As far as the gun settlements or possible gun settlements are concerned, I would like to extend Epstein's comments about the possible relevance of public nuisance doctrine, and private nuisance doctrine as well.
It seems to me that this is one area of tort law in which formal black-letter
legal doctrine clearly needs to be revised to prevent tort law from taking
over areas that properly belong to regulation and the law-making process
more generally. If private nuisance is defined in a black-letter way, as
Epstein and a California statute each suggest, as involving any conduct by
any defendant that is "injurious to health,"[59] then any behavior by any
company that might be subject to health regulation could itself be challenged as a private nuisance. Clearly, however, the jurisdiction of private
nuisance law should not extend so far. Indeed, one California court has
resisted the literal reading of § 3479, perceiving that such a reading would
convert nuisance into a monster that would devour all of tort law.[60]

The language in public nuisance cases sometimes extends even more
broadly. One sees rhetoric in public nuisance opinions indicating that anything is a public nuisance if it interferes "with the interests of the community or the comfort and convenience of the general public."[61] (If so, then
the behavior of the defendant can be regarded as a public nuisance and can
be challenged in a lawsuit brought by a local government.) The trouble is
that such language is so broad as to render public nuisance coextensive with
the so-called police power that is enjoyed by state and local law-making
authorities generally. Clearly enough, within constitutional limitations, if
there is conduct that is inconsistent with "the interests of the community,"
that conduct may properly be dealt with by local ordinances or state
statutes; but the conduct should not for this reason alone be subject to challenge in a lawsuit brought by a local city attorney's office, invoking the public nuisance doctrine. One is reminded of Dean Prosser's interesting
comments on the "nuisance" terminology: "It has meant all things to all
people, and has been applied indiscriminately. . . . Few terms have afforded

59. Calif. Civ. Code, sec. 3479 (West 2001).
60. *City of San Diego* v. *U.S. Gypsum Co.*, 32 Cal. Rptr. 2d 876 (Ct. App. 1994).
61. See, for example, *Venuto* v. *Owens-Corning Fiberglas Corp.*, 99 Cal. Rptr. 350, 355 (Ct. App. 1971). Quotation from Prosser (1971, p. 583).

so excellent an illustration of the familiar tendency of the courts to seize upon a catchword as a substitute for any analysis of a problem."[62]

Especially, then, for public nuisance, there seems to be an obvious problem of black-letter doctrine that is extremely overbroad and that needs to be revised to prevent it from being exploited by an intelligent and ambitious city attorney's office. The Epstein chapter suggests that the pattern of decided cases shows that the public nuisance doctrine can be kept within reasonable limits. The example he draws is of a street obstruction that interferes with the small interests of a large number of travelers. Yet this example clearly does not exhaust the range of activities that have been regarded as public nuisances. The list, as Prosser points out, also includes brothels, unlicensed prize fights, and public profanity.[63] But even if the example of street obstructions is supplemented by considering these other examples, we are still far from the example of the national distribution of guns—conduct that is not really tied to one local area. At the least, the public nuisance doctrine requires a geographically circumscribed instance of conduct, or pattern of conduct, on the part of the defendant. And one departs unacceptably from that traditional understanding by allowing public nuisance doctrine to apply to the design features of all guns sold or the distribution practices that might be engaged in nationwide by gun manufacturers.

In closing, let me comment on Rosenberg's elegant chapter. In its dramatic endorsement of a complete collectivization of litigation, rather than the more traditional individualized approach, Rosenberg's chapter seems influenced by work that has recently been done by his Harvard colleagues Louis Kaplow and Steven Shavell, who I think would endorse Rosenberg's proposal as in line with their general approach to private-law problems and their belief in the primary relevance of the efficiency goal.[64] The problem I have with Rosenberg's chapter is that I think it needs somewhat more heft than it currently contains by way of real-world support. As Rosenberg makes clear, although he talks about the goal of efficient litigation, for him that goal is really only an intermediate goal. His ultimate goal is the efficient deterrence of defendants—the expectation of efficient litigation is an expectation he wants companies to entertain so that they will be efficiently deterred.

His chapter rests on a model of the following sort. The defendant is considering engaging in conduct that has an expected harm of $400 mil-

62. See Keeton and others (1984, p. 616).
63. Keeton and others (1984, pp. 643–44).
64. Kaplow and Shavell (2001).

lion. The cost of preventing that harm would be $300 million. Given the current inefficient litigation system, that system on its own would be able to generate liability of only $250 million. If, indeed, the likely harm is $400 million, but the anticipated cost of liability (because of inefficient litigation) is only $250 million rather than $400 million, then the defendant will not be induced by the threat of liability to adopt the efficient level of precautions—$300 million.

I understand the example clearly. Still, as I look back on what has happened in American tort law during the past forty years—the era of modern tort law and of modern aggregate litigation—I would like to see more real-world examples of a situation like the one just described. Rosenberg, for example, might be in the position of saying that Bendectin was in fact a defective drug, but that its producer, Merrill, was in a position to anticipate that plaintiffs would not be able to invest in litigation in a way that would enable them to succeed in proving Bendectin's defectiveness. If this were the case, then one could say that Merrill produced a bad drug because of the expectation that it could get away with a bad product in light of the inefficiencies of the litigation system. But as far as I know, this is not at all an accurate narrative of the Bendectin situation. Indeed, I really do not know of any real-world situations in the past thirty years that fit the scenario Rosenberg describes. If Rosenberg does know of any situations, it would be wise for him to identify them and describe how the tort system might indeed have malfunctioned and in malfunctioning might have induced an inefficient level of deterrence. Certainly, that would considerably strengthen the persuasiveness of Rosenberg's model. To repeat, I understand the model well enough, and I find it of substantial interest. But I need to know more about its real-world applicability before I would be willing to endorse a recommendation as dramatic and unorthodox as Rosenberg's.

References

American Law Institute. 1965. *Restatement of Torts Second*. Philadelphia.

Bulow, Jeremy, and Paul Klemperer. 1999. "The Tobacco Deal." In *Brookings Papers on Economic Activity: Microeconomics 1998*, edited by Martin Baily, Peter Reiss, and Clifford Winston, 323–94.

Coase, Ronald H. 1960. "The Problem of Social Cost." *Journal of Law and Economics* 3 (1): 1-44.

———. 1988. *The Firm, the Market, and the Law*. University of Chicago Press.

Dagan, Hanoch, and James J. White. 2000. "Governments, Citizens, and Injurious Industries." *New York University Law Review* 75 (2): 354–87.

Epstein, Richard A. 1973. "A Theory of Strict Liability." *Journal of Legal Studies* 2 (1): 151–204.

———. 1979. "Nuisance Law: Corrective Justice and Its Utilitarian Constraints." *Journal of Legal Studies* 8 (1): 49–102.

———. 1984. "The Legal and Insurance Dynamics of Mass Torts." *Journal of Legal Studies* 13 (3): 475–506.

———. 1985. "Product Liability as an Insurance Market." *Journal of Legal Studies* 14 (3): 645–70.

———.1997. "Takings, Exclusivity and Speech: The Legacy of *PruneYard* v. *Robins*." *University of Chicago Law Review* 64 (Winter): 21–56.

———. 1999. *Torts*. Aspen Law and Business.

———. 2001. "Standing and Spending: The Role of Legal and Equitable Principles." *Chapman Law Review* 4 (Spring): 1–18.

———. 2002. "Class Actions: The Need for a Hard Second Look." *Justice Report* 4 (May).

Farnsworth, E. Allan. 1990. *Contracts*. 2d ed. Aspen Law and Business.

Freeman, Jody. 1997. "Collaborative Governance in the Administrative State." *UCLA Law Review* 45 (October): 1–27.

Hobbes, Thomas. 1985. *The Leviathan*. Penguin Classic Edition.

Kaplow, Louis, and Steven Shavell. 2001. "Fairness Versus Welfare." *Harvard Law Review* 114 (February): 961–79.

Keeton, Page W., and others. 1984. *Prosser & Keeton on the Law of Torts*. 5th ed. West Publishing.

Lott, John R. Jr. 1998. *More Guns, Less Crime: Understanding Crime and Gun Control Laws*. University of Chicago Press.

Lott, John R. Jr., and William M. Landes. 1999. "Multiple Victim Public Shootings, Bombings, and Right-to-Carry Concealed Handgun Laws: Contrasting Private and Public Law Enforcement." John M. Olin Law and Economics Working Paper 73. University of Chicago Law School (April).

Michelman, Frank. 1997. "The Common Law Baseline and Restitution for the Lost Commons: A Reply to Professor Epstein." *University of Chicago Law Review* 64 (Winter): 57–69.

Nagareda, Richard. 2002. "Autonomy, Peace and Put Options in the Mass Tort Class Action." *Harvard Law Review* 115 (3): 747–830.

O'Brien, Thomas C. 2000. *Constitutional and Antitrust Violations of the Multistate Tobacco Settlement*. Policy Analysis 371. Washington: Cato Institute (May).

Prosser, William. 1971. *Handbook of the Law of Torts*. 4th ed. West.

Shavell, Steven. 1984. "Liability for Harm versus Regulation of Safety." *Journal of Legal Studies* 13 (2): 357–74.

———. 1987. *Economic Analysis of Accident Law*. Harvard University Press.

Contributors

Kenneth S. Abraham
University of Virginia
  Law School

John E. Calfee
American Enterprise Institute
  for Public Policy Research

Philip J. Cook
Duke University

J. David Cummins
University of Pennsylvania

Patricia Danzon
University of Pennsylvania,
  Wharton School

Richard A. Epstein
University of Chicago
  Law School
The Hoover Institution

Joni Hersch
Harvard Law School

Daniel P. Kessler
Stanford University

Thomas J. Kniesner
Syracuse University

Jim Leitzel
University of Chicago

Jens Ludwig
Georgetown University

Randall Lutter
American Enterprise Institute
  for Public Policy Research

Elizabeth Mader
American Enterprise Institute
  for Public Policy Research

Mark B. McClellan
Stanford University

David Rosenberg
Harvard Law School

Peter Schuck
Yale Law School

Gary T. Schwartz*
University of California,
    Los Angeles, Law School

* Deceased.

W. Kip Viscusi
Harvard Law School

James Wootton
U.S. Chamber of Commerce

Index

JOINT CENTER

AEI-BROOKINGS JOINT CENTER FOR REGULATORY STUDIES

Director
Robert W. Hahn

Codirector
Robert E. Litan

Fellows
Robert W. Crandall
Christopher C. DeMuth
Thomas W. Hazlett
Randall W. Lutter
Clifford M. Winston

In response to growing concerns about the impact of regulation on consumers, business, and government, the American Enterprise Institute and the Brookings Institution established the AEI-Brookings Joint Center for Regulatory Studies. The primary purpose of the center is to hold lawmakers and regulators more accountable by providing thoughtful, objective analysis of existing regulatory programs and new regulatory proposals. The Joint Center builds on AEI's and Brookings's impressive body of work over the past three decades that evaluated the economic impact of regulation and offered constructive suggestions for implementing reforms to enhance productivity and consumer welfare. The views in Joint Center publications are those of the authors and do not necessarily reflect the views of the staff, council of academic advisers, or fellows.